(MIS)INT̶E̶R̶P̶R̶E̶T̶I̶N̶G̶
GENESIS

how the

CREATION MUSEUM

Misunderstands the Ancient
Near Eastern Context of the Bible

BEN STANHOPE

SCARAB PRESS

Suggested citation:

Stanhope, Ben. *(Mis)interpreting Genesis: How the Creation Museum Misunderstands the Ancient Near Eastern Context of the Bible.* Louisville, KY: Scarab Press, 2020.

Scarab Press
Louisville, Kentucky

Fulfilled by
Amazon KDP
Monee, Illinois

First edition, 2020
2 4 6 8 10 9 7 5 3 1

(Mis)interpreting Genesis: How the Creation Museum
Misunderstands the Ancient Near Eastern Context of the Bible

ISBN: 978-0-578-82369-0

1. Biblical Studies. 2. Interpretation.

Bible quotations are the author's translation unless otherwise noted.

Contains illustrations and elements referenced on back matter
attributions page.

Cover design Benjamin Stanhope

Author and publisher inquiries at bjstanhope@Gmail.com

For Briana,

עצם מעצמי ובשׂר מבשׂרי

CONTENTS

TABLE OF FIGURES

Acknowledgments

I owe gratitude to the biblical scholar Michael S. Heiser. Through his work, I first fell in love with ancient Israelite religion, and his publications were formative in my academic development. I also owe a special thanks to the linguist Charles Loder for reviewing an early draft of this work. Semitics is a staggeringly difficult field, and the church often fails to appreciate the years of sacrifices its scholars make in the pursuit of its service. Dave O'Holleran contributed many important corrections, and Michael Jones provided a great deal of encouragement. Foremost of all, John Holzmann labored with me for years and provided the most valuable criticisms and keen editorial support. Although our views sometimes differed in substantial ways, and all final decisions were my own, his involvement was of tremendous benefit.

INTRODUCTION

PETERSBURG KENTUCKY, 2018

O N a rainy Sunday afternoon, my wife and I drive up to a gateway flanked by two silhouettes of stegosauruses. From the parking lot, we can spot the projecting neck of a large sauropod dinosaur. We have come to the Creation Museum in northern Kentucky, the 27 million dollar incarnation of young-earth doctrine upheld by the organization Answers in Genesis.

As we enter the main building, we are immediately drawn to colorful displays and panels about dragon legends from around the globe. Overhead, a great Chinese dragon snakes its way through the portico in the direction of the admittance counter. Despite the grim weather outside, I find that the entrance line is surprisingly long, mostly families with excited children in tow. Even a few Mennonite bonnets bob their way among the crowd.

Joining the line, I gaze at a large display panel, entitled, "Not the Stuff of Legends." On its left is a depiction of a *brachiosaurus* being attacked by human hunters with spears. On the right swims a *Liopleurodon*. Verses from the biblical book of Job and the titles "Behemoth" and "Leviathan" accompany these illustrations in support of the museum's belief that men lived alongside these ancient reptiles in the early post-flood world.

Our tickets in hand, my wife and I turn the corner and find ourselves standing in the shadow of a mastodon skeleton towering at the forefront of the museum hall. To our left, a sign next to the gift shop advertises Ken Ham's book, *The LIE: Evolution*. The sound of a large aquarium pulls your ear. Above it, an animatronic child and raptors are playing together near the water's edge. I can immediately appreciate why the general culture and news media have seen this museum as little more than a comedy goldmine, and I fail to suppress my own grin. However, my smile quickly transforms to a somber sympathy as I reflect on what I know to be the museum's motives.

For centuries, our civilization has rested on the metaphysical foundations of Genesis' creation account. Even those Westerners who have never darkened the door of a church or synagogue, or think the Bible is fairytale nonsense, have undoubtedly unconsciously sublimated the fruits of its worldview through our shared cultural heritage stretching back twenty centuries to imperial Rome. Much of the Creation Museum stands as a warning that we cannot obliterate that heritage from the foundations of our civilization and expect all to carry on unchanged. Although I reject much of the Creation Museum's theology, I sympathize with their concern that society is bulldozing metaphysical walls without first asking why our ancestors built them in the first place.

I was born into an evangelical missionary family. Some of my earliest memories include playing with dinosaur figures in my tropical Dominican backyard and flipping through young-earth picture books like Duane Gish's classic *Dinosaurs by Design*. In grade school, I can remember using class essay projects as an excuse to write against evolution or to argue that sauropod dinosaurs might still be living deep in the Congo jungles. I remained strongly committed to the views taught by Answers in Genesis throughout most of high school, and I admired the teachings of the creationist Kent Hovind.

Growing up in church, I had always encountered the early chapters of Genesis from a posture of either scientific embattlement or merely in the form of basic Sunday school level overviews for the sake of sermon messages. After hearing hundreds of sermons on Genesis throughout my life, I thought I understood Genesis pretty well—to the point that it frankly bored me. However, into my late teens, I finally began to read Genesis for myself without sermon training wheels, and something strange occurred. I realized that, despite the fact that these texts were supposed to set the foundation of my beliefs about the nature of all reality and despite having spent my entire young life in the pew in conservative, grape juice communion drinking Bible-believing churches, my sense of mastery was a colossal sham. The story I was reading was much more profoundly cryptic than the tame, packaged version I had been taught. These inaugural chapters came from a world and culture I did not understand. A barrage of questions pounded me as I read:

What was Genesis 1:7 talking about when it said there are waters "above" the sky? Where was the "evening and morning" light on the first three creation days coming from if the sun, moon, and stars *weren't even made until day four*? When God says, "Let *us* make man in our image," to whom does the "us" refer? Why was the villain in Eden a talking snake of all things, and why does the author have Eve striking up a conversation with it with no background information as if we are just supposed to accept that sort of thing as reasonable?

If Adam and Eve were the only original humans, why does Genesis 4 seem to imply there were already cities on earth right after their first child Cain killed his twin? Who is Cain afraid of finding him? Where did he get his wife, and how did he build a city by himself in 4:17? If Adam and Eve were *already* created immortal, what was the purpose of there even being a "Tree of Life" in the garden story? After Adam and Eve sin, why does God announce in 3:22, "The man has now become like one of us, knowing good and evil"? What does it mean to "know good and evil," and how is it not blasphemy to say Adam's sin made him "like God"? For that matter, was the serpent lying or not?

Assuming no death can exist in a perfect world as young-earth creationists had always taught me, what happens if an elephant in Eden accidentally stepped on a frog? Would the frog magically reassemble somehow like a video recording thrown in reverse? And if God had created all of nature originally free of all death and predation of any kind, why do scorpions look the way they do—with their bulbous pincers, segmented plate armor, and arching stingers full of complex poisons? Did God only give scorpions all these nasty bits after Adam sinned? What did they look like before the Fall? Why is the introduction of animal predation and death never even remotely mentioned in Genesis 3 when God is listing out all the consequences of the Fall? Was God too busy talking about the introduction of weeds to find this important enough to mention? Is Genesis 1 even describing a "perfect world" when it says the original creation was "very good"?

My comfortable boredom with Genesis was mercilessly shattered.

As a kid, it's easy to fantasize about finding yourself in the enchanted desert caves of the *Arabian Nights* or exploring the glyphic tombs of Egypt. With its lost garden, divine trees, serpent, and passing mentions of exotic divine creatures like the cherubim, this cosmic history, coming down to us from untold antiquity in a Middle Eastern script on desert scrolls, inspired in me the same fascination.

The desire to explore these mysteries eventually drove me to obtain my bachelor's degree from Boyce College of the Southern Baptist Seminary, where I became more deeply acquainted with the evangelical intellectual tradition and learned to translate Hebrew, the language of the Old Testament. Eventually, my desire for advanced training in the Bible took me to Northern Germany, where I was accepted into a program in manuscript studies at the University of Hamburg.

In Germany, I was introduced to the great manuscript cultures of the world. During the short winter days, I would take a train from the countryside into the city at sunset and eventually meet my small band of classmates from countries across the globe. Over the months, a rotation of experts would introduce us to the mysteries of ancient Egyptian papyri, Sanskrit palm-leaf manuscripts, Medieval Jewish magic amulets, Quranic calligraphy, bamboo manuscripts from Chinese tombs, Ethiopia's biblical traditions—unparalleled in beauty, or the earliest Greek manuscripts of the church. I wished that I might live a hundred lifetimes to study each of these fields. However, I had come for my first love, the Hebrew Bible. I was introduced to scientific archaeometry by a pair of Dead Sea Scrolls scientists, fulfilled my dream of traveling the ancient cities of Ephesus and Jerusalem, and would eventually conduct and publish my research thesis on Egyptian symbols adorning seal artifacts once belonging to the biblical kings of Judah in the days of the prophets.[1]

As someone who deeply values the Hebrew Scriptures, I have written to engage the average churchgoer and curious secular readers. My thesis is that archaeological and linguistic discoveries about the Bible's original context clearly show that a great deal of mainstream young-earth interpretation of biblical creation texts is wrong. I also aim to demonstrate that these archaeological and linguistic discoveries should correct our understanding of the biblical authors' core intended messages.

No shortage of books exists that discuss the scientific evidence for evolution or the geological evidence for the age of the earth. The

---

[1] Benjamin Stanhope, "First Temple Hebrew Seals and Bullae Identifying Biblical Persons: A Study of their Iconographic and Historical Significance" (M. A. Thesis, Hamburg University, Dec 2019). Available: https://independent.academia.edu/BenStanhope.

subject of this book is unique, however, in that it is a serious *biblical-interpretive critique* of the Creation Museum. Why do I target the Creation Museum specifically? Do I have a peculiar vendetta towards them? Am I simply trying to be provocative? No. I have chosen to target the Creation Museum largely because I believe they have done the finest job of any institution in making the issues involved dramatically tangible and clear to the public. Some of the ideas I critique in this book are popular in mainstream evangelicalism in general, but the Creation Museum is evangelicalism's flagship embodiment of these ideas and therefore makes for a fine space to discuss them.

This book is divided into three sections: The first confronts the widespread young-earth creationist assertion that the biblical authors described creatures that mainstream paleontology says disappeared millions of years ago. The leaders of the young-earth movement claim the author of the book of Job must have seen a living sauropod dinosaur called Behemoth and some great marine reptile like a mosasaur, called Leviathan. Answers in Genesis has even speculated in print that a creature the original King James Version curiously translates as a "unicorn" might be an extinct species of giant rhinoceros. Indeed, many young-earthers, like Ken Ham and Jason Lisle, have even suggested that "fiery flying serpents" mentioned by the prophet Isaiah are possibly a reference to a species of pterosaur that was still alive in the eighth century BC Judean desert!

A serious study of these cryptids will show that they are depicted in some fascinating artifacts and texts from ancient Syria and Egypt. However, I argue that none of these creatures are what young-earthers have long asserted them to be when they are understood in their ancient cultural context.

Section two, "Reading Genesis like an Ancient Israelite" forms the bulk of the book. It shows examples of how modern scholarship of the Bible's literary context has unveiled new information that helps us understand the first chapters of Genesis as its original audience would have understood them.

I first explain how the syntax of Genesis 1:1 allows interpretive room for a billions of years old *universe*. Following this is a survey of the Old Testament's cosmology—how its authors and readers perceived the physical universe. Here, I compare the Bible's description of the natural world to texts and art from neighboring civilizations like Egypt, Babylon, and Canaan. While the Hebrew Scriptures teach a dramatically different theology than that believed by its surrounding cultures, the Bible's cosmology is remarkably similar to what you will find in most ancient cultures. It is my firm conclusion that the Bible's physical cosmology powerfully contradicts young-earth interpretations.

Following this, I address the first three chapters of Genesis. This portion examines the original, ancient Near Eastern meaning of the seven days of creation. It is my argument that concordist old and young-earth creationists have both failed to adequately understand the literary and theological motivations of the author of Genesis due to their desire to interpret this document in light of modern science.

From here follows an examination of the significance of the long lifespans that Genesis says the patriarchs enjoyed before the Flood. I have argued, from the biblical material itself, that the lifespan numbers are largely symbolic. Young-earthers are mistaken when they try to use these lifespans to construct historical-geological chronologies upon which to build "scientific" understandings of ancient history.

Finally, young-earthers who follow the Creation Museum model famously teach that all animals were vegetarian before Adam and Eve fell—that there was no death in the animal kingdom before Adam sinned. The last chapter of this section firmly argues that this interpretation doesn't conform with modern analysis of ancient Semitic religion, particularly of five passages found in Genesis, Isaiah, and Romans. Contrary to what has often been claimed, cutting-edge research on several overlooked verbs in Genesis 1 demonstrates that nature "red in tooth and claw" was indeed the original "very good" state of creation.

The last section of this book seeks to draw together the conclusions from these previous sections to show how changing some of our false core assumptions about the Bible can dramatically improve our ability to understand it. Since most of my readers are practicing Christians, I first argue that Paul didn't teach the Holy Spirit typically acts as a supernatural Bible commentary for believers like most evangelicals believe. I likewise offer an important biblical caveat that any articulation of divine inspiration must integrate if believers want to avoid generating the pattern of interpretive errors documented throughout this book. Apart from what proceeds from these respectful critiques which I believe Christians will find valuable, I write as a textual analyst. I avoid writing with the tone of a theologian and seek to maintain a generally religiously neutral tone.

Appendix A documents and refutes displays in the Creation Museum and Answers in Genesis' publications that purport to show artifact and folklore evidence of men and dinosaurs coexisting. It likewise offers an alternative explanation for why dragon legends are found universally in traditional cultures. Appendix B critiques Answers in Genesis' use of flood legends—often cited in support of their belief in a global flood. Finally, Appendix C surveys about fifty traditional cosmologies around the world to show that ancient cultures universally tend to share the same general cosmological assumptions that I argue characterize the thinking of the biblical authors throughout this book.

SECTION I

PROPOSED CLAIMS OF EXTINCT ANIMALS IN THE BIBLE

"Contrary to what many may think, what we know now as dinosaurs get more mention in the Scriptures than most animals!"

—Ken Ham, CEO Answers in Genesis

CHAPTER 1

WHAT WAS LEVIATHAN?

MAINSTREAM paleontologists believe a chasm of some sixty-six million years separates the extinction of the dinosaurs from the first arrival of modern humans. Young-earth creationists maintain that human beings and dinosaurs were created on the same day of the biblical creation week and lived alongside each other.[1] Ken Ham, the CEO of Answers in Genesis, believes, "Contrary to what many may think, what we know now as dinosaurs get more mention in the Scriptures than most animals!"[2]

While growing up, I was taught that Leviathan, the sea monster described in the book of Job, was a member of the animal kingdom—some marine reptile like a plesiosaur or mosasaur that Job had witnessed firsthand. This claim can be found ubiquitously throughout young-earth literature. A large sign in the Creation Museum's portico quotes the description of the creature Leviathan given in the book of Job, accompanied by the image of a *Liopleurodon*. The caption reads, "While dragon legends may be fanciful retellings of actual events, God's Word tells us about two real dragon-like creatures."[3] Answers in Genesis' *New Answers Book* elaborates: "Job 41 describes a great animal that lived in the sea, Leviathan.... This 'dragon' may have been something like...the 82 ft. (25 m) *Liopleurodon*."[4]

---

[1] Ken Ham, "Dinosaurs and the Bible," *Answers in Genesis*, Nov. 5, 1999. Last featured Jan. 5, 2015. Accessed May 8, 2017, www.answersingenesis.org/dinosaurs/dinosaurs-and-the-Bible/.
[2] Ibid.
[3] On the sign entitled, "Not the Stuff of Legends!"
[4] Ken Ham, "What Really Happened to the Dinosaurs" in Ken Ham (ed.) *The New Answers Book 1: Over 25 Questions on Creation/Evolution and the Bible* (Green Forest, AR: Master Books, 2006), 159.

Henry M. Morris, often considered the founder of the modern creation science movement, claimed, "It is important to remember that Job lived during the early generations after the Flood and that he no doubt had seen many animals that later became extinct.... [L]eviathan fits what we know about some large marine reptiles, such as the plesiosaur...."[5] A more recent book by a geologist at the Institute for Creation Research contends that Leviathan "may be a description of a semiaquatic dinosaur like the Spinosaurus."[6]

The most substantial description we find of this creature comes to us from Job 41. The ESV reads:

Can you draw out Leviathan with a fishhook[?]...
Can you fill his skin with harpoons or his head with fishing
    spears?...
Around his teeth is terror.
His back is made of rows of shields, shut up closely as with a
    seal....
His sneezings flash forth light, and his eyes are like the eyelids of
    the dawn.
Out of his mouth go flaming torches; sparks of fire leap forth.
Out of his nostrils comes forth smoke, as from a boiling pot and
    burning rushes.
His breath kindles coals, and a flame comes forth from his
    mouth....
Though the sword reaches him, it does not avail, nor the spear,
    the dart, or the javelin.
He counts iron as straw, and bronze as rotten wood....
His underparts are like sharp potsherds; he spreads himself like a
    threshing sledge on the mire.
He makes the deep boil like a pot.... Behind him he leaves a
    shining wake....
On earth there is not his like, a creature without fear....
    he is king over all the sons of pride.

[5] Henry M. Morris, *The Biblical Basis for Modern Science: The Revised and Updated Classic!* (Green Forest, AR: Master Books, 2002), 332-333.
[6] Tim Clarey, *Dinosaurs: Marvels of God's Design: The Science of the Biblical Account* (Green Forest, AR: Master books, 2015), 71.

One can hardly ignore the repeated references to Leviathan as a fire-breather: "His sneezings flash forth light.... Out of his mouth go flaming torches.... Sparks of fire leap forth...and a flame comes forth from his mouth."

Believing that the Job author is being literal, the sponsors of the Creation Museum and other young-earth authors believe these verses provide us evidence that there must have lived alongside man a species of marine reptile that possessed the biological capability of *literally breathing fire.*[7]

For them, a non-literal interpretation of this fire-breathing dragon dishonors the divine authority of the Bible. They cite textual reasons for why they believe Job *must* be attempting to describe a natural animal and point out that we can't know a great deal about the physiology of ancient marine reptiles since we only have fossils to go by. They then compare Leviathan's flaming maw with creatures we know like the electric eel and the bombardier beetle (which shoots boiling chemicals out of its abdomen). They consider these creatures proof-of-concept that fire breathing is at least biologically possible.

The Answers in Genesis website argues, "Certain beetles shoot out burning chemicals, so is a fire-breathing dragon really that far-fetched?"[8] Ken Ham presents the same argument,[9] and Henry Morris argued the same.[10] The astrophysicist Jason Lisle says:

> Leviathan sounds an awful lot like a plesiosaur...But could it really breathe flame? Well,...think of the other amazing creatures that God has created like the bombardier beetle.... Or think about an electric

---

[7] Besides ensuing citations, see Darek Isaacs, *Dragons or Dinosaurs? Creation or Evolution?* (Alachua, FL: Bridge Logos, 2010), 162; Durwood B. Hatch, *God Did It: Not the Big Bang and Evolution* (Oklahoma: Tate Publishing, 2010), 192; James Edward Gilmer, *100 Year Coverup Revealed: We Lived with Dinosaurs* (Bloomington: AuthorHouse, 2011), 51; Tim Chaffey and Jason Lisle, *Old Earth Creationism on Trial: The Verdict is in* (Green Forest: Master Books, 2008), 175-176.

[8] "Dragons: Fact or Fable?," *Answers in Genesis*, Accessed May 8, 2017, www.answersingenesis.org/dinosaurs/dragon-legends/dragons-fact-or-fable/.

[9] "Dinosaurs for Kids," YouTube video, 1:26:23, recorded presentation given by Ham, posted by "Answers in Genesis," Dec 18, 2014, www.youtube.com/watch?v=B-g_hk_KKro. Relevant comments stated 29 minutes into presentation.

[10] C.f. Morris, *The Biblical Basis for Modern Science*, 359.

eel.... In fact, most animals produce methane anyway, which is a flammable gas. If you just had a way to ignite it, you could do it.[11]

Far be it from me to discourage any exciting new research attempting to extrapolate the pyrotechnic potentialities of ancient reptilian belching, but I want to show you why we know, beyond doubt, that Leviathan is *not* a member of the animal kingdom. Leviathan isn't just a mere sideshow in our journey through the Bible's view of creation. It is appropriate to begin with him because uncovering his identity is key to understanding a major theme in Israel's creation theology that will be featured throughout this book.

The first clue to unveiling the dragon's identity comes to us from a biblical text that literalists have far too long neglected. Psalm 74:14 reads:

> You crushed the heads of Leviathan and gave him for food to the inhabitants of the wilderness.

In past decades, the great majority of young-earth creationists who published books claiming there are dinosaurs in the Bible held science degrees but had no formal education in Hebrew.[12] This generated many

---

[11] Stated 14:30 minutes into "Dinosaurs and the Bible, Part 1," *Answers in Genesis*, 00:18:00. Video Lecture uploaded March 2009, www.answersingenesis.org/media/video/animals/dinosaurs-and-Bible/.

[12] Henry M. Morris completed a bibliography of 130 creationist books in 1995 that can be found on the ICR website: "The Young Earth Creationist Bibliography," *ICR.org*, www.icr.org/article/YoungEarth-creationist-bibliography/. Originally published in *Acts & Facts* 24.11 (1995). Accessed June 29, 2017.

Morris points out that over 70% of the bibliography was authored by scholars with earned doctorates who take a literal view of the days of Genesis. He compiled the list, he says, in order to demonstrate the scope of creationist publishing.

I looked up every author, as they appeared, to see whose biographical data I could acquire in order to confirm which ones had or didn't have formal biblical training. The following numbers should be understood as tentative and suggestive: Book-by-book (in the interest of overall impact of published material) we have 89 authors (repeated or not) whose education biography was accessible enough for me to determine if they possessed accredited training involving biblical studies. Only 15 out of the known 89 did—about 17%. Having looked at the incomplete bios of those in the "doubtful" category (most of these were science PhDs who

imbalances in young-earth literature and is undoubtedly the reason why its authors usually failed to notice a crucial detail in this passage. Namely, is *Leviathan* in the above passage singular, or plural? Are we dealing with multiple Leviathans, each with a single head? Or are we dealing with *one* Leviathan that has multiple heads—a sort of hydra? It's easy to see how one might skim through this verse without ever asking the question.

As anyone who has had first semester Hebrew will tell you, it turns out, grammatically, this passage is indisputably describing a single creature with multiple heads.[13] It is describing a hydra. In the Hebrew phrase, "heads of Leviathan" (רָאשֵׁי לִוְיָתָן), the term "head" (רֹאשׁ) appears in the plural state marked by what is called a *sere-yod* in conjunction with the singular noun "Leviathan."[14]

Why is it significant that we have a biblical text that speaks of Leviathan as multi-headed? Because the Israelites weren't the only people group in the surrounding lands of the ancient Near East who described the dragon in this way. Leviathan was also spoken of on ancient stone tablets written by another civilization north of Israel in Syria.

---

could have done an unmentioned theology undergrad but very likely didn't), I strongly suspect the actual percentage was lower.

Those in the bibliography with a confirmable background in biblical studies were Cooper, DeYoung, Leupold, Lubenow, Jobe, Pearcey, T. Sharp, Bebber, Watson, Whitcomb, and Wilson.

[13] Thus: Richard E. Averbeck, "Ancient Near Eastern Mythography as it Relates to Historiography in the Hebrew Bible: Genesis 3 and the Cosmic Battle," *The Future of Biblical Archaeology* (2004), 340; John Walton and Tremper Longman III, *How to Read Job* (Downers Grove: Intervarsity, 2015), 80; Walter C. Kaiser, Peter H. Davids, F. F. Bruce, Manfred Brauch, *Hard Sayings of the Bible* (Downers Grove: InterVarsity, 1996), 278; Johannes Botterweck, Helmer Ringgren, Heinz-Josef Fabry (eds.), *Theological Dictionary of the Old Testament Vol VII* (Grand Rapids: Eerdmans, 1995), 508; Mark David Futato, *Interpreting the Psalms: An Exegetical Handbook*. Handbooks for Old Testament Exegesis (Grand Rapids: Krugel, 2007), 54.

[14] E.g. see discussion of this construct in Russell T. Fuller, *Invitation to Biblical Hebrew: A Beginning Grammar* (Grand Rapids: Kregel, 2006), 61-7.

ENTER UGARIT

Before continuing the hunt for Leviathan, a digression is in order.

I imagine that, like me growing up, most Christians were taught to be suspicious of claims about new advancements in Scriptural understanding. The idea is that if nineteen centuries of godly men didn't land on some interpretive insight about a text—an interpretation only now being advanced by modern scholars—then the modern interpretation is probably wrong. Its novelty alone speaks against it.

Though I appreciate the motive behind this attitude and think that it is wise to tread carefully when people claim new insights into the most studied book in human history, there is a weakness with this approach. Namely, there is the fact that nearly all the statements of faith and articulated theologies behind religious denominations and ancient sects were formulated before scholars ever discovered and deciphered the hundreds of thousands of lines of ancient Near Eastern literature that put the Hebrew Bible into its cultural and linguistic context.

Until modern archaeology of the Near East began to emerge around the middle of the nineteenth century, we had minimal access to the Hebrew Bible's historical context—especially of the early chapters of Genesis. In the early 1800s, scholars didn't even agree whether the Egyptian hieroglyphs were true vocally representative writing, much less had anyone significantly deciphered them. The vast majority of cuneiform texts—the primary document form of the great Mesopotamian civilizations like Babylon, had yet to be unearthed from the desert sand. The Babylonian creation account wouldn't be published until 1876. The Dead Sea Scrolls wouldn't be discovered until the end of World War II, and they took decades to piece together and publish!

Another example of how our knowledge of the Bible has dramatically increased in relatively recent church history is the discovery of the Ugaritic texts.

Ugarit was an ancient port city in what is today Syria that archaeologists began excavating in the late 1920s. It is difficult to overemphasize the importance of this find to biblical studies because Ugarit's language is among the closest ancient tongues to Biblical Hebrew ever discovered. The two languages are therefore rich in mutual cognates—that is, words that share the same linguistic derivation.

The discovery of Ugaritic-Hebrew cognates has been useful to biblical scholars because there are over a thousand unique Hebrew words in the Bible that only appear once or a few times, or that were accidentally split in two by a confused scribe, or that contain letters uncertainly transmitted, and so, have uncertain meanings.

Figure 1. The Ugaritic alphabet impressed on a clay tablet.

After the discovery of the Ugaritic material, scholars could hunt around in those texts for counterparts to these difficult Hebrew words and, in so doing, discover more solid understandings of their meanings that several thousand years of Christian and Jewish manuscript scholars had not previously enjoyed access.

Besides granting a better understanding of previously obscure words, the Ugaritic texts have also been useful to biblical scholars because the people of Ugarit were Baal worshipers—the primary religion that the biblical authors fought against. As modern readers, we can gain a greater appreciation for what the Bible is saying when we have a better understanding of its primary religious arch-nemesis.

Finally, Ugarit and ancient Israel shared many of the same cultural idioms. That is to say, as linguistic cousins living in the same part of the world, they breathed the same cultural air. As one scholar puts it, "The Hebrew Bible did not 'borrow' from Northwest Semitic culture: it *is* Northwest Semitic culture."[15]

An excellent example of the Bible's shared Northwest Semitic culture is what scholars refer to as the chaos dragon.

LEVIATHAN/LITANU: THE CHAOS DRAGON

---

[15] Ola Wikander, "From Indo-European Dragon-Slaying to Isaiah 27.1: A Study in the *Longue Durée*" in Tommy Wasserman, Greger Andersson and David Willgren (eds.), *Studies in Isaiah: History, Theology, and Reception*. Library of Hebrew Bible/Old Testament Studies 654 (Oxford: Bloomsbury T&T Clark, 2017), 120.

Let's compare some poetry from one of the Ugaritic tablets with an allusion to Leviathan in Isaiah.

The Ugaritic passage is older here by many centuries. I say that by no means to suggest that the Bible was based on the Ugaritic texts (that would be highly historically unlikely) but, simply, to note that the Ugaritic would not have been based on the biblical texts.

KTU 1.5:1:2	ISAIAH 27:1
[Y]ou smote *Litanu*, the fleeing [Ugaritic: *brh*] serpent, Annihilated the twisting [*'qltn*] serpent, the dominant one who has seven heads[16]	In that day Yhwh will punish, with his greatly fierce and mighty sword, Leviathan the fleeing [Hebrew: *brh*] serpent, Leviathan the twisting [*'qltn*] serpent, and he will slay the dragon [*tannin*] that is in the sea.

The first important similarity between these two texts is that the consonants for the Ugaritic dragon named *Litanu*, or LTN in Ugaritic, are contained within the consonants comprising the word *Leviathan*, LWYTN in Hebrew. (Note that most Middle Eastern alphabets are consonantal and omit symbols for vowels.)

Notice also that, like Psalm 74, *the Ugaritic dragon is a hydra*. It has seven heads. However, the most important features that demonstrate their mutual identification are the cognate titles "fleeing serpent," and "twisting serpent." As the Ugaritologist Ola Wikander at Lund University writes, these terms are so rare that, "it is quite unthinkable that the combination of…these two specific words should have arisen by chance both in Ugaritic and Hebrew literature, and so a historical connection must be postulated."[17] The connection between Leviathan and *Litanu*, therefore, "is rather well-known in modern exegetical

---

[16] Quoted with commentary in Aïcha Rahmouni, *Divine Epithets in the Ugaritic Alphabetic Texts*. Trans., J.N. Ford, Handbook of Oriental Studies. Section I, The Near and Middle East (Leiden: Brill, 2008), 300. For those unfamiliar with Ugaritic, the abbreviation "KTU," I will be using refers to the numbering system in M. Dietrich, O. Loretz, and J. Sanmartín (eds.), *The Cuneiform Alphabetic Texts from Ugarit, Ras Ibn Hani and Other Places* (Münster: Ugarit-Verlag, 1995).

[17] Wikander, "Dragon-Slaying to Isaiah 27.1," 117.

scholarship,"[18] and is considered by scholars to be "indisputable."[19] These stock phrases for speaking about the chaos dragon must have circulated throughout Northwest Semitic culture for many centuries. Interestingly, the Ugaritic text, Psalm 74, and Isaiah 27 all depict the deity (Yhwh or Baal) smiting the dragon.

In the beautiful Psalm 74:12-17, God even smites Leviathan *as a part of creating the world* and the establishment of the sea and dry land:

> Yet God my King is from of old;
>> working sustaining deeds in the midst of the earth.
> You divided, by your strength, Sea;
>> **you broke the heads of the sea monsters in the waters.**
> **You crushed the heads of Leviathan;**
>> **you gave him for food to the inhabitants of the wilderness.**
> You cleft open fountain and river;
>> you dried ever-flowing streams.
> **Yours is the day, yours also the night;**
>> **you have set in place moon and sun.**
> **You have established all the boundaries of earth**
>> **you have fashioned summer and winter.**

In his Grace Theological Seminary doctoral thesis, Richard Engle points out that the last four lines "duplicate vocabulary and concepts from Genesis 1-2."[20] The evangelical Hebrew scholar Michael Heiser, agrees

---

[18] Ibid. Williams points out the Leviathan parallel to new students of Ugaritic in the first lesson of his popular grammar. Michael Williams, *Basics of Ancient Ugaritic: A Concise Grammar, Workbook, and Lexicon* (Grand Rapids: Zondervan, 2012), 20. Rahmouni also states, "As is well known, the parallel pair *btn brh* // *btn 'qltn* is the exact semantic equivalent of the Biblical Hebrew נחש ברח // נחש עקלתון (Isa. 27:1), which explicitly refers to לויתן 'Leviathan,' the Hebrew equivalent of Ltn." *Divine Epithets*, 143. Niehaus comments, "The verbal parallel alone between the Ugaritic and the Hebrew is astonishing.... It shows how stock phrasing can survive over many centuries—a common enough phenomenon in the ancient Near East, the more remarkable here because of an intercultural context." Jeffrey Jay Niehaus, *God at Sinai: Covenant and Theophany in the Bible and Ancient Near East* (Grand Rapids: Zondervan, 1995), 113.
[19] Averbeck, "Ancient Near Eastern," 338.
[20] Richard W. Engle, "Psalm 74: Studies in Content, Structure, Context and Meaning" (D. Th. thesis, Grace Theological Seminary, 1987), 99.

that most of "the language in [these] verses…can be found in Genesis 1 (Gen 1:4-5, 9-10, 14-18)."[21]

Therefore, Psalm 74 envisions Leviathan being defeated at the creation of the world. But then, in Isaiah 27, we saw that God will smite Leviathan, "the fleeing serpent . . . the twisting serpent," "in *that day*"—not just at creation, but at the end of days.

If we are to take Psalm 74 literally, why doesn't the creation account in Genesis also speak of God slaying a dragon in conjunction with creating the world? And why does Leviathan have multiple heads, breathe fire, and, for that matter, why would God beat up a poor *Liopleurodon* at the end of days in Isa 27:1?

If taken literally, these descriptions of Leviathan are contradictory. Therefore, it is clear that Psalm 74 and Isaiah 27 are probably speaking in literary and symbolic terms, not narrating the ancient equivalent of a National Geographic special.

WHAT DOES THE DRAGON SYMBOLIZE?

Job uses Leviathan in parallel with other dragons found in the Ugaritic texts—the Hebrew names *Tannin* and *Yam*. Moreover, these names are used interchangeably with the name *Rahab* and the title *fleeing serpent*. Notice the interchangeability of these titles in Job:

Job 7:12: Am I *Yam* (Sea) or a *tannin* (sea-serpent) that you would set watch over me?

Job 9:13: God won't withdraw his anger; the helpers [i.e. the *tannin*] of *Rahab* are humbled beneath him.

Job 26:12-13: By his power, he upheaved the sea [Hebrew: *yam*]. By his wisdom, he smote *Rahab*.
…his hand pierced the fleeing [*brh*] serpent

You will notice in the last passage that *Rahab* is called by the same title Isaiah gives Leviathan and that the Ugaritic texts give *Litanu*—the "fleeing serpent." It is also important to note that Job mentions *Yam*

---

[21] Michael S. Heiser, *The Unseen Realm: Recovering the Supernatural Worldview of the Bible* (Bellingham: Lexham Press, 2015), 153.

because *in the Ugaritic texts* the "twisting serpent" *Litanu* is also used in conjunction with both *Yam* and *Tannin*:

Surely I destroyed *Yam*, beloved of El,
  surely I made an end of River, the mighty god.
Surely I lifted up the Dragon [*tannin*] of the two flames
I destroyed the twisting ['*qltan*] Serpent,
  the Tyrant with the seven heads.[22]

Earlier in the same text, this "tyrant" is referred to as *Litanu*.[23] Therefore, *Yam, Litanu, Rahab, Tannin,* and *Leviathan* are all overlapping names.[24] The title "dragon of the two flames" in the text above may even imply that the Ugaritic *Litanu* was fiery—an idea which would give us another conceptual parallel to the fire breathing in Job 41.[25] We also have ancient Near Eastern artifacts depicting seven-headed dragons both emanating flame and exhaling fire as they fight various gods.[26]

It should be clear by now that each of the biblical and Ugaritic texts we have looked at associate this monster with the sea (the title *Yam* means "sea" in Hebrew and Ugaritic). But why is God waging a battle against the sea in Isa 27:1, Job 26:12-13, and Psalm 74?

In the Ugaritic texts, *Litanu* was the god of the chaotic waters of the sea that ever surround and threaten to overcome the terrestrial world.[27] After Baal slays this enemy and is about to celebrate by building his palace, one of the gods exclaims, "Yam is indeed dead! Baal shall be

[22] KTU 1.3:III:38-46, quoted in John Day, *God's Conflict with the Dragon and the Sea: Echoes of a Canaanite Myth in the Old Testament* (Cambridge: Cambridge University Press, 1985), 13-14.
[23] KTU 1.5:I:3. See comments in Rahmouni, *Divine Epithets*, 300.
[24] Averbeck likewise notes this in the Baal literature. Averbeck, "Ancient Near Eastern Mythography," 341.
[25] Rahmouni, *Divine Epithets*, 310. The title *tnn 'istm lh* "the dragon of the two flames" occurs only once in the Ugaritic texts, so its full meaning is enigmatic. Rahmouni compares the syntax of the title with others and concludes that there may be a relation to Job 41 and Mesopotamian fire-dragon art.
[26] The first is a cylinder seal from Tell Asmar in Baghdad. The second is etched on a Sumerian shell inlay. These are depicted in Bernard F. Batto, *In the Beginning: Essays on Creation Motifs in the Ancient Near East and the Bible*. Siphrut 9 (Winona Lake: Eisenbrauns, 2013), 32.
[27] Christoph Uehlinger, "Leviathan" in K. van der Toorn, Bob Becking, and Pieter Willem van der Horst (eds.), *Dictionary of Deities and Demons in the Bible (DDD)* (Leiden: Brill, 1999), 511-515.

king!"[28] Baal's domination over the destructive forces of the sea, therefore, demonstrated his *kingship* over the created realm.[29] This same kingship symbolism can be found by reexamining Psalm 74.

Psalm 74 opens with a description of how the Babylonians have just conquered Judah. Its authors find themselves exiled in Babylonia lamenting that these foreign pagans have raided and torched Yhwh's temple (v. 7). They long for God to correct this injustice and return them to their homeland: "Why, O God, do you cast us off forever?... Remember your congregation, which you have purchased of old.... How long, O God will the enemy scoff?" The tone of the poem then becomes hopeful as the psalmist reflects how, at the foundation of the world, Yhwh "divided" the Sea—smashing the heads of Leviathan before creating the sun and moon and "establishing all the boundaries of earth" (v. 17).

This story is important because it remarkably parallels how the Babylonians themselves believed the world was created.

In the mid-nineteenth century, archaeologists excavating in ancient Nineveh shook the world of biblical studies when they discovered clay tablets recounting the Babylonian myth of creation. These ancient tablets tell of how the king of the Babylonian pantheon, Marduk, acquired his throne.

Like Yhwh's defeat of Leviathan and Baal's battle with *Litanu*, Marduk had an epic brawl with a watery, primeval chaos dragon, in this version, named Tiamat. After defeating this foe, we read, "with his merciless club [Marduk] smashed her skull."[30] Then, slicing Tiamat's colossal body in two, Marduk used her upper half to create the sky and her bottom half to form the earth. After setting the celestial bodies in the heavens, Marduk then uses the dragon's spit to form clouds. Her head becomes a mountain, and the Tigris and Euphrates rivers, central

---

[28] KTU 1.3:XXXII. Quoted in John C. L. Gibson, *Canaanite Myths and Legends*, 2 ed. (London: T & T Clark, 1956), 45.

[29] Cf. the "lordship" and "king of beasts" comments in Henry Rowold, " מי הוא ?לי הוא!: Leviathan and Job in Job 41:2-3," *Journal of Biblical Literature* 105.1 (1986), 108.

[30] *Enuma Elish*, IV.130. Translation: L. W. King, *Enuma Elish: The Seven Tablets of Creation*, vol. 1 (London: Luzac and Co., 1902), 75.

to the ancient Mesopotamian world, gushed forth from her eye sockets.[31]

Recall that Job 41:2 asks, "Can you put a cord through [Leviathan's] nose, or pierce his jaw with a hook?" A common motif in Mesopotamian art for gods that wage battle against the chaos dragon and its monstrous minions shows the deity standing on top of these defeated enemies who come to represent aspects of the god's power. Maul directs us to two images shown in Figure 2.[32] The left shows an engraving from a Babylonian cylinder seal (c. ninth century) wherein Marduk stands over a pedestal symbol of the defeated sea and its associated chaos dragon. The cylinder seal engraving on the right shows the god Adad with tamed chaos dragons leashed, apparently through the mouth or nose.[33]

Figure 2. Marduk and Adad standing over defeated chaos dragons. Images from Robert Koldewey, *Mitteilungen der Deutschen Orient-Gesellschaft* 5 (1900), 13, 14 (images 2 and 3).

In Babylonian religion, the chaos dragon needed to be defeated, and her waters were ever restrained by Marduk in order for life on earth to be created and sustained. When we read Psalm 74 in this context, we see it

---

[31] *Enuma Elish* IV.93-V.66. I owe this reference to B. Alster, "Tiamat," in *DDD*, 867.

[32] Stefan M. Maul, "Der Sieg über die Mächte des Bösen: Götterkampf, Triumphrituale und Torarchitektur in Assyrien" in Erich Zenger (ed.), *Ritual und Poesie: Formen und Orte religiöser Dichtung im Alten Orient, im Judentum und im Christentum*. Herder's Biblical Studies 36 (Freiburg: Freiburg, 2003), 67.

[33] Ibid.

as a slap in the face of the pagan gods. It takes this same epic story, erases hotshot gods like Baal or Marduk and inserts Yhwh. Yhwh is the *real* dragon slayer! He is the one who defeated the oceanic forces of chaos and created the world, and he alone—not Baal or Marduk—deserves worship as its rightful king.

Did the Old Testament writers believe that God fought a literal dragon to create the world? The author of Genesis 1 sure didn't seem to think so. He talks directly about God piercing the chaos and separating the sea. However, there is no hint in Genesis 1 of any such crucial battle with the dragon that personified these in Near Eastern mythology.[34] Therefore, unless we want to say the author of Psalm 74 and the author of Genesis 1 held contradictory views of the means through which God created the world, we must conclude that the author of Psalm 74 is using leviathan *as a figurative symbol,* most likely to emphasize Yhwh's kingship over creation.

LEVIATHAN IN JOB 41

We may now return to the museum display with which we kicked off this chapter.

A sign in the Creation Museum portico reads:

> Some Christians suggest that these are mythical monsters, but the mention of Behemoth and Leviathan in the book of Job follows the descriptions of about a dozen real animals. Furthermore, why would God tell Job to consider two beasts that did not even exist?[35]

---

[34] Indeed, Genesis 1 is widely recognized (especially by conservatives) as a conscious denial of this *chaoskampf* cosmogony. See, David T. Tsumura, *Creation and Destruction: A Reappraisal of the Chaoskampf Theory in the Old Testament* (Winona Lake: Eisenbrauns, 2005), 143; Kenneth A. Mathews, *The New American Commentary*, vol. 1A (Nashville: Broadman & Holman Publishers, 1996), 157; This popular polemical interpretation was defended by Gerhard F. Hasel, "The Polemic Nature of the Genesis Cosmology," *Evangelical Quarterly* 46 (1974), 87; It is likewise expressed by scholars like J. Richard Middleton, "Created in the Image of a Violent God? The Ethical Problem of the Conquest of Chaos in Biblical Creation Texts," *Interpretation* 58.4 (2004), 352. Also alluded to by Mark S. Smith, *The Priestly Vision of Genesis 1* (Minneapolis: Fortress Press, 2010), 108.

[35] On the sign entitled, "Were Dinosaurs Dragons."

These objections are weak because the author of Job 41 is referencing Leviathan in a literary manner similar to the other biblical authors and cultures of the ancient Near East: as a personification of the watery chaos that ever threatens the created order. This mythological interpretation is especially supported by the fact that, in the very same book, Job 26:12-13 even recounts a primordial battle between God and this foe similar to Baal's fight against the Ugaritic *Litanu*.

Therefore, in Job 41, Leviathan's placement at the end of a list of natural animals emphasizes the fact that the author has progressed from praising God by describing his dominion over natural animals in creation to praising God by describing his dominion over a Near Eastern stock motif of natural chaos itself. It caps off these chapters by expressing God's dominion over *all creation* collectively. Symbolically, it is by God's domination of this "super-monster" that the inhabitable world is sustained.

CONCLUSION

In summation, the evidence that Leviathan is not a Jurassic Park escapee includes the following:

1) In Psalm 74, God's defeat of Leviathan precedes the creation of the world. If literal, this would contradict the creation account in Genesis 1.

2) Isaiah says Leviathan will be killed *again* at the eschaton. (What? Is there a surviving *Liopleurodon* out there in the Atlantic that God is going to give a knuckle sandwich at the eschaton?)

3) He has the cognate titles of an earlier Near Eastern chaos dragon (and however old you think Job is, it's obvious that Job's allusions to figures like Yam and Rahab reference earlier known Semitic dragon motifs).

4) In addition to *breathing fire* in Job 41 (!), in Psalm 74, Leviathan has multiple heads (undoubtedly seven like his Ugaritic

counterpart). There are no seven-headed reptiles in the fossil record.

With the Ugaritic texts now on the table, I think it is time young-earth leaders amend their views of Job 41. Their interpretation contradicts how Leviathan is used in other biblical passages, and consequently, obscures the literary meaning of the creature as a personification of chaos.

But what of Leviathan's mysterious twin? Is the creature Behemoth a dinosaur?

CHAPTER 2

WAS BEHEMOTH A DINOSAUR?

YOUNG-EARTH creationists frequently claim Behemoth was a dinosaur—usually some sort of long-necked sauropod.[1] A sign in the Creation Museum portico quotes the biblical description of the creature next to a picture of a brachiosaur fending off humans trying to hunt it with spears.[2]

Ken Ham argues that the biblical phrase, "He is first of the works of God" implies that the cryptid must be greatest in size of all the animals: "Behemoth is very much like *Brachiosaurus*, one of the large dinosaurs."[3]

Henry M. Morris also wrote, "Note the description of behemoth in Job 40:15-24, and observe how impossible it is to apply these words to either the elephant or hippopotamus…. Every sentence is appropriate in describing…a huge dinosaur…. [N]o other animal we are aware of, living or extinct, fits the bill."[4]

---

[1] In addition to ensuing citations see, for example, Gary Parker, *Building Blocks in Science: Laying a Creation Foundation* (Green Forrest: Master Books, 2007), 47; Ken Ham, *Dinosaurs for Kids* (Green Forrest: Master Books, 2009), 48; Joe White and Nicholas Comninellis, *Darwin's Demise: Why Evolution Can't Take the Heat* (Green Forrest: Master Books, 2001), 59; Darek Isaacs, *Dragons or Dinosaurs? Creation or Evolution?* (Alachua, FL: Bridge Logos, 2010), 55; Ray Comfort, *Nothing Created Everything: The Scientific Impossibility of Atheistic Evolution* (Los Angeles: WND Books, 2009), 61.

[2] On the sign entitled, "Not the Stuff of Legends".

[3] Ken Ham, *The New Answers Book 1: Over 25 Questions on Creation Evolution and the Bible,* Ken Ham (ed.) (Green Forest, AR: Master Books), 160.

[4] Henry M. Morris, *The Biblical Basis for Modern Science: The Revised and Updated Classic!* (Green Forest, AR: Master Books, 2002), 333.

Not only can one find this idea defended in sources like the *Journal of Creation*,[5] but it's also taught in educational material aimed towards kids. One of Answers in Genesis' speakers, who leads a children's workshop for the organization's conferences, has written a catchy song titled, "Behemoth is a Dinosaur." Video of one of these workshops shows a roomful of engaged children clapping and singing along as lyrics project on a screen backdropped by various images of brachiosaurs:

> Behemoth is a dinosaur,
>   a dinosaur is he.
> "He eateth grass as an ox."
> "His tail's like a cedar tree."
> "His bones are strong as bars of iron."
> "He's chief in the ways of God."
> Could behemoth be a dinosaur,
>   a mighty sauropod?[6]

Our suspect in question appears in Job 40:15-23. The ESV reads:

> Behold, Behemoth, which I made as I made you;
>   he eats grass like an ox.
> Behold, his strength in his loins,
>   and his power in the muscles of his belly.
> He makes his tail stiff like a cedar;
>   the sinews of his thighs are knit together.
> His bones are tubes of bronze,
>   his limbs like bars of iron.
> He is the first of the works of God;
>   let him who made him bring near his sword!
> For the mountains yield food for him
>   where all the wild beasts play.
> Under the lotus plants he lies,
>   in the shelter of the reeds and in the marsh.

---

[5] Allan K. Steel, "Could Behemoth have been a Dinosaur?," *Journal of Creation* 15.2 (2001), 42–45.

[6] Video of this can be seen about 15 minutes into the documentary *Friends of God*. Alexandra Pelosi, *Friends of God: A Road Trip With Alexandra Pelosi*, HBO, Jan 25, 2007. The song can be found on Buddy Davis' *Creation Musical Adventures*, Answers in Genesis. Track 20, 2013, MP3.

For his shade the lotus trees cover him;
    the willows of the brook surround him.
Behold, if the river is turbulent he is not frightened;
    he is confident though Jordan rushes against his mouth.

The fact that Behemoth appears adjacent to and paired with a fire-breathing, seven-headed chaos dragon should, perhaps, caution us against automatically presuming that he must be a natural animal. Immediately, it should be apparent there are many pieces of evidence to suggest that the Creation Museum is wrong when it claims we should identify Behemoth as something like a brachiosaur or *Argentinosaurus*.

A SUPER-BULL?

The name Behemoth is built on a common Hebrew word most frequently (though not exclusively) used for cattle, *behemah*. The *oth* ending functions as an "intensive" form. Linguistically, the connotation suggests that this is a sort of super-bull, or "super-ox," as the Hebraist Bernard F. Batto notes.[7] There is nothing in the passage that describes him as reptilian—something we would reasonably expect if this were a dinosaur.

Second, what is impressive about a sauropod like a brachiosaur? If you had to brag about one in a poem what chief feature would come to mind that would be worth mentioning? How about the fact that its head hung several stories in the air, that its entire biomorphology is framed around feeding from the tops of trees! If the author of Job wanted to brag about brachiosaur's features, you would think he would have mentioned these distinctions rather than the comparatively pitiful and opposite line: "He feeds on *grass* like an ox."[8] For the author to omit the business about Behemoth's alleged thirty feet of neck seems about as unlikely as me bragging about a giraffe's features in a poem and forgetting to mention its neck.

---

[7] B. F. Batto, "Behemoth" in K. van der Toorn, Bob Becking, and Pieter Willem van der Horst (eds.) *Dictionary of Deities and Demons in the Bible (DDD)* (Leiden: Brill, 1999), 165.
[8] The Hebrew term translated 'grass' here is not ambiguous. It occurs 21 times in the Bible, usually with reference to being consumed by cattle and horses.

BEHEMOTH'S TAIL

Despite the difficulties, young-earthers have a perfectly understandable reason for invoking a dinosaur in this passage. They point us to the enigmatic line, "He stiffens his tail like a cedar."[9] No known living animal possesses a tail that might call a cedar to mind. A brachiosaur certainly does. What other animal could it possibly be?

There is one minor complication.

This line about the creature's tail probably doesn't refer to a tail. It's much more likely a euphemism for his male organ. That explanation may not preach easily on Sunday morning, but it isn't some new-spun liberalization by pointy-headed academics. It's very ancient, emphasized in most academic commentaries, and is firmly supported by the lexical evidence.

The portion of the poem describing Behemoth's body uses what scholars call list or bicola parallelism,[10] a classic Hebrew literary technique in which each line echoes the thought of the previous (40:16-18):

Behold, his strength in his **loins**,
  and his power in the muscles of his **belly**.

He extends his **tail** like a cedar;
  the sinews of his **thighs** are knit together.

His bones are tubes of **bronze**,
  his limbs like bars of **iron**.

The following four arguments favor the idea that Behemoth's tail is a euphemism for his reproductive anatomy:

1) If you've read much biblical poetry, you'll be familiar with the fact that it frequently operates through repetition. That is, the biblical poets like to state an idea in a short line then repeat or

---

[9] E.g., ESV, CSB, HCSB, ISV, NET, JPS.
[10] As noted by David Bernat, "Biblical *Wasfs* Beyond Song of Songs," *Journal for the Study of the Old Testament* 28.3 (2008), 335.

expand on the same idea in the following line. Most of Job 40 is written according to this form of verse structure. Notice that the word "tail" is paralleled with the Hebrew word translated "thighs" in the following line. This word "thighs," *pachad* in Hebrew, only appears once in the Bible, but we know its meaning through Aramaic and a cognate Arabic word.

In Aramaic literature, the word our modern English translations translate as "thighs" actually refers to the testicles.[11] "Thighs" is a literally correct translation, but the point of the term is that it was a polite designation for what exists between the thighs. This is why the KJV translates this word "stones," and why ancient Jewish scholars like Rashi and Ibn Ezra interpreted it as "testicles."[12] The ancient Latin Vulgate likewise uses the word *testiculorum*, and some modern Hebrew experts have also opted for direct translations implying the testicles.[13] The best data we have on the meaning of this Hebrew term effectively place the word translated "tail" in couplet parallelism to *testicles*. Therefore, a literal interpretation of *tail* doesn't fit the bill.

2) In his technical article discussing the poetic structure of this passage in the *Journal for the Study of the Old Testament*, David Bernat points out that a euphemism for the masculine organ makes sense of the otherwise problematic verb connected with behemoth's "tail"—that he "extends" it or "stiffens" it.[14] Explaining it as his male appendage creates a clever use of double meaning in the poem. The Hebrew verb *chafaiz* refers to ideas like "extending," "moving" or "stiffening" as most translations render it in the passage. But we know the word frequently also connotes meanings like "desire," and "delight."[15]

---

[11] Bernat (Ibid., 336) points us to *Onqelos* and *Pseudo-Jonathan*, which use the term in translating Lev 21:20.

[12] Ibid.

[13] See Robert Alter, *The Wisdom Books: Job, Proverbs, Ecclesiastes; A Translation with Commentary* (New York: W. W. Norton & Co., 2010), 169-170. Mitchell translates the passage, "His penis stiffens like a pine," and, "his testicles...."
Stephen Mitchell, *The Book of Job* (New York: Harper Perennial, 1992), 126-27.

[14] Bernat, "Biblical *Wasfs*," 226.

[15] For example, God "delights" in truth in Psa 51:6. Other examples of this use include Gen 34:19, Num 14:8, Deut 21:14, or 1 Sam 2:25.

A sexual euphemism makes sense of both these meanings and logically supports the surrounding verses extolling features of strength: "Behold! His strength is in his *loins*.... The sinews of his *testicles* are knit...."

3) Bernat also points out that the term translated "strength" here (as in, "his *strength* is in his loins") also refers to sexual virility in other biblical passages. He cites Gen 49:3, Deut 21:17, and Psa 105:36 as examples of this.[16]

4) Ancient post-biblical Hebrew used this same word "tail" as a euphemism for the male appendage.[17]

If the author of Job was referring to Behemoth's male appendage, why not just say it rather than using a confusing euphemism?

The main answer to this objection is that it would be weird if Job *didn't* use a euphemism. There is no specific word for the male appendage in the Bible. As a rule, for cultural reasons, biblical literature is remarkably creative about referring to sexual anatomy.

In the Dead Sea Community Rule Scroll, the author uses the word "hand" as a euphemism for the male body part.[18] If you wade into the Hebrew, the Bible apparently uses this euphemism in Isaiah.[19] More examples include the general word "flesh" (Exod 28:42), several different terms for "nakedness" (Lev 18:6; Hab 2:15), "secret parts" (Deut 25:11), "spout" (Deut 23:1), the general word "loins" (1 Kgs 12:10), and, strange enough, possibly even the word "feet" (Ruth 3:3-4; Isa 7:20; Ezek 16:25).[20] Later, with the Jewish Talmud and Mishna, the number of Hebrew euphemisms for this body part greatly increases.[21]

It's important I don't overstate my case; we don't have any other Bible passages that use this particular euphemism, "tail." At the same

---

[16] Bernat, "Biblical *Wasfs*," 336.

[17] As noted by Scott C. Jones, "Corporeal Discourse in the Book of Job," *Journal of the Society of Biblical Literature* 132.4 (2013), 861.

[18] 1QS 7:13-14. See also 11QT 46:13. I owe these references to Bernat, "Biblical *Wasfs*," 335-6.

[19] See Isa 57:8. This euphemism is likewise probably used in Song 5:4.

[20] Most of these examples are taken from Elon Gilad, "Why Hebrew has so Many Words for 'Penis,'" *Haaretz*. Jul 22, 2015. Accessed May 8, 2017, www.haaretz.com/jewish/features/.premium-1.667193.

[21] Ibid, Gilad.

time, the fact that Job would use a euphemism here is something we ought to expect, and the parallel structure of the Hebrew poetry anticipates it.

WHAT IS BEHEMOTH?

So what is Behemoth? Given that he appears in literary dyad with a dragon used in ancient literature as a personification of aquatic chaos, Behemoth is likely a mythic chaos counterpart to Leviathan. Not only is this how early Jewish texts understood the creature,[22] but it would correspond quite nicely with a reference made in an Ugaritic text that we've already encountered in relation to Leviathan:

> Surely I lifted up the Dragon.
> I destroyed the twisting Serpent,
> the Tyrant with the seven heads.
> I destroyed Arshu, beloved of El,
> I put an end to El's calf Atik.[23]

Consider the situation we have on our hands in the above text.

The Ugaritic version of Leviathan just so happens to be paired with a mythical bull called "the calf of god." (The god *El* in the Ugaritic pantheon was the highest deity.)

---

[22] Notably, 4 Ezra 6:49-52 and the Apocalypse of Baruch 24:4 speak of Behemoth and Leviathan being devoured by the people of God at the last day. See Mulder's survey on the mythological significance of these creatures in early Jewish literature. Michael Mulder, "Leviathan on the Menu of the Messianic Meal: The Use of Various Images of Leviathan in Early Jewish Tradition" in Koert van Bekkum, et al. (eds.) *Playing with Leviathan: Interpretation and Reception of Monsters from the Biblical World*. Themes in Biblical Narrative 21 (Netherlands: Brill, 2017), 118-130. Citing the same Jewish traditions, Pope writes, "The eschatological interpretation tends to confirm the mythological character of both beasts." Marvin Pope, *Job: A New Translation with Introduction and Commentary by Marvin Pope*, The Anchor Bible vol. 15 (New York: Doubleday, 1965), 321.
[23] Translation John N. Day, "God and Leviathan in Isaiah 27:1," *Bibliotheca Sacra* 115 (1998), 428.

When we look at the main biblical passage that talks about Leviathan, what do we find? He, too, it seems, is paired with a 'super-bull'—an intensified form of *behemah*, a common Hebrew word for cattle.

It seems remarkably unlikely that this similar pairing in both the biblical and Ugaritic texts is merely a coincidence. As a result, many if not most scholars like John Day, former professor of Old Testament at Oxford University, or Nili Wazana at the Hebrew University of Jerusalem, have found the view that Behemoth was a kind of super-bull to be the most reasonable interpretation.[24] If the Job passage is describing a literal wild ox, this creature was likely seen as an earthly counterpart a mythic divine being.

We don't know much about the divine bull Atik, but we do have precedence for divine bulls in other ancient Near Eastern texts. In the Epic of Gilgamesh, for example, the goddess Inanna sends, to defeat the heroes Gilgamesh and Enkidu, a tremendous "bull of heaven"—a bull so great that it "drank the water of [a] river in great slurps. With each slurp it used up one mile of the river, but its thirst was not satisfied."[25] This is reminiscent of what we read of Behemoth (40:23): "Behold, if the river is turbulent he is not frightened; he is confident though Jordan rushes against his mouth."

Also, Job 40:21 says that Behemoth dwells, "in the shelter of *the reeds* and in the marsh." Psa 68:30 similarly describes bulls as dwellers "*among reeds*," and the Ugaritic texts likewise use the same cognate term *reeds* to describe the bulls that inhabited marshy regions around a place called Lake Huleh.[26]

Finally, I have emphasized how strongly the passage praises the virility of Behemoth, referring to his reproductive organs twice and how "his strength is in his loins." This, too, aligns well with a bovine

---

[24] See Elmer B. Smick, "Mythology and the Book of Job," *Journal of the Evangelical Theological Society* 13.2 (1970), 106; Batto, "Behemoth," 165; John Day, *Yahweh and the Gods and Goddesses of Canaan* (Sheffield: Sheffield Academic Press, 2000), 103; Nili Wazana, "Anzu and Ziz: Great Mythical Birds in the Ancient Near Eastern, Biblical, and Rabbinic Traditions," *Journal of the Ancient Near Eastern Society* 31.1 (2009), 112; Allan Dyssel, "Sea Monsters and Other Mythical Creatures Associated with the Primeval Flood in the Old Testament: A History of Denial," (D.Th., University of South Africa, 2017), 71.

[25] "Gilgamesh and the Bull of Heaven: a translation," *Electronic Text Corpus of Sumerian Literature* (1999), B55-B63, etcsl.orinst.ox.ac.uk/section1/tr1812.htm.

[26] See Pope, *Job*, 322.

identification because in the agrarian cultures of the ancient Near East, bulls were a stock symbol of power and fertility.[27]

CONCLUSION

Based on the connotation of the etymology, Ugaritic parallel evidence, biblical parallel language of dwelling "among reeds," and the fact that an allusion to the reproductive virility of bulls fits comfortably within the everyday experience of ancient agricultural civilization, it seems most likely that Behemoth was conceived of as a supernatural bovine creature. His placement next to Leviathan in a similar poetic structure implies that he too is perhaps a literary personification of chaos.

The truth claim of the passage is not about early post-Flood zoology. Rather, as with Leviathan, the author is most likely using this creature of mythic origins to teach us a lesson about God's domination over the cosmic order and man's frailty by comparison.

---

[27] This theme is frequently confirmed throughout Renate Marian Van Dijk, "The Motif of the Bull in the Ancient Near East: An Iconographic Study" (M.A. thesis, University of South Africa, 2011).

CHAPTER 3

KING JAMES' UNICORNS

MANY religious skeptics have attempted to mock the Bible by pointing out the multiple passages in the King James translation that make mention of unicorns. If you have never encountered these in your modern translation, several examples follow:

Deut 33:17: "His glory is like the firstling of his bullock, and his horns are like the horns of **unicorns**."

Job 39:10: "Canst thou bind the **unicorn** with his band in the furrow? or will he harrow the valleys after thee?"

Psa 29:6: "He maketh them also to skip like a calf; Lebanon and Sirion like a young **unicorn**."

Psa 92:10: "But my horn shalt thou exalt like the horn of an **unicorn**: I shall be anointed with fresh oil."

What do some young-earth creationists make of these passages? According to an Answers in Genesis article,[1] a video featured on their website,[2] and the *New Answers Book*,[3] the *re'em* (רְאֵם), translated

---

[1] Elizabeth Mitchell, "Will the Real Unicorn Please Stand Up?," *Answers in* Genesis, Jun 15, 2011. Accessed May 8, 2017, www.answersingenesis.org/extinct-animals/will-the-real-unicorn-please-stand-up/.

[2] Video posted in, "Unicorns in the Bible?," *Answers in* Genesis, Feb 3, 2015. Accessed May 8, 2017, www.answersingenesis.org/kids/videos/unicorns-Bible/.

"unicorn" in the King James, might be a prehistoric creature called an *Elasmotherium*. *Elasmotherium* was a Eurasian genus of giant rhinoceros reckoned by paleontologists to have gone extinct around 29,000 years ago at the end of the Pleistocene.

Many creationists feel compelled to identify the biblical cryptid with the prehistoric giant because it seems to them that the unicorn in the Bible has a single horn—the most prominent characteristic of *Elasmotherium*.

The author of an Answers in Genesis article says, "There is ample support for the possibility that the creature in view here really did have just one horn."[4] Ken Ham complained that a new *Elasmotherium* fossil had been dated at 29,000 years old and points out that, "We've written articles and even a book chapter defending the biblical unicorn and pointing out that it could very well have been an *Elasmotherium*…—the same extinct creature that news outlets are calling a 'Siberian unicorn!'"[5]

The Hebrew grammar shows this proposed identification is impossible.

In Deut 33:17, our old friend, the Hebrew plural noun construct, continues to be the banana peel on which Answers in Genesis has slipped. The singular *re'em* (רְאֵם) in that passage is bound to the plural-possessive form for horn (קַרְנֵיו). It is therefore grammatically impossible for a single-horned *Elasmotherium* to be what the ancient Hebrews were talking about.

So what is the *re'em*? In Deut 33:17, you will notice that this creature is used in poetic parallel with the term "bullock." It turns out that we also have a cognate word for this animal in an ancient language related to Hebrew called Akkadian. The Akkadian word *rimu* refers to a species of wild ox, and for this reason, modern biblical linguists (including those who translated the *New* King James version) translate it as such. The term unicorn in the original King James is simply a mistranslation for the wild ox (sorry if that's boring).

[3] Elizabeth Mitchell, "Unicorns in the Bible" in Ken Ham (ed.), *The New Answers Book 3: Over 35 Questions on Creation/Evolution and the Bible* (Green Forest, AR: Master Books, 2009), 320.
[4] Mitchell, "Will the Real Unicorn Please Stand Up?"
[5] Ken Ham, "Giant Siberian 'Unicorn' Discovered," *Ken Ham Blog*, Apr. 5, 2016. Accessed May 7, 2017, www.answersingenesis.org/blogs/ken-ham/2016/04/05/giant-siberian-unicorn-discovered/.

CONCLUSION

I bring up the unicorn example in brief here, not because it is particularly important as a thing in itself, but to demonstrate a point we will bring into the next chapter: A degree in astrophysics or medicine isn't necessarily transferable to Semitic literature analysis, and in texts that are culturally contextualized, interpretations can start getting out of hand very fast if we aren't careful.

To further illustrate this problem, I turn now to another example.

CHAPTER 4

MAKING SENSE OF ISAIAH'S FLYING SERPENTS

S OME popular young-earth authors have claimed that pterodactyls may have made a cameo appearance in the Bible. A display case in the Creation Museum certainly suggests this.[1]

According to Ken Ham, "There is…mention of a flying serpent in the Bible: the 'fiery flying serpent' (Isa 30:6). This could be a reference to one of the pterodactyls, which are popularly thought of as flying dinosaurs, such as the Pteranodon, Rhamphorhynchus, or Ornithocheirus."[2]

In an Answers in Genesis lecture, the physicist Jason Lisle has asserted the same claim: "What about flying reptiles like pterodactyl? Does the Bible mention things like that? Well, you know it does…. Isaiah talks about a fiery flying serpent…. [T]he Bible definitely talks about dinosaur-like creatures, no question of it."[3] Brian Thomas, one of the lead writers for the Institute for Creation Research, has also published a similar thesis.[4]

---

[1] Under the label "Romans and Dragons." The sign speaks of Ammianus Marcellinus mentioning Herodotus' flying serpents and asks, "Could these reptiles be the same as the creature called a 'fiery flying serpent' in Isaiah 30:6?"

[2] Ken Ham, "What Really Happened to the Dinosaurs" in Ken Ham (ed.), *The New Answers Book 1: Over 25 Questions on Creation/Evolution and the Bible* (Green Forest, AR: Master Books, 2006), 159.

[3] Stated six minutes into "Dinosaurs and the Bible, Part 2," *Answers in Genesis*, 00:14:33. Video Lecture uploaded March 2009, www.answersingenesis.org/media/video/animals/dinosaurs-and-Bible/.

[4] Brian Thomas, *Dinosaurs and the Bible* (Oregon: Harvest House, 2015), 46ff.

In *The New Answers Book*, Bodie Hodge, a speaker and writer for Answers in Genesis, takes the adjective "fiery" as a literal reference to fire breathing and points to the bombardier beetle comparison again.[5] One of the primary passages these gentlemen are referring to is Isa 30:6:

> An oracle upon the beasts of the Negev: In a land of trouble and suffering, in the domain of the lioness and lion, the viper and flying serpent [*saraph meofaif*], they will carry their riches on the shoulders of young donkeys, and upon the humps of camels take their treasures to a people that won't profit them.

Altogether, there are only five passages in the Old Testament that use this noun they are interpreting in Isaiah 30 as a possible pterosaur. The noun *saraph* appears in Num 21:6-8, Deut 8:15, Isa 6:2-6, 14:29, and 30:6.

What will become apparent is that there are two different categories of *saraphs* in the Bible. The first category refers to a natural creature that lives in a desert ecosystem. The second refers to a divine being that most readers will recognize by name—the mysterious *seraphim*. (Just as English marks the plural with the ending *s*, Hebrew designates it with the ending *im*.)

Both of these creatures, spelled the same in ancient Hebrew, were closely related in ancient biblical religion, and we must understand them with reference to each other.

SARAPH AS A NATURAL ANIMAL

Numbers and Deuteronomy provide us further context of what a *saraph* is when it is used to refer to a natural animal:

Num 21:6-8
Then the Lord sent fiery serpents [*nachashim seraphim*], and they bit the people so that many of Israel's people died.... And the Lord said to Moses, "Make for yourself a fiery serpent [simply, a *saraph* in

---

[5] Bodie Hodge, "Dragons…Were They Real?" in Ken Ham (ed.), *The New Answers Book Volume 4: Over 30 Questions on Creation/Evolution and the Bible* (Green Forest, AR: Master Books, 2013), 31-32.

Hebrew] and set it upon a pole, and it will be that all who are bitten, when they look at it, will live."

Deut 8:15

"…who led you through the great and terrible desert, with its fiery serpent [*nachash saraph*], and scorpion, and drought…"

What can we isolate from these two passages?

First, whatever it is, this creature lives in arid wilderness. Second, a leading treatment on the subject published in the *Journal for the Study of the Old Testament* points out that these two passages both use the word *saraph* as a descriptive identifier. How do we know? Because they both directly connect it with the more common word for snake—*nachash*, in Hebrew.

The Hebrew *nachash saraph* literally means "snake of fieriness." Though English reverses the word order, we qualify things like this in our own language all the time. For example: a "rattle snake," "corn snake," "sea snake," "garter snake," etc.[6]

Third, like the Isaiah passage that young-earthers cite, it is also obvious in both of the above texts that this snake is capable of killing with its venom, here described as "fiery."

"Fiery" is undoubtedly a reference to the intense burning sensation caused by its bite and likely the fact that a viper bite wound looks like incinerated flesh. The ancient Egyptians also used this same "fiery" language, specifically for the cobra.[7] All of these features check out as belonging to some sort of common desert snake, such as the red spitting cobra indigenous to the Judean Negev.

So why does the Isaiah passage describe it as flying? To understand this, it is necessary to now examine the divine being to which the noun *saraph* can also refer.

---

[6] See Philippe Provençal, "Regarding the Noun שָׂרָף in the Hebrew Bible," *Journal for the Study of the Old Testament* 29.3 (2005), 372.

[7] Currid collects many examples: The *Book of the Gates* speaks of a fire-spitting serpent named Kheti. The *Book of Am Duat* speaks of twelve *uraei* spitting forth fire to light the path of the sun. The *Story of the Shipwrecked Sailor* tells of a snake of deadly flame and another text entreats the crown god: "O Fiery Snake!" John D. Currid, *Ancient Egypt and the Old Testament* (Grand Rapids: Baker Books, 1997), 147-8.

SARAPH AS A DIVINE BEING

Those familiar with Isaiah will recognize that the term *saraph* sounds like a term the prophet uses in the throne room scene of chapter 6 to describe a category of divine beings. Isa 6:1-3 reads:

> In the year that King Uzziah died, I saw the Lord sitting on a throne, high and lifted up; and the train of his robe filled the temple. *Standing Seraphim were above him, each with six wings—six wings to each.* With two he covered his face, with two he covered his feet, and with two he did fly. And one cried to another, saying:

> "Holy, holy, holy is Yhwh of hosts!
> The whole earth is full of His glory!"

Archaeologists have long collected and cataloged ancient seal artifacts from Israel and Judah that were created during the period this passage was written. These seals were the main area of research in my own academic background. Important ancient individuals often had artisans carve semiprecious stones, often not much larger than a fingernail, with various icons as well as the bearer's name. These stone stamps were often worn in rings or as necklaces and were used to create impressions in lumps of clay for document security and verification in the ancient world. This is somewhat similar to how we use our seals today on legal documents. Occasionally, the art on these little stones depicts *seraphim* stylistically.

Figure 3. Hebrew seal ring, clay impression, and clay sealed papyrus documents. Illustrations by author.

Figure 4. Hebrew seraph seals. The left is a green stone in Clark Collection, "belonging to Elishama son of the king" (note Jer 41:1 and 2 Kgs 25:25). The middle is dark red jasper and inscribed as belonging to the family name Maaseyahu. Currently held in the *Cabinet des Médailles*, Paris. Right is limestone, "Belonging to Gaddiyahu" in the Moussiaf collection.

At first glance, you might think the seals pictured in Figure 4 were discovered in Egypt, but the script is paleo-Hebrew. The great Swiss Egyptologist and biblical scholar Othmar Keel provides images of over a dozen Hebrew seals with winged serpents like these.[8] In Iron Age Judah, the vast majority of seal art is Egyptian in style. As surprising as this may seem, it is clear that this borrowing of Egyptian motifs was not perceived by orthodox Jews of the period as sacrilegious since the images were often reinterpreted in ways that harmonized them with Yahwistic theology.

For example, the biblical historical authors were big fans of King Hezekiah. This personal confidant of the prophet Isaiah is said to have torn down the pagan altars in his kingdom, even going so far as to destroy Moses' bronze serpent when he saw people honoring it with incense (2 Kgs 2:4). According to 2 Kgs 2:5-6: "Hezekiah trusted in Yahweh, the God of Israel. There was no one like him among all the kings of Judah, either before him or after him. He held strong to Yahweh and did not stop following him."

---

8   Othmar Keel, *Jahwe-Visionen und Siegelkunst: Eine neue Deutung der Majestätsschilderungen in Jes, Ez 1 und 10 und Sach 4*, Stuttgarter Bibel-Studien 84/85 (Stuttgart: Verlag Katholisches Bibelwerk, 1984), 102; 104; 109. See also William A. Ward, "The Four-Winged Serpent on Hebrew Seals," *Rivista Degli Studi Orientali* 43.2 (1968), 135-43.

However, a strange puzzle emerges from this lavish praise. Modern archaeology has discovered at least 12 different seal impressions with inscriptions mentioning Hezekiah during his reign. The left of Figure 5 depicts one of these seal impressions discovered by archaeologists near the Temple Mount in 2009. The inscription states that the seal "Belongs to Hezekiah (son of) Ahaz, king of Judah," and bears Egyptian ankhs and the sun disk of the Egyptian god Ra.

What gives? Has the Bible lied to us about Hezekiah's singular devotion to Yahweh? Why would such a godly king put an image of a pagan sun god on the very emblem of his royal administration?

The short answer is that in the ancient Near East it was common to borrow attributes, titles, and even symbols of competing gods and to apply them to one's own god, often as a way of elevating one's god above the competition. Even Hezekiah's advisor Isaiah images Yahweh as the dawn sun in 58:8 and 60:1. In 60:19, Isaiah goes so far as to claim that God's glory will replace the luminescence of the sun at the New Creation. Psalm 139:9 speaks of the "winged dawn." It has been argued that the Hebrew of Amos 4:13 speaks of Yahweh bringing the "winged dawn,"[9] and Malachi 4:21 (Hebrew: 4:2) would write in the Persian period that Yahweh is "the Sun of Righteousness with healing in his wings." Other examples of passages that directly image Yahweh as the sun are Deut 33:2, 2 Sam 23:3b-4, and Ps 84:11.

With the understanding that it was not considered sinful to symbolize Yahweh as a winged sun disk in Egyptianized styles in Iron Age royal Judah, let us return to the issue of the winged serpent. The seal to the right in Figure 5 is especially significant to our investigation.

---

[9] John B. Whitley, "עיפה in Amos 4:13: New Evidence for the Yahwistic Incorporation of Ancient Near Eastern Solar Imagery," *Journal of Biblical Literature* 134.1 (2015), 127-138.

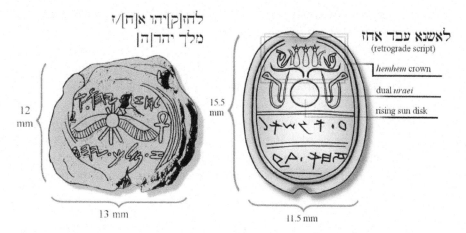

לחז[ק]יהו א[ח]ז/ז
מלך יהד[ה]

לאשנא עבד אחז
(retrograde script)

hemhem crown

dual *uraei*

rising sun disk

12 mm

15.5 mm

13 mm

11.5 mm

Figure 5. Left: Eighth century clay bulla, "Belonging to Heze[k]iah, (son of) 'A[h]az, king of Jud[ah]. Right: Eighth century Hebrew seal, "belonging to Ashna, minister of Ahaz." Digital illustrations by author.

I have shown in a recent study that this seal features a sun disk wearing a composite Egyptian crown known as the *hemhem*.[10] The *hemhem* crown embodies several mythic symbols most frequently associated with the sun's emergence over the horizon in Egyptian art.[11] In other words, this motif connects well with many biblical passages that specifically refer to Yahweh as a rising dawn sun.

Benjamin Sommer at The Jewish Theological Seminary in New York has specialized in biblical texts describing visual appearances of God. He agrees that the seal shown in the right of Figure 5, "portrays Yhwh symbolically as a sun disk wearing a crown (a typical representation in Israelite-Judean art). Yhwh is thus portrayed as king, and surrounding him are the seraphs."[12] Sommer therefore believes this seal parallels the

---

[10] § 3.3.3 of Benjamin Stanhope, "First Temple Hebrew Seals and Bullae Identifying Biblical Persons: A Study of their Iconographic and Historical Significance" (M. A. Thesis, Hamburg University, Dec 2019). Available: https://independent.academia.edu/BenStanhope.

[11] The most outstanding recent study is Katja Goebs, "Crown (Egypt)" in van der Toorn et al. (eds), *Iconography of Deities and Demons in the Ancient Near East*. Electronic Pre-Publication 14 April 2015 (Zürich: University of Zürich, 2015), 10-1. Online [cited 22 Aug 2019]: http://www.religionswissenschaft.unizh.ch/idd.

[12] Benjamin Sommer, "Seraphs," *Bible Odyssey* presented by *The Society of Biblical Literature*. Accessed May 8, 2017, www.Bibleodyssey.org/en/tools/ask-a-scholar/seraphs.

divine enthronement vision we find in Isaiah 6. Why should we take this parallel seriously? Sommer continues:

> The text on [this seal] states that it belonged to a courtier of King Ahaz named Ashna. In light of the similarity between the seal and Isaiah 6, it is worth noting that Jerusalem in the eighth-century B.C.E. was a very small town, that both Isaiah and Ashna lived during the reign of King Ahaz, and that Isaiah enjoyed very close connections to the royal court in which Ashna served (see Isa 7-9). Consequently, it is inconceivable that Isaiah and Ashna did not know each other.[13]

I don't think it's a coincidence that the passages to which many creationists point as referring to venomous winged serpents happen to be found in Isaiah, exactly at the time when flying cobra divine beings were a common Judean artistic motif.

As we saw in passages like Num 21:6-8, the Hebrew noun *saraph* often refers to a mundane type of desert snake. In fact, the biblical word likely originates from an Egyptian root associated with venomous snakes.[14]

As for their divine counterparts shown on the above seals, if we look at Egyptian art overlapping with this period, we find many examples that depict these serpents with human limbs and heads reminiscent of the anthropomorphization in Isaiah's throne room vision. (Isaiah 6:6 tells us the seraphim had "hands.") Given the sometimes contradictory ways ancient art adds and omits these features (sometimes in the same image), Keel has observed that it is evident the wings and humanoid features were fluidly interchanged, and are even implied when not explicitly shown in the art. Examples of this can be seen in Figure 6.[15]

---

[13] Ibid.

[14] See T. N. D. Mettinger entry "Seraph" in K. van der Toorn, Bob Becking, and Pieter Willem van der Horst (eds.) *Dictionary of Deities and Demons in the Bible* (*DDD*) (Leiden: Brill, 1999), 743.

[15] Top left, from the Papyrus of Amon-hotep, plate 26 in Alexandre Piankoff and Natacha Rambova, *Mythological Papyri,* Bollingen Series XI.3 (New York: Pantheon, 1957). Top right, from the tomb of Ramesses VI (adapted from reproduction in Keel, *Jahwe-Visionen,* 78). Upper middle image from the papyrus of Her-Uben B, produced in Piankoff, *Mythological Papyri,* 75. Lower middle image from the Papyrus of Amon-hotep in Piankoff, plate 26. Bottom image reproduced in Keel, *Jahwe-Visionen,* 78.

Figure 6. Human body parts were fluidly interchanged with the divine serpent motif in Egyptian art, even implied when not explicitly depicted. Notice the bottom image has identical creatures depicted both with and without arms in the same scene. Likewise, the two middle register images depict the same scene of serpents towing the solar barge, though interchanging the presence of human legs. Like the Ashna seal, the top right image also depicts serpents flanking a god symbolized by the disk, but here they have human arms.

Due to the linguistic evidence, the function of the seraphim, and the archaeology, *biblical scholars have established that the divine beings praising God upon his throne in Isaiah were probably serpentine.*[16] To us moderns used to picturing angels (though seraphim aren't technically angels in Hebrew) as pale blondes and serpents as usually synonymous with evil incarnate, this realization may come as a shock, but snakes were often positively associated in ancient desert cultures with divinity and wisdom. These associations were made for many reasons. For example, a snake's ability to shed its skin was taken in the biblical world as a symbol of rejuvenation, and consequently, of immortality and the gods.[17] Still, by the time that the ancient Jewish book of Enoch was written (which is quoted occasionally in the New Testament), we read of "Gabriel, one of the holy angels, who is in charge of Paradise, the serpents and the Cherubim" (1 Enoch 20:7-8).[18] Later (61:10 and 71:7), Enoch says the

---

[16] As Mettinger observed, "[T]here is now an emerging consensus that the Egyptian uraeus serpent is the original source of the seraphim motif." "Seraph" in *DDD*, 743. See also Lowell Handy, *Among the Host of Heaven: The Syro-Palestinian Pantheon as Bureaucracy* (Winona Lake: Eisenbrauns, 1994), 155.

[17] The classic example of serpent shedding representing immortality in the Near East is found in the *Epic of Gilgamesh* (Tablet XI) where the hero travels to the edge of the earth to find a mythical plant purported to grant renewed youth. On his journey home, Gilgamesh stops to bathe and a serpent steals the plant, sloughing behind its skin as a symbol of its newly gained revitalization.

Joines notes that in the Adapa legend, *Ningishzida*, the serpent-god, offers Adapa the food of immortality. The common Semitic root for serpent (*hawwa*) has also been linked with the same root for 'life,' and Eusebius reports that the Phoenicians and Egyptians associated the serpent with indefinite renewal. K. R. Joines, "The Serpent in Gen 3," *Zeitschrift für die Alttestamentliche Wissenschaft* 87 (1975), 2.

Lurker agrees: "[T]he snake, because it sloughs its skin, became a symbol of survival after death, as in Chapter 87 of the Book of the Dead." Manfred Lurker, *The Gods and Symbols of Ancient Egypt* (Britain: Thames and Hudson, 1980), 108.

Even in modern times, we still use the caduceus—two serpents intertwined on a pole—as a symbol for healing (i.e. rejuvenation). The caduceus can be found on Mesopotamian amulets and seals and was later inherited by the Greeks—an ancient Near Eastern symbolic tradition that Moses' bronze *seraph* serpent seems to be sharing in Num. 21. See discussion of the origin and history of the caduceus in Leslie S. Wilson, *The Serpent Symbol in the Ancient Near East: Nahash and Asherah: Death Life and Healing* (Lanham: University Press of America, 2001), 183-194.

[18] Translation: Matthew Black and James C. VanderKam, *The Book of Enoch or I Enoch: A New English Edition with Commentary and Textual Notes* (Leiden: Brill, 1985),

seraphim and cherubim surround God's throne, suggesting that the author may be conceptualizing *serpents* and *seraphim* interchangeably in the same vein as the eighth century BC artwork we've examined above.

We can now return to our original question: Do Egyptian serpent motifs help us to identify Isa 30:6's flying serpents in the desert? Provençal's paper concludes:

> The Uraeus-serpents of Ancient Egypt are often depicted with wings, and are commonly portrayed as cobras having two wings extending from their hoods. In other words, the winged serpents [of Isa 30:6] may be understood as mythological pendants to cobras whose outstretched hoods are depicted as wings.[19]

What does Provençal mean? *Uraeus* is a technical term for Egyptian royal guardian cobras (like those worn in the pharaoh's crown). When

Figure 7. Egyptian winged cobra. E. A. W. Budge, *The Gods of the Egyptians*, vol. 2 (London: Gilbert and Rivington, 1904), 65.

he says that divine winged serpents were seen as "mythological pendants to cobras," he means that normal cobras were viewed in the ancient Near East as the earthly counterpart to winged versions in the spiritual realm. (The cobra is particularly appropriate in that its expanding hood figuratively suggested the wings of the divine version.)

Occasionally, we make connections somewhat like this when we name animals in English. The *basilisk* lizard takes its name from the basilisk of Greek mythology. We speak of the *griffon* vulture, the *angelfish*, or the South American *harpy* eagle harking back to old Greek legend.

We know the Egyptians associated the cobra's hood with wings because their religious art depicted them as wings. For example, golden amulets of winged cobras were found around the neck of King Tut's mummy. The Egyptian Museum in Cairo currently houses a colorful statue of such a human-headed winged cobra (the goddess Weret-Hekau)

---

37. Note: The translators insert a parenthetical suggestion in the text that the serpents are seraphim. I have omitted this to avoid redundancy.

[19] Provençal, "Regarding the Noun שָׂרָף," 375-6.

discovered in the tomb of Amenhotep II. Likewise, winged cobras without human heads are frequently depicted on burial chamber friezes like those found guarding Amon-hir-khopshef's tomb. Most famously, the armrests of King Tut's throne are also formed from dual winged cobras.

CONCLUSION

Contextual study shows that Isaiah's "flying serpent" was a cultural nickname for the cobra. Likely, the Egyptian cobra and red spitting species indigenous to the Negev. We have the archaeological data to demonstrate this. There is nothing in the Egyptian or Judean literary and artistic material that might lead us to interpret the winged cobra motif (or the Old Testament's mundane inclusion of this creature among scorpions and vipers) as referring to a pterosaur like the Creation Museum suggests.

SECTION II

READING GENESIS LIKE AN ANCIENT ISRAELITE

How is it that complex and admirable ancient civilizations could have developed and flourished, initially, if they were predicated upon nonsense? (If a culture survives, and grows, does that not indicate in some profound way that the ideas it is based upon are valid? If myths are mere superstitious proto-theories, why did they work?...)

We appear to have made the presumption that stories such as these – myths – were equivalent in function and intent (but were inferior methodologically) to empirical or post-experimental description. It is this fundamentally absurd insistence that, above all, has destabilized the effect of religious tradition upon the organization of modern human moral reasoning and behavior.

–Jordan B. Peterson, Professor of Psychology, University of Toronto. *Maps of Meaning: The Architecture of Belief* (New York: Routledge, 1999), 19-20.

CHAPTER 5

DOES GENESIS 1:1 DESCRIBE THE ABSOLUTE BEGINNING?

I'LL be discussing the ancient meaning of the six-day creation of the earth in a later chapter, but perhaps a more interesting (and much more rarely asked question) is whether or not Genesis takes a stance on how old the universe itself is. The Creation Museum and Answers in Genesis believes it does.

As you walk through the Creation Museum, this unfolds in a drama. The museum depicts the fall of man into sin then expels you into a concrete room of looping grey film of atom bomb explosions, images of starving children, and goring wolves. This then leads down an alley depicting the devastation of addiction and adultery. A video shows a pastor snaking evolutionary teaching into Genesis before his congregation. A sidewall is sculpted to mimic the side of a church that is being demolished by a massive wrecking ball engraved with the words "millions of years." In large letters, another wall is adorned with a post-modern declaration: "Today man decides truth." The word "truth" has been crossed out with a scrawl of graffiti and is amended to embrace full nihilism: "Today man decides ~~truth~~ *whatever.*" After this unsettling depiction of cultural collapse, you are taken into a contrasting, hopeful, white room of flat screens and ubiquitous signs extolling the first clause of Genesis: "*In the beginning* God created the heavens and the earth."

Answers in Genesis understands these words to be what grammarians call an absolute temporal clause. They hold that the phrase "In the beginning…" encompasses the creation of the entire universe—of space-time itself. This is their logical basis for dating the *entire cosmos* at 6,000 years old, contrary to the some 13.7 billion years espoused by the majority of modern cosmologists.

In his book, *Taking Back Astronomy*, the popular young-earth astrophysicist Jason Lisle, who helped develop the Creation Museum planetarium, writes:

> The Bible implicitly teaches us about the age of the universe. In other words, it gives us sufficient information so that we can compute approximately how long ago God created the universe.... [W]e can conclude that the earth, the entire universe, and everything in it were created approximately 6,000 years ago.[1]

What's the problem with this position? Science aside, issues arise from the Hebrew text itself.

First, not a single one of our vowel-marked Hebrew manuscripts (called the Masoretic texts) mark Gen 1:1 with the word "the" (as in: "In *the* beginning"). This means the museum's planetarium and astrophysical models are, in part, predicated on a single word in the Hebrew Bible that doesn't exist. The word *the* is inferred.

A second problem is that a huge number of Hebrew grammarians, including evangelical Christians and conservative Jews reaching back to the Middle Ages, have come to reject the traditional translation.

A sampling of leading modern Hebraists who oppose it includes Robert Alter at the University of California, Berkeley,[2] Martin Baasten at the University of Leiden,[3] Mark S. Smith from NYU and Princeton,[4] Ellen van Wolde from Radboud University,[5] Robert Holmstedt at the University of Toronto,[6] Michael S. Heiser at Logos Bible Software,[7]

---

[1] Jason Lisle, *Taking Back Astronomy: The Heavens Declare Creation and Science Confirms It* (Green Forest, AR: Master Books, 2006), 40.

[2] Robert Alter, *The Five Books of Moses: A Translation with Commentary* (New York: Norton, 2004), 17.

[3] Martin F. J. Baasten, "First Things First: The Syntax of Gen 1:1-3 Revisited" in Martin F. J. Baasten, and Reinier Munk (eds.), *Studies in Hebrew Literature and Jewish Culture Presented to Albert Van Der Heide on the Occasion of His Sixty-Fifth Birthday* (Dordrecht: Springer, 2007), 169-88.

[4] Mark S. Smith, *The Priestly Vision of Genesis 1* (Minneapolis: Fortress Press, 2010), 44-45.

[5] See comments on the translation of Gen 1:1 in Ellen van Wolde, "Why the Verb ברא Does Not Mean 'to Create' in Genesis 1.1-2.4a," *The Journal for the Study of the Old Testament* 34.1 (2009), 7.

[6] Cited in the proceeding argument.

66

John Hobbins at Wisconsin-Oshkosh,[8] Francis Andersen at Fuller Seminary,[9] Bruce Waltke at Knox Seminary,[10] William P. Brown at Columbia Theological Seminary,[11] Miles Van Pelt at Reformed Theological Seminary,[12] Benjamin Sommer at Jewish Theological Seminary,[13] Jack Sasson at Vanderbilt University,[14] Richard E. Averbeck at Trinity Evangelical Divinity School,[15] Christine Hayes at Yale,[16] or Jon Levenson at Harvard.[17]

---

[7] Michael S. Heiser, "There's a Lot to Think About When Translating Genesis 1:1-3," *The Naked Bible Blog*, 2011. Accessed May 1, 2017. www.drmsh.com/theres-a-lot-to-think-about-when-translating-genesis-11-3/.

[8] John Hobbins, "A Response to Ellen van Wolde on Genesis 1," *Ancient Hebrew Poetry*, 2009. Accessed Feb 12, 2017. www.ancienthebrewpoetry.typepad.com/ancient_hebrew_poetry/2009/10/a-response-to-ellen-van-wolde-on-genesis-1.html.

[9] Francis Andersen, "On Reading Genesis 1-3" in Michael Patrick O'Connor and David Noel Freedman (eds.), *Backgrounds for the Bible* (Winona Lake: Eisenbrauns, 1987), 141.

[10] Bruce K. Waltke and M. O'Connor, *An Introduction to Biblical Hebrew Syntax* (Winona Lake: Eisenbrauns, 1990), 156.

[11] William P. Brown, "'Let There Be Light!' The Genesis of Biblical Cosmology," *Journal of Cosmology* 9 (2010), 2187-2193.

[12] Van Pelt is Professor of Old Testament and Biblical Languages and Academic Dean of Reformed Theological Seminary, Jackson. He endorses Holmstedt's work in Miles Van Pelt, "Exegetical Evidence for Non-Solar and Non-Sequential Interpretations of Genesis 1 and 2 Creation Days," in Timothy D. Finlay and William Yarchin (eds.), *The Genre of Biblical Commentary: Essays in Honor of John E. Hartley on the Occasion of His 75th Birthday* (Oregon: Wipf and Stock, 2015), 202.

[13] Benjamin D. Sommer, "An Anthology of Beginnings," *Parashat Bereishit 5776*. Produced by Jewish Theological Seminary (2015), www.jtsa.edu/an-anthology-of-beginnings.

[14] Jack M. Sasson, "Time…to Begin," in Michael Fishbane, Emanuel Tov and Weston W. Fields (eds.), *"Sha'arei Talmon": Studies in the Bible, Qumran, and the Ancient Near East Presented to Shermaryahu Talmon* (Winona Lake: Eisenbrauns, 1992), 187-88.

[15] Richard E. Averbeck, "A Literary Day, Inter-Textual, and Contextual Reading of Genesis 1-2" in J. Daryl Charles (ed.), *Reading Genesis 1-2: An Evangelical Conversation* (Massachusetts: Hendrickson, 2013), 9.

[16] Hayes is emphatic about this 29 minutes into "Lecture 3. The Hebrew Bible in its Ancient Near Eastern Setting: Genesis 1-4 in Context," YouTube Video,

I don't list these names to try to intellectually browbeat you into submission, but to illustrate that the view advanced by AiG has some serious opposition based on textual grounds.

In this chapter, I will briefly explain how modern research into the first few verses of Genesis casts serious doubt on the traditional grammatical assumptions made by many young-earth advocates concerning this passage. My thesis is that Genesis 1:1 doesn't comment on the age of the universe itself nor on the age of the materials from which the earth was made.

"IN THE BEGINNING"? OR "WHEN GOD BEGAN"?

To start, an example of the translation of Genesis 1:1 that young-earthers usually favor can be found represented in the ESV:

> [1]In the beginning, God created the heavens and the earth. [2]The earth was without form and void, and darkness was over the face of the deep. And the Spirit of God was hovering over the face of the waters. [3]And God said, "Let there be light," and there was light.

This fits well in the stream of common, traditional translations. It makes Gen 1:1 into a full sentence in its own right. The first verse here stands as a grammatically complete thought—an independent clause. We will therefore call this the "independent clause" translation.

By contrast, a translation that many Hebrew experts believe is closer to the actual grammar of the text is exemplified by the New Jewish Publication Society (NJPS) version. We will call it the "dependent clause" translation because *it takes the first verse of Genesis as an incomplete sentence,* unlike the traditional view. That is, it takes the first verse of Genesis as only the beginning of a sentence that extends across three verses:

47:42, university lecture, Dec 2012. Posted by "Yale Courses," May 8, 2017, www.m.youtube.com/watch?v=ANUD8IK12ms.

[17] This argument features prominently throughout Jon D. Levenson, *Creation and the Persistence of Evil: The Jewish Drama of Divine Omnipotence* (Princeton: Princeton University Press, 1988).

[1]When God began to create the heaven and earth—[2]the earth being unformed and void, with darkness over the surface of the deep and a wind from God sweeping over the water—[3]God said, "Let there be light"; and there was light.

The difference between these two is subtle but the impact profound.

The independent clause translation exemplified by the ESV starts out assuming that, before Gen 1:1, there was no matter. In *the* beginning God created matter—understood to be encapsulated in the phrase, "heavens and the earth." Because, according to this translation, space-time itself is understood to have been created on the first day, old-earth creationists like Hugh Ross view Genesis 1:1 as a reference to the Big Bang, and young-earth creationists assume that they can whip out a calculator and use genealogies from Adam to Christ to chalk up a reasonable ballpark of how old the cosmos is.

The Jewish Publication Society translation suggests both of these views are wrong because it implies that Genesis 1:1 says nothing about the absolute beginning of the physical universe. You will notice in the NJPS Bible that matter is already on the table and waiting before the first verse even opens. *When God begins* his creating, the chaotic matter he uses to do so—the "unformed and void" earth is already there. We are never told when this material of creation was brought into existence. Perhaps it had been sitting around for five minutes, perhaps fourteen billion years. The grammar of this translation doesn't allow us to know.

ASSESSING THE POSITIONS

On what grounds does the Creation Museum prefer the independent clause translation over the dependent clause one? Certainly, the first and primary reason is that it is traditional. It has held sway throughout most of church history and has prevailed in the majority of the Bibles we all grew up with (though English translations like the NRSV and NAB are exceptions).

More significantly, in 2013, I wrote a piece about the Creation Museum that garnered enough attention to motivate an online response from several of the organization's scientists, and a scholar from my own school named Joshua Wilson contacted me to inform me that he had, several years before, written a doctoral dissertation defending the translation that the Creation Museum prefers. His own summary of the arguments in his thesis appeared soon after in an article published on the Answers in Genesis website, titled, "Have we Misunderstood Genesis 1:1?"[18] Although these issues concern Hebrew grammar, Wilson's article should permit anyone to understand the big picture.

Because Wilson was arguing against the dependent clause translation (recall that a *dependent clause* is a group of words that don't express a complete thought), he looked at 210 clauses in the Old Testament that are of the same variety as the dependent clause camp claims Gen 1:1 to be. Observing these 210 other grammatical specimens, he came to the following four conclusions:[19]

1) A Hebrew mark (called a *soph passuk*), which post-biblical scribes invented to mark the end of a verse, separates Gen 1:1 from 1:2. In 97% of cases, dependent clauses of this sort aren't separated with this mark. All things equal, this would imply that the dependent clause translation of Gen 1:1 has a 97% chance of being wrong!

2) In their structure, the first several verses of Genesis are separated by a certain type of Hebrew prefix. In over 98% of other cases, such dependent clauses aren't set off in this manner.

3) In no other dependent clause in the Bible do we find the two features above occurring together.

4) The dependent clause translation makes Gen 1:2 into a parenthetical aside. Such parenthetical syntax doesn't occur in any of the other dependent clause cases Wilson examined.

To put all the above in a nutshell, Wilson argues that, while it is grammatically *possible* that Gen 1:1 could be a dependent clause (i.e., it

[18] Joshua D. Wilson, "Have we Misunderstood Genesis 1:1?" *Answers in Depth*, Sept 11, 2013. Accessed March 8, 2017, www.answersingenesis.org/hermeneutics/have-we-misunderstood-genesis-11/.
[19] Joshua D. Wilson, "A Case for the Traditional Translation and Interpretation of Genesis 1:1 Based Upon a Multi-Leveled Linguistic Analysis" (PhD diss., The Southern Baptist Theological Seminary, 2010), 110-111.

wouldn't violate any laws of grammar if it was), the syntax would be so extremely rare and cumbersome that the traditional translation is astronomically the more likely option. In his Answers in Genesis piece, he writes, "The dependent-clause understanding of Genesis 1:1 is not grammatically easy; it is difficult and awkward. The traditional understanding of Genesis 1:1 is grammatically easy, and the most basic principle for understanding any language is to follow the ease of the grammar."[20]

There's no disputing Wilson's observation that the dependent clause translation is exceptionally cumbersome. Why then do Hebraists at universities like Yale, Princeton, and Harvard insist it is superior, despite its transparently cumbersome nature? One reason has to do with important discoveries in Hebrew grammar.

GENESIS 1:1 AS A RESTRICTIVE RELATIVE CLAUSE

In preparing his own doctoral dissertation, Robert Holmstedt, currently at the University of Toronto and a current director of the Holmstedt-Abegg Hebrew Syntax database, analyzed every type of relative clause in the Hebrew Bible.[21] Sorting through this massive amount of data, he claims to have demonstrated that Genesis 1:1 is a *restrictive relative clause*.

A restrictive relative clause is a clause that gives essential information that defines a corresponding noun or noun phrase. For example:

Students **who study hard** will do well in this class.

In this above sentence the bolded phrase "who study hard" helps to describe the noun "students." Relative clauses are introduced with a relator pronoun like *who, that, which, where,* or *when* and help to define or describe a noun. In that sense, they serve as adjectives. However, some relative clauses merely add information; others provide essential information.

In the sentence "Sandra, **who had just won a marathon**, ate two dozen cookies," the relative clause "who had just won a marathon" provides some useful context to the statement that she ate two dozen

---

[20] Wilson, "Have we Misunderstood," n.p.
[21] Robert D. Holmstedt, "The Relative Clause in Biblical Hebrew: A Linguistic Analysis" (PhD diss, University of Wisconsin-Madison, 2002).

cookies, but it is not essential to the meaning of the primary statement concerning the number of cookies she consumed.

In the sentence "Students **who study hard** will do well," the phrase "who study hard" obviously narrows or *restricts* our understanding of which students will do well. In other words, the comparative sentence "Students will do well in this class" absolutely does *not* communicate the same message as: "Students *who study hard* will do well." The one implies that *all* students will do well in the class. The other says only that those *who study hard* will do well. This relative clause provides essential information that restricts the meaning of the sentence. Therefore, the phrase "who study hard" forms a *restrictive* relative clause.

In the same way, Holmstedt has argued that Gen 1:1 is not a sentence in its own right but, as a restrictive relative clause, the phrase "God created the heavens and the earth" merely helps to define what type of "beginning" the author has in mind. This is not *the* absolute beginning, but merely that "beginning *in which* God created the heavens and the earth."

How can it be argued that Genesis 1:1 is a restrictive relative? Three features of Hebrew grammar necessitate this:

1) Hebrew reference grammars widely recognize in biblical Hebrew that a noun may be modified by a relative clause, even when the relative clause includes no explicit relative word (*who, when, that, which, whose, etc.*).[22] This means the fact that we see no relative word like *which* or *when* in Gen 1:1 is of no significance for determining whether that verse is a relative clause. This observation is not controversial, being widely recognized by partisans on both sides of the debate. It is partially the reason why Wilson agreed that Genesis 1:1 *could* be a relative clause even though he believed it was extremely unlikely.

---

[22] For these clauses, called 'asyndetic' or 'bare' relatives in reference grammars, Holmstedt cites examples like the following: Gen 14:13; Exod 4:13; 9:4; 14:11; 15:17; 8:20; Lev 7:35; Num 7:13; Deut 32:11; Josh 7:21; Judge 8:1; 1 Sam 6:9; 1 Kgs 13:2; Isa 1:20; 6:6; Jer 2:6; Ezek 22:24; Hos 5:14; Jon 1: 10; Mic 5:2; Hab 1:5; Zeph 2:1; Zech 6:12; Mal 2:16; Psa 5:5; 74:2; 118:22; Prov 8:32; Job 1:1; 3:3; 8:21; Eccl 10:5; Lam 1:14; 3:1; Ezra 1:5; Neh 8:10; 2 Chr 15:11; Exod 4:13; Lev 7:35; Deut 32:25; Jer 36:35; Mic 5:2; Psa 4:8; 56:4, 10; Job 3:3; 6:17, 18:21; Lam 1:21; 1 Chron 29:3; 2 Chron 20:22. Robert D. Holmstedt, "The Restrictive Syntax of Genesis i 1," *Vetus Testamentum* 58 (2008), 59-60.

2) When nouns are modified in Hebrew they often take on an ending called the "bound form" (i.e. as an indication that they are "bound" to the modifier). Holmstedt's comprehensive study of Hebrew relative clauses made the important discovery that when a relative clause modifies a noun in its bound form, the relative clause is *always* restrictive.[23] The noun "beginning" ראשית in Genesis 1:1 happens to be a word which takes the same form whether it is grammatically bound or not, therefore it *may* be in bound form.[24] This fact, combined with feature (1) above, demonstrates that the author of Genesis 1:1 chose to craft this passage such that it *can* be read as the noun "beginning" in bound form being modified by the relative clause "[in which] created God the heavens and the earth." Since Holmstedt's thesis discovered clauses following this format of a bound noun modified by a relative clause are *always* restrictive, by not negating the restrictive relative reading in his selection of the wording, the author employs this grammatical formula to designate this passage as restrictive relative.

3) Holmstedt also found that when a relative clause in Hebrew omits its relative word (*who, when, that, which, whose,* etc.), the relative clause is *always* restrictive.[25] The fact that Genesis 1:1 *can* be read as a relative clause, according to feature (1) above, and

---

[23] For example, in all 217 cases of nouns in construct with the relative word *asher* meaning *that* or *which* in the Hebrew Bible, "all of them present restrictive relatives." Holmstedt also cites 87 passages illustrating this phenomenon with the relative *Ha*. Holmstedt, "The Relative Clause," 119-25.

[24] Indeed, in 78% of occurrences of the noun ראשית the term is bound in construct. E.g., Lev 23:10; Num 24:20; Deut 21:17; Deut 26:10; Neh 10:37; Psa 78:51. Ogunlana considers this significant evidence that the term is likely being used in construct here. Babatunde Ogunlana, "Inspiration and the Relationship Between Genesis 1:1-2:4A and *Enuma Elish*," Paper presented to Jos-Bukuru Theological Society, Jos, Nigeria (July 11, 2013), 6.

[25] "The Restrictive Syntax," 62. Holmstedt provides the following examples: Gen 15:13; 26:10; 29:25; 42:28; 43:18; 49:27; Exod 4:13; 14:11; Lev 7:35; Deut 32:35; 1 Sam 14:21; Isa 1:30; 30:9; 41:24; 42:16; 43:19; 45:1; Jer 2:8, 11; 36:2; Ezek 13:3; Jon 1:10; Mic 5:2; Hab 1:5, 6, 8, 14; 2:5; Psa 4:8; 5:5; 7:16; 7:9; 9:16, 18; 12:6; 7:1; 8:3, 44; 25:12; 33:12; 35:8; 56:4, 10; 58:5; 65:5; 74:2; 81:6; 103:5; 118:22; 119:136; 129:6; 141:9; Job 6:17; 18:21; 29:16; 36:27; Prov 8:32; Lam 1:14; Neh 8:10; 1 Chr 12:24; 15:12; 16:15; 2 Chr 1:4; 15:11; 20:22; 24:11; 29:27.

indisputably does not contain a relative word means that it grammatically *must* be a restrictive relative clause.

Therefore, according to features (2) and (3) above, the author of Genesis 1:1 used two different techniques to mark the passage as restrictive relative. These rules governing relative clauses are nothing short of grammatical laws without exceptions throughout the *entire corpus* of the Hebrew Bible and are exhibited throughout the hundreds of parallel examples Holmstedt provides. He therefore concludes the traditional translation is, "grammatically indefensible. Period. End of Story."[26]

Given these recent developments in our understanding of relative clause grammar in biblical Hebrew, I suggest a translation of the opening of Genesis informed by elements from Holmstedt, the NJPS, and the Semitist Robert Alter:

1 In the initial period[27] in which God created the heavens and the earth[28]—

2 the earth being welter and waste,[29]

---

[26] Robert D. Holmstedt, "Genesis 1.1-3, Hebrew Grammar and Translation," *Ancient Hebrew Grammar*, Nov 11, 2011. Accessed May 8, 2017, www.ancienthebrewgrammar.wordpress.com/2011/11/11/genesis-1-hebrew-grammar-translation/. To date (Feb 2018), I have been unable to find any published studies challenging Holmstedt's analysis.

[27] Following Holmstedt's translation in "The Restrictive Syntax," 65. The restrictive relative grammar would literally read, "In beginning that/which created God the heavens and the earth…." Because this is not grammatically coherent in English, "in the initial period" is a suitable equivalent.

[28] It is highly likely that 'earth' in these verses should actually be translated 'underworld'—a meaning that this Hebrew word often designates. An article published by the National Association of Professors of Hebrew by Noegel has revealed impressive evidence that across Akkadian and Ugaritic literature the phrase, "the heavens and the earth" (הַשָּׁמַיִם and הָאָרֶץ) had a long-established cultural history as a specified merism for the heavens and the underworld—the totality of creation. This reading makes far more sense in the cosmogonic context of the passage and has great explanatory power when applied to the use of this merism elsewhere in the Bible. Scott B. Noegel, "God of Heaven and Sheol," *Hebrew Studies* 58 (2017), 119-144.

[29] The clever alliteration "welter and waste" for the Hebrew *tohu wa-vohu* here is taken from Robert Alter's translation. *The Five Books of Moses*, 17. In a widely cited

and darkness was over the face of the deep,
and a wind of God[30] was fluttering over the face of the waters—

3 God said, "Be light!"[31]
And light there was.

Notice in this restrictive relative translation how the main noun "initial period" is being modified by the essential clause information that follows ("in which God created the heavens and the earth..."). Notice also that the restrictive clause translation renders 1:1 into an incomplete thought. As an incomplete thought, 1:1 is necessarily grammatically dependent on what follows. The strong majority of scholars who take this translation agree that verse 3 should be understood as the main clause, making these three verses one long sentence.[32] As Wilson correctly observes, with the dependent clause translation:

No longer is Genesis 1:1 the first act of creation. Rather, Genesis 1:1, along with 1:2, becomes a description of the context in which the first act of creation takes place: the creation of light in Genesis 1:3. According to this interpretation then, the elements of Genesis 1:2 were already present before God began creating.[33]

---

study, Tsumura concludes more precisely that these terms refer to things being in a state that was "unproductive and uninhabited." David Toshio Tsumura, *The Earth and the Waters in Genesis 1 and 2: A Linguistic Investigation.* JSOTSup 83 (Sheffield: Sheffield Academic Press, 1989), 17ff.

[30] "Spirit of God" is how this Hebrew phrase is translated elsewhere and the author is likely intending a double entendre, difficult to represent in English. On the literary level, "wind of God" appears slightly favorable in the sense that it is the means used by God to drive back the sea in Gen 7:24-8:1 and passages like Exod 14:21. Wind was also a weapon Baal equipped himself with when fighting the chaos sea in the Ugaritic texts.

[31] The longer traditional translation, "Let there be light," fails to capture the dramatic beauty in the terseness of this proclamation in Hebrew where it only occupies two brief words: "*Yehi or!*"

[32] As Baasten states, "The rules of Biblical Hebrew syntax are such that if a clause begins with a temporal phrase or a temporal subordinate clause, the main clause often starts with a *wayyiqtol* form.... The most obvious answer, therefore, is that the main clause in Gen 1:1-3 starts with the *wayyiqtol* form in verse 3." Baasten, "First Things First," 178-9.

[33] Wilson, "Genesis 1:1," 6. Wilson's statement applies regardless of whether or not verse 2 is itself dependent on verse 3.

THE DEPENDENT CLAUSE TRANSLATION AND GENESIS' LITERARY CONTEXT

What about Wilson's objection—that the parenthetical stage setting of the second verse runs so long and is so complex that it is awkward? As I have agreed above, there is no question that the dependent clause translation is cumbersome. However, as astonishing as it may seem, far from being an argument against the dependent clause translation, I actually believe the rareness of its syntax is a second powerful argument *in its favor*. How can that be? This wordy style conforms beautifully with Genesis' original literary context—the style in which other surrounding cultures in Mesopotamia began their creation stories.

The Babylonian creation story *Enuma Elish* likely dates as far back as the second millennium BC. Since biblical scholars widely believe that Genesis 1 was edited during or after Judah's Babylonian captivity, it is plausible that Genesis 1's editor(s) were familiar with it. Interestingly, tablet I, lines 1-10 opens the Babylonian account with similar complex back-dropping following a dependent clause as we have observed in Genesis 1:

Dependent temporal clause	When on high heaven was not named, and the earth[34] beneath a name did not bear –
Parenthetical information	primeval Apsu [fresh water] was their progenitor, life-giving Tiamat [salt water], the bearer of all; their waters together they mingled, no canebrake yet formed, no marsh discoverable – when of the gods none had appeared, names were not borne, destinies not decided,
Main clause	the gods were given shape within them, Laḫmu and Laḫamu made to appear, names they bore.[35]

---

[34] As noted in a previous footnote, the Semitic merism "heaven" and "earth" here likely refers to the heavens and underworld (as in Genesis 1:1-2). See Noegel, "God of Heaven and Sheol," 138-144.

As the Assyriologist E. A. Speiser points out, like Genesis 1:1-3, this passage begins with a dependent temporal clause and follows with 6 lines of parenthetical clauses before arriving at the main clause in lines 9-10.[36] Overly complex? Or literary style?

There is another Akkadian creation text that scholars widely recognize as having important similarities to the Genesis creation account—*Atrahasis*. Like Genesis, *Atrahasis* has humanity created from the earth to cultivate the ground and features a description of the Great Flood. Incredibly, it too opens with a dependent clause followed by a parenthetical clause before it arrives at its main clause:

Dependent temporal clause	When the gods like men Bore the work and suffered the toil—
Parenthetical information	The toil of the gods was great, The work was heavy, the distress was much—
Main clause	The Seven great Anunaki [gods] were making the Igigi [lower gods] suffer the work....[37]

Another creation story discovered in the ruined capital of the Assyrian empire called KAR 4 dates to about 800 BC. Its opening lines also take the general literary style we have been observing. Again, those who allege that Genesis 1 should not be translated as a dependent clause because its resulting parenthetical lines are awkwardly long should observe where this same structure is several times longer in this creation text:

---

[35] This exceptionally beautiful translation is produced by the Semitist John Hobbins. I present it here in a slightly modified format of the original: John Hobbins, "Genesis 1:1-3: How it all Began," *Ancient Hebrew Poetry*, Apr 2008. Accessed May 8, 2017, www.ancienthebrewpoetry.typepad.com/ancient_hebrew_poetry/2008/04/genesis-11-3-ho.html.

[36] E. A. Speiser, *Genesis: Introduction, Translation and* Notes (New York: Doubleday, 1964), 12, 19. Hamilton agrees that on the dependent translation, "Gen. 1:1…is the equivalent of the first two lines of *Enuma elish.*" Victor P. Hamilton, *The Book of Genesis: Chapters 1-17*, The New International Commentary on the Old Testament (Grand Rapids: Eerdmans, 1990), 104.

[37] W. G. Lambert, A. R. Millard, and Miguel Civil (eds.), *Atra-Hasis: The Babylonian Story of the Flood* (Winona Lake: Eisenbrauns, 1999), 43.

Dependent temporal clause	When heaven had been separated from the earth, the distant trusty twin,
Parenthetical information	(And) the mother of the goddesses had been brought into being; When the earth had been brought forth (and) the earth had been fashioned; When the destinies of heaven and earth had been fixed; (When) trench and canal had been given (their) right courses, (And) the banks of the Tigris and Euphrates had been established
Main clause	(Then) Anu, Enlil, Šamaš, (and) Ea, the great gods, (And) the Anunnaki, the great gods, Seated themselves in the exalted sanctuary and recounted among themselves what had been created.[38]

Scholars have long recognized that this format is standard to the Mesopotamian creation account genre.[39] Benjamin D. Sommer, Professor of Bible and Semitic Languages at The Jewish Theological Seminary specifically recognizes Genesis 1:1-3's syntactical similarity to

---

[38] Trans. Alexander Heidel, *The Babylonian Genesis: The Story of Creation.* 2 ed. (Chicago: University of Chicago Press, 1951), 68-9.

[39] In addition to previously cited and ensuing examples, see Hermann Gunkel, *Genesis.* Trans. Mark E. Biddle, Mercer Library of Biblical Studies (Macon: Mercer University Press, 1997), 1. Westermann wrote, "'When this and this was not yet...then...', and its formula is found in Gen 2:4bff., it forms the introduction of the Enuma elish epic, and occurs often in Sumerian and Egyptian." Claus Westermann, *Genesis 1-11: A Commentary.* Trans. John J. Scullion (Minneapolis: Augsburg Publishing, 1984), 93. In a more recent doctoral thesis, Vail writes of the relative clause: "Genesis 1:1-2 shows parallels to *Enuma elish*. The two texts have similar introductory statements.... Second, both texts contain uncreated waters." Eric M. Vail, "Using 'Chaos' in Articulating the Relationship of God and Creation in God's Creative Activity" (PhD diss., Marquette University, 2009), 104.

the Babylonian account and *Atrahasis*.[40] Mark S. Smith, Professor of Old Testament Language and Exegesis at Princeton Theological Seminary, agrees that "other creation narratives similarly open with [such] clauses…. Despite the length of such a sentence, it falls entirely in line with the openings of creation accounts from Mesopotamia."[41]

However, of all the parallel texts, there is one that towers over the others in relevance. You may have heard before that Genesis contains a so-called "second creation account" in Genesis 2:4b-7. Incredibly, even that passage follows the general format scholars are endorsing for translating Genesis 1:1-3. That is, like Genesis 1:1:1-3, it opens with a dependent temporal clause followed by an extended parenthetical insertion before it reaches the main clause:

Dependent temporal clause	4bWhen the Lord God made earth and heaven—
Parenthetical information	5Now no plant of the field was yet in the earth and no herb of the field had yet to grow, since the Lord God had not caused it to rain upon the earth and there was no man to work the ground 6(but a mist went up from the earth and watered the whole face of the ground)—
Main clause	7The Lord God formed man from dust of the ground….

Looking at this passage, the respected Hebraist Bill T. Arnold agrees in the *New Cambridge Bible Commentary*, "The syntax of 2:4b-7 is not unlike that of 1:1-3."[42]

So, the dependent clause opening of Genesis is indeed odd and cumbersome when we compare it across the syntax of the Bible as a whole, but it is *typical* in a generic sense when we compare it to other creation narratives from Genesis 1's ancient Mesopotamian literary

---

[40] Footnote 9, Benjamin D. Sommer, *The Bodies of God and the World of Ancient Israel* (Cambridge: Cambridge University Press, 2009), 245.

[41] Smith, *The Priestly Vision*, 45.

[42] Bill T. Arnold, *Genesis*, New Cambridge Bible Commentary (Cambridge: Cambridge University Press, 2009), 56.

context and the "second creation account" occurring in the immediately following chapter. This correspondence seems so unlikely to be a mere coincidence (since its literary formula is so unusual) that the Hebraist Jack M. Sasson at Vanderbilt Divinity School cites it as part of the reason he believes the dependent clause translation is now "beyond dispute." [43]

CREATIO EX NIHILO

When I first encountered the grammatical problems in the opening of Genesis, I was greatly disturbed. If Genesis 1:1 doesn't teach that the universe had a definite beginning, then the Bible might actually teach that the universe is eternal. If the Bible teaches that the universe is eternal, it contradicts current science in a fundamental way. Much worse than this, if the Bible teaches the universe is eternal, one of its core assumptions about reality would be philosophically incoherent.

I think most young-earth apologists would agree that theistic philosophers like Thomas Aquinas, Maimonides, and Al-Ghazali have logically proven that time and causality had to have a beginning. The observations of these thinkers are foundational to modern monotheistic apologetics. Wilson, of course, agrees and goes so far as to claim that the doctrine that God created from nothing is "central to the theology of God." [44]

However, is it the case that the doctrine of God's creation from nothing (usually called by its Latin name, *creatio ex nihilo*) lives or dies upon our translation of the first verse of Genesis? Have we driven a cold knife into the very heart of this ancient teaching? Most of the scholars advocating the dependent clause translation have attempted to assure us that this is not the case.

They give at least two reasons: First, while the dependent clause translation of Genesis doesn't say that God created *ex nihilo*, it also certainly doesn't do anything to disqualify the idea either. The dependent clause translation suggests that the first verse of Genesis opens with the material of creation already present, waiting to be shaped. But that doesn't imply that the material is, itself, uncreated and

---

[43] Sasson, "Time…to Begin," 187-88.
[44] Wilson, "A Case for the Traditional Translation," 9.

eternal. All it means is that we don't know how old it is. The text is silent on the issue.

For Christians, the second reason the doctrine of *creatio ex nihilo* isn't threatened by the dependent clause translation is that there are New Testament passages that teach—or at least lean towards teaching a doctrine of creation *ex nihilo*. These New Testament verses aren't chronologically contextualized enough for someone to attempt to date the universe (as young-earthers attempt to do with Gen 1:1), but the doctrine of creation *ex nihilo* is based on far more than a single verse in the entire Bible.

Rev 4:11 says, "You created all things, and by your will they existed and were created." Woodenly translated, John 1:3 says, "All things through Him emerged." In his leading historical survey of the doctrine, the late Gerhard May, Professor of Church and Doctrinal History at the Johannes Gutenberg University of Mainz, pointed out that the New Testament never explicitly goes out of its way to defend *creatio ex nihilo* simply because it wasn't a subject of controversial interest in its context. At the same time, he concluded: "What the New Testament statements about the creation intend is quite legitimately interchangeable with the idea of *creatio ex nihilo*."[45]

CONCLUSION

In plain summation, what implications may we draw?

The opening verses of Genesis *do not* describe creation from nothing (though they don't contradict the idea, either). The Hebrew syntax of the creation account *does not* allow us to establish when the matter of the universe or the pre-earth materials were brought into being in the author's mind. For all we know, this matter may have existed for as long as the majority of cosmologists think it has.

Whatever one's opinion about the Bible's relationship to science, young-earth cosmological models based on the assumption that the universe came into being only thousands of years ago have a reasonable likelihood of being wrong, not merely because they contradict the vast

---

[45] Gerhard May, *Creatio Ex Nihilo: The Doctrine of 'Creation out of Nothing' in Early Christian Thought*. Trans. A. S. Worrall (New York: T&T Clark, 2004), 26.

consensus of modern cosmology, but because these models are predicated on an incorrect translation of the first verse of the Bible.

CHAPTER 6

ANCIENT HEBREW HEAVENLY COSMOLOGY

As we saw in the last chapter, young-earth creationists assume we can look at Genesis 1 and use it to inform accurate astrophysical models.
In the following chapters, I will argue that we shouldn't interpret Genesis through the filter of modern astrophysics and cosmology because the biblical authors shared the same general cosmology as the rest of their ancient neighbors. Specifically, the Old Testament authors assumed the earth is round, flat, and covered by a sky dome that retained above it a literal cosmic ocean.

I understand that last sentence will be massively suspect and uncomfortable for many traditionalists. My own journey from being a young-earth creationist to embracing the Bible's ancient cosmology was no exception. In college, I was exposed to lectures on Israelite cosmology by the great Hebraist Michael Heiser. These led me to read John Walton's *The Lost World of Genesis One*, Wayne Horowitz's *Mesopotamian Cosmic Geography*, and several articles on Israelite cosmology written by a scholar named Paul Seely in the *Westminster Theological Journal*.

It took me years of uncomfortable, incremental exposure to these sources before the cognitive dissonance finally forced me to change my views. I don't believe important worldview modifications should be made haphazardly. At the same time, I'm not going to protect you from your Bible. I believe the Bible should be handled honestly on its own terms, and the evidence for its cosmology is formidable.

For those that believe in biblical divine inspiration, there are several reasons why I believe understanding Israelite cosmology is to your benefit rather than a thing to be feared: First, if your theology forces you to contort and massage the biblical texts to make them conform to modern astrophysics, your theology is forcing you to misinterpret the Bible. An issue like cosmology is so fundamental to the ancient Hebrew worldview that understanding it accurately yields major and rapid gains in our ability to comprehend and enjoy the Bible at a higher resolution.

Second, if you believe in biblical inspiration, you are only setting yourself up for worldview fragility and biblical-exposure-anxiety if your definition of that doctrine only comes from pure theological theorizing. If you want a sturdy worldview that aids and doesn't impede you from enjoying your Bible then your doctrine of divine inspiration *cannot* just come from the idealistic theorizing of theologians who typically aren't trained to read the Bible in its comparative cultural context. Rather than devising a theory of inspiration and forcing it on the text from the top-down, one should instead start with gritty case studies at the level of the text before abstracting principles about how it behaves.

I provide critical observations for thinking through this issue in section three, but the following rabbit trail may suggest something of the point.

An Object Lesson from Ancient Anatomy

Have you ever noticed there is no unique word for the *brain* in the Old Testament? Astonishing as it may sound to us moderns, the biblical authors were ignorant of the brain's function. Similarly, historians of medicine recognize, "Like the Babylonians and Assyrians, the Egyptians appear to have had no understanding of the brain or of psychological function. Emotion and knowledge were related to the heart...."[1] Another historian of neuroscience, for example, draws our attention to how the Egyptians considered the brains so unimportant that they would discard them during embalming, although they carefully

---

[1] M. Trimble and E. H. Reynolds, "A Brief History of Hysteria: From the Ancient to the Modern," in Michael J. Aminoff, François Boller, Dick F. Swaab (eds.), *Handbook of Clinical Neurology vol. 139* (Amsterdam: Elsevier, 2016), 5. Also, Edward H. Reynolds and James V. Kinnier Wilson, "Neurology and Psychiatry in Babylon," *Brain* 137.9 (2014), 2617: "[The Babylonians] had no knowledge of brain (or psychological) function [so] most of the above neuropsychiatric disorders were viewed as supernatural."

preserved other organs like the heart for continued use in the afterlife in canopic jars alongside a person's mummy.[2] Similarly, whenever one would expect the biblical authors to use the word *brain,* they substitute words for other organs like the heart. When biblical characters use their rational faculties—their reason—we are often met with the formula: "He said in his heart." We moderns take this as nothing more than a bit of poetic language, but the ancients intended it quite literally.

As the Old Testament scholar John Walton has pointed out, the Bible not only attributes the seat of human consciousness to the heart but to the kidneys as well—such as in passages like Psa 16:7, Psa 7:9, Jer 17:10, Prov 23:16, and Jer 11:20.[3] If you look these up, you will see that your translation has probably rendered the Hebrew word for kidneys translated by words like "mind," "conscience," or "heart," marking the literal Hebrew in your Bible's footnotes. According to Psa 7:9, "the righteous God tests the hearts and kidneys" of people.

When David prays in Psalm 26, "Examine me, O Lord, and prove me; try my kidneys . . .," he literally thinks there is a sense in which his inner psyche resides in his kidneys in the same way that his ancient Near Eastern neighbors did.[4]

If inspiration includes the idea that the Bible is true in absolutely everything that it affirms about science in *every sense* (even incidental, cultural side references like this), then how should a believer in this doctrine expect this verse to have been written?

Maybe God could have: 1) not let David write this statement because his scientific-cultural context disposes him to express it in a physiologically inaccurate way. Or, 2) he could have given David a divine lesson about brain science that would have scientifically catapulted him ahead of his Near Eastern neighbors by centuries so he

---

[2] Stanley Finger, *Origins of Neuroscience: A History of Explorations into Brain Function* (Oxford: Oxford University Press, 1994), 9-10.

[3] John Walton, *The Lost World of Genesis One: Ancient Cosmology and the Origins Debate* (Downer's Grove: IVP Academic, 2009), 18-9.

[4] See G. Eknoyan, "The Kidneys in the Bible: What Happened," *Journal of the American Society of Nephrology,* 16.12 (Dec 2005), 3464-3471. Kopple agrees that "The kidneys were viewed as the seat of conscience and of ethical feelings and yearnings, and the source of mortality and ethical activity. The kidneys were believed to be associated with the innermost parts of the personality." J. D. Kopple, "The Biblical View of the Kidney," *American Journal of Nephrology* 14 (1994), 279-81.

could write the verse in a way that was physiologically correct but would have been obtuse to any other ancient Hebrew.

The second option seems self-evidently absurd. The first option—that God might have written the entire Bible skirting around the scientifically ancient assumptions of the biblical authors, seems unreasonably restrictive and would place our cultural context above the cultural context of the ancient people that the Bible was originally addressed to. Neither is what we find going on in the text.

It turns out David doesn't care about biological science in Psalm 26. Scientific nephrology is a thousand miles away from his point and criticizing the truth-value of his statement on that ground would be rather pathetic and ridiculous. If you consider yourself an adherent of divine inspiration and this information about kidneys in your Bible hasn't opened up a nihilistic void beneath your feet and hurled you into an existential crisis of faith, then I'm going to suggest that the Hebrew Bible's beautiful ancient cosmology probably won't do you much spiritual harm either.

THE SKY DOME AND WATERS ABOVE

I have broadly represented the Old Testament's conception of the world in Figure 8.[5] The Hebrews believed creation exists in a bubble surrounded by cosmic waters. The solid firmament above was a feature common to the Near Eastern world of its authors and anthropologists

---

[5] This illustration draws on the attempts of previous scholars, including Nahum Sarna, *Understanding Genesis: The Heritage of Biblical Israel* (New York: Schocken Books, 1966), 5. Incorporating the iconography of Leviathan and the Seraphim is an idea I owe to the illustration in Othmar Keel, *Altorientalische Miniaturkunst: Die ältesten visuellen Massenkommunikationsmittel. Ein Blick in die Sammlungen des Biblischen Instituts der Universität Freiburg Schweiz* (Universitätverlag Freiburg Schweiz: Vandenhoeck & Ruprecht Göttingen, 1996), 15. Foremost of all, I have benefited from a graphic entitled, "Ancient Hebrew Conception of the Universe" produced by Karbel Multimedia for Logos Bible Software (2012), which has been published in Barry, Mangum, Brown, and Heiser (eds.), *NIV Faithlife Study Bible: Intriguing Insights to Inform Your Faith* (Grand Rapids: Zondervan, 2017). I have also fruitfully consulted a survey of Hebrew cosmology by John R. Roberts, "Biblical Cosmology: The Implications for Bible Translation," *Journal of Translation* 9.2 (2013), 1-53.

have found that it is almost universal among premodern cultures.[6] We are first introduced to it in Gen 1:6-8:

> And God said, "Let there be a firmament [*raqia*] in the midst of the waters and let it separate water from water." And God made the firmament and separated between the waters which are below the firmament and **the waters which are above the firmament**. And it was so. And God called the firmament [*raqia*] heavens [*shamayim*]. And it was evening and it was morning, a second day.

---

[6] A worldwide survey of cosmologies is conducted in Appendix C of this study as demonstration of this point.

ANCIENT ISRAELITE COSMOLOGY

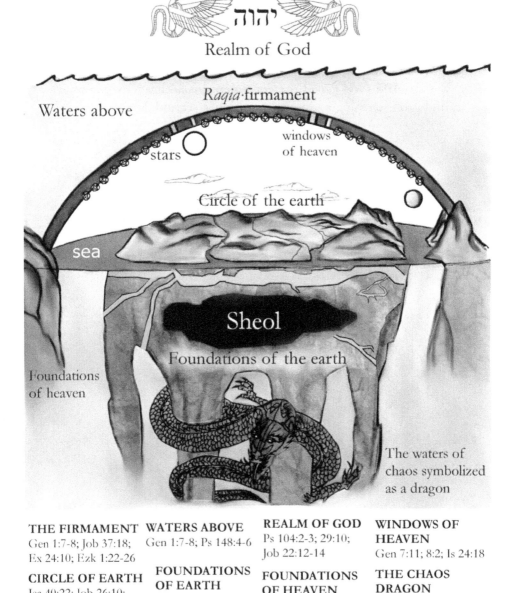

THE FIRMAMENT	WATERS ABOVE	REALM OF GOD	WINDOWS OF
Gen 1:7-8; Job 37:18;	Gen 1:7-8; Ps 148:4-6	Ps 104:2-3; 29:10;	HEAVEN
Ex 24:10; Ezk 1:22-26		Job 22:12-14	Gen 7:11; 8:2; Is 24:18
CIRCLE OF EARTH	**FOUNDATIONS**	**FOUNDATIONS**	**THE CHAOS**
Isa 40:22; Job 26:10;	**OF EARTH**	**OF HEAVEN**	**DRAGON**
Prov 8:27	Job 9:6; Ps 75:3;	Job 26:11; 2 Sam 22:8	Ps 74:13-15; Job 7:12;
	102:25		9:13; 26:12-13

Figure 8. The Israelite conception of the world. Illustration by author.

Following the influence of a book by the young-earth creationist Joseph C. Dillow, years ago, many top-name young-earth publications were brimming with hydrological graphs and mathematical equations attempting to demonstrate that Gen 1:7-8 describes a "pre-diluvian vapor canopy."[7]

The vapor canopy model was basically believed to have been an water-shell hanging over the globe's atmosphere that was alleged to filter out harmful UV rays and caused an oxygen surplus on earth—what some young-earthers claimed as the explanation for how men like Methuselah were able to live nearly 1,000 years. The canopy doesn't exist today because it was depleted to create the Great Flood. (That was the theory, anyway.)

Unfortunately, a widely ignored passage in the book of Psalms landed this theory a mortal blow when it was continuously pointed out by young-earthers like Russell Humphreys that the "waters above" were still described as loitering over the sky *after* the Flood.[8] Psa 148:4-6 is quite clear about this, "Praise Him you heavens of the heavens and *you waters which are above the heavens!* Let them praise the name of Yhwh, for he commanded and they were created. *He has established them forever....*"

To their credit, the majority of young-earthers have abandoned the vapor canopy model because the meteorological science could never get off the ground, and contradicting Bible verses like these became so

---

[7] Joseph C. Dillow, *The Waters Above: Earth's Pre-Flood Vapor Canopy* (Moody Press: Chicago, 1982). Morris popularized this theory. See Henry M. Morris's chapter "Water and the Word: Biblical Hydrology and Meteorology" in *The Biblical Basis for Modern Science: The Revised and Updated Classic!* (Green Forest, AR: Master Books, 2002), 270-299; also the first chapter of Scott M. Huse, *The Collapse of Evolution*, third edition (Grand Rapids, Baker Books, 1997). The revival of modern creationism in the 60s with Morris and Whitcomb's classic *The Genesis Flood* was especially interested in promoting the vapor canopy. John C. Whitcomb and Henry M. Morris, *The Genesis Flood: The Biblical Record and its Scientific Implications* (New Jersey: Presbyterian and Reformed Publishing, 1961). Noting this, Creationists like Rush and Vardiman, who helped dismantle the theory, alluded to its popularity in the 90s. David E Rush and Larry Vardiman, "Pre-Flood Vapor Canopy Radiative Temperature Profiles" R.E. Walsh and C. L. Brooks (eds.), *Proceedings of the Second International Conference on Creationism* (Pittsburgh: Creation Science Fellowship, 1990), 231.
[8] D. Russell Humphreys, *Starlight and Time: Solving the Puzzle of Distant Starlight in a Young Universe* (Green Forrest: Master Books, 1994), 61.

glaringly problematic. The Answers in Genesis website advises Christians now to reject the view.[9]

So creationists today propose different theories to explain the "waters above." Some commentators like Younker and Davidson have argued that the "waters above" are just rain clouds.[10] In addition to the cultural-contextual reasons we will review towards the end of this chapter, this cloud interpretation doesn't work because Gen 1:17 opens saying, "God set" the celestial bodies "*in* the firmament [Hebrew: *raqia*]." Since the "waters above" are "*above* the firmament [*raqia*]" only a few verses over in Gen 1:7, identifying clouds with the "waters above" would imply that the author of Genesis thought clouds were more distant than the sun, moon, and stars.[11]

Because the cloud interpretation and the canopy model couldn't account for the biblical data, and there is logically nowhere else left to go in the sky but up, modern creationists have therefore resorted to trying to push the waters into outer space somewhere. It's what's hot right now in YEC astronomy. Two influential young-earth scientists, Larry Vardiman and Russell Humphreys, have argued that the *raqia*

---

[9] See Bodie Hodge, "The Collapse of the Canopy Model," *Answers in Genesis*, Sept 2009. Accessed May 8, 2017. www.answersingenesis.org/environmental-science/the-collapse-of-the-canopy-model/.

[10] Randall W. Younker and Richard M. Davidson, "The Myth of the Solid Heavenly Dome: Another Look at the Hebrew רָקִיעַ *RĀQIAʿ*," *Andrews University Seminary Studies* 1 (2011), 143-44. This position is also taken by Vern S. Poythress, "Rain Water Versus a Heavenly Sea in Genesis 1:6-8," *Westminster Theological Journal* 77 (2015), 181-91.

[11] I have created a fuller lecture critique of Younker and Davidson's article on this point: Ben Stanhope, "The Biblical Flat Earth: Responding to Objections," video presentation, Jun 19, 2018, Posted by "Ben S," Jul 20, 2018. http://m.youtube.com/watch?v=c8Jz4tvlhZM.

An additional defeater for Younker and Davidson's argument comes with a close reading of Genesis 6:1-7. The fact that the *raqia* initially starts in the midst of the sea ("*betoq hamayyim*"), with waters already under and over it, shows that when the author says the waters are above the *raqia* as the final resulting act of their separation, he means this literally as in the initial condition. Not only are clouds never described as existing above the sky or *raqia* in the Bible as their argument proposes, but it's exegetically inconsistent to switch from a literal interpretation at the start of the *raqia* creation sequence then interpret that same concomitant resulting state as some sort figurative statement in the second part of that sequence. The initial state of the described sequence in Genesis 6:1-7 defines the waters above as literal.

must be "the fabric of space" and the "waters above" an expanding interstellar shell of ice particles some 20 million light-years away![12] John Hartnett, a creationist physicist, has proposed that the waters are "a shell of water in the outer regions of the solar system."[13] Answers in Genesis' *Answers Research Journal* has even published an article titled, "Thoughts on the *Raqia* and a Possible Explanation for the Cosmic Microwave Background." That author deals with the "waters above" by literally consigning them to the edge of the universe![14]

All of this is unnecessary. When ancient Jews modestly gathered and sang, "Praise Him, you waters above the heavens" (Psa 148:4) they were not singing about unobservable cosmic ice particles at the edge of the space-time continuum. The scientists proposing these ideas are intelligent, but, because they are scientists and not biblical scholars, their theories are uninformed by the Bible's ancient context.

Following is another quotation from the creation myth of Babylon, *Enuma Elish*. Recall from our previous investigation of Leviathan that this myth relates how the god Marduk slays a primeval chaos dragon named Tiamat. After Marduk kills Tiamat, he uses parts of her body to construct heaven and earth:

ENUMA ELISH, TABLET IV.136-140	GENESIS 1:7-8
[Marduk] split her in half like a dried fish. Then he set half of her up and made the Heavens as a roof. He stretched out a skin and assigned a guard [to hold it in place].	And God said, "Let there be a firmament in the midst of the waters and let it separate water from water." And God made the firmament and separated between the waters which are below the firmament and the

[12] Larry Vardiman and D. Russell Humphreys, "A New Creationist Cosmology: In No Time at All Part 1," *Acts & Facts* 39.11 (2010), 12-15; Brian Thomas, "What Were the 'Waters Above the Firmament'?" *Acts & Facts* 45.5 (2016), 20.

[13] J. Hartnett, *Starlight Time and the New Physics* (Powder Springs: Creation Book Publishers, 2007), 94.

[14] Danny R. Faulkner, "Thoughts on the *rāqîa'* and a Possible Explanation for the Cosmic Microwave Background," *Answers Research Journal* 9 (2016), 57-65.

He ordered them not to let her waters escape.[15]	waters which are above the firmament. And it was so. And God called the firmament heavens.

You will notice that these two passages are very different. Genesis 1 really was something unique in its ancient context.[16] The author behind Genesis 1 was aware of other ancient creation myths and takes shots at them theologically, but Genesis doesn't borrow its creation story from anyone.

All this said, I'm showing you these texts because they both illustrate an idea that was present in the ancient Near East at large. In the *Enuma Elish* story, Marduk cuts the cosmic dragon Tiamat in half. The bottom half he uses to make the flat, solid earth. With the other half of her corpse, he makes the sky—establishing it like the covering of a tent. We are told that Marduk then uses an apparently watertight skin and stations guardians for the sake of preventing Tiamat's upper waters from escaping. Later, he establishes a heavenly realm for the gods above this.[17]

It is wrong to assume ancient creation myths were principally concerned with material origins the way modern scientific theories are. Ancient creation stories frequently are not concerned about material origins.[18] Despite this, we can say that *Enuma Elish* genuinely does

---

[15] Translation by Wayne Horowitz, *Mesopotamian Cosmic Geography*, Mesopotamian Civilizations 8 (Winona Lake: Eisenbrauns, 1998), 112.

[16] Towards the end of the nineteenth century, it was popular for scholars to claim that the Israelites borrowed from *Enuma Elish* when they wrote Genesis. Experts now generally agree this view is wrong. See Victor Hurowitz, "The Genesis of Genesis: Is the Creation Story Babylonian?" in Sarah Yeomans (ed), *From Babylon to Baghdad: Ancient Iraq and the Modern West* (Washington DC: Biblical Archaeology Society, 2009), 2-10. Arnold believes, "[I]t must be admitted that many of the similarities are common to most ancient cosmogonies, and Gen 1 is not genetically related to the *Enuma elish*, nor is it necessarily a direct polemic against it." Bill T. Arnold, *Genesis*, New Cambridge Bible Commentary (Cambridge: Cambridge University Press, 2009), 30.

[17] In accordance with comments in Horowitz, *Mesopotamian Cosmic Geography*, 112.

[18] See Vern Poythress, "Biblical Studies: Three Modern Myths in Interpreting Genesis 1," *Westminster Theological Journal* 76 (2014), 321-350. My thinking here has also been profitably tempered by two articles by Noel K. Weeks: "The Bible and

assume that a very real cosmic ocean is somehow retained by the sky, prevented from flooding the earth.[19]

THE FIRMAMENT

The noun *raqia* in the Genesis passage, which I have been translating as "firmament," occurs in its verbal form 11 times in the Old Testament and refers to "beating out," "stamping out," or "spreading" by pounding. Frequently, it is used with reference to metal.[20] For example, Exod 39:3 says, "They hammered out (*raqa*), gold sheets." Num 16:39 says, "They hammered out plating for the altar." Jer 10:9 uses the term to refer to plated silver. Similarly, in a language close to Hebrew called Phoenician, we find a cognate noun *mrqa*, which refers to a metal "platter" or "bowl."[21]

In the third century BC, the Old Testament was translated by seventy Jewish scholars into a Greek Bible called the Septuagint. The Septuagint was important because it served as the primary Bible of the New

---

the 'Universal' Ancient World: A Critique of John Walton," *Westminster Theological Journal* 78 (2016), 1-28, and "Cosmology in Historical Context," *Westminster Theological Journal* 68 (2006), 283-293.

[19] Horowitz's commentary is representative. Horowitz, *Mesopotamian Cosmic Geography*, 262:

> Explicit statements that the heavens are made of water are found in Babylonian texts. Examples include Ee IV 137-46, where Marduk builds the heavens out of the watery corpse of Tiamat and Inamgisuanki, where the Akkadian name for heaven, *šamê*, is explained as *ša mê* 'of water.' ...In Ee IV 139-40, Marduk stretches out a skin and assigns guards to keep the waters of heaven from draining downward onto lower regions of the universe. These traditions may be compared with Genesis 1, where the primeval waters are divided in two, with the upper waters positioned above the firmament (רקיע), and Psa 104:3 and 148:4, which speak of waters above the heavens.

[20] According to Amzallag, "It has no other meaning in Biblical Hebrew, except for 'to stamp with foot' (רקע ברגל) encountered only in the book of Ezekiel (Ezk 6, 11; 25,6). Even there, it evokes a mild and repetitive beating, so that it should be considered as a figurative derivation of the primary metallurgical meaning." Nissim Amzallag, "Copper Metallurgy: A Hidden Fundament of the Theology of Ancient Israel?," *Scandinavian Journal of the Old Testament* 27.2 (2013), 162.

[21] See the Brown-Driver-Briggs entry on רָקַע. Francis Brown, S. R. Driver, and Charles A. Briggs (eds.), *A Hebrew and English Lexicon of the Old Testament* (Oxford: Clarendon Press, 1906), 955-6. Refers to 391 BC inscription from Idalion.

Testament authors and early church. When these ancient Jewish scholars made this translation, they selected a very rare term for expressing the meaning of the word *raqia*. They picked the Greek word *stereoma*, which indisputably emphasizes firmness and solidity.[22]

Addressing his fellow professional Bible translators in the *Journal of Translation*, the senior linguist John R. Roberts concludes from the linguistic data that "the Hebrew makes it explicit" that the biblical firmament—the *raqia* "should be conceived of as a solid dome with a surface."[23]

The Israeli scholar Nissim Amzallag, in the department of Bible, Archaeology, and Near Eastern Studies at the Ben-Gurion University of the Negev, believes the term *raqia*, "designates the firmament as a piece of metal."[24]

Interestingly, the verbal form of *raqia* is used in Job 37:18 to refer to the creation of the skies—comparing its creation to the cast bronze plates from which mirrors were hammered out in the ancient world. [25] Here is the passage in three of its most popular English translations:

ESV: "Can you, like him, spread out (*tarqia*) the skies, hard as a cast metal mirror?"

NASB: "Can you, with Him, spread out the skies, Strong as a molten mirror?"

---

[22] A database search of the word στερεωμα in all its forms over eight centuries (8th-1st) of Greek texts returns only 16 occurrences out of all extant Greek literature. Gary Martin, "*Raqi'a*: Form and Function of the 'Firmament' as a Celestial līmes/līmen in Israelite Cosmology," graduate seminar paper, Washington University (2013), 18, www.faculty.washington.edu/garmar/Raqia.pdf. That στερεωμα refers to "firmness"/"hardness" is readily apparent in its extrabiblical uses and verbal form. Young-earth creationists acknowledge this but argue that the Jewish scribes selected the word because they had been influenced by the solid spheres of Greek astronomy (for example, Younker and Davidson, "The Myth of the Solid Heavenly Dome," 129).

[23] Roberts, "Biblical Cosmology," 41.

[24] Amzallag, "Copper Metallurgy," 162.

[25] Besides all the examples discovered of them at archaeological sites, Exod 38:8 tells us that the Tabernacle bronze laver and its base were constructed by melting down the mirrors of serving women.

NIV: "Can you join him in spreading out the skies, hard as a mirror of cast bronze?"

Some creationists attempt to translate this passage as referring to God spreading out the clouds, not the sky. However, the verb typically refers specifically to beating out metal and certainly does here where the context is pounding out a bronze plate. It doesn't make much sense to compare the hardness of clouds to metal. Likewise, Clines points out that the "spreading" of clouds is an ongoing and daily occurrence that would tend to imply a repeated, ongoing action of the verb.[26] However, ancient mirrors were only "spread out" by hammering during their initial manufacture after casting. It therefore makes more sense that the verb refers to a single past action—the initial creation of the sky.[27]

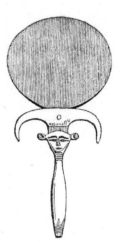

Figure 9. Egyptian metal mirror. Frohnmeyer and Benzinger, *Bilderatlas zur Bibelkunde* (Stuttgart: Theodor Benzinger, 1905), 147 (image 314).

It is important to emphasize that an association of the sky with metal is not unique to ancient Israel. Egyptologists have long known this idea is found in Egyptian texts and art.[28] An excellent recent study by Almansa-Villatoro in the *Journal of Egyptian Archaeology* emphasizes that the ancient Egyptians believed the sky was specifically made of iron as a container for the heavenly ocean upon which the sun

---

[26] David J. A. Clines, *Job 21-37*. Word Bible Commentary 18A (Nashville, TN: Thomas Nelson, 2006), 882.

[27] Ibid.

[28] E.g. E. A. Wallis Budge, *The Gods of the Egyptians*. Vol. 1 (London: Methuen, 1904), 502, 511. W. M. Müller, *The Mythology of All Races. Vol. 12: Egyptian* (New York: Cooper Square, 1964), 35. James K. Hoffmeier "Some Thoughts on Genesis 1 & 2 and Egyptian Cosmology," *Journal of the Ancient Near Eastern Society* 15 (1983), 45. Amsallag states, "This singular belief is not restricted to Ancient Israel. In Egyptian cosmology as well, the firmament is identified as a giant plate of copper hammered by Ptah, the smith-god." Amsallag, "Copper Metallurgy," 163. See also discussion of the firmament in Joanne Conman, "It's About Time: Ancient Egyptian Cosmology," *Studien zur Altägyptischen Kultur* 31 (2003), 33-34.

daily sailed.[29] Undoubtedly, the Egyptians inferred this because meteors, which they assumed to be fallen pieces of the firmament, occasionally fell in their lands and were harvested for their precious iron long before the Iron Age. Archaeologists have discovered numerous Egyptian artifacts made of the celestial metal, such as a famed ornate dagger found in the folds of King Tut's mummy.[30]

The Egyptian name for iron *(bia n pt)* accordingly means "metal of heaven."[31] A common theme in the Pyramid Texts (PT) speaks of the necessity for the Pharaoh to ascend to the afterlife by first "splitting" through the sky's "metal" (i.e. PT 257). PT 469 and 584 similarly speak of the king forcefully pushing his way through the "iron door in the starry sky" and other texts liken this necessity for the king to break through the iron firmament to breaking out of an egg (PT 757, 669).[32]

The primeval egg seems to have been related to the sky goddess Nut, whose name is sometimes spelled with an egg determinative and whose primary symbol was a water jar. Almansa-Villatoro cleverly recognized that the Egyptian sign used to write the noun iron (Gardiner sign N41—a containment of water) is also strangely used in writing terms relating to water and women. This is likely because, since very early in Egyptian thought, the sky goddess was intimately connected to iron— the "metal of heaven" and the great heavenly waters upon which the solar bark sails before its daily consumption and rebirth from the archetypal womb of the goddess.[33]

Amongst the ancient Sumerians along the Tigress and Euphrates rivers, scholars have noticed that multiple terms for iron and tin seem to etymologically contain the term for heaven—AN.[34] Accordingly, the Assyriologist Samuel Noah Kramer affirmed that for the Sumerians, "The earth was a flat disk surmounted in the shape of a vault. Just what this heavenly solid was thought to be is still uncertain; to judge from the

---

[29] M. Victoria Almansa-Villatoro, "The Cultural Indexicality of the N41 Sign for *bjз*: The Metal of the Sky and the Sky of Metal," *The Journal of Egyptian Archaeology* 105.1 (2019), 73–81.

[30] Ibid., 74. On the use of meteorite iron in ancient Egypt see Diana Johnson et al., "Analysis of a Prehistoric Egyptian Iron Bead with Implications for the Use and Perception of Meteorite Iron in Ancient Egypt," *Meteoritics & Planetary Science* 48.6 (2013), 997-1006.

[31] Almansa-Villatoro, "The Cultural Indexicality," 74.

[32] Ibid., 74-6.

[33] Ibid., 77.

[34] Ibid., 78.

fact that the Sumerian term for tin is 'metal of heaven,' it may have been tin."[35] Comparison with the Egyptian term "metal of heaven" seems to strengthen this interpretation.[36]

The opening of a Sumerian text called *Gilgamesh, Enkidu and the nether world* speaks of a time when heaven was "separated" from earth—when the two were "divided" from each other. Indeed, it can virtually be inferred that "The idea of a separation of heaven and earth is present in all ancient Near Eastern mythologies."[37] The Hittites to the north spoke of this cosmic separation occurring by means of a cleaver of copper.[38] Almansa-Villatoro points out that in the Luwian language, the hieroglyph for sky is a bowl (the sign CAELUM ▽), and that at Yazilikaya, a sacred sanctuary in the capital of the Hittite Empire in modern central Turkey, there is a central relief of two bullheaded gods upholding the sky as a great starry bowl as a variant of this symbol.[39] An inscription by the carver labels the image "heaven" and "earth."[40] Likewise, a papyrus of the Aegean poet Sappho (c. 620-570 BC) refers to the dawn ascending into "the bowl."[41]

---

[35] Samuel Noah Kramer, *The Sumerians: Their History, Culture and Character* (Chicago: University of Chicago Press, 1963), 113.

[36] Almansa-Villatoro, "The Cultural Indexicality," 78.

[37] Gerhard F. Hasel, "The Significance of the Cosmology of Genesis 1 in Relation to Ancient Near Eastern Parallels," *Andrews University Seminary Studies* 10 (Andrews University Press, 1972), 7.

[38] Harry A. Hoffner Jr., "Song of Ullikummi," in *Hittite Myths*. Society of Biblical Literature Writings from the Ancient World 2 (Atlanta: Scholars Press, 1990), 59. Hasel quotes this text as, "When heaven and earth were built upon me [Upelluri, an Atlas figure] I knew nothing of it, and when they came and cut heaven and earth asunder with a copper tool, that also I knew not." Hasel, "The Significance of the Cosmology," 8.

[39] Relief 28/29 of Chamber A of the rock sanctuary. Almansa-Villatoro ("The Cultural Indexicality," 77) refers to the drawing in K. Bittel, R. Naumann, and H. Otto, *Yazilikaya: Architektur, Felsbilder, Inschriften und Kleinfunde, I* (Leipzig, 1941), 61. See interpretation and comparison with the Hittite monument Eflatun Pinar in A. César González García and Juan Antonio Belmonte (eds.), "Thinking Hattusha: Astronomy and Landscape in the Hittite Lands," *Journal for the History of Astronomy* 42.4 (2011), 468.

[40] Calvert Watkins, "The Golden Bowl: Thoughts on the New Sappho and its Asianic Background," *Classical Antiquity* 26.2 (2007), 320.

[41] Almansa-Villatoro "The Cultural Indexicality," 77. Referring to Watkins, "The Golden Bowl," 306.

A related concept we see in the Bible is that the firmament is visually comparable to some sort of blue stone. In Exodus 24, Moses, Aaron, and Israel's elders ascend Mount Sanai. Verse 10 tells us that upon doing so, "they saw the God of Israel, and under his feet was pavement like lapis lazuli,[42] like the body of the heavens in clarity."[43]

In Ezekiel 1 the *raqia* is said to be crystalline or ice-like in color. In a vision, Ezekiel sees God seated on his throne above the firmament upheld by cherubim whose four faces represent the cardinal quarters of the Babylonian compass.[44] The message of the vision is that God's reign extends over the whole of the earth even though the Jews are sitting in exile in Babylon:

> And a form was over the heads of the living creatures: a firmament (*raqia*) *like the fearful color of crystal*...and there was a voice from over the firmament (*raqia*) which was over their heads.... And from over the firmament (*raqia*) which was over their heads was the form of a throne of lapis lazuli stone in appearance. And from up above, upon the likeness of the throne, was an image in the appearance of a man...and the appearance of amber.... This was the appearance of the likeness of the glory of the Lord. When I beheld it, I flung myself upon my face....

We know this passage is describing a representation of the sky because, as a noun, the Bible uses this word *raqia* 17 times across Genesis, the Psalms, Ezekiel and Daniel.[45] In *every single* other case, it refers to the sky. Likewise, the context of this passage is Babylonian, and it is remarkably similar in its enthronement description to a Babylonian text depicting

---

[42] Following the translation of *sappir* noted by Peter Kingsley, "Ezekiel by the Grand Canal: Between Jewish and Babylonian Tradition," *Journal of the Royal Asiatic Society* 2.3 (1992), 339.

[43] In the Ugaritic texts, we are likewise told that Baal's palace on a mountain called Zaphanu has paved brick constructed of "the clearness of lapis lazuli." See Michael S. Heiser, "The Divine Council in Late Canonical and Non-Canonical Second Temple Jewish Literature" (PhD diss. University of Wisconsin-Madison, 2004), 2.2.

[44] See Michael Heiser, "Ezekiel's Vision, Part 2," *PaleoBabble*, 2008. Accessed May 28, 2017, www.michaelsheiser.com/PaleoBabble/2008/08/ezekiels-vision-part-2/.

[45] Found in Gen 1:6-8, 1:14-15, 1:17, 1:20; Psa 19:1, 150:1; Ezek 1:22-23, 25-26, 10:1; and Dan 12:3.

Marduk seated on his lapis lazuli throne over the solid lower heavens of Babylonian cosmology, similarly surrounded by the gleam of amber.[46]

The view that the heavens are stone is stated point-blank in the religious texts of Israel's neighbors. One Akkadian text reads:

> The Upper Heavens are *luludanilu*-stone. They belong to (the god) Anu. He settled the 300 Igigi (gods) inside.
> The Middle Heavens are *saggilmud* stone. They belong to the Igigi. Bel sat on the high [platform] inside,
> *The Lower Heavens are jasper. They belong to the stars. He drew the constellations of the gods on them.*[47]

A different tablet repeats the same phrase about the lower heavens.[48] In these texts, we are told the undersurface of the sky looking up from the earth is Jasper—a glassy, often translucent type of chalcedony. The text is probably talking about a sky-blue variety known from Persia.[49] Upon this firmament, the stars are "drawn," perhaps similar to the concept of them being literally "*set in* the firmament" in Gen 1:17.

There are other biblical passages containing related notions. In Genesis 28, Jacob has a dream about 'stairs' physically reaching to the sky.[50] Upon the steps in his vision, Jacob sees the angels ascending and

---

[46] See Kingsley's paper discussing VAT 8917 in the Berlin Vorderasiatisches Museum, Kingsley, "Ezekiel by the Grand Canal," 339-346.

[47] KAR 307:30-33. Quoted from Horowitz, *Mesopotamian Cosmic Geography*, 4.

[48] Ibid., 4.

[49] Ibid., 13. Some may be confused by the reference to upper and middle heavens made out of two different types of stone. What's going on here is conceptually similar to what certain Native American tribes like the Navajo believed. Some Mesopotamians thought that above the solid sky was another solid sky—like the stories of a house. The second story had its own sky ceiling with yet a third story on top of it. The gods live on the middle and upper stories, not the bottom. We know from other texts that *saggilmud* stone is blue and *luludanilu* was probably of a reddish hue.

[50] These were probably the stairs of a ziggurat. A ziggurat in Sippar, for example, was similarly referred to by the title "The Staircase to Holy Heaven." H. W. F. Saggs, *Civilization Before Greece and Rome* (New Haven: Yale University Press, 1989), 57. The Hebrew term "stairs" in this passage is a *hapax legomenon* but appears cognate with the Akkadian *simmiltu*. According to Ross, "In the myth of 'Nergel and Ereshkigal' communication between the netherworld and heaven takes place via the long stairway of heaven that leads to the gate of Anu, Enlil, and Ea.... The most that can be said is that a word used in ziggurat settings is cognate to the

descending. Waking up trembling, he says, "This is the gate of heaven!" In this story, we see implied again a sense that heaven has geography—that it could be reached by ascending steps.

A similar intimation can be found in Job 22:12-14. In this text, Eliphaz is accusing Job of doubting God's omniscience. The ESV translates:

> Is not God high in the heavens? See the highest stars, how lofty they are! Therefore you say, 'What does God know? Can he judge through the deep darkness? Thick clouds enwrap him so that he does not see, and he walks on the dome [literally: "circle"] of heaven.

THE HEAVENLY WATERS

The material composition of the *raqia* in the minds of the ancient Hebrews was probably ambiguous. However, this is less important than its function of retaining a heavenly ocean in Genesis 1.

Israel's God abides over a heavenly flood in Psa 104:2-3: "He stretches out the heavens like a tent cloth. He lays the beams of his upper chambers in the waters."[51] Jer 10:13 says, "When God's voice thunders, there is a tumult of waters in the heavens." As emphasized, Gen 1:7 also mentions these "waters above," and the psalmist declares, "praise him you waters above the heavens!"

When the Bible talks about the throne of God resting above a flood in the sky, it is relating an idea common in the ancient Near East. Professor of Judaic studies J. Edward Wright at the University of Arizona points out that Egyptian texts also mention the heavenly waters

---

word used here, a word that fits the way of communication between heaven and earth." Allen P. Ross, "Studies in the Life of Jacob Part 1: Jacob's Vision: The Founding of Bethel," *Bibliotheca Sacra* 142 (1985), 224-37.

[51] According to Schwab, "The 'beams' in view here are more likely foundation beams needed to secure God's palace on the celestial ocean." Mark Futato and George M Schwab, *Cornerstone Biblical Commentary: Psalms, Proverbs*, ed. Philip W. Comfort (Carol Stream: Tyndale, 2009), 330. Alter makes the same identification. Robert Alter, *The Book of Psalms: A Translation with Commentary* (New York: W.W. Norton & Company, 2007), 363. Barker agrees, "The imagery portrayed here is that of a celestial palace whose foundation beams are laid in the waters. Presumably, based on the context of 'light' (2a), 'heavens' (2b), 'clouds' (3b), and 'wind' (3c), the waters are heavenly waters (cf. Amos 9:6).

frequently. One hymn speaks of "the Nile in heaven."[52] A hymn to Ra calls them "the watery abyss of the sky."[53] A coffin text calls them "the Celestial waters," and, "the pool of the firmament."[54] Commenting on a fragment of Egyptian art, Othmar Keel writes, "The heavenly ocean is called *kbhw-Hr*, the 'cool' or 'upper waters of Horus,' the sky god. A surrounding wall shown in one associated artifact may represent the 'firmament' which contains the upper waters."[55]

Citing a handful of texts and artistic depictions, James P. Allen, the previous president of the International Association of Egyptologists and professor of Egyptology at Brown University, confirms that the ancient Egyptians believed in celestial waters suspended over heaven:

> Looking at the sky without telescopes, the Egyptians saw only an undifferentiated background of blue by day, or black by night—the same qualities visible in the river Nile. Understandably, therefore, the Egyptians concluded that the sky, like the Nile, was composed of water. The waters of the sky were thought to surround the earth and extend infinitely outward in all directions. The world existed as a single void inside this endless sea…. By day the sun sailed across the surface of the sky-ocean….[56]

---

[52] Hymn to Aton from the period of Amenhotep IV. Quoted in J. Edward Wright, *The Early History of Heaven* (Oxford: Oxford University Press, 2000), 11.

[53] Ibid., 12. Originally from a hymn to Ra prefixed to the *Book of the Dead*.

[54] Ibid., 12-13. *Coffin Text* §74 and 761.

[55] Othmar Keel, *The Symbolism of the Biblical World: Ancient Near Eastern Iconography and the Book of Psalms*. Trans. Timothy J. Hallett (Winona Lake: Eisenbrauns, 1997), 37.

[56] James P. Allen, "The Celestial Realm," in David P. Silverman (ed.), *Ancient Egypt* (Oxford: Oxford University Press, 1997), 114.

Figure 10. Papyrus art symbolically depicting the cosmos. Adapted from "The god Seb supporting Nut on heaven" in E. A. W. Budge, *The Gods of the Egyptians*, vol. 2 (London: Gilbert and Rivington, 1904), 96.

Other people of the ancient Near East seem to have applied this same logic in order to derive the common conclusion that the heavens retained cosmic waters.[57]

Clearly, if the heavenly waters mentioned in Genesis are evidence for revelation about a modern astrophysical view of the universe, as young-earth creationists usually claim, then they are left with the theological difficulty of admitting the Egyptian and Babylonian religions were apparently divinely inspired as well.

---

[57] *Genesis Rabba* XIII:10 reads: "Rabbi Joshua said: [The earth drinks] from the upper waters, for it is written, 'And drinketh water as the rain of heaven cometh down' (Deut. 11, 11); the clouds, however, mount up to heaven and receive them [the waters] as from the mouth of a bottle, for it is written, 'They gather up water into its cloud.'" Quoted from H. Freedman and Maurice Simon (eds.), *Midrash Rabbah: Complete in Ten Volumes. Translated into English with Notes* (New York: Soncino Press, 1983), 105. Horowitz also argues that the etymology of several Sumerian words indicates that the waters above were associated with rainfall. Horowitz, *Mesopotamian Cosmic Geography*, 262.

THE SUPPORTS OF HEAVEN

Most of us have come across the Bible's language about the "pillars of earth," but it is significant to recognize that the Bible also alludes to pillars upholding the sky.

Job 26:11 tells us "the *pillars of heaven* quake" at God's rebuke. 2 Sam 22:8 says the *"foundations of heaven"* shook." Keel notices that the parallel passage to 2 Sam 22:8 in Ps 18:7 interchanges the phrase "foundations of the heavens" with "foundations of the mountains" because the two are identical.[58] In biblical cosmology, the heavens also have "ends" (i.e. a rim). Isa 13:5 and Psa 19:6 talk about the "ends of the heavens." Deut 4:32 seeks to encompass the entire earth with the phrase, "from one end of the heavens to the other," and other passages, like Isa 5:26 and Psa 22:27, similarly refer to the "ends of the earth." Further, if the earth shakes, then the heavens, which rest on the earth, shake also. Joel 2:10 says God will "shake" heaven and earth. Isa 13:13 says, "I will make the heavens tremble and shake the earth from its place...."

Figure 11. Shu upholds the sky. E. A. W. Budge, *The Gods of the Egyptians*, vol. 2 (London: Gilbert and Rivington, 1904), 98.

How do young-earthers explain such language? An Answers in Genesis piece assures us that these passages must not be literal: "We know that the earth does not literally have foundations and a cornerstone like a building; instead, God uses this figurative language to create a mental picture...."[59] Indeed, modern readers are predisposed to impose their scientific preconceptions onto the text and conclude that

---

[58] Keel, *The Symbolism of the Biblical World*, 22.
[59] Erik Lutz, "Contradictions: Hanging on Pillars of Nothing?," *Answers in Genesis*, Aug 9, 2011. Accessed July 28, 2017, www.answersingenesis.org/astronomy/earth/contradictions-hanging-on-pillars-of-nothing/?sitehist=1501457736342.

this language is merely metaphor, but it was not so with the ancients. Paul Seely writes of the Egyptians:

> [The Pyramid] Text 1156c mentions that "his (the god Shu's) right arm supports the sky"; and 2013a says, "Thou art a god who supports the sky." Various of the Coffin Texts (ca. 2050 to 1800 BC) reiterate these ideas of the sky needing support, e.g., spells 160, 366, 378, and 664. Pyramid Text 1040c more prosaically points to the two mountain ranges on the east and west sides of the Nile as the "two supports of the sky." ...Text 299a implies that if the supporting arms of Shu were hacked off, the sky would fall.[60]

In the ancient Egyptian *Trial of Horus and Seth*, the goddess Neith threatens that she will "become very angry and cause the heaven to touch the ground."[61]

The most prevalent Egyptian idea paralleling the biblical pillars was that four, massive cardinal supports suspended the sky. One text reads, "I set the glory for thee and fear of thee in all lands, the terror of thee as far as *the four supports of heaven*."[62] Another text reads: "I rise like the sun disc and shine like Ra, as *the heaven is firm upon its supports*."[63] In fact, after completing a renovation project on the Karnak temple in Luxor, Thutmose III's scribe stated in an inscription that the renovations were done, "in order that this temple might be established like the heavens, abiding upon their four pillars."[64] Concerning this roof-like firmament, it's frequently pointed out by Egyptologists that the hieroglyph for sky even depicts a roof: *pt—* ▱.[65] As Seely mentions above, the

[60] Paul Seely, "The Firmament and the Water Above: Part I: The Meaning of *raqia`* in Gen 1:6-8," *Westminster Theological Journal* 53 (1991), 233.
[61] D.L. Couprie, trans., in *Heaven and Earth in Ancient Greek Cosmology: From Thales to Heraclides Ponticus*. Astrophysics and Space Science Library 374 (New York: Springer, 2011), 213.
[62] James Prichard, *Ancient Near Eastern Texts Relation to the Old Testament*, (*ANET*) 2 ed. (Princeton: Princeton University Press, 1969), 374.
[63] Ibid., 257.
[64] Quoted in Wright, *Early History of Heaven*, 15.
[65] This has been noted by James K. Hoffmeier, "Thoughts on Genesis 1 & 2," 45; Wright, *The History of Heaven*, 10; James Atwell's mention of it in "An Egyptian Source for Genesis 1," *Journal of Theological Studies* 51 (2000), 456. Also James P. Allen, *Genesis in Egypt: The Philosophy of Ancient Egyptian Creation Accounts*. Yale Egyptological Studies 2 (Yale University Press: New Haven 1988), 4.

Egyptians theologically attributed the supporting of this sky to the god Shu (the anthropomorphized embodiment of air), upholding the heavens with his arms. More materially, they literally identified mountains as serving this function. For example, Coffin Text 160 says, "I know that mountain of Bakhu upon which the sky leans."[66] Keel likewise produces images from the Book of the Dead showing the gate the sun enters between twin mountains at the earth's horizon.[67]

These cosmological ideas are also found in Mesopotamian literature. The *Epic of Gilgamesh*, whose origins we can trace back to before 2000 BC, tells the story of the king Gilgamesh who resolved to travel to the literal end of the world in order to seek out a legendary man who was long ago granted eternal life by the gods. The texts (Tablet I.40-42), tell us that Gilgamesh found the immortal one beyond "the ocean...as far as the sunrise" at "the edges of the world."[68] Gilgamesh traveled until he "reached Mount Mashu, / which daily guards the rising and setting of the Sun, / above which only the dome of heaven reaches" (Tablet IX.37-40).[69] After reaching these twin mountains supporting the sky, Gilgamesh is confronted by two half-man, half-scorpion guardians who allow him to take the subterranean tunnel through the mountains that the sun takes in its rising. These mountain sky pillars that the sun passes through at the eastern and western opposite ends of the earth are also mentioned on Tablet V.9-11 of the *Enuma Elish* creation story. In the Ugaritic texts, we find these mountains as well: "Now you shall head out to mount *TRGZZ*, to mount *TRMG*, the twin mounds at the edges of the earth...."[70]

I don't think it's a coincidence that the biblical notion of heavenly supports is similar to Egyptian, Mesopotamian and Ugaritic literature. The Torah has the Jews spending centuries in Egypt. As the archaeology

---

[66] Prichard, *ANET*, 12.

[67] Keel, *The Symbolism of the Biblical World*, 22, 24. Figures 10-13.

[68] Dalley, *Myths from Mesopotamia*, 51.

[69] Maureen Gallery Kovacs, *The Epic of Gilgamesh* (Stanford, CA: Stanford University Press, 1989), 76. George's important edition translates line 40 more in keeping with tent language: "Their tops [abut] the fabric of the heavens." George, *The Babylonian Gilgamesh Epic*, 669.

[70] KTU 1.4:VIII:1-4. Translation quoted from Mark S. Smith, "The Structure of Divinity at Ugarit and Israel: The Case of Anthropomorphic Deities versus Monstrous Divinities" in Gary Beckham and Theodore J. Lewis (eds.) *Text, Artifact, and Image: Revealing Ancient Israelite Religion* (Providence: Scholars Press, 2006), 44.

likewise demonstrates, throughout Judean history, Egyptian motifs and even literature also flowed into Judah.[71] Additionally, much of the Hebrew Bible was greatly shaped by Mesopotamian civilizations like Babylon and Assyria, and Ugaritic literature is closely related to the Hebrew's linguistic-cultural context.

STRETCHING OUT THE HEAVENS

The Babylonian creation myth uses the language of securing a tent for the heavens. In tablet V.59-62, we are told that the god Marduk twisted the chaos dragon's tail and "fastened it as the Great Bond."[72] He then hoisted the skin upwards, securing the "bonds" of heaven and tethering its "lead ropes." We likewise find tent language describing the heavens frequently in the Old Testament. A dozen times, we read of the heavens being "stretched out."

For example, Psa 104:2 says God, "stretches out the heavens like a tent." Isa 40:22 says God "spreads them out like a tent to live in."

The young-earth astronomer Jason Lisle thinks the Bible's tent spreading language here describes the astronomical expansion of the universe. In *Taking Back Astronomy*, he writes:

> God "stretches out the heavens like a curtain, and spreads them out like a tent to dwell in." This would suggest that the universe has actually increased in size since its creation. God has stretched it out. He has expanded it (and is perhaps still expanding it). This verse must have seemed very strange when it was first written…. It must have been hard to believe at the time…. Most astronomers today believe that the universe is expanding. This expansion is a very natural result of the physics that Einstein discovered—general relativity.[73]

---

[71] Hoffmeier states, "In the years following their occupation of Canaan there was ongoing contact with Egypt. There is no reason to doubt that there could have been literary influence on Hebrew cosmology as there was in other areas of Hebrew literature." Hoffmeier, "Some Thoughts on Genesis 1 & 2," 48.

[72] L. W. King, *Enuma Elish: The Seven Tablets of Creation*, vol. 1 (London: Luzac and Co., 1902), 77.

[73] Jason Lisle, *Taking Back Astronomy: The Heavens Declare Creation and Science Confirms It* (Green Forest: Master Books, 2006), 28.

Despite these claims, as will become obvious in what follows, the language and concepts of the Bible were not culturally strange at all to the Israelites. There is a far better interpretation than what Lisle proposes. These passages sound bizarre to us moderns only because we come to them inserting our assumptions about an atmospheric sky into the text, but they made perfect sense to ancient Israelites whose very word for firmament alludes to "stretching out" with connotations like hammered metal.[74]

Biblical scholars recognize that this tent language is intended to convey the idea that the world is God's tabernacle tent.[75] However, Lisle wants us to believe that the Israelites had songs containing coded references to Einsteinian general relativity theory (i.e. the expansion of the space-time universe) that made no sense to them in their original context. But why should we insert modern astrophysics into these passages when ancient parallels already explain the meaning?

On Tablet IV.139 of the Babylonian creation story, we are told that Marduk, "stretched out the skin" of Tiamat, tethering it with rope in tent building fashion in conjunction with fashioning the covering of heaven. The Akkadian word for "stretching" (*isduud*) is present in the ancient texts,[76] and the stretching of this skin serves the same function of retaining the waters in the Babylonian myth as it does in the Bible. Did the priests of Marduk discover relativity physics as well?

ANCIENT INTERPRETATION OF BIBLICAL COSMOLOGY

JEWISH
To demonstrate beyond doubt how alien to the world of the Bible young-earth interpretations like those proposed by Dr. Lisle are, I want to share a handful of examples of how ancient Jews understood them. If

---

[74] In Isa 42:5; 44:24 and Psa 136:6 the verbal form of *raqia* is used for cosmological 'spreading out' of the earth. Isa 44:24 uses it in parallel with the spreading of the sky.

[75] This connection is implied in Psalms like 78:69. See L Michael Morales, *The Tabernacle Pre-Figured: Cosmic Mountain Ideology in Genesis and Exodus* (Leuven: Peeters, 2012), 78-9.

[76] I'm indebted to the linguist Charles Loder for showing me the entry for the verb in Martha T. Roth, et al. (eds.), *Chicago Assyrian Dictionary* 17.1 (Illinois: Oriental Institute, 1989), 20.

there was some sort of "strange" scientific code for an atmospheric model in the Bible, the ancients sure don't show evidence of noticing it.

One apocalyptic text called 3 Baruch (written in the first few centuries after Christ) tells us about the Tower of Babel and how its builders were attempting to ascend to heaven. 3:6-8 reads:

> And appearing to them, the Lord changed their languages; by that time they had built the tower 463 cubits (high). And taking an auger [i.e. a drill], they attempted to pierce the heaven, saying "Let us see whether the heaven is (made) of clay or copper or iron." Seeing these things, God did not permit them (to continue), but struck them with blindness and with confusion of tongues....[77]

In a different source, the *Babylonian Talmud*, the rabbis tell us that the scheming men of Babel said: "Let us build a tower, ascend to heaven, and cleave it with axes, that its waters might gush forth."[78] This text seems to retain the heavenly waters above as an element of this tradition.

Another ancient Jewish passage that assumes a solid sky and explicitly alludes to its heavenly ocean can be found in a text called Genesis Rabba, compiled during Judaism's classical period between AD 300-500. It preserves a handful of rabbinic speculations about the thickness of the heavenly vault:

> The thickness of the firmament equals that of the earth: compare, "It is He that sitteth above the circle (Hebrew: *chug*) of the earth" (Isa 40:22) with, "And He walketh in the circuit (Hebrew: *chug*) of the heaven" (Job 22:14): the use of '*chug*' in both verses teaches that they are alike. Rabbi Aha said in Rabbi Janina's name: [It is as] thick as a metal plate. Rabbi Joshua son of Rabbi Nehemiah said: It is about two fingers in thickness. The son of Pazzi said: The upper waters exceed the lower ones by about [the measure of] thirty xestes [for it is written], "And let it divide the waters from the waters (Hebrew: *la-*

[77] James H. Charlesworth (ed.), *The Old Testament Pseudepigrapha: Volume One Apocalyptic Literature and Testaments* (Massachusetts: Hendrickson, 1983), 665.
[78] *Sanhedrin* 109a. I. Epstein (ed.), *The Babylonian Talmud: Seder Nezikin. Sanhedrin II.* H. Freedman (trans.) (London: Soncino, 1935), 748.

mayim)".…. Our Rabbis said: They are half-and-half [that is, equal].[79]

Again, we can see from this passage that the Rabbis believed the *raqia* was a literal retaining vault. Rabbi Janina even thought (undoubtedly from the etymology) that it was as "thick as a metal plate." Many early Rabbinic texts explicitly interpret the firmament of Genesis 1 as solid. For example Genesis Rabba 4:2:

> Our rabbis said the following in the name of Rabbi Hanina, while Rabbi Phinehas and Rabbi Jacob son of Rabbi Bun said it in the name of Rabbi Samuel son of Nahman: When the Holy One, blessed be He, ordered: "Let there be a firmament in the midst of the waters," the middle layer of water solidified and the…heavens… were formed.[80]

As can be observed in these two examples, the Rabbis additionally continued to maintain there was a literal ocean above the sky. Some speculated that it was "half-and-half" in volume to the earth's oceans because the Gen 1:6 phrase "divide waters from waters" tends to imply a half-and-half separation. The Dead Sea Scroll book of Jubilees comes to this same half-and-half conclusion. As there is the earthly ocean, there is a heavenly ocean (2:8):

> And on the second day he created the *raqia* between the waters, and he divided the waters on that day. *Half* of them rose above the *raqia*, and *half* of them descended under the *raqia*, which was in the midst over the face of all the earth.[81]

After the Old Testament period, the Greeks did eventually influence many Jews to modify aspects of their cosmology, and several hybrids emerged. However, one still finds belief in a solid firmament in Jewish

---

[79] *Parashah 4, Midrash* 5. Wilfred Shuchat reproduces this and other similar passages in Raphael Posner (ed.), *The Creation According to the Midrash Rabbah* (Jerusalem: Devora, 2002), 159.

[80] Quoted in Moshe Simon-Shoshan, "'The Heavens Proclaim the Glory of God…': A Study in Rabbinic Cosmology," *Bekhol DeraKhekha Daehu* 20 (2008), 73.

[81] Author's translation:

"וביום השני עשה את הרקיע בין המים ויבדלו המי ביום ההוא חציים עלה מעל לרקיע וחציים ירד מתחת לרקיע אשר בתווך על פני כל הארץ."

authors like Josephus (Antiquities, 1.1.30) because the Greek model usually held that the stars were "fixed like nails" to a crystalline sphere encompassing the earth.[82] Aristotle popularized this view in his work *On the Heavens* (II.8), and this Aristotelian cosmology was maintained by the Roman Stoics who were the dominant intellectual school during the New Testament period.[83]

We catch a snapshot of the transition in Jewish thought in the *Babylonian Talmud*:

> The Sages of Israel maintain: The sun travels beneath the sky by day and above the sky by night [i.e. it is hidden above the wall of the firmament]; while the Sages of the nations of the world maintain: It travels beneath the sky by day and below the earth at night. Said Rabbi: And their view is preferable to ours, for the wells are cold by day but warm at night.[84]

The Palestinian Talmud, Rosh Hashanah 58a, as well as the text Exodus Rabba (15:22) even postulate a system of 365 windows in the perimeter of the sky dome that the sun travels through to make its ambulation behind the heavenly vault possible.[85]

Genesis Rabba 6:8 asks, "How do...the sun and moon set?" The Rabbis disagreed:

---

[82] Aëtius writes that "Anaximenes held that stars are fixed like nails in the crystalline substance." Quoted W.K.C. Guthrie, *A History of Greek Philosophy: Volume 1, The Earlier Presocratics and the Pythagoreans* (Cambridge: Cambridge University Press, 1962), 135.

[83] Jonathan T. Pennington, *Cosmology and New Testament Theology* (New York: T&T Clark, 2008), 16-18.

[84] *Pesahim* 94b. Quotation from Gerald J. Blidstein, "Rabbinic Judaism and General Culture: Normative Discussion and Attitudes," in Jacob J. Schacter (ed.) *Judaism's Encounter with Other Cultures: Rejection or Integration?* (Lanham, MD: Rowman & Littlefield, 1997), 45.

[85] Yerushalmi Rosh Hashana 3.58a reads, "The Holy One, Blessed be He, created 365 windows of which the world makes use, 182 in the east and 182 in the west and one in the middle of the firmament." Exodus Rabbah 15.22 states, "God created 365 windows in the firmament, 183 in the east and 192 in the west. Some he created for the sun, and some he created for the moon." Translation Simon-Shosan, "Heavens Proclaim," 88.

R. Judah says, behind the dome and above it. The rabbis say, behind the dome and below it…. R. Simeon b. Jochai said: We do not know if they fly up in the air, if they scrape the firmament, or if they travel as usual; the matter…is impossible for humans to determine.[86]

These divergent theories are also found in the tractate Bava Batra 25a-b in the Talmud:

It was taught in *Beraita* [i.e. oral law]: R. Eliezer says, the world is like an exedra [a type of Greek semicircular architectural recess], and the northern side is not enclosed, and when the sun reaches the north-western corner, it bends back and rises above the firmament. And R. Joshua says, the world is like a tent, and the northern side is enclosed and when the sun reaches the north-western corner, it circles around and returns on the other side of the dome, as [Eccl. 1:6] says….[87]

1 Enoch is a Jewish work that the New Testament authors occasionally quote and frequently allude to. Within this text, we are told how the biblical figure Enoch is given a tour of the cosmos. In his study, *The Early History of Heaven*, the scholar of early Judaism J. Edward Wright quotes 2 Enoch 3:3: "[The angels] placed me on the first heaven and showed me a very great Sea, greater than the earthly sea." According to Wright: "This is the celestial ocean believed since ancient times to be just above the atmosphere. This text thus incorporates the ancient Near Eastern traditions about the celestial ocean into the Greco-Roman multiple heaven model."[88] The *Testament of Levi* found among the Dead Sea Scrolls contains a similar affirmation: "And I entered from the first heaven, and I saw there a great sea hanging."[89]

Similarly, in Genesis Rabba 4:1, 2 we read, "The Holy One, blessed be He, roofed over His world with naught but water…. [God's] handiwork [heaven] was in fluid form, and on the second day, the *raqia* congealed."[90]

---

[86] Ibid., 72-3.

[87] Ibid.

[88] Wright, *History of Heaven*, 175.

[89] *Testament of Levi* 1:8-10. See Charles' footnote. R. H. Charles (ed.), *The Apocrypha and Pseudepigrapha of the Old Testament, Volume Two*. Biblical Apocrypha Series (Berkeley: Apocryphile Press, 2004), 304.

[90] Trans. Simon-Shoshan, "The Heavens Proclaim," 72-3.

In his careful survey of Rabbinic cosmological literature, the Hebrew University Rabbinic expert Moshe Simon-Shoshan concludes:

> The rabbis' view of the nature and structure of the heavens closely parallels Ancient Near Eastern perceptions on the matter, both in its broader conception and in many of its details. Though the rabbi's main source was certainly the Bible, they very likely had indirect access to other Ancient Near Eastern traditions about the heavens. Several of the rabbis' ideas about the heavens that have no source in the Bible have precedence in various Mesopotamian sources.[91]

CHRISTIAN AND LATER SOURCES

Historians like Efthymios Nicolaidis of the National Hellenic Research Foundation and the philologist Kevin van Bladel at Yale have documented how, up into the Byzantine Empire, many of the church fathers of the Near East long maintained belief in general aspects of this cosmology based on indigenous tradition and biblical interpretation.[92]

John Chrysostom, one of the most prolific authors in the Early Church and the Archbishop of Constantinople—the capital of the Byzantine Empire, held a "cosmology [that] was simple: a flat earth covered by a single heaven in the form of a vault. Heaven is immobile; it is the stars that move, and their movement serves to determine time."[93]

Proponents of similar views included Mar Aba the Great, the head Bishop of the Assyrian Church of the East,[94] Narsai, the head of the school of Nisibis and foremost writer in the Assyrian Church of the East,[95] Diodorus, the fourth century Bishop of Tarsus,[96] Theodore of

---

[91] Ibid., 88.

[92] See Efthymios Nicolaidis, *Science and Eastern Orthodoxy: From the Greek Fathers to the Age of Globalization*, trans. Susan Emanuel, (John Hopkins University Press: Baltimore, 2011), 24-40. Kevin Van Bladel, "Heavenly Cords and Prophetic Authority in the Quran and Its Late Antique Context," *Bulletin of the School of Oriental and African Studies, University of London* 70.2 (2007), 226. www.jstor.org/stable/40379198.

[93] Nicolaidis, *Science and Eastern Orthodoxy*, 25.

[94] Cosmas called Mar Aba by his Greek title Patricius and attributes these teachings of "the true science" to him in passages like 2.2 and 8.25 of his *Typography*. Van Bladel, "Heavenly Cords," 238.

[95] Ibid., 226.

Mopsuesta, the Turkish teacher of Nestorius, Severian, the Bishop of Gabala in Syria, who published six sermons against a spherical cosmology,[97] or Cosmas Indicopleustes, a Syrian trained Christian who published his infamous work *Christian Typography* vehemently arguing for a flat earth cosmology from Scripture.[98]

I do not wish to give the reader a false impression. Young-earth apologists are quite accurate when they point out that by the time Christianity expanded throughout the broader world, the vast majority of the educated early church believed in the round earth of previously established Hellenistic science, especially in the West. However, apologists have frequently misled the public by failing to recognize that things were not so simple, especially in the Middle East. Like the Syrian branch of Christianity it polemicizes against, even the Arabian Qur'an, written in the seventh century, doesn't hold a spherical cosmology.[99]

Additionally, although the broader early church embraced Greek spherical cosmology, they did not deduce from their Bibles what we would recognize as an atmospheric cosmology. Among our ancient sources that comment on cosmology, we continue to find frequent references to the solidity of the heavens.

In his commentary on Genesis, the church father Origen (c. 184-253) is emphatic that the firmament is "without doubt, firm and solid.... [T]his heaven, that is, the firmament, is corporal."[100] In the second century, Theophilus calls it a "lid" and "dome-shaped covering."[101] Augustine says that the firmament is "solid and...constitutes an

---

[96] This was affirmed by Diodorus in his *Against Fate*. Though this work has not survived, it is paraphrased in Photius, *Bibliothèque*, codex 223: "Two heavens there are, one visible and the other invisible; one below, the other above: the latter serves as roof to the universe, the former as covering to our earth—not round or spherical, but in the form of a tent or arch." John Louis Emil Dreyer, *History of the Planetary Systems from Thales to Kepler* (New York: Cosimo Classics, 2007), 212.

[97] E.g. quoting Isaiah 40:22, he writes, "The Scripture says it has a top, which a sphere has not." J. L. E. Dreyer, "Medieval Cosmology" in Milton K. Munitz (ed.), *Theories of the Universe: From Babylonian Myth to Modern Science* (New York: The Free Press, 1957), 119.

[98] See Nicolaidis, *Science and Eastern Orthodoxy*, 24-40.

[99] See Appendix C of this book.

[100] Origin, *Homilies on Genesis and Exodus*. trans. Ronald E. Heine, Fathers of the Church 71 (Washington: Catholic University of America Press, 1982), 49.

[101] *Theophilus to Autolycus*, 2.13. Quoted Alexander Roberts and James Donaldson (eds.), *Ante-Nicene Christian Library: Vol. III. Tatian, Theophilus, and the Clementine Recognitions* (Edinburgh: T&T Clark, 1867), 80.

impassable boundary between the waters above and the waters below."[102] Quoting Genesis 1:7, Ambrose, the fourth century Bishop of Milan, writes, "that here the specific solidity of this exterior firmament is meant."[103] Cyril, the fourth century Bishop of Jerusalem, wrote in his *Catechesis* 9:5:

> For what fault have they to find with the vast creation of God?— they who ought to have been struck with amazement on beholding the vaultings of the heaven: they who ought to have worshipped Him who reared the sky as a dome, who out of the fluid nature of the waters formed the stable substance of the heaven. For God said, *Let there be a firmament in the midst of the water.* God spoke once for all, and it stands fast, and falls not. [104]

In the fourth century, Saint Basil the Great recognized that the scientific opinion of his day contradicted the idea that there was a heavenly ocean over the physical heavens, so he found himself forced to defend Genesis 1 by proposing the idea that the firmament is concave with a flat outer surface upon which the heavenly waters must rest. Like many Christians today, he was "unwilling to disregard the literal meaning of the Genesis text just because it seemed absurd to natural philosophers [i.e. his day's scientists]."[105]

When it came to the "waters above," Thomas Aquinas also had a difficult time trying to make sense of them. When reading Thomas, it is clear that the science of his day made the literal reading impossible, and he lists the reasons why in his *Summa Theologica* (I.68). He imagines an objector stating: "[W]ater is heavy by nature, and heavy things tend naturally downwards, not upwards...and fluids cannot rest on a sphere,

---

[102] Augustine, *Genesi Ad Litteram*, II.10. Translation from Johannes Quasten, et al. (eds.), *The Literal Meaning of Genesis Volume 1*. Ancient Christian Writers (Mahwah: Paulist Press, 1982), 61.

[103] Ambrose, *Hexaemeron*, IV.15 in J.J. Savage (trans.), *Hexameron, Paradise, and Cain and Abel*. The Fathers of the Church, vol. 42 (Washington: Catholic University of America, 2003), 60.

[104] Philip Schaff and Henry Wallace (eds.), *Nicene and Post-Nicene Fathers: Second Series, Volume VII Cyril of Jerusalem, Gregory Nazianzen*. Trans. Edward Hamilton Gifford (New York: Cosimo Classics, 2007), 52.

[105] See Adam David Rasmussen, "How St. Basil and Origen Interpret Genesis 1 in the Light of Philosophical Cosmology" (PhD diss., The Catholic University of America, 2013), 141.

as experience shows. Therefore, since the firmament is a sphere, there cannot be water above it."[106] Thomas eventually tries to resolve this issue by arguing that when Moses talked about the heavenly waters he may have been "condescending" to his audience. It must not have been apparent to the Jews that air was an actual, real substance like the other elements, so Moses was forced to use the word *water* though his true meaning was air. Thomas concludes: "On account of the air…being invisible, Moses includes [it] under the name of water, and thus it is evident that waters are found on each side of the firmament…."[107]

Maimonides, the great Medieval Jewish scholar, was also aware that a literal reading of the "waters above" was scientifically problematic in his day. He therefore opted for the same sort of explanation as Thomas, claiming the phrase "indicates extraordinary mysteries," that, "the portion above the firmament is only water by name, not in reality."[108]

Finally, even by the time of the Reformers, the tension between the ancient Hebrew and Greek models continued. Martin Luther admitted this in a lecture on Genesis:

> But what is most remarkable is that Moses clearly makes three divisions. He places the firmament in the middle, between the waters. I might readily imagine that the firmament is the uppermost mass of all and that the waters which are in suspension, not over but under the heaven are the clouds which we observe, so that the waters separated from our waters on the earth. But Moses says in plain words that the waters were above and below the firmament. Here I, therefore, take my reason captive and subscribe to the Word even though I do not understand it.[109]

---

[106] Thomas Aquinas, *Summa Theologica* I.68.1-3. Quoted Fathers of the English Dominican Province, *The "Summa Theologica" of St. Thomas Aquinas Part 1*, vol. 2. (London: R. & T. Washbourne, 1912), 498-507.

[107] Ibid.

[108] This passage was drawn to my attention by Greenwood, *Scripture and Cosmology*, 153. Originally in Moses Maimonides. M. Friedländer (trans.), *The Guide for the Perplexed* (New York: Dover, 1904), 215.

[109] Greenwood (*Scripture and Cosmology*, 153) draws our attention to this passage in Jaroslav Pelikan (ed.), *Luther's Works, Volume 1: Lectures on Genesis, Chapters 1-5*, trans. George V. Schick (St. Louis: Concordia, 1958), 26. In Luther's time, the Aristotelian idea of heavenly spheres was still maintained.

Luther warns believers against being swayed by the scientists of his day who claimed there are no waters above the crystalline sphere, telling us that, "if some things are beyond our comprehension like those before us concerning the waters above the heavens, we must believe them rather than wickedly deny them or presumptuously interpret them in conformity with our understanding."[110]

CONCLUSION

When I went looking for creationist articles responding to the mainstream analysis I have here presented, the name of the apologist J. P. Holding (whose work I have often benefited from in other areas) continually arose in publications by Answers in Genesis.

Holding argued that the cosmological texts of the Bible are "equivocal." By this, he means that the Bible is sufficiently vague about the physical structure of the universe that it doesn't directly affirm either a scientifically ancient or modern cosmology.[111] The difficulties which commentators like Basil, Thomas, Maimonides, and Luther had with reconciling the Bible's heavenly vault and upper waters with the emerging discoveries of astronomy is powerful historical evidence that Holding's view is wrong.

The early church's problem with the firmament wasn't that Genesis is vague. Rather, Genesis is too clear. They admitted the difficulty of weaseling their way out of its scientific implications. Basil proposed a sort of *ad hoc* flat table over the concave sky. Luther threw his hands up. Origen, Thomas, and Maimonides resorted to claiming that the heavenly waters may not actually be water even though the passage has them being separated from the primordial sea in parallel fashion (how's that for a "plain, literal" reading)![112]

I have argued that we are demonstrably wrong when we interpret the "waters above" as anything other than a literal celestial ocean. If we try to massage, nudge and cajole the Bible to make them into rainclouds, or astrophysical ice particles, or if we throw up our hands and cry

---

[110] Pelikan, *Luther's Works*, 42-43.

[111] James Patrick Holding, "Is the *Raqiya'* ('Firmament') a Solid Dome? Equivocal Language in the Cosmology of Genesis 1 and the Old Testament: A Response to Paul H. Seely," *Journal of Creation* 13.2 (Nov 1999), 44-51.

[112] Regarding Origen's interpretation see Rasmussen, "How St. Basil and Origen Interpret," 139.

"mystery!," we are demonstrating that our theology protects us from the Bible. It seems clear that such rationalizations are attempts to censor the Bible into conformity with modern science.

CHAPTER 7

THE ANCIENT HEBREW CONCEPTION OF THE EARTH

ISAIAH'S CIRCLE OF THE EARTH

IT's 2013. I just worked an eight-hour graveyard shift, and I'm sitting in the back of a theology class stabbing into my palm with a pencil to prevent myself from falling asleep. At some point, a student raises his hand to ask our professor about evolution, and I perk a bit from my drooling stupor. The professor admits, "I'm not a biologist so I can't speak on the subject scientifically, but I can tell you the theological costs." He goes on to argue for the necessity of an historical Adam then assures us that the Bible is scientifically accurate in amazing ways in other areas: "For example, look at Isaiah. Isaiah said God 'sits above the circle of the earth, and its inhabitants are like grasshoppers.' Now, how could Isaiah have known that the earth was a circle in a time when everyone else thought it was flat unless this had been divinely shown to him?"

I mention this story because this idea is commonly repeated among evangelicals.[1] Henry Morris even went so far as to declare that the specific Hebrew term translated "circle" in the Isaiah passage "means to be made spherical."[2]

---

[1] For example, the second chapter of Jason Lisle, *Taking Back Astronomy: The Heavens Declare Creation and Science Confirms It* (Green Forest: Master Books, 2006), 26-40.

[2] Henry M. Morris, *The Remarkable Record of Job* (Green Forest: Master Books, 2000), 40.

I think it would be exciting if Isa 40:22 were a supernatural astrophysical revelation that dramatically set Israel centuries apart from the rest of the ancient world. Unfortunately, when I began to read Wayne Horowitz's *Mesopotamian Cosmic Geography* that same summer, I quickly discovered that there's nothing scientifically special going on in this verse because we have plenty of polytheistic ancient Near Eastern writings before and after Isaiah which also describe the earth as a circle (i.e. a disk).

On top of this, Morris was wrong. The Hebrew word translated "circle" here (as in, "circle of the earth") doesn't specify a sphere. In Isa 44:12-13, a form of this Hebrew word is used to refer to the compass of a craftsman. In Job 26:10 and Prov 8:27 the same term is used again to describe the "circle of the earth" being "inscribed"—another reference to the two-dimensional shape one draws with a compass.

Certainly, we should contextualize Isaiah's circle of the earth with these parallel passages. An indication that Isaiah is referring to a flat disk can also be found in the immediate passage itself if we would only read one verse further:

> He sits over the circle of the earth, so its inhabitants are like grasshoppers; who stretches out the skies like a canopy and spreads them out like a tent to dwell in.

Isaiah views the earth like the flat ground over which the heavenly tent is erected. We even have a drawing of this flat earth from roughly the period of Genesis 1's redaction. A clay tablet called the Babylonian Map of the World depicts the earth disk inscribed with a compass upon which identified geographies are plotted (Figure 12). Encircling the earth disk is the ocean, which the text identifies by name four times.[3] This is the "Bitter River" which Gilgamesh crossed to reach the immortal man Utnapishtim—the Babylonian survivor of the Great Flood.

---

[3] Wayne Horowitz, *Mesopotamian Cosmic Geography*. Mesopotamian Civilizations 8 (Winona Lake: Eisenbrauns, 1998), 27.

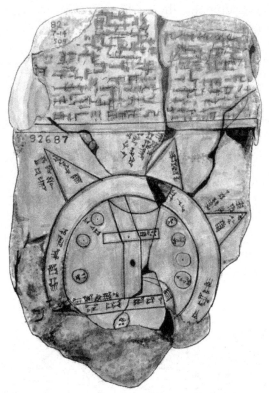

Figure 12. The Babylonian Map of the World. 600-500 BC, British Museum 92687. Illustration by author.

Irving Finkel, the British Museum curator of the tablet who was instrumental in discovering an important missing fragment of the map's face in 1995, tells us that the (originally eight) exterior triangles at the outer rim of this cosmic sea depict, "a ring of vast mountains that marks the rim of the world."[4] These mountains, called *nagus*, are described on the whole of the tablet's reverse and would have been conceived of as "unimaginably remote" in the map's original context (see Figure 13).[5] Finkel confirms that "The world in the map is portrayed as a disc, and

---

[4] Irving Finkel, *The Ark Before Noah: Decoding the Story of the Flood* (New York: Double Day, 2014), 263.
[5] Ibid., 268.

we can therefore assume that the world itself was generally visualised in the same way at the time the map originated."[6]

According to Ulla Koch-Westenholz's *Mesopotamian Astrology*, the Babylonians never recognized the movements of the celestial bodies as spheric, "even in the latest and most advanced stages of Babylonian mathematical astronomy."[7] Wright agrees: "All Babylonian astronomy presupposed a flat earth and either did not recognize or ignored the influence of latitude on celestial observation."[8]

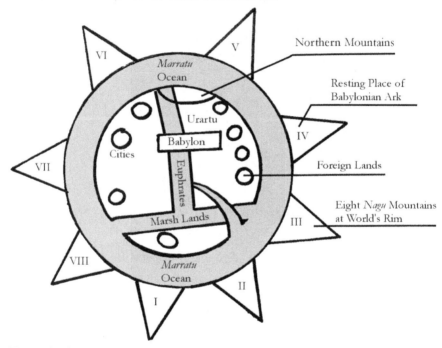

Figure 13. Reconstruction of the Babylonian Map (incorporating Finkel's important discovered numbering of the *nagu* mountains). Illustration by author.

In addition to the Babylonian map, the Babylonian flood tablets compare the earth to a round boat (called a coracle) over the cosmic

---

[6] Ibid., 269. See also the analysis in Othmar Keel, *The Symbolism of the Biblical World: Ancient Near Eastern Iconography and the Book of Psalms*. Trans. Timothy J. Hallett (Winona Lake: Eisenbrauns, 1997).

[7] Ulla Koch-Westenholz, *Mesopotamian Astrology: An Introduction to Babylonian and Assyrian Celestial Divination*. The Carsten Niebuhr Institute of Near Eastern Studies 19 (Denmark: Museum Tusculanum Press), 21.

[8] J. Edward Wright, *The Early History of Heaven* (Oxford: Oxford University Press, 2000), 99.

sea.[9] We also have five Neo-Assyrian sources telling the story of a king who lived before the Flood named Etana. The Etana legend tells of how the ancient monarch was carried upwards by an eagle and was shown the world from the sky. As he ascends higher and higher, Etana proclaims, "The land has turned into the garden of a gardener. The sea has become like the waters of an irrigation ditch." After this, Etana compares the shape of the ditch to "an animal pen."[10] This description of the earth and sea as a garden encircled by a watering ditch corresponds well with the Babylonian map's representation.

Among the Egyptians to Israel's west, the circular earth can also be found in art. A fourth century BC sarcophagus from the necropolis of Saqqara depicts the disk of the earth surrounded by the encompassing cosmic sea. Over this terrestrial circle is depicted the personified sky supported by the hands of the god Shu.[11]

This sort of cosmology pictured on the Babylonian map and in Egyptian art is what Prov 8:27 and Job 26:10 have in mind when they say God "has inscribed a circle on the face of the waters," and what Isaiah means when he says, "God sits over the circle of the earth."

If you read Genesis 1 carefully, you can see this concept in the text. After God divides the waters above and below the sky, verse 9 tells us, "God said, 'Let the waters under the sky collect to one place [אֶל־מָקוֹם אֶחָד], and let the dry land appear.' And it was so." How do you have a situation in which land appears but all the waters under the sky are collected in "a single place?" The Babylonian and Egyptian civilizations to the left and right of ancient Israel seem to offer the most plausible explanation.

Interestingly, many creationists who read the Genesis passage have noticed this language it uses and have also concluded that it is describing a single giant landmass. Filtering the text through modern science, some conclude it must be describing the original supercontinent

---

[9] Finkel, *The Ark Before Noah*, 172.

[10] Horowitz, *Mesopotamian Cosmic Geography*, 63.

[11] This image, which is featured on the cover of Keel's book, is pictured and discussed in Othmar Keel and Silvia Schroer, *Creation: Biblical Theologies in the Context of the Ancient Near East*, trans. Peter T. Daniels (Winona Lake: Eisenbrauns, 2015), 79-80.

named Pangea.[12] A sign in the Creation Museum proposes that the Flood therefore first catalyzed the continental drift that created our present world.[13] Surely the fact that the Bible alludes to Pangea is evidence that God revealed modern science within it! Again, the problem with this argument is that it would imply that Israel's pagan neighbors also had divinely inspired science. It also doesn't make any sense because the Bible *still* subscribes to this same cosmology *after the Flood* in Isaiah and Proverbs.

Recall again that the Babylonian map shows the earth disc encompassed by a ring of ocean called the *Marratu*—the "Bitter River." This river-like ring of ocean encompassing the earth disk is also explicitly shown in Egyptian art where it is often symbolized as the chaos serpent Apophis as the circular *ouroboros* biting his tail.[14] Keel has noted this same idea of the river-ocean ring demarcating the edges of the world is undoubtedly reflected in the Psalms where the terms 'sea' and 'river' are often cosmically paralleled.[15] Emphasizing that the whole earth is Yahweh's, Psalm 24:2 thus reads: "For he has founded it upon the seas, and upon the rivers [*nhrwt*] established it." The Hebrew of Psalm 93:3-4 praises Yahweh for his superiority over the "roar" and "waves of the rivers [*nhrwt*]," the "breakers of *Yam* (=sea)." Psalm 72:8 reads: "Let him dominate from sea upon sea, and from the River [*nhr*] upon the ends of the earth." The Ugaritic chaos serpent in the Ba'al Cycle is likewise interchangeably titled, "Prince Sea" [*zbl ym*] and "Judge River" [*tpt nhr*].[16] The cosmic ocean-river ring only makes sense if the earth was seen as a disk.

JOB: "HE HANGS THE EARTH ON NOTHING"

---

[12] For example, Hugh Ross (who doesn't believe in a global flood, and isn't a young-earther), Hugh Ross, *The Genesis Question: Scientific Advances and The Accuracy of Genesis*, 2 ed. (Colorado Springs: NavPress, 2001), 36.

[13] Under the label, "The Flood Rearranges the Earth."

[14] Noted in Keel, *Symbolism of the Biblical World*, 44. The similarity between Apophis and Leviathan and their mutual descriptions as coiled serpents is briefly discussed in chapter 9.

[15] The following citations I draw from Keel, *Symbolism of the Biblical World*, 22.

[16] E.g. KTU 1.2:III:23.

What other passages do concordists use to defend their belief that the Bible's cosmology is scientifically advanced for its time? Besides Isaiah's "circle of the earth," a favorite passage is Job 26:7:

He stretches *Zaphon* over chaos/void (Hebrew: *tohu*);
he suspends the earth over naught (*bli-mah*).

Often, it is taught that this verse especially teaches that the earth hangs in empty space as modern astronomy has discovered. Jason Lisle writes:

Job 26:7...states that God "hangs the earth on nothing."...—something quite unnatural for the ancient writers to imagine. Indeed, the earth does float in space. We now have pictures of the earth taken from space that show it floating in the cosmic void...just as the Bible teaches.[17]

Again, reading this text in the context of the modern space program is a bad idea. Within this passage's following verses, we read of God inscribing the earth's horizon on the surface of the primordial waters and of the "pillars of the earth" (v. 10-11). Immediately before, the text is speaking of the underworld. In the immediately following verse after this, we read of God defeating the sea, *Yam*—cutting the dragon *Rahab* into pieces. These themes imply that we should interpret this verse in light of the ancient Near Eastern cosmology we have been tracing.

You will notice that the first line of verse 7 refers to God stretching out *Zaphon*. In Hebrew, *Zaphon*, could either refer to a cosmic mountain, upon which God was frequently said to dwell, or it could refer to the northern sky. Since we are dealing with poetry, it seems reasonable to suspect that both meanings are at play: In the case of the first meaning, the *tohu* over which God's mountain spans seems to refer to the waters under the earth referenced in verses 5 and 10-12—sandwiching the passage (*tohu* is also used of the primordial waters of chaos in Gen 1:2).

In the case of the second meaning, "northern sky," the use of *tohu* could refer to the void between the firmament and the earth or the initial separation of the sky from watery chaos at creation. Considering the way *tohu* is used in the first line, the second parallel line in the couplet, "he suspends the earth over naught," is probably not emphasizing God's hanging the earth in a literal vacuum.

---

[17] Lisle, *Taking Back Astronomy*, 28.

In accordance with a main theme of the passage's chapter, and especially verse 10, most scholars view this nothingness as alluding to the abyss of chaotic waters over which is suspended the terrestrial creation in Job's cosmology.[18]

THE ISRAELITE CONCEPTION OF THE EARTH

I have argued above that young-earth creationists have misinterpreted the two main passages used to support the idea that the Bible contains modern cosmology (Isa 40:22, and Job 26:7). If this is so, what *did* the Israelites believe about terrestrial cosmology?

First, we have seen how the Babylonians conceived the earth as a disk. In his book *Scripture and Cosmology*, Kyle Greenwood has pointed out that the book of Daniel reflects this general conception through the words of the Babylonian king Nebuchadnezzar.[19] Nebuchadnezzar tells Daniel (ESV 4:10-11):

> The visions of my head as I lay in bed were these: I saw, and behold, a tree in the midst of the earth, and its height was great. The tree grew and became strong, and its top reached to heaven, and it was visible to the end of the whole earth.

These elements are repeated in Daniel's following interpretation (4:20-24).

The cultural background of this cosmic tree imagery is well established.[20] The influential Mesopotamian Erra Epic speaks of a primeval world tree whose roots reach to the extreme bottom of the underworld to mingle with the cosmic deep, and whose bough literally

---

[18] Thus the interpretation in Keel, who notes that Near Eastern texts often marvel and theologize upon the question of what the pillars of the earth themselves ultimately stand upon. Keel, *Symbolism of the Biblical World*, 55.

[19] Kyle Greenwood, *Scripture and Cosmology: Reading the Bible Between the Ancient World and Modern Science* (Downer's Grove: InterVarsity Press), 76.

[20] See Silviu Bunta, "The MESU-tree and the animal Inside: Theomorphism and Theriomorphism in Daniel 4," *Scrinium* 3.1 (2007), 364-384. This cosmic tree imagery is also found with greater description in Ezekiel 31. See Daniel I. Block, *The Book of Ezekiel: Chapters 25-48*. The New International Commentary on the Old Testament (Grand Rapids: Eerdmans, 1998), 185ff.

reached to heaven.[21] Because the ancients believed the earth was a disk, Nebuchadnezzar and Daniel assume that if an object of sufficient size were stationed at the center of the earth (its top reaching the firmament) then the whole population of the earth could see it. This conception would be impossible had Nebuchadnezzar presumed the correct (but bizarre), idea that the earth is a sphere with people living parallel lives upside down in distant lands, prevented from falling off by some invisible force. It corresponds well, however, with the contextual sources we looked at above. Simply imagine setting the Babylonian map tablet on a table and placing a miniature toy tree in its center, and you would likely have Nebuchadnezzar's notion.

Figure 14. Unfinished *Kudurru* from the twelfth century, discovered in Susa. Currently held at the Louvre.

Additionally, the Bible also frequently speaks of the "pillars" and "foundations" of the earth: "The pillars of the earth are Yhwh's, upon which he has set the world" (1 Sam 2:8); "When the earth quakes and all its inhabitants, I bear up the pillars" (Psa 75:3); "My own hand laid the foundations of the earth" (Is 48:13). Other such passages include Mic 6:2, Jer 31:37, Psa 18:15; 82:5; 104:5, Isa 24:18; 51:13, or Prov 8:29.

Keel and Schroer point us to a carved boundary marker dating to the twelfth century BC, discovered in the Elamite city of Susa in modern Iran (Figure 14).

Referred to as the "Unfinished *Kudurru*," and currently held in the Louvre, the piece depicts the earth upheld by four pillars that reach down from the underworld into the cosmic sea beneath. The chaotic waters are symbolized by the great dragon coiled around its base. Another corresponding serpent "encloses the peak of the entirety…. The two serpents symbolize the upper and

---

[21] *Erra Epic* I:150-53.

lower oceans."[22] On the level directly under the heavenly waters above are "the symbols of the gods that can be recognized in the constellations."[23] The middle register depicts the earth in a procession of worship and the register beneath this likely depicts the fortress walls of the city of the underworld.[24]

If the earth is held up by pillars what is holding up the pillars at their base? This is the question that God puts to Job (38:6): "on what were its foundations sunk?" It appears the artist who carved this *Kudurru* may not have been sure of the answer to that mystery either, at least in the material sense. The four pillars surrounding the stone simply terminate where they intersect with the body of the serpent—suspended over chaos.

SHEOL AS A LITERAL GEOGRAPHY

The final tier concluding our tour of Israelite cosmology is the underworld. We moderns often have a hard time accepting that anyone might be denied access to heaven. It was not so with the ancients. Among the Homeric Greeks, the Assyrians, the Babylonians, and the Canaanites, it was believed that everyone, usually even the virtuous and heroes, went to a form of hell at death. Though not the New Testament's fiery torment, their conception of the underworld was remarkably dismal. In the *Odyssey*, the disconsolate ghost of the hero Achilles tells the Ithacan king that he would rather be among the poorest on earth than lord over all the dead.[25] In the *Epic of Gilgamesh*, the hero Enkidu describes his visions of the "House of Darkness" before his life slips away. There, in the "House of Dust," dust covers the lock of exit. Bereft of light, the shades of the dead are clothed in feathers like birds. Dirt and clay are their food, and heaps of mortal crowns litter the ground like trash.[26]

The similar idea that *Sheol* is geographically under the earth will be familiar to most casual Bible readers. For example, in Num 16:30-33 we read, "If Yhwh creates something new and opens the mouth of the

---

22 Keel and Schroer, *Creation*, 81.
23 Ibid., 82.
24 Ibid.
25 *Odyssey*, II:486.
26 *Epic of Gilgamesh*, VII.4.29-40.

earth and swallows them up and all that belongs to them, and they go down alive into *Sheol*, you will know that these men provoked Yhwh." In other words, the Hebrew Bible not only significantly shares in its Near Eastern context with respect to its heavenly and earthy physical cosmology, but also spoke in many similar terms about its underworld.[27]

CONCLUSION

The Old Testament's cosmology interfaces closely with its surrounding cultural context. When it comes to the three-tier cosmology of the Scriptures—heavens, earth, and the underworld—we see repeatedly that the ancient Near East is the appropriate context for understanding the Hebrew authors. In some cases, it is especially foolish to apply a modern scientific interpretation because the biblical conception assumes a flat earth. Too often, we have used our theology to distort the Bible because we deduced philosophically what we think it should (and should not) be permitted to say.

---

[27] Because Hebrew belongs to the West Semitic family of languages, we see many of the same cognate terms used in their texts that we see in the Bible. Upon death one's soul (*n-b-sh* in Ugaritic, *n-p-sh* in Hebrew), or spirit (*r-ch*, like the Hebrew *r-ch*) descended into the earth to the realm of the dead—the Hebrew word for death being the same as the name of the Semitic god of the dead, *Mot*. In the Hebrew Scriptures, these inhabitants of the underworld are called the *rephaim* 25 times and also the *metim*. Both of these terms for the inhabitants of the underworld also occur in the Ugaritic texts—*rpum* and *mtm*. We also have Ugaritic texts that call these disembodied human dead a cognate for the Hebrew term which we usually translated "god"—*'lim*. Amazingly, when the witch at Endor in 1 Samuel 28 raises Samuel's spirit, she likewise uses a similar noun: "I see an *elohim* coming up out of the earth." See H. Rouillard's entry, "Rephaim" in *DDD*, K. van der Toorn, Bob Becking, and Pieter Willem van der Horst (eds.) (Leiden: Brill, 1999), 692-700.

CHAPTER 8

EDEN: THE COSMIC MOUNTAIN OF GOD

I have a message I will tell you, a word I will recount to you,
a word of tree and whisper of stone,
a word men know not and the earth's masses do not understand,
the converse of heaven with underworld, of watery depths with stars.
I understand the lightning which the heavens do not know.
Come, and I will reveal it in the midst of my divine mountain Zaphan,
on the holy mount of my inheritance.[1]

–The Ba'al Cycle, KTU 1.3:IV:13-20

WHAT exactly was Eden? That archetypal realm calls forth so many dreamlike oddities and questions that scholars of religion have long sought out any cipher which Near Eastern archaeology might unearth. Especially in the past century, much has been accomplished that has allowed us to push back some of the shadows cast by the millennia between us and the biblical authors, but this information rarely filters down to the pew. Perhaps part of the reason why this is the case is that the religious generally shy away from the idea that the *theology* of Israel might be illuminated with the texts of Israel's neighbors.

I believe taking a brief break from evaluating the claims of young-earth creationists in order to understand the context of Eden will be useful for establishing the arguments of the following chapters—that

---

[1] Author's paraphrase of Mark S. Smith and Wayne T. Pitard, *The Ugaritic Baal Cycle Volume II: Introduction with Text, Translation and Commentary of KTU/CAT 1.3-1.4.* Supplements to Vetus Tesamentum 114 (Leiden: Brill, 2009), 278.

the Bible's ancient Near Eastern context is our primary key for its accurate interpretation. This context will also prove of great interest to those curious about Genesis' early chapters.

However, before we can make sense of Eden's original function, we must first understand a little about God's divine family that originally convened there.

Israel's Divine Council

In his influential publications on the divine beings in the Bible, the Semitic language expert and former Logos Bible Software Scholar-in-Residence, Michael S. Heiser has specialized in a strange category of heavenly creatures called, "the sons of God." These entities show up frequently in the Psalms and Job: "Where were you when I laid the foundations of the earth…when the mourning stars sang together and all the *sons of God* shouted for joy?" (Job 38:4-7) These creatures were not just run-of-the-mill messengers. In God's divine family, they maintained an occupational tier above the angels.[2] Deut 32:7-9 alludes to their role as it reflects on the aftermath of the Babel event.

Our oldest and best manuscripts read:[3]

---

[2] As Heiser observes: "[I]n the Hebrew Bible, the sons of God are actually never called angels. That is, there are no passages in which *beney elohim* (and similar phrases) occur in parallel with *mal'akim* ("angels"). Later Jewish texts, such as the Septuagint…in some instances rendered *beney elohim* as *angeloi* ("angels"), but such translation decisions are not driven by the distinctive Hebrew vocabulary." Michael S. Heiser, *The Unseen Realm: Recovering the Supernatural Worldview of the Bible* (Bellingham: Lexham Press, 2015), 24. Meier's *DDD* entry agrees that "Where English 'angel' is the undifferentiating term for all of God's supernatural assistants, *mal'ak* originally could be applied only to those assistants whom God dispatched on mission as messengers." S. A. Meier, "Angel I" in *Dictionary of Deities and Demons in the* Bible, K. van der Toorn, Bob Becking, and Pieter Willem van der Horst (eds.) (Leiden: Brill, 1999), 47.

[3] Some manuscripts have "sons of Israel" instead of "sons of God." This reading is incoherent since Israel did not exist yet until long after this period in the story and was not included in the Table of Nations. The additional technical textual-critical reasons why "sons of God" is the superior reading are elaborated by Michael S. Heiser, "Deuteronomy 32:8 and the Sons of God," *Bibliotheca Sacra* 158 (2001), 52-74. Also, Ellen White, *Yahweh's Council: Its Structure and Membership.* Forschungen sum Alten Testament 2 (Tübingen: Mohr Siebeck, 2014), 34-49, 65.

Remember the days of old. Dwell upon the years from generation to generation. Ask your father, and he will show you, your elders, and they will tell you: When the Most High divided up the nations, when he separated the sons of Adam, he set the borders of the people according to the number of the *sons of God*. *But* Yhwh's portion is *his people*, Jacob *his* allotted inheritance.

You will notice the odd line, "when the Most High divided up the nations…he set the borders *according to the number of the sons of God*." What is interesting about this statement is that Genesis 10 gives us the list of this "Table of Nations" after the Babel event. If you tally up the nations in that list, you will see that there are seventy—implying that biblical religion must have had seventy corresponding sons of God.[4] The sons of God show up in religious texts outside of the Bible. At Ugarit, they were called by the same cognate phrase as in Hebrew, and we are told there were *seventy* of them in those texts.[5] So, Israel, like Ugarit, had seventy divine "sons of God."

Deuteronomy tells us that after Babel, God handed over the nations to be administrated by these seventy divine beings and kept Jacob (who would become Israel) for himself. The fact that these entities held geographically allotted governing jobs is reiterated in Psalm 82, which faults them for corruption in this office:

God stands in the divine council. In the midst
    of the gods [*elohim*], he issues [this] judgment:

"How long will you [addressing the plural gods]
    judge unjustly and favor the wicked?"…

"Defend the poor and orphan.
    Grant justice to the afflicted and needy.
    Deliver the poor and needy.
    Remove them from the hand of the wicked

---

[4] Heiser, "Deuteronomy 32:8," 2, 23-4.

[5] KTU 1.4:VI:46 speaks of the "seventy sons of Asthirat." N. Waytt, "The Seventy Sons of Athirat, the Nations of the World, Deuteronomy 32.6b, 8–9, and the myth of divine election" in N. Waytt (ed.), *The Archaeology of Myth: Papers on Old Testament Tradition* (New York: Routledge, 2010) 69-77.

They are confused, and they do not understand.
In darkness they walk. All the foundations of the
earth shake.

I have said you are gods [*elohim*],
and sons of the Most High, all of you.

But you shall die like men
and as one of the princes, you will fall."

Arise O God! Judge the earth.
For you shall inherit all nations.

Many theologians try to argue that these "sons of the Most High" here
are just the human elders of Israel and not a category of divine beings.
Their motivation for this interpretation is that God plainly calls these
creatures "gods" ("I have said you are *elohim*"), and they are afraid that
affirming the existence of literal other gods, who rule over territories,
would imply that this passage is teaching polytheism. I sympathize with
this concern, but Heiser's work has demonstrated that such fears are
misguided. Not only were these creatures made by God and granted
their office by him, but God is announcing his decree to kill them, "like
men." They are clearly inferior to "the Most High."

The term *monotheism* has been excellent historically for expressing the
absoluteness, uniqueness and unchallengeable authority of Israel's God,
but as the Princeton expert in ancient Israelite religion Mark S. Smith
has frequently warned, it's also a surprisingly modern word coined by
philosophers in the seventeenth century.[6] In his doctoral thesis on
monotheism and Israelite religion, Nathan McDonald also cautions,
therefore, that we should be careful not to use the term in a manner that
oversimplifies the complexity of ancient Israelite religion.[7]

---

[6] Mark S. Smith, "Mark S. Smith – The Birth of Monotheism," YouTube video,
1:59:52, lecture presented to the Tangier Global Forum, Feb 20, 2018. Posted
by "Tangier Global Forum," Jan 27, 2017.
https://www.youtube.com/watch?v=PvOT6Kj8Yxk
[7] See Nathan McDonald, *Deuteronomy and the Meaning of 'Monotheism'* (Tübingen:
Mohr Siebeck, 2003), 1-21.
The average reader may be wondering how Israel could believe in the existence
of other *elohim* since there are places in Deuteronomy and Isaiah which have
Israel's God declaring, "there is no god beside me" (ex. Deut 32:39). Both

There are numerous reasons why Psalm 82 cannot be talking about human judges. For one, contrary to what is often claimed, there is no other place in the Bible that calls living human beings *elohim*.[8] However, Heiser has shown that the biggest reason we know these must be heavenly beings is that Psalm 82 alludes to the same event we saw described in Deut 32:8. Notice the following three parallels:

DEUTERONOMY 32:8	PSALM 82
Called, "sons of God"	Called, "gods" and "sons of the Most High."
God, "divided up the nations according to their number."	"All the nations of the earth shake" These sons of the Most High judged unjustly, and in the final line, the psalmist asks God to take back "all nations" from them.
God, handed the nations over to the "sons of God," but Yhwh's portion is his people, "Jacob His allotted *inheritance*."	Ends: "Arise O God! Judge the earth. For you shall *inherit* all nations."

Deut 32:8 describes how God divided the nations among the sons of God, taking the nation of Israel for his own people. Later, in Psalm 82, God is seen judging these same beings for conducting this administration unjustly. The seventy sons of God can't be the ancient

McDonald's above cited study and Heiser's dissertation have demonstrated that these phrases are Hebraic statements of incomparability. Such statements are not literal denials of the existence of other *elohim*, especially considering the Old Testament frequently affirms the existence of *elohim* in regards to four other categories of entities. See Heiser, "What is / are (an) Elohim?" Presented at the Evangelical Theological Society (2010), www.thedivinecouncil.com/WhatisareanelohimETS2010.pdf.

[8] Heiser outlines the reasons why this is the case in Michael S. Heiser, "Should the Plural אלהים of Psalm 82 Be Understood as Men or Divine Beings?" Presented to the Annual Meeting of the Evangelical Theological Society (2010), 1-14, www.thedivinecouncil.com/ETS2010Psalm82.pdf.

seventy human elders of Israel in the Deuteronomy passage because Israel was never given authority over the nations and didn't even yet exist after the fall of Babel.

A third parallel passage Heiser points us to in Deut 4:19 demonstrates this point beyond doubt. There, Moses says the law was given lest you, "lift your eyes to heaven when you see the sun, and the moon and the stars, all the host of heaven and are driven to worship them and serve those that Yhwh your God *has allotted for all nations under all heaven.*" This same inheritance language of "allotment" among "all nations" implies that the same language in Deut 32:8 must be referring to heavenly beings as well. Because Psalm 82 recalls the same event as Deut 32:8, Psalm 82 must likewise, therefore, be referring to heavenly beings.[9]

This is why the "sons of the Most High" of Psalm 82 are clearly said to reside "in the heavens" in Psalm 89:

PSALM 82	PSALM 89
v.1 "God stands in the *congregation of El.*"	v.6 "The heavens praise your doings, Yhwh...*in the assembly of the holy ones.*"
v. 1 "In the *midst of the gods* he judges"	v.8 "...God [is] dreaded in *the great holy council*, and feared by *all that surround* him.
v.6 "I said, 'You are *gods.*'" "*sons of the Most High.*"	v.7 "For who *in the clouds* can be compared to Yhwh, who among the *sons of God/gods.*"[10]

---

[9] I am aware of Jesus' use of Psalm 82 in John 10. Understanding that Jesus is referring to divine beings in John 10:34 actually solves the incoherencies created by the view that he is merely alluding to human judges. See, Michael S. Heiser, "Jesus' Quotation of Psalm 82:6 in John 10:34: A Different View of John's Theological Strategy," Paper presented to the Society of Biblical Literature (2012).
[10] The term here, *beny elim*, occurs at least once in an Ugaritic text and once in Phoenician in similar divine council contexts.

The simplest solution is to assume that *bn 'ilm* was understood as an idiomatic periphrasis for 'the gods', i.e. 'the divine beings'. The one occurrence of *bn 'lm* in a Phoenician text...(*KAI* 26 A III 19) is probably to be understood similarly: 'the whole circle of the divine beings'.... That upon reflection ancient Israelites might specify either a singular or a plural referent is suggested by the

The biblical authors believed in a category of created, heavenly *elohim*. These were higher than angel messengers and held geographic governance over the people of foreign nations. However, they are presented as God's inferiors.

EDEN: THE MEETING PLACE OF THE SONS OF GOD

As I have argued in the previous cosmological survey and the appendix of this book, ancient people tended to assume that heaven was a physical geography over the sky and that some mountains possibly connected with it. Mountains were frequently viewed as cosmic gates. Upon them the divine beings dwelt and descended and ascended between heaven and earth.[11] For this reason, Babylonian ziggurats and Egyptian pyramids were built as artificial mountains, and temples were often constructed on mountain summits as places for the gods to rest on earth, especially in the Near East.[12]

The very shape of a mountain is a natural symbol of hierarchy and exultation, and their lofty association with heaven made them ideal places for the gods. Babylonian sanctuaries are called names like "Mountain of the House," "House of the Mountain of all Lands," and

---

occasional substitution of *'elim* (plural) or *'Elyon* (singular) for the ambiguous *(ha)elohim*.

S. B. Parker, "Sons of (the) God(s)" in *DDD*, 794.

[11] Several examples: Niehr mentions that in Hurrian and Hittite tradition the mountain Namni and Hazzi were "already venerated as a divine abode." At Ugarit, the divine abode was identified with Jebel al-Aqra. H. Niehr, "Zaphon," in *DDD*, 927. We've also excavated about thirty shrines and temples on Mount Hermon in Lebanon. In Jewish literature like Enoch, this mountain was where the Watchers descended to earth in order to have relations with human women.

[12] There is a fascinating book on this subject produced by a seminar held by the Oriental Institute. In it, 18 scholars examining global civilizations as widespread as Asia, the Near East, and Mesoamerica explore the functions of their temples. At the risk of being simplistic, it is remarkable that certain themes, such as cosmic mountains, temples serving as resting places for the gods, and temples being constructed as microcosms, are globally present in cultures as alien from the Near East as India and Mayapan. Deena Ragavan (ed.), *Heaven on Earth: Temples, Ritual, and Cosmic Symbolism in the Ancient World*. Oriental Institute Seminars 9 (Illinois: Oriental Institute, 2013). In regards to the Ancient Near East, see the erudite study by L Michael Morales, *The Tabernacle Pre-Figured: Cosmic Mountain Ideology in Genesis and Exodus* (Leuven: Peeters, 2012), 3-14.

"Link between Heaven and Earth."[13] The great British Museum Assyriologist, Irving Finkel, states that the ziggurat mountain temple, "was a ladder to heaven to allow the king's voice…the best chance of being heard…. [I]ts function as a royal 'hot line' to heaven is beyond dispute."[14]

Figure 15. Ziggurat of Ur at Imam Ali Air Base, Iraq.

Why do I point all this out? Because the Bible itself shares this association of mountains with the divine realm. Isa 2:2 and Mic 4:1 speak of "the mountain of the house of Yhwh." We read that Yhwh's holy abode and temple rests on Mount Zion. The Ten Commandments were delivered to Moses upon Mount Sinai, and in Exodus 24, the elders of Israel encountered a vision of God and shared a meal upon this peak. Passages like Psalm 48 say that God dwells on, "the heights of the North."

Many might be surprised to learn that Eden was also located on top of a mountain. We know this because Ezek 28:13-16 plainly says, "You were in Eden, the garden of God…the holy mountain of God." Why

---

[13] Morales, *The Tabernacle Prefigured*, 1-11.
[14] Irving Finkel, *The Ark Before Noah: Decoding the Story of the Flood* (New York: Double Day, 2014), 236.

was Eden additionally a lush, well-watered garden? The reason again is surely that garden imagery was extremely common in ancient Near Eastern temples where the gods dwell on earth. For ancient desert people, water and its produce were go-to symbols of abundance. *Of course*, VIPs like the gods *must* live in a well-watered garden paradise devoid of the daily lack faced by mortals.

Scholars therefore agree that Eden, like the other mountain abodes, was a Near Eastern "cosmic mountain"—a functional equivalent to the inner sanctum of a temple where God and his divine sons congregated to administrate the affairs of the cosmos. This conclusion is clear in the Bible itself, but it is especially obvious once you observe that the biblical language that describes Eden is in many ways indisputably similar to how surrounding nations described the meeting place of their gods.

Ugarit's highest creator deity went by the same simple name as the biblical God—El (the word *el* being a generic Semitic term simply meaning "god"). The similarities detailed below may seem to imply that the Semitic El and Israel's God were originally the same. Indeed, the two were often worshiped with the same cultural forms and titles. However, experts like John Day from Oxford University and the famous scholar T.N.D. Mettinger have forcefully argued from the earliest evidence that the God of Israel must have emerged independently from El given essential differences in the nature of both gods.[15] Here, however, the similarities are our chief concern.

THE SIMILARITIES BETWEEN EDEN AND THE UGARITIC COSMIC MOUNTAIN

In the Ugaritic texts, we read that the god El and his own "sons of god" (the spelling is cognate) met to govern the cosmos at the "source of the two rivers" (*mbk nhrm*), in the "midst of the fountains double-deep" (*qrb*

---

[15] See John Day, *Yahweh and the Gods and Goddesses of Canaan*. Journal for the SOTSup 265 (New York: Sheffield Academic Press, 2000), 14; T.N.D Mettinger, "The Elusive Essence: YHWH, El and Baal and the Distinctiveness of Israelite Faith," in E. Blum, C. Macholz and E.W. Stegemann (eds.), *Die Hebräische Bibel und ihre zweifache Nachgeschichte: Festschrift für Rolf Rendtorff zum 65* (Neukirchen-Vluyn: Neukirchener Verlag, 1990), 393-417.

'apq thmtm) on the peak of a northern mountain of assembly.[16] The second highest god of this pantheon, Baal, likewise dwelt on a mountain in the North called *Zaphanu*.[17]

There are direct biblical parallels to these ideas in Eden.

Genesis 2:10 tells us that, "a river flows from Eden to water the garden, and from there it divides to become four branches." In parallel to the Ugaritic "midst of the double-deep," Ezek 28:2 refers to Eden as the "throne of God," "in the heart of the seas."[18] And Gen 2:6-15 tells us that a ground flow (like the Ugaritic "fountains") welled up "from the land and watered all the face of the earth." Both of these were beautiful, well-watered places.

In parallel to mount *Zaphanu* in the Ugaritic texts, we are told in Psa 48:1-2 that Yhwh dwells in the "heights of *Zaphon*." Isa 14:13 calls Yhwh's abode, the "mount of assembly," which is in the "heights of *Zaphon*." *Zaphon* and *Zaphanu* are, in fact, cognates. In both the Bible and Ugaritic texts, these are spoken of as the dwelling place of the divine,[19] a sort of Semitic version of mount Olympus.

There is also a great deal of language in the Ugaritic texts mentioning El and his council members issuing decrees from their dwelling tents[20]—an idea paralleled in biblical texts like Exodus 33, where Yhwh was said to dwell in a tent from which his decrees were mediated through Moses. We likewise read in the Ugaritic texts of the "tents of El" and the "domed tent" of El. The same cognate biblical word

---

[16] See Michael S. Heiser, "Divine Council" in John D. Barry and Lazarus Wentz (ed.), *The Lexham Bible Dictionary* (Bellingham, WA: Lexham Press, 2012), 2.

[17] See KTU 1.3:V:5-7; 1.6:I:32-34.

[18] According to Mullen, "it is impossible to divorce the reference [in Ezk 28:2] from the picture of 'El's dwelling." E. Theodore Mullen Jr., *The Divine Council in Canaanite and Early Hebrew Literature*. Harvard Semitic Monographs 24 (Chico, CA: Scholars Press, 1980), 150.

[19] See Morales, *The Tabernacle Prefigured*, 9.

[20] One Ugaritic text reads: "Then they set face / Toward El at the sources of the Two Rivers, / In the midst of the pools of the Double-Deep. / They entered (= rolled back the tent flap) the tent(s) of El and went into / The tent-shrine of the King, the Father of Years." Quoted in Richard J. Clifford, "The Tent of El and the Israelite Tent of Meeting," *The Catholic Biblical Quarterly* 33.2 (1971), 222-3. Comparisons of Yhwh and the Ugaritic El issuing tent decrees are produced by Mullen, *The Divine Council*, 132-8.

"tabernacle" is applied to the Ugaritic gods in their texts.[21] In one passage, the Ugaritic "tent of El" is connected to the cosmic mountain.[22] This is significant because Zion, conceptually paralleled with the cosmic mountain *Zaphon, is also called Yhwh's tent* in Isa 33:20, and Moses was shown Yhwh's tent upon the mountain Sinai. Moses was then commanded by God to, "set up the Tabernacle in accordance with the fashion in which you were shown on the mountain" (Exod 26:30).

This idea that an earthly temple is supposed to mimic the divine mountain dwelling of the gods was common among the Canaanites and their temple architecture, and we have also found it among the Sumerians, Egyptians, and Babylonians.[23] In his leading treatment on the cosmic mountain motif, Morales agrees that this "idea that temples on earth had their counterparts in heaven, thus corresponding to heavenly archetypes, was common in the ancient Near East."[24]

I have emphasized how, in the Ugaritic texts and the Bible, the divine beings who met on the cosmic mountain are called by the same cognate title, "sons of God." Heiser also provides us with some of the titles that the divine seventy are called in the Ugaritic texts, several of which I reproduce from his dissertation here.[25]

'dt 'ilm – "assembly of El / the gods"[26]
dr 'il – "assembly (circle) of El"[27]

---

[21] For example, KTU 15.3:XVIII-XIX: "The circle of El (go) to their tabernacles [*miskanatihumu*]."

[22] "Then he set face / Toward the Benign One, El the Compassionate, / In the midst of the Mount... / He entered the tent(s) of El and went into the tent-shrine of the King, the Father of Years. Quoted in Clifford, "The Tent of El," 223.

[23] J.A. Davies, *A Royal Priesthood: Literary and Intertextual Perspectives on an Image of Israel in Exodus 19:6*, JSOTSup 395 (London: T&T Clark, 2004), 142. Weinfeld also produces three quotations from Babylonian material conveying this idea. Moshe Weinfeld, "Sabbath, Temple and the Enthronement of the Lord - The Problem of the *Sitz im Leben* of Genesis 1:1-2:3," in André Caquot and Mathias Declor (eds.), *Mélanges bibliques et orientaux en l'honneur de M. Henri Cazelles* (Kevelaer: Butzon & Bercker, 1981), 505.

[24] Morales, *The Tabernacle Prefigured*, 12.

[25] The first three of this list with its assembled citations are from Michael Heiser, "The Divine Council in Late Canonical and Non-Canonical Second Temple Jewish Literature" (PhD diss., University of Wisconsin-Madison, 2004), 2.1.

[26] G. del Olmo Lete and Joaquín Sanmartín. *A Dictionary of the Ugaritic Language in the Alphabetic Tradition (DULAT)*. Trans. Wilfred G. E. Watson. Handbuch der Orientalistik 67 (Leiden: Brill, 2003). *DULAT* 1:152. See KTU 1.15:II:7, 11.

dr bn 'il – "assembly (circle) of the sons of El"[28]
phr kbkbm – "the assembly of the stars"[29]

Phrases similar to these also occur in biblical texts in the same conceptual environments. Psalm 82:1 uses the cognate phrase "assembly of El," Jer 23:18 speaks of standing "in the council of Yhwh," Job 15:8 refers to the "council of God." Psa 89:8 calls the sons of God the "council" and "assembly of the holy ones." The biblical sons of God too even possessed astral associations. Job 38:7 speaks of the sons of God as the "morning stars."

Why belabor all this parallel data between the Bible and ancient Baal literature? There are several reasons. First, many seminary-trained pastors, apologists, and creationists believe and teach that ancient Israel's theology was so utterly alien and descended culturally pristine and foreign from heaven that it is illegitimate to use the theology of Israel's neighbors to illuminate the religion of the Bible. Though this view is true in major and important respects, in many others it is demonstrably wrong: Both Israel and Ugarit had a highest god called El. They shared seventy "sons of El," called by similar divine titles. Both religions talk about the multi-headed chaos dragon and use the same cognate titles for him. In both religions, their divine beings met on a mountain called by the same name, in tents called by the same name, in a well-watered mountain at the source of several rivers watering the earth—upon which the temples of both religions were connected to mimic a heavenly archetype.

In recent years, Old Testament Scholars like John Walton, Michael Heiser, and Tremper Longman have been gaining influence in encouraging the church to take the Bible's ancient cultural context seriously because we can use the parallel concepts in these texts to see if their interface sheds light on scripture.

In retaliation, I have heard many podcasts and seen endless popular books and articles by evangelicals that caution us against the perceived abominations of evangelical Old Testament scholars. Some of these

---

[27] *DULAT* 1:279-280. See KTU 1.15:III:19; 1.39:VII; 1.162:XVI; 1.87:XVIII.

[28] *DULAT* 1:279-280. See KTU 1.40:XXV, XXXIII-XXXIV.

[29] KTU 1.43:II-III. See the section: "The Astral Background of El's Family in Ugaritic and Israelite Literature and Baal's Outsider Status" in Mark S. Smith, *The Origins of Biblical Monotheism: Israel's Polytheistic Background and the Ugaritic Texts* (Oxford: Oxford University Press, 2001), 61ff.

critics freely, perhaps proudly, admit to being illiterate in the Ugaritic, Babylonian, and Egyptian comparative literature, but they feel qualified to speak confidently because they are convinced they have theologically worked out what God would and would not do when revealing himself to ancient Israel.

They are wrong.

As unique as Israel's theology was, with its unchallengeable God, its religion still shares many of the categories, symbols, and much of the language and conceptual framing of its surrounding context. However, we are making here only a passing glance at a theme that we will take up again in the next chapter. To return to our original intention, we may briefly use this data to piece together a coherent picture of what Eden was.

RECONSTRUCTING EDEN

People often wrongly assume that Eden covered the entire globe at creation. The truth is Genesis says Eden was a limited place and the garden was an even smaller geography within it. Genesis 2:8-10 tells us, "God planted a garden *in* Eden." "A river issues from Eden to water the garden," and this river divided into four heads that intersected with other named geographies. So Eden was a particular, well-watered mountain, where gleaming precious "stones of fire" and others like jasper, sapphire, emerald, and amethyst probably adorned the summit according to a tradition in Ezekiel.[30] There, among euphonious rivulets

---

[30] Ezek 28:14 says that on the garden mountain God's fallen cherub once, "walked among stones of fire." In verse 16, again: "I have destroyed you, O guardian cherub, from among the stone of fire." 1 Enoch 18:7 describes a mountain of flame colored stone. In the next verse, he then refers to a mountain reaching heaven, over which is the throne of God made of precious stones. Its summit is described as burning with fire. H. J. van Dijk looks at the listing of precious stones given in Ezek 28:13 that is usually preceded with the translation, "every precious stone was your covering." He rejects this translation, "covering," due to the absence of the *dagesh forte* and proposes the root actually refers to a "hedge" or "fence." On this reading, the passage would refer to the walls of the garden being made of precious stone. H. J. van Dijk, *Ezekiel's Prophecy on Tyre (Ez. 26,1-28,19) A New Approach*. Biblica et orientalia 20 (Rome: Pontifical Biblical Institute, 1968),

and the filtered light of lush copses, in the glow of the deep morning mist, the sons of God gathered to administrate the affairs of the cosmos, terrestrial and empyrean. To use the wording of Job 1:6, here "the sons of God came to present themselves before Yhwh." We have a couple of illustrations in the Bible of how this was likely conceived to play out in the heavenly realm.[31] The biblical God doesn't need help in his administration, but he apparently enjoys including others in it anyway. Even humanity was created to carry out a divine job description on the Creator's behalf.

As will be discussed in a later chapter, the man and woman were not created inherently immortal originally, but they had access to the Tree of Life that would prevent them from dying as long as they ate from it.[32]

Although I must restrain myself from unpacking his full argument since it would take us too far afield of our purpose, specialists on ancient Israel's divine beings, especially Heiser, have argued from passages like Genesis 3, Isaiah 14, and Ezekiel 28 that Lucifer should be categorized as a seraph throne guardian.[33] Lucifer's classification as a

---

116-117. Precious stones are frequently correlated with the divine abode in passages like Isa 54 and Rev 4:1-6.

[31] 1 Kgs 22:16-23 is a classic example. In that passage, the divine council comes to an agreement about how to dispose of the king Ahab. Dan 7:9 speaks of God taking his seat among other thrones in a divine council context. Dan 4:7 speaks of the "decree of the Watchers" concerning Nebuchadnezzar's fate. Heiser points out that Dan 2:25-26 parallels the phrase, "the Most High is sovereign" with the phrase, "heaven is sovereign." The Aramaic subject-verb agreement of the second phrase alludes to a plurality within heaven. *The Unseen Realm*, 54.

[32] Van Ee's study concludes: "Genesis 2-3, like Mesopotamian literature, does not contain a description of humans as originally immortal.... In the Hebrew Bible, humans had the possibility of gaining immortality, but it was not reached because of disobedience. Thus, death may have been a possibility for humans in the original state, but it was not necessarily their destiny." Joshua John Van Ee, "Death and the Garden: An Examination of Original Immortality, Vegetarianism, and Animal Peace in the Hebrew Bible and Mesopotamia" (PhD diss., University of California, 2013), 176.

[33] See Heiser's extended discussion in chapter ten of *The Unseen Realm*, which primarily draws on H. J. van Dijk's linguistic commentary. Though none to my knowledge have developed this argument to the extent that Heiser has, a number of scholars have likewise noticed the serpent's connection in Genesis 3 to the taxonomy of the seraphim and the job function of the cherubim. According to Ronning, "In both passages [Gen 3 and Isa 6], the serpents speak, and by their speech show knowledge of both human and divine affairs, as would be expected from those who are privy to the divine council." John L. Ronning, "The Curse of

serpentine seraph would suggests that there are deep and clever literary associations at play with how the Genesis author parallels Eden's villain with a natural snake. Contrary to those who mock the Bible as infantile for containing a "talking snake," linguistic and cultural contextual analysis of the image of the serpent demonstrates the profound literary and cultural sophistication of the biblical author for including it.[34]

Considering the serpent was originally a member of God's divine entourage and was an intelligent being possessing speech like the seraphim in Isaiah 6, there was likely nothing abnormal with Eve conversing with it in the story because she had often presumably seen the serpent immortals coming and going on the mountain regularly. But this traitor concealed in his heart a plan for corrupting God's adored new imagers. At his encouragement, the man and woman broke the divine law, and so, they had to be expelled from the sacred mountain and the loyal members of the assembly. They were cut off from the Tree of Life which was the antidote granting them and their offspring immortality, and they lost the immediate presence of God in the inner sanctum of his temple—Eden.

CONCLUSION

Like the inner sanctum of a temple, Eden was the link between heaven and earth—the place where God and his divine council members dwelt on earth. In the next chapter, we will further expand upon these themes of temple imagery as they relate to the seven days and the creationism debate.

---

the Serpent (Genesis 3:15) in Biblical theology and Hermeneutics," (PhD diss. Westminster Seminary, 1997), 134. Batto likewise comments that the Edenic serpent is, "a semidivine creature with wings and feet like the seraphs of Isa 6:2, whose function was to guard sacred persons and sacred objects...." Bernard F. Batto, *In the Beginning: Essays on creation Motifs in the Ancient Near East and the Bible.* Siphrut 9 (Winona Lake: Eisenbrauns, 2013), 47. Although she doesn't come to Heiser's conclusions, the possible overlap between the cherubim and seraphim has been noted between Ezek 1:11 and Isa 6:2 in Alice Wood, *Of Wings and Wheels: A Synthetic Study of the Biblical Cherubim.* Beihefte zur Zeitschrift für die alttestamentliche Wissenschaft (New York: Walter de Gruyter, 2008), 134.

[34] The examination of these associations is the subject of Heiser, *The Unseen Realm*, 83-91.

CHAPTER 9

THE MEANING OF THE SEVEN DAYS OF CREATION

CREATION AS A TEMPLE

MOST Bible readers are aware that the Old Testament frequently uses the number seven as a symbol for completion and sacred order. However, you may not have noticed before that Genesis 1 has the number seven woven into the structure of creation through literary patterns beyond just its divisions of days. Many important words and phrases in Genesis 1 repetitively turn up in sequences of seven when counted up in the original Hebrew. Jeff Morrow at Seton Hall University summarizes these patterns that have long been marveled at by biblical scholars:[1]

In Hebrew, Gen 1:1 contains seven words; 1:2 has fourteen words (2x7), and "God" occurs thirty-five times (5x7) in the seven-day account. The term "earth" occurs twenty-one times (3x7); "heavens/firmament" twenty-one times (3x7); the phrase "and it was so" appears seven times, as well as the phrase, "God saw it was good." The important words "light" and "day" are found seven times in the first natural paragraph, and there are seven references to light in the fourth paragraph. In the section dealing with the creation of animals, the Hebrew word for "living beings" occurs seven times. In the seventh

---

[1] Jeff Morrow, "Creation as Temple-Building and Work as Liturgy in Genesis 1-3," *Journal of the Orthodox Center for the Advancement of Biblical Studies* 2.1 (2009), 1-13. These structures of sevens are also emphasized by John R. Roberts, "Biblical Cosmology: The Implications for Bible Translation," *Journal of Translation* 9.2 (2013), 3.

paragraph, which deals with the seventh day, there occur three consecutive sentences that each contains seven words and the phrase "seventh day" in the center. Moreover, the Hebrew words in the seventh paragraph total thirty-five (5x7).

This list goes on beyond these examples.[2] In fact, Genesis 1 breaks its literary patterns for the sake of contriving these sets of seven. For example, the phrase "it was good" is missing in verses 6-8. Verse 9 omits the formulaic description of its creative act, and verse 20 doesn't conclude with the phrase, "and it was so" as one would expect.[3]

The author of Genesis 1 was far more artistically cunning than most modern readers, even Christians (perhaps even especially Christians), give him credit on a surface reading. A divine symmetry is woven into the cosmos of the text. It both speaks in unmistakable expression and whispers esoteric. The days are not lone expressions of this but stand in unity and proportion with the deeper meaning formed by the whole.[4]

In this chapter, it will be demonstrated that the creation in seven days was selected to communicate a theological message to the original reader. I will also contend that this information is significant when considering whether they should be taken as a sequentially accurate account of the material formation of the cosmos as scientific concordists like most young-earth creationists assert them to be.

In short, most scholars agree that the primary message behind the days of the creation week is that the world is God's temple. For Genesis' original audience, that would have been something they deeply needed to hear. How so? Although current opinion is not as unified as it used to be, mainstream scholarship generally still holds that Genesis' creation account was edited into its present form after the Babylonians conquered Jerusalem.[5] The sources for Genesis are certainly far more

---

[2] See Gordon J. Wenham, *Genesis 1-15*. Word Biblical Commentary Vol. 1 (Waco, Texas: Word Books, 1987), 7.

[3] Noted by Morrow, "Creation as Temple-Building," 3.

[4] This staggering care and proportion with which the Genesis 1 author writes has been praised by Bill T. Arnold, *Genesis*. New Cambridge Bible Commentary (Cambridge: Cambridge University Press, 2009), 30.

[5] As Brueggemann stated, "The text is likely dated to the sixth century B.C. and *addressed to exiles.*" Walter Brueggemann, *Genesis: Interpretation A Bible Commentary for Teaching and Preaching* (Louisville: Westminster John Knox Press, 1982), 24-5. A sixth century priestly source was also accepted by Westermann, in Claus Westermann, *Genesis: A Practical Commentary*. Text and Interpretation, trans. David

ancient than this, but they were likely assimilated together as a coherent literary whole in this shadow of devastating defeat.

Imagine being in the shoes of the scribe likely behind the Hebrew creation account. The Jews thought their Scriptures had promised their kingdom could never be dethroned, but Yhwh's temple was sacked and came crashing down at the hands of idolaters. His people were now forced to live in a foreign land under the dominion of a foreign god. We moderns usually have a cartoonish comprehension of polytheism. To the ancients, the Babylonian warrior god Marduk was no pushover on the developing world stage. We have tablets that consider that cosmic dragon slayer so mighty that they border on sounding proto-monotheistic.[6] When the Temple fell, it looked like Marduk had eaten Yhwh's lunch. Perhaps Israel's Warrior Savior wasn't the strongest among the gods after all? One doesn't imagine the Judean worldview crises would have been helped as thousands of its highest officials were marched as prisoners into the expansive Babylonian metropolis capital with its 230-foot (70 meters) high temple to Marduk fissuring the sky.

Finkel reflects, "[T]he Judaean deportees must have found themselves with nothing substantive at all to define their culture or hold their identity together."[7] How do a people rapidly losing their traditions in a foreign land, who cannot even look to a carved image of their God to aid their memory, expect to hold together their religious and national identity? It is probably from these hopeless ashes that the ancient creation narrative of Genesis flashed forth in renewal like a phoenix,[8]

E. Green (Grand Rapids: Eerdmans, 1987), 2-3. Smith outlines the state of scholarship on this issue and agrees:

> Many biblical scholars date Genesis 1 to the sixth century BCE. For years, I have questioned whether this is true; indeed, I have been skeptical as to whether we have enough evidence to pin down the time of the writing of Genesis 1. Still, over the course of working on Genesis 1 in this study, I have come to the tentative conclusion that a sixth century date remains the best theory.

Mark S. Smith, *The Priestly Vision of Genesis 1* (Minneapolis: Fortress Press, 2010), 41.

[6] This has been noticed by Finkel in Tablets VI and VII of *Enuma Elish*. Irving Finkel, *The Ark Before Noah: Decoding the Story of the Flood* (New York: Double Day, 2014), 241. See similar comments in Jan Assmann, *Of Gods and Gods: Egypt, Israel, and the Rise of Monotheism* (Madison: University of Wisconsin Press, 2008), 60.

[7] Finkel, *The Ark Before Noah*, 241-242.

[8] "In sum, the author of Genesis 1 wrote as an elite figure in a colonized society dominated by a foreign power." Smith, *The Priestly Vision*, 43.

implying that Genesis 1 is a defiant declaration that Yhwh is still the true Cosmic Architect and that he hasn't been dethroned. All creation is his sanctuary, and he has ultimate right of dominion over it all.

What justification do we have for reading into the seven days the idea that the whole of the world is Yhwh's temple? The first is that the construction of the Israelite Tabernacle and the world both use similar language. Indeed, the parallels between the construction of the world and the Tabernacle are overwhelming:

1) Moses builds the Tabernacle in Exod 40:17-33. *Seven times* in the building process, it is repeated that Moses carried out the construction of a given part, "just as Yhwh had commanded Moses."[9] In other words, the Tabernacle, like the world, was constructed in *seven stages* of divine commands.

2) The Tabernacle priests were ordained in a *seven-day* process (Lev 8:33-35).

3) Gen 2:2 says, "God finished the work...." Exod 40:33 reads, "When Moses had finished the work..."

4) Gen 2:3 says that after the completion of creation, "God blessed the seventh day...." After the completion of the Tabernacle in Exod 39:43 we read that, "Moses blessed them...."

5) After the blessing, Gen 2:3 speaks of God "sanctifying" creation. Exod 40:9 speaks of Moses "sanctifying" the Tabernacle "and all its furnishings."[10]

6) God's presence was in Eden as it was in the Tabernacle. We are told that he would "walk" about in the garden (Gen 3:8). Commentators note that this same Hebrew verb is strangely used of God "walking about" in the Tabernacle in Lev 26:12, and Deut 23:15.

7) We are told that Adam and Eve were to "work and keep" the garden. These same two Hebrew verbs are only used together elsewhere to describe the job obligations of the priests who kept the Tabernacle and later Temple (Num 7–8; 8:25–26; 1 Chron 23:32; Ezek 44:14).

8) The furnishings of the Tabernacle were created to resemble garden imagery. Many scholars believe the seven-branched

---

[9] These seven places are verses 19, 21, 23, 25, 27, 29, and 32.
[10] Points 3-6 are taken from listing in Morrow, "Creation as Temple-Building," 5-6.

lampstand was modeled after the Tree of Life. Later, Solomon's Temple in 1 Kings 6 greatly enhanced the garden imagery with its architectural carvings,[11] and the sanctity of both places was guarded by the cherubim.

Among scholars, the association between these two accounts "is certain."[12] In addition to these, interesting parallels that help us understand the theological meaning of the days of Genesis are also found in the inauguration process for the Temple of Solomon:[13]

1) The construction of Solomon's Temple took *seven years* (1 Kgs 6:38).
2) The Temple was dedicated during a *seven-day festival* that fell on the *seventh month* of the year (1 Kgs 8:2).
3) Solomon's speech during the dedication of the Temple included *seven petitions* (1 Kgs 8:31-53).
4) We are told God rested on the seventh day of creation. It is well documented that after the inauguration of a temple in ancient Near Eastern religion, the deity would come to rest (i.e. cease

---

[11] For more on these points, see Morrow (ibid.) and Gregory K. Beale, "Eden, the Temple, and the Church's Mission in the New Creation," *Journal of the Evangelical Theological Society* 48.1 (2005), 7-10.

[12] L. Michael Morales, *The Tabernacle Pre-Figured: Cosmic Mountain Ideology in Genesis and Exodus* (Leuven: Peeters, 2012), 84. Waltke agrees, "The Garden of Eden is a temple-garden, represented later in the tabernacle." Bruce K. Waltke, *Genesis: A Commentary* (Grand Rapids: Zondervan, 2001), 85. Weinfeld writes, "The fact that with the completion of the instructions for the building of the Tabernacle in P, there appears a commandment on the Sabbath (Ex. 31:12-17), shows also the connection which existed between Creation and the Building of the Temple." Moshe Weinfeld, "Sabbath, Temple and the Enthronement of the Lord - The Problem of the *Sitz im Leben* of Genesis 1:1-2:3" in André Caquot and Mathias Declor (eds.), *Mélanges bibliques et orientaux en l'honneur de M. Henri Cazelles* (Kevelaer: Butzon & Bercker, 1981), 502. Smith likewise affirms this interpretation and refers to seven additional scholars, like Fishbane and Levenson, who have developed upon it. Smith, *The Priestly Vision*, 179. This thesis is also prominently defended in John H. Walton, *The Lost World of Genesis One: Ancient Cosmology and the Origins Debate* (Downers Grove: InterVarsity Press, 2009), 78-85.

[13] The following four examples are derived from Morrow, "Creation as Temple-Building," 6-8.

from work) within it.[14] This association with rest and the Temple can also be seen in passages like Psa 132:13-14, where we are told that God "rests" on Zion.

It is interesting that in addition to the elaborate garden carvings in Solomon's Temple and the menorahs reminiscent of the Edenic trees, a colossal bronze bowl filled with 16,000 gallons of water sat outside called the *yam* (recall, this is the common Hebrew word for "sea"). Considering this abundance of creation imagery, Morales' leading study states, "The Temple of Solomon likely conveyed to its visitors a typological Garden of Eden...."[15] Many passages connect this temple imagery with creation. For example, in Psa 78:69, we read that God, "built his sanctuary like the heavens, like the earth which he has established forever."[16]

THE DAYS ARE LITERAL, BUT THAT'S NOT THE POINT

Creation is the archetype, and the Temple was considered a symbolic incarnation of that cosmic order. The seven days in Genesis were certainly selected primarily for their valuable theological-symbolic content.

Over half a millennium before Moses, the seven-day temple dedication shows up in Sumerian literature. Nineteenth century

---

[14] Batto reviews a number of texts. In the *Theology of Memphis* we read, "And so Ptah *rested* after he had made everything as well as all the divine order." In the Ugaritic myth, after Baal is revivified and order restored, the creator god El announces, "Now I can sit and rest, / Even my inmost being can rest." The theme also figures into the opening plot of *Atrahasis* and in *Enuma Elish*. Bernard F. Batto, "The Sleeping God: An Ancient Near Eastern Motif of Divine Sovereignty," *Biblica* 68.2 (1987), 157-177. This subject has also been treated by John Walton, *The Lost World of Adam and Eve: Genesis 2-3 and the Human Origins Debate* (Downers Grove: IVP Academic, 2015), 48. Weinfeld observes that "the sanctuary of El in Ugarit is conceived, as in Babylonia and as in Israel, as a seat of rest. Thus we read of El who places his feet on his footstool and says:...'Now I will sit and rest' (CTA 6 111:18).... [T]he throne of Baal is also called a throne of rest:... He 'Chased him from his throne of kingship, from the restful seat of his dominion' (CTA 3 D:46-47)." Weinfeld, "Sabbath, Temple and Enthronement," 504.
[15] Morales, *The Tabernacle Pre-Figured*, 19.
[16] For this reference, I am indebted to Smith, *The Priestly Vision*, 70.

archaeologists in Iraq discovered two large cylinders covered in Sumerian texts over 4,000 years old. The second of these, called Gudea Cylinder B, extensively details a dedication festival of seven days for a temple called Eninnu.[17] Like Genesis, that earthly temple is associated with creation itself in the text.[18]

Likewise, nearly a millennium before Genesis 1 was edited, even Baal was said to have completed his house on top of the cosmic mount *Zaphanu* in seven days according to the Ugaritic texts (KTU 1.4:VII:16-40).[19] On one tablet, we read of the busy forge kept burning during the week of its construction: "Behold! a day and a second…. A third, a fourth day the fire consumed in the mansion [and] the flames in the palace. A fifth, a sixth day the fire consumed…." Finally:

> …[O]n the seventh day
>   the fire escaped from the mansion,
>   the flames from the palace.
> The silver had turned into plates,

---

[17] As Frey states, "There seem to exist striking similarities between the Gen 1 creation account and ancient Near Eastern temple building texts such as the Gudea temple building and dedication text." Mathilde Frey, "The Sabbath in the Pentateuch: an Exegetical and Theological Study" (PhD diss. Andrews University, 2011), 64. Hurowitz discusses this at length in Victor Hurowitz, *I have Built You an Exalted House: Temple Building in the Bible in Light of Mesopotamian and North-West Semitic Writings*. JSOT Series 115 (Sheffield: A&C Black, 1992), 32-57. The number seven is also emphasized in lines 562-577, 602-616, and 781-798 in "The Building of Ningirsu's Temple (Gudea, Cylinders A and B)" in the Electronic Text Corpus of Sumerian Literature (ETCSL), etcsl.orinst.ox.ac.uk/cgi-bin/etcsl.cgi?text=t.2.1.7#.

[18] This is drawn to our attention by Walton, *The Lost World*, 80. Lines 820-823 of the ETCSL read: "The house is a great mountain reaching up to the skies. It is Utu [the sun] filling the midst of the heavens; Eninnu [i.e. the temple] is the white Anzud bird spreading its talons upon the mountain land."

[19] Looking at the Ugaritic example and the seven days of Solomon's temple, Fisher observed: "Now it is extremely interesting that it took seven days to build the house of Baal 'in the midst of the heights of Sapan'. Baal's house is also of cosmic proportions, and from it he controls the Heavens. If these temples were constructed in terms of 'seven' it is really no wonder that the creation poem of Genesis 1 is inserted in a seven-day framework." L. R. Fisher, "The Temple Quarter," *Journal of Semitic Studies* 8.1 (1963), 40. Weinfeld agrees: "A relationship between the building of the Temple and the *seventh day* is found in the Ugaritic Baal Epic…which seems to be associated with creation as well…." Moshe Weinfeld, "Sabbath, Temple and the Enthronement," 504.

The gold had been turned into bricks.
Mightiest Baal did rejoice, (saying):
"I have built my mansion of silver,
    my palace of gold.[20]

The point is not that Genesis 1 is directly borrowing from these texts. Historically, that would be implausible. The point is that the Bible *is* Near Eastern culture like them and these motifs were as natural to the Hebrew's own thinking as they were to other Semitic nations and the Mesopotamians.

Therefore, it turns out that the seven days of Genesis, which the church has been in an insecure frenzy over for centuries, were chiefly selected by the biblical authors because they were a common cultural form for the inauguration period of a temple.

Genesis 1's original audience, recently defeated by Babylon, and going through a religious identity crisis wouldn't have been aided by knowledge about velociraptors, geological history, or astrophysics, and it's a bit comical when modern readers want to drag these issues into the text. The Hebrews needed something to preserve their identity, to know that their God was still enthroned over the whole of his cosmic sanctuary (even Babylonia).

To be clear, I am asserting that the author of Genesis 1 had a theological-cultural agenda behind his use of the seven days. This does not mean the author and his ancient audience wouldn't have taken those days to be literal 24-hour periods.

Despite all my criticisms of young-earthers, I am in full agreement with the Creation Museum that old-earth interpretations that try to read millions of years out of the days of Genesis 1 are dismally unimpressive, and rather obvious attempts at contorting the text into conformity with modern science. Genesis 1 is a temple building text. Were the sequences of seven days involved in building the Tabernacle and Solomon's Temple non-literal? When we read that Baal built his dwelling place in seven days, do the Ugaritic texts *really mean* that Baal built his house over periods of millions of years?

If young-earthers engaged with Baal literature more often, I believe they would find a powerful ally to their cause in a religious text called KTU 1.115:XIV. This tablet contains a ritual instruction which speaks

---

[20] Quoted John C. L. Gibson, *Canaanite Myths and Legends*, 2 ed. (London: T & T Clark, 1956), 63.

of, "(an offering of) a turtle dove…(on) day one (*ym 'ahd*)."[21] The phrase "day one" here is an exact linguistic parallel to the way the days in Genesis are worded. It is also probably significant that the literary context of this Ugaritic parallel breathes the same priestly context as Genesis 1. The implication is that the days of the creation account are literal like the cognate use is here in the Ugaritic. Likewise, as young-earth creationists have been reminding us for centuries, the literalness of the creation days is also powerfully implied by how Genesis 1 prefixes each day numeration with the phrase, "evening and morning."

As scientifically untenable as many old-earthers may find young-earth creationism, a wincing interpretation that tries to read the days of the creation account as poetic sequences of millions of years is part of the problem, not the solution. It's a manner of handling the text that is reminiscent of when young-earthers insist that the "waters above" in the Psalms are intergalactic ice particles at the edge of the space-time continuum.

The Creation Museum is certainly correct that the days are not a poetic description of millions of years. It is my task to argue, however, that the real problem with the young-earth view is to be found in how it has largely failed to frame the seven days within the context of two facts: 1) The *primary motive* for the author's use of seven days is to communicate *temple theology* within the symbols of his culture. And, 2) Genesis 1 is *clearly not* a sequentially accurate account of the origins of the material world.

GENESIS 1 AS A POLEMIC AGAINST THE GODS

Concerning the first point above, we have seen why it is nearly universally accepted among Old Testament scholars that the seven days of Genesis were associated with temple theology. The parallels with its account and other temple texts are undeniable. Concerning the second point, there are at least two reasons why it is a bad idea to assume Genesis 1 is a sequentially accurate account of the origins of the material world.

First, I have argued that the author of Genesis 1 conveys roughly the same material cosmology as his neighbors. He recounts the creation of a sky boundary retaining a heavenly sea. Unless the entire modern space

---

[21] Quoted from Smith, *The Priestly Vision*, 81.

program has been an elaborate hoax by NASA to launder money to our Illuminati overlords like the Flat Earth Society claims, this is not scientifically accurate.

Second, I will be outlining a brief handful of examples illustrating how Genesis 1's arrangement intentionally borrows elements from the creation stories of its milieu. Usually, when Genesis 1 does this, it is for polemical purposes.[22] That is, many of the odd features we observe in the creation account exist, not because they were amazing scientific revelations, but because the Genesis author was borrowing and reshaping the themes of other creation stories as a clever strategy of taking jabs at competing religions.

In the first place, is it plausible that the author of Genesis 1 would have been aware of how his neighbors thought about creation as a precondition for even being able to construct such a polemic against those views? The evidence implies a sonorous *yes*. This is because Genesis 1 shows every indication of having passed through the editorial hands of the highly educated priestly elite of Jewish society. (Even if the document is indeed among those sources in the Torah claimed to go back to Moses, there are still clear indications that the book of Genesis later came to be edited into its modern form in Mesopotamia.)

We have already seen a brief glimpse of how Egyptian iconography was showing up in Israel during Isaiah's time before Genesis 1 was edited. Anyone acquainted with Isaiah will immediately recognize that he is highly internationally informed. Following that period, Smith adds that "Scholars have noted that the seventh and sixth centuries BCE witnessed great literary production and crosscultural influence across the eastern Mediterranean and Middle East."[23]

By the time we get to Ezekiel, we can see that prophet is "exceedingly literate"[24]—"keen to absorb the rich Babylonian culture surrounding him while at the same time lending an eager ear to the vibrant cultural amalgam of other exiled communities – Phoenicians,

---

[22] As the evangelical Egyptologist Hoffmeier puts it, "The apologetic or polemical nature of Genesis 1-2 cannot be denied." James K. Hoffmeier "Some Thoughts on Genesis 1 & 2 and Egyptian Cosmology," *Journal of the Ancient Near Eastern Society*, vol. 15 (1983), 39.

[23] Smith, *The Priestly Vision*, 42.

[24] Ibid.

Edomites, Egyptians, Elamites, Aramaeans, and many others…."[25] This point is important because Genesis 1 seems most likely to have been compiled in roughly the period in which Ezekiel was operating. The bottom line is that, like Isaiah, or Ezekiel, the highly educated priestly figure that produced Genesis 1 probably would have also been aware of how his international neighbors thought about the world and its creation.[26]

THE WATERS OF CHAOS

In chapter six, it was detailed how the author of Genesis 1 decided to open his account using an odd style of syntax customary in Mesopotamia. The stage curtains roll back to reveal things originally in a state of watery chaos. In this respect, Genesis 1 sides with the common opinion of the ancient Near East.[27] The first sentence of the Hebrew syntax tells us that the earth was "chaos and void, and darkness was upon the face of the *deep*." That is, "the face of the *waters*." After this, God divides the waters to form the cosmic bubble in which he will establish dry land. This land is formed on the third day by pushing back the waters "to one place" (v.9).

For decades, a handful of Egyptologists have been suggesting interaction with Egyptian ideas may be present within Genesis 1.[28] This initial state of watery chaos out of which the world emerged was a staple in Egyptian art depictions and mythology, and all four major versions of our Egyptian cosmological texts have creation emerging from a primeval watery abyss, usually deified as the god Nun. Reminiscent of Gen 1:10's first emergence of dry land, the Pyramid and Coffin texts

---

[25] Jonathan Ben-Dov, "The Resurrection of the Divine Assembly and the Title El in the Dead Sea Scrolls" in Andrea Ercolani and Manuela Giordano (eds.), *Submerged Literature in Ancient Greek Culture*, (Berlin: De Gruyter, 2016), 10.

[26] Smith agrees, citing the case of Ezekiel, whom he believes, "reflect[s] knowledge of priestly tradition as well as various facets of Phoenician and Egyptian culture." He may have also known "wider currents of thought about the universe…as reflected in works as diverse as the Mesopotamian creation account…, the Egyptian Memphite Creation text, and the Phoenician cosmogony of Philo of Byblos." Smith, *The Priestly Vision*, 42

[27] Richard E. Averbeck, "A Literary Day, Inter-Textual, and Contextual Reading of Genesis 1-2" in J. Daryl Charles (ed.), *Reading Genesis 1-2: An Evangelical Conversation* (Massachusetts: Hendrickson, 2013), 9.

[28] An erudite survey of this is presented by Gordon H. Johnston, "Genesis 1 and Ancient Egyptian Creation Myths," *Bibliotheca Sacra* 165 (2008), 178-94.

speak of the first dry ground surfacing in the form of a sacred hill, "in the midst of Nun."[29]

It is curious that, like the Hebrews, the Egyptians also personified the sea encompassing the earth disk as a great reptile of chaos, attesting to the unspeakable antiquity of the symbol. We have a 3,000-year-old Egyptian papyrus depicting this monster, named Apophis, chasing his own tail in the symbol of the *ouroboros* (which quite possibly contextualizes why the Hebrew Leviathan is given the titles of "wreath" shaped and "fleeing"—i.e. his own mouth).[30] "Every morning the sun-god Re and his helpers had to defeat this marine reptile."[31]

Among the Babylonians, we also see this initial state of watery chaos personified in the reptilian goddess Tiamat, whom Marduk must defeat to create the world. This old motif about a god waging battle with the marine dragon is explicitly attributed to Israel's God in passages like Psalm 74 in the form of the Hebrew version Leviathan.

Likely, Genesis 1 is also interacting with this motif because the Hebrew term for "the deep" (*tehom*) in its opening verses, "occurs in the Ugaritic texts not only in god-lists, but also in mythological contexts."[32] Smith likewise refers to texts from archaeological sites in Mari and Aleppo that use this word *tehom* in the context of the divine battle motif, showing that a combat with *Tehom* was a general "old West Semitic idea and not just a Mesopotamian one."[33] This linguistic parallel and the attested, incredible distribution of the chaos dragon across the Near East is significant in its silence in Genesis 1. There is no hint at all in the Genesis creation account that God participates in any sort of struggle with this watery *tehom*. He simply commands, and it obeys.

By remaining within this ancient Near Eastern motif about an original state of chaotic waters, with all its cultural filigree of symbolic content, the author of Genesis is able to polemically elevate his God above all others: "In this way, God can be viewed as a power beyond

---

[29] Ibid., 182-4.

[30] This is the proposal of Marjo Korpel and Johannes de Moor, "The Leviathan in the Ancient Near East," in Koert van Bekkum, et al. (eds.), *Playing with Leviathan: Interpretation and Reception of Monsters from the Biblical World.* Themes in Biblical Narrative 21 (Netherlands: Brill, 2017), 7.

[31] Ibid., 6-7.

[32] Smith, *The Priestly Vision*, 69.

[33] Ibid.

conflict, indeed the unchallenged and unchallengeable power beyond any powers."[34]

There is a second probable polemic against the sea in Genesis 1. In verse 21, we see God creating the "great sea monsters" in conjunction with the sea's other creatures. The Hebrew term used for these "monsters" is *tannin*. As encountered in our opening study of Leviathan, *tannin* was a generic term for the chaos monsters of Ugaritic literature, used interchangeably with the dragon *Litanu* or *Yam*. In the Bible, this word is used in the same manner, particularly as a synonym for Leviathan (Job 7:17, 41:25). The author of Gen 1:21 is possibly playing off this connotation to polemically imply that the "*tannin*, so greatly feared, is depicted as no more than a sea creature."[35]

A fuller sense of this idea shows up in the parallel creation text, Psalm 104. Verses 24-26 read:

How many are your works Yhwh!... There is the sea, great and vast, wherein are swarming creatures without number, beasts both small and great. There the ships go, and Leviathan, whom you have formed to play in it.

Check the footnotes in your modern translation and you will notice the last sentence of the above can take on a double meaning in Hebrew. The poetry has been written such that the subject of "to play" might also be Yhwh: "Leviathan, whom you have formed to play *with*."[36] It appears that when Gen 1:21 has God creating "the great sea monsters" it may be carrying on in the same polemical tradition as passages like

---

[34] Ibid.

[35] Kenneth A. Mathews, *The New American Commentary*, vol 1A (Nashville: Broadman & Holman Publishers, 1996), 157. This popular polemical interpretation was defended by Gerhard F. Hasel, "The Polemic Nature of the Genesis Cosmology," *Evangelical Quarterly* 46 (1974), 87. It is likewise expressed by scholars like J. Richard Middleton, "Created in the Image of a Violent God? The Ethical Problem of the Conquest of Chaos in Biblical Creation Texts," *Interpretation* 58.4 (2004), 352. Also alluded to by Smith, *The Priestly Vision*, 108.

[36] As Kwakkel notes, this translation gains plausibility by the fact that Job 40:29 uses the same Hebrew term when God asks Job whether he can stand to "play" with Leviathan. Gert Kwakkel, "The Monster as a Toy: Leviathan in Psalm 104:26" in Koert van Bekkum, *Playing with Leviathan*, 84.

Psalm 74 and 104.[37] The terrible sea and its monster are not adversaries to be overcome, but God's mere playthings.

HOW CAN THERE BE DAY AND NIGHT BEFORE THE SUN?

Next in the creation story, we encounter something which Jews and Christians have been scratching their heads over for centuries. According to the grammar of Gen 1:1-3, the first thing God commands into being is light: "And God called the light day and the darkness he called night, and there was evening and there was morning, a first day" (v. 5). Following this, on days two and three, we read about "evening and morning, a second day…evening and morning, a third day." What's strange about all this? It isn't until we get to *day four that God even makes the sun, moon, and stars!* Like the light created on day one, we are informed these luminaries were also made, "to divide between the day and night" (v.18).

Where was the light on the first three days coming from? Were the editors of Genesis so oblivious (as some critics accuse) that they didn't notice the fact that they put the creation of day and night in verse 4 *before* the creation of the sun in verse 14? Were ancient Jews not clued in on the fact that you can't have night and day without the sun?

Some popular old-earth scholars have argued that the fact that day and night exist in Genesis before the creation of the sun must indicate that Genesis 1 is dischronologized—that it is not concerned with relating things as they were conceived to have happened in sequential order. They argue that the sun must have actually existed on days one through three but was not depicted as created until day four for literary reasons. From this basis, they then attempt to weasel their way around the somewhat embarrassing fact that Genesis 1 has trees (day three) created before the sun (day four)! I don't find this argument convincing. Other biblical texts imply that the light summoned forth on the first day proceeded not from the sun, but from God himself.

Returning to the creation hymn Psalm 104, we find that the first five verses contain the following lines:

…With honor and majesty you are clothed.
Garbed in light as with a cloak,

---

37 The mention of ships going about at sea likely emphasizes God's initial act of taming the waters for the sake of creation's habitably (referred to in verses 6-9 and symbolized by the appearance of Leviathan). Ibid., 88.

stretching out the heavens like a curtain.

…

He established the earth upon its foundations,
    that it not be removed forever and ever

Smith likewise points us to another passage from Isaiah.[38] In 60:19, we find God's emanating light replacing the sun:

No longer shall the sun be for your light by day,
    and neither shall the moon give light for brightness to you.
But Yhwh will be for you an everlasting light,
    and your God for your glory.

This notion that Yhwh is emanating in "clothed light" in Psa 104:2 and Gen 1:3 before the creation of the luminaries is interesting because the idea shows up as a motif in a few of the creation stories of Israel's neighbors. In the opening of the Babylonian story, we read of Marduk being conceived from within the primeval waters. The text then begins describing this glorious new son of the gods who would eventually create the heavens and earth:

The son UTU (the Sun), the son UTU (the Sun),
The son, the sun, the sunlight of the gods!
He wore (on his body) the auras of ten gods.
    had (them) around his head too….[39]

Here we see the new god Marduk called the sun. The same mundane Semitic term used of Marduk being "clothed" in luminous auras is used of Yhwh being "clothed" in light in Psalm 104.

A still yet curious example is Egyptian. As I have already alluded, a handful of Egyptologists have been pointing out for years that Genesis 1, at least *structurally*, shares more in common with Egyptian creation myths than any other texts we've been able to recover from the ancient world.[40] Most strikingly, a hieroglyphic text called the *Memphite Theology*

---

[38] Smith, *The Priestly Vision*, 76-7. What follows is the author's translation.

[39] Smith trans. ibid., 78. Tablet I.101-103.

[40] See structural comparison between Genesis 1 with Babylonian and Egyptian cosmogony in James Atwell, "An Egyptian Source for Genesis 1," *Journal of Theological Studies* 51 (2000), 449.

is the only other text that seems to contains the idea that creation occurred by the power of divine speech.[41] Comparing these texts to the structure of the Genesis 1 account, the Egyptologist John Strange believed that, "The similarities in detail and structure are too close to be accidental."[42] The archaeologist J. D. Currid agreed, "There exists such a magnitude of parallels that it could not be by mere chance."[43] I remain skeptical as to whether the relevant Egyptian material would have served as a *direct* influence, but it is undeniable when reading the parallel literature that Genesis 1 indeed accords with many of the general currents of thought which the Egyptian texts participate in. It is also significant that the period leading up to the editorial finalization of Genesis 1 saw a peak of Egyptian activity and trade in Judah's archaeological record,[44] and my research has supported Judean knowledge of Egyptian creation symbolism on seal art before this period (recall from chapter 4 that the royal seal of King Hezekiah's administration represents Yahweh in the form of the Egyptian sun disk).

The Old Testament scholar Gordon H. Johnson emphasizes that Egyptian myth circulated during this period has the god Atum emerging into existence from the primordial waters. As a manifestation of his self-creation, he declares, "I lighten darkness!" Fascinatingly, as in Genesis, it is not until later at the apex of the Egyptian story that the actual sun is formally created (capping off its account with the first sunrise).[45]

---

[41] See Johnston, "Genesis 1 and Ancient Egyptian," 187-9.

[42] John Strange, "Some Notes on Biblical and Egyptian Theology," in *Egypt, Israel, and the Ancient Mediterranean World* (Leiden: Brill, 2004), 345. I owe this reference to Johnston, "Genesis 1 and Ancient Egyptian," 185.

[43] J. D. Currid, "An Examination of the Egyptian Background of the Genesis Cosmology," *Biblische Zeitschrift* 35 (1991), 39. I likewise owe this reference to Johnston, "Genesis 1 and Ancient Egyptian," 191.

[44] "The archaeological record is full of evidence supporting connections between Egypt and the southern Levant. Imported Egyptian pottery and artifacts are commonly found at many sites in the southern Levant, including all the major Philistine cities, Jerusalem, and throughout the Negev.... [T]he late Iron II (750-600 BCE...) shows a clear peak in Egyptian activity and relations." Joshua Theodore Walton, "The Regional Economy of the Southern Levant in the 8th-7th Centuries BCE" (PhD diss., Harvard University, 2015), 93.

[45] See Johnson, "Genesis 1 and Ancient Egyptian," 186-7. Atwell specifies the same parallel, stating that, "just as there is a certain tension in the Genesis 1 narrative between the creation of light initially and the heavenly bodies only subsequently, so in ancient Egypt there is a tension between Re identified with

In reflection, as the first lines of Genesis 1 open, the shadows of the primeval state successively dispel to reveal dim forms. The Hebrew words describing the chaos have been selected for their long-o sounds that fill the back of the throat—words full, deep, and ancient like the darkness. Our anticipation builds as we await the main clause, which comes in brief utterance piercing through chaos: "And God said, *'yehi or'*"—"Be light!" The emergence of light, shining forth from God himself, as the first creative act in the Hebrew account, is surely an idea pregnant with inexhaustible theological, even artistic, content. Wisdom, the priesthood, the logos, truth, order, the good—all of these are legitimate ideas we could trace within its iridescence. But unlike the Egyptian myth where the breaking forth of light was taken as a symbol of the god's self-generation, it may be significant that reading Gen 1:3 in the context of other Israelite priestly texts plausibly implies that this light summoned forth was conceived to have existed with God from all eternity.[46] Therefore, this feature of the account, which elevates Yhwh as the true origin of all light, likely served a polemical function in its original context.

CREATION OF THE SKY

Next in line in the Genesis account, we see God separating the heavens from the earth in quite a literal sense. Brief summation will suffice: For the Sumerians, "earth had been separated from heaven" when the god Enlil pulled the earth downwards and his father An, "carried off the heaven."[47] In Babylonia, Marduk raises the firmament like the roof of a tent. In Hittite myth, we read of it being fashioned by the god: "When heaven and earth were built upon me [Upelluri, an Atlas figure] I knew nothing of it, and when they came and cut heaven and earth asunder with a copper tool, that also I knew not."[48] The Egyptian texts praise the god Shu who "raised Nut [the sky-goddess]."[49] Hasel likewise noted

---

Atum, the origin of all order, and Re born daily of Nut, the sky goddess, as a subsequent if principal part of that order." Atwell, "An Egyptian Source," 457.

[46] This is hypothesized by Johnson, "Genesis 1 and Ancient Egyptian," 186-7.

[47] Translation quoted in Gerhard F. Hasel, "The Significance of the Cosmology in Genesis I in Relation to Ancient Near Eastern Parallels," *Andrews University Seminary Studies*, X:1 (1972), 8.

[48] Ibid.

[49] Ibid.

how Phoenician mythology describes this event in terms of the splitting of the world egg.[50]

The firmament was unspeakably immense and played an indispensable function in ancient cosmology. Without it, there could be no created world. Its separation from earth was such a ubiquitous theme in creation stories that the author of Genesis would have worked counterintuitive to his purpose by failing to address it. Namely, God's establishment of heaven created the necessary preconditions for creation to occur and demonstrated authority over the constant ravishes of cosmic chaos. God's establishment of the firmament is superior here to most other religious texts in how he accomplishes it by mere command.

CREATION OF MAN

A final major theme is worthy of attention for getting a feel of the creation account's literary goals. Moving forward to the creation of man, we again see the Bible intentionally interacting with its milieu. According to Gen 1:26: "God said, '*Let us* make man in our image as our likeness, and let them have dominion....'" For centuries, Christians have been quoting the cryptic plural language in this passage as a reference to the Trinity speaking amongst itself. In reality, God is not addressing the other persons of the Trinity in this particular text, but is speaking to his divine council "sons of God." We can be fairly confident of this because this same plural language parallels how an Assyrian tablet from c. 800 B.C. has humanity formed:

> Let us slay (two) Lamga [craftsmen] gods. With their blood let us create mankind.[51]

Both this text and Gen 1:26 are grammatically analogous. In the Assyrian text, a class of gods called the Anunnaki are announcing their plan to the other members of a divine council. The Genesis author likewise adopts this same form of address (what grammar geeks call the cohortative) to depict Israel's God expressing his intentions to his own heavenly entourage. This style of divine council "let us..." language is

---

[50] Ibid.

[51] Alexander Heidel, *The Babylonian Genesis: The Story of Creation*, 2 ed. (Chicago: University of Chicago Press, 1951), 69.

very common in Mesopotamian literature.[52] However, it is significant that in Genesis, when God actually creates humanity, the act is accomplished with singular verbs. Unlike what we see in other creation stories, this indicates that Israel's God solicited no help in carrying out the creation of human beings.

The vast majority of modern biologists and geneticists believe humanity physically came about through millions of years of evolution. Genesis 1 contradicts this by siding with virtually every other creation account in the Near East. These claimed that humanity was created by the God/gods, fully formed, *de novo* from the ground.

The Hebrew name Adam is an etymological pun with the soil (*adamah*) from which the man was "shaped" by God in Genesis 2. Thus, Adam literally means "earthling." Likewise, the Sumerians believed that humanity was created from shaped clay at the instruction of the god Enki.[53] The old Epic of Gilgamesh legend has the goddess Aruru fashioning the hero Enkidu by pinching off and shaping a piece of clay.[54] Among the Egyptians, humanity is sometimes shown in art and texts to have been shaped on the potter's wheel by a ram-headed deity named Khnum.[55] Drawing on older motifs, Babylonian sources like *Atrahasis* tell of how the gods killed a rebel among them. Ea then took the blood of this creature and mixed it with a piece of pinched off clay to shape seven pairs of humans.[56] Although the Ugaritic texts don't explicitly divulge how humanity was made, we likely catch a glimpse of what they thought in a passage where El shapes a female healing figure out of clay to save the king Kirta.[57] In Job 33:6, Job's friend Elihu uses language cognate to these texts when he says, "I too was pinched off from clay."

---

[52] E.g. Ibid., pages 19 (line 40, 46), 23 (line 121, 125, 127), 48 (lines 51, 53), 53 (line 164), 69 (line 26).

[53] See Samuel Noah Kramer, *History Begins at Sumer* (New York: Anchor, 1959), 109.

[54] *Gilgamesh* I.2.

[55] See Bernard F. Batto, *In the Beginning: Essays on creation Motifs in the Ancient Near East and the Bible*. Siphrut 9 (Winona Lake: Eisenbrauns, 2013), 21.

[56] Ibid., 28-9.

[57] KTU 1.16:V:28-30. For a linguistic comparison of this text to Akkadian parallels see: Edward L. Greenstein, "God's Golem: The Creation of the Human in Genesis 2" in Henning Graf Reventlow and Yair Hoffman (eds.), *Creation in Jewish and Christian Tradition*. JSOTSup 319 (Sheffield: Sheffield Academic Press, 2002), 223.

Like Genesis, the Mesopotamian stories also have humanity created for the primary purposes of agriculture and religious service. Specifically, in *Atrahasis*, man is created because the gods are sick of the toil of farming and want slaves to take over the job and feed them. As the gods declare in an Assyrian tablet, "They will…take in their hands hoes and baskets, to benefit the House of the great gods."[58] These accounts are all similar insofar as they have humans being shaped *de novo* from the earth and link man's purpose to farming (with the connotation of priestly service in the verbs "guard" and "keep" in Gen 2:15). However, the biblical account features some massive points of dissimilarity and certainly polemicizes against them.

Genesis declares an astonishingly high view of humanity. Whereas in the Mesopotamian myths man is invariably created as a field laborer to feed the gods, Gen 1:29 specifically tells us that God created vegetation to feed man. Instead of declaring humanity a species of slaves, Genesis 1 has the opposite, speaking of humanity with technical royal language—as vice-regents. In other words, humans were created to bear God's authority and image on earth as his representative.[59]

WHY GENESIS 1 SEEMS TO HAVE THINGS CREATED IN A STRANGE ORDER

Before drawing all the data together to derive some conclusions, there is a final and important feature in Genesis 1 that has major implications in the creationism debate. We have already seen that its account was meticulously crafted to convey sacred order. This aesthetic in the text has awed biblical scholars for centuries. According to Gerhard von Rad: "Nothing is here by chance."[60] Brown comments: "No other text is so

---

[58] From KAR 4 in Richard J. Clifford, *Creation Accounts in the Ancient Near East and in the Bible*. The Catholic Bible Quarterly Monograph Series 26 (Washington: Catholic Bible Association, 1994), 50.

[59] Ibid., 143. As is widely known, viewing the Hebrew terms "image" and "likeness" as language of vice-regency is firmly supported by an Aramaic-Akkadian inscription of the statue of an Assyrian emperor. The text uses these cognates to designate the delegated authority of his servant. See Smith, *The Priestly Vision*, 99-100.

[60] Gerhard von Rad, *Genesis: A Commentary (Revised Edition)*. The Old Testament Library (Philadelphia: Westminster Press, 1972), 47. I owe this and the following reference to Smith. *The Priestly Vision*, 128.

densely structured in the Hebrew Bible; every word seems to bear the mark of extensive reflection."[61] Another commentator observes, "The most prominent literary feature in Genesis 1 is its recurring formulaic structure and symmetry."[62]

The days of Genesis 1 were certainly understood as literal, and I have bristled against the common old-earth thesis that different days of the account should be brought together and interpreted as describing the same event in time (an idea commonly associated with what is called the "Framework Hypothesis"). Despite all these words of caution, *there is* strong evidence, widely noticed among academic commentators, that Genesis 1's days are structured according to a symmetrical literary schema corresponding to the author's care for proportion and symmetry that we see elsewhere.[63]

As can be observed in Figure 16, the creation days are treated by the author in a revolving sequence. That is, God orders a domain then returns during the second half of the week to fill it in mirrored sequence. We moderns have huge hang-ups over the fact that Genesis has the earth formed before any star, trees created before the sun, all the stars contemporaneous with the moon, all birds formed before insects, etc. I do not wish to minimize the fact that Genesis 1 contains ideas contradicting accurate material cosmology. It does. At the same time, we should appreciate that the ordering of its account, which the church has been biting its nails over for centuries, is most probably the product of the Genesis author simply wanting to make his literary schema symmetrical.

You read that correctly.

---

[61] William P. Brown, *Structure, Role, and Ideology in the Hebrew and Greek Texts of Genesis 1:1-2:3.* SBL Dissertation Series 132 (Atlanta: Scholars Press, 1993), 249.

[62] Arnold, *Genesis*, 30.

[63] Variations of the following chart can be found advocated among commentators like Bruce Waltke, *Genesis*, 57; Smith, *The Priestly Vision*, 89; Bernard W. Anderson, "A Stylistic Study of the Priestly Creation Story," in George W. Coats and Burke Long (eds), *Canon and Authority: Essays in Old Testament Religion and Theology* (Philadelphia: Fortress, 1977), 157; Clare Amos, *The Book of Genesis*, Epworth Commentaries (Peterborough: Epworth Press, 2004), 9; William P. Brown, *The Seven Pillars of Creation: The Bible, Science, and the Ecology of Wonder* (New York: Oxford University Press, 2010), 38; David Toshio Tsumura, *Creation and Destruction: A Reappraisal of the Chaoskampf Theory in the Old Testament* (Winona Lake: Eisenbrauns, 2005), 34, or Gordon J. Wenham, *Word Biblical Commentary*, 7.

The evidence in favor of Genesis 1 being intentionally constructed according to a symmetrical literary schematic is the fact that there are so many alternate, coherent ways that the author could have ordered things that would have ruined the pattern we can see in the below chart:

GOD ESTABLISHES ORDER	GOD FILLS DOMAIN
Day 1 "Let there be light" (v. 3)	**Day 4** "Let there be lights" (v. 14)
Day 2 Formation of the heavenly *raqia* by separation from "waters below" (v. 6-8)	**Day 5** Creatures that fly "on the face of the heavenly *raqia*" and swim in the waters (v. 20-23)
Day 3 Earth and plants(v. 11-13)	**Day 6** Terrestrial animals and man (given plants of the earth v. 29-30)

Day 7
Sabbath

Figure 16. The mirrored structure of Genesis 1.

Genesis 1 could have logically had the earth created after the sun. There is no obvious reason why the waters couldn't have been divided on day one. Why didn't the author choose to include the birds and fish in the creation of day five with the creation of other animals on day six? Why not have the moon created at the same time as the earth as modern astronomers have suggested? Why not have the stars made before the other luminaries? Why not have sea creatures occupy the totality of day five and reserve the creation of birds with the other land creatures on day six since birds depend on berries and insects that grow on the earth? Logistically, why couldn't the earthly "creeping" animals of day six be interchanged with the birds on day five?

The tremendous number of alternate workable combinations makes it seem remarkably suspicious that the text's creative acts just happen to conform to this mirrored structure.

Second, it is also significant that the arguments that have been brought against the existence of this intentionally mirrored structure are unconvincing.[64]

CONCLUSION

---

[64] I am not advocating the Framework Hypothesis insofar as I take the author to be intending literal and sequential days. In my assessment, the best single objection raised against this proposed literary schema I present here is the fact that there is an apparent discrepancy between the juxtaposition of days two and five. That is, although God separates the lower waters on the second day, he does not name them "sea" until the third day in conjunction with forming the earth. This would imply that the fish made to dwell in the sea ought to have been created on day six, not day five. In response to this objection, I think it's plausible that the author may have tolerated this discrepancy because the second day still has the lower waters acting as a legitimate parallel to the fish of day five, and he wanted to track with the deep theological tradition reflected in the Psalms which have the sea "defeated" through the emergence of land. Psalms 74:13-14, 77:16, 89:9-11 and 104:6-9 speak of the sea "trembling," "fleeing," and being "crushed" by God. Particularly, the allusions in 77:16 and 104:6-9 explicitly associate this defeat of the sea with the emergence of dry earth.

Besides this, McCabe's first monograph raises two other objections against this literary schema (Robert V. McCabe, "A Critique of the Framework Interpretation of the Creation Account (Part 1 of 2)," *Detroit Baptist Theological Seminary Journal* 10 [2005], 49-51). The first is that 1:1 contains a reference to the creation of heaven and earth which has been omitted from charts like the one I have produced here, and second, that man on day six doesn't seem to parallel the vegetation of day three. I have argued his first objection is predicated on a falsified analysis of the syntax of 1:1-3 (see chapter six of this book). His second objection is resolved by taking both man and animals to be paralleled with *both* the earth and vegetation on the obvious grounds they are *both* created from the earth and are both explicitly given vegetation for food.

A 2007 paper by Chaffey (another writer on this subject for Answers in Genesis) contributes the objection that the preexistence of the waters before day two, "by itself…destroys the alleged parallelism of the text." This argument is unimpressive because these waters are in no way said to be formed or parsed into anything until day two (as argued in chapter six of this book, creating is not synonymous with bringing something into being *ex nihilo* for the Genesis author). Likewise, Chaffey's objection that birds spend most of their time on land seems negligible since 1:20 explicitly defines their domain as the *raqia* firmament of day two. Timothy R. Chaffey, "A Critical Evaluation of the Framework Hypothesis," Liberty University student paper (2007), 62-7.

The seven days of creation were literal for the author of Genesis 1 and culturally encoded the theological message that all creation is God's temple. Religious Jews and Christians with a traditionalist view of inspiration like the Creation Museum feel obligated to believe these creation days are scientifically accurate. However, their view of inspiration cannot be reconciled with fundamental aspects of Genesis' cosmology like the heavenly firmament and the celestial ocean. On the other hand, religious Jews and Christians that aren't theologically bothered by Genesis' ancient cosmology, on the grounds that their view of inspiration allows for the Bible to be accommodated to the scientific place of its authors, will likely not have a theological problem with the literalness of the creation days either. They may simply point out that the literalness of the days is only symbolically incidental to the text's main point.

Second, we have seen that Genesis 1 adopts many of the same themes as the creation accounts of its neighbors. In certain cases, there is evidence that it does this in a polemical fashion to elevate its God. Due to their theological commitments, most young-earth creationists will argue that Genesis 1 is scientifically correct when it asserts with all its Near Eastern neighbors that the earth was originally formless water. They will also argue that it is scientifically accurate when it asserts with its Near Eastern neighbors (and against the assessment of the vast majority of relevant scientists) that humanity was materially formed *de novo*. The problem here, again, is that we can be certain Genesis 1 is *not* correct (in the scientific sense) when it asserts with its Near Eastern neighbors that there is an expanse overhead, retaining a celestial ocean, which the stars are "set" in. The fact that Genesis 1 conforms to falsified Near Eastern assumptions in its astronomy should, at the very least, encourage Christians to be cautious with building scientific models off its biology or geology.

Third, it is interesting that, after all these years of debate, insecurity, and evangelicals feeling scientifically embattled over the strange ordering of the creation days (like the sun formed *after* trees), it turns out the whole show was probably largely a product of the church's failure to appreciate that the priestly author was trying to be symmetrical to convey the supreme order of creation.

These observations have long raised a question that I've mulled over in my mind: How would it even be coherent for the Genesis author to go about discrediting the myths of the nations by producing an account chronologically commensurate with science that would only be discovered thousands of years down the pike? Besides the fact that we can show Genesis doesn't do this, attempting to polemicize with a scientifically accurate sequential model of the material origins of the cosmos probably wouldn't have accomplished its goals, and conceivably would have interfered with them. By its nature, miraculous information of that sort would have presented no means (and therefore little interest) for its original readers to assess whether or not the account was superior in that dimension. Considering the original intended audience wouldn't have had the technical capability or impetus for appreciating such a thing, it doesn't seem obvious that this expectation old and young-earth creationists bring to the text should even be granted as theologically reasonable.

I suspect Genesis 1 is poor as an accurate account of the universes' chronological, material formation. However, with regards to what Genesis 1 *was actually written to be*, it only shows evidence of having succeeded fantastically well.

CHAPTER 10

THE NUMEROLOGICAL LIFESPANS OF THE PATRIARCHS

I
N the genealogies in Genesis 5 and 11, we find it claimed that early humanity lived astonishingly long lifespans. At 969 years old, one imagines a wizened Methuselah breathlessly spluttering into the bonfire over his birthday cake. Adam lived 930 years, Noah to 950!

Writing in a blog post entitled, "Christian academics telling God what He got wrong!" Ken Ham has rebuked Jim Stump, the Senior Editor at BioLogos, for floating the idea that these lifespans were symbolic.[1] Ham finishes the piece by entreating his readers, "I urge you not to be taken in by such elaborate ideas, which are nothing more than fallible sinful man's attempts not to take God at His word! How arrogant is finite man in thinking he can tell God what He got wrong."[2]

Young-earth interpreters like Ham traditionally take the long lifespans in Genesis to be literal. This assumption is the backbone of young-earth chronology. It is the primary basis for calculating the date of the flood to the middle of the second millennium and the creation of the earth at about 6,000 years ago. In the view of probably most Christians, the intended literalness of these lifespans seems so obvious in the Bible that it appears outrageous to doubt. Clearly, anyone proposing mere symbolic interpretations of these numbers is probably only doing so to make them palatable with Darwin.

---

[1] Ken Ham, "Christian Academics Telling God What He Got Wrong," *Answers in Genesis, Ken Ham Blog,* Jan 2014. Accessed Jun 8, 2017, www.answersingenesis.org/blogs/ken-ham/2014/01/25/christian-academics-telling-god-what-he-got-wrong/.
[2] Ibid.

It is my task in this chapter to take up the outrageous position—to convince you of a thesis that you probably currently believe is impossible: Not only is a literal interpretation of the Genesis genealogical lifespans inferior, it actually contradicts the Bible itself upon close inspection. In order to demonstrate this claim, I will argue two corresponding points: 1) Interpreting the long lifespans in Genesis as literal generates contradictions in the biblical narratives. And, 2) the long lifespans in Genesis are contrived with arithmetic formulae and are often clearly symbolic.

THE LITERAL INTERPRETATION AND INTERNAL CONTRADICTIONS

Let us first examine some evidence for my first claim: Interpreting the long lifespans as literal generates contradictions in the biblical narratives.

In conducting research for this book, I compiled every modern journal article and academic commentary on the patriarchal genealogies I could access over a period of weeks. While doing so, I was informed that a doctoral dissertation at Dallas Theological Seminary had just been published by a scholar named Craig Olson entitled, "A Proposal for a Symbolic Interpretation of the Patriarchal Lifespans."[3] When I obtained a copy of this new research, it became clear to me that it renders some assumptions in most past research on this topic obsolete.

Most significantly, the second chapter of Olson's thesis presents all sorts of arguments demonstrating that a literal interpretation of the long lifespans in Genesis results in contradictions and inconsistencies in the biblical stories that are, in at least several cases, so glaring that it is difficult to imagine the authors of the Bible could have overlooked them. The fact that the biblical authors were not bothered by these blatant inconsistencies would seem to imply that they consciously generated them and were therefore indifferent about their literal consistency. Consider five examples from Olson's thesis:

In Genesis 25:8 we read: "Abraham breathed his last and died at good old age, an old man full of years." Abraham is the first person in the Bible to be described as having obtained fullness of age. However, if the lifespans in Gen 5 and 11 are literal, this passage is bizarre because

---

[3] Craig Olson, "A Proposal for a Symbolic Interpretation of Patriarchal Lifespans" (PhD diss. Dallas Theological Seminary, 2017).

Abraham's great, great, great, great grandfather Eber was still alive and kicking at Abraham's death and even outlived him at 464 years (Gen 11:14-17). In fact, Abraham, who died in "good old age full of years," still had a spry great, great, great, great, great, great, great grandfather still living named Sheliah, along with *his* grandfather Shem (Gen 11:10-14).[4]

Second is a related point. If literal, these genealogies imply every one of the patriarchs born back to Noah lived at the same time as Abraham![5] This is strange because the Bible otherwise appears to treat these men like they were long dead by this time. Joshua 24:2 and 14-15 speaks of Abraham's "ancestors" having lived "long ago" מעולם and claims they worshiped foreign gods. This would be an odd way of describing Abraham's contemporaries, and it seems unlikely that paganism would have crept into Noah's family line while survivors of the flood like Noah and his son Shem were still alive.

Indeed, except for Jacob blessing Joseph's sons, none of the patriarchs is ever recorded as having related to his grandchildren.[6] This isn't a mere weak argument from silence. The whole point of patriarchal tribal culture is that the oldest surviving male ancestors should have still been the revered rulers and chief consultants of their family lines. Did no one really live with, visit, care for, or see fit to consult their ancestor so wise and venerable as Noah? Jacob founded the nation of Israel. Why do we never see him consulting with or meeting Abraham to whom the promise of this nation was once given? Why does Eber never appear in the Abrahamic narratives about the formation of the Hebrew people considering they were named after him? Where were any of these patriarchs at the rape of Dinah tragedy, or the supposed death of Joseph and the later famine in that story?

Third, the call of Abraham story gives us a more concrete example. If you remember, the story goes in Genesis 18 that Abraham is sitting in front of his tent in the heat of the day by the trees of Mamre, and three mysterious visitors come to him with a message from God. They tell him in a year he will bear a son. Abraham was incredulous. As Gen 18:11 says, "Now Abraham and Sarah were old, advanced in years. The way of women had ceased to be with Sarah." Abraham responded

---

[4] Ibid., 48-9.

[5] Olson presents a convenient graph of this data (Ibid, 213).

[6] Ibid., 55.

(17:17): "Will a son be born to a man *a hundred years old*? Will Sarah bear a child at the age of *ninety*?" Sarah, who overheard this conversation on the other side of the tent even laughs at the absurdity of it. "Then the Lord said to Abraham, 'Why did Sarah laugh and say, 'Will I really have a child, now that I am old?' Is anything too difficult for the Lord? I will return to you at the appointed time next year, and Sarah will have a son.'" So, of course, a year passes and this miracle does come true. Sarah names the baby Isaac, meaning laughter in Hebrew—a testament to the miraculous power of God visited to her in her old age!

Here's the problem: If the numbers given in the Genesis 5 and 11 genealogies are literal, this wasn't actually a miracle. Why not? Because Abraham's own dad, Terah, fathered either Abraham or one of his bothers at 130 years old (Gen 11:32, 12:4, Acts 7:4).[7] The Bible never hints that this birth was a miracle. In fact, not only his father but Abraham's own grandson Jacob fathered multiple children between the ages of 84 to 105![8]

So why is that one of the most central legends in the Torah, about the very formation of the Hebrew people, makes such a big deal about the miracle of Abraham and Sarah having a son at the ages of 90 and 100 if their relatives both after and immediately before them had children at older ages? A literal interpretation detracts from the whole point of the birth of Isaac story as a miracle.

This issue, that 90 and 100 in Abraham's day were considered "very old" and too old to have children is the basis for a fourth example. If you do some simple addition, Abraham's grandson Jacob not only fathered children as late as 105, but he was apparently a virgin until 77 years old when he fell in love with Rachel and was up for 7 years of labor to pursue a sexual relationship with her. That means he waited until age 84 before he started fathering 12 kids in a mere 7 years.

We know something of ancient marriage in the ancient Near East. In the first millennium, at least, it has been estimated that Mesopotamian women typically married between 14 and 20, and men between 26 and 32.[9] In the patriarchal period, Dinah must have been raped around at

---

[7] Ibid., 52.

[8] This calculation is derived by noting that Benjamin was born after the Dinah incident at Shechem (Gen 34:16-20). Ibid., 56.

[9] Martha T. Roth, "Age at Marriage and the Household: A Study of Neo-Babylonian and Neo-Assyrian Forms," *Comparative Studies in Society and History* 29.4 (1987), 747.

least 13 or 14, and Judah can be calculated as marrying at age 18 or 19.[10] In light of the Abraham narrative, and what we know about ancient marriage, the Jacob timeline seems incongruent on multiple levels if taken literally.

A similar fifth example of how the lifespans seem intentionally exaggerated when considered in light of their associated narratives can be observed with Isaac. If you remember the stolen blessing story of Jacob and Esau, the whole motive for why Isaac wants to bless Esau is that he was supposedly near death. (27:2-4): "Behold I am old; I do not know the day of my death…. Bring me some food…that I may bless you before I die." Esau then reiterates in verse 41, "The days of mourning for my father are approaching." This entire story is based around how Isaac is so old that he can't even see well enough to tell his sons apart. What is the problem with this? Chronology places Isaac at 137 years old when this story takes place. However, Gen 35:28-9 claims he died at 180—43 years later.[11] Was Esau an old man on the verge of death or not? A literal gap of 43 years seems to create an incongruence in the story.

The problems produced by a literal interpretation of the patriarchal lifespans in Genesis are considerable. It implies all the patriarchs would have been contemporaries of Abraham, a claim that the rest of the Bible doesn't seem to support, and it creates tension with Abraham's claimed "good old age, full of years." It inexplicably nullifies the miraculousness of the birth of Isaac story central to the call of Abraham. Additionally, the claim that 90 and 100 were too old to have kids in Abraham's day doesn't cohere with Jacob waiting until 77 to marry and fathering 12 kids in 7 years starting at ages 84-105. A literal interpretation also has Isaac astonishingly outliving his deathbed by 43 years!

EVIDENCE FOR A SYMBOLIC INTERPRETATION

Now let us consider what evidence can be produced for my second claim: The long lifespans in Genesis are arithmetically formulaic and often symbolic.

In order to demonstrate this, I draw your attention to the genealogy in Genesis 5 tabulated in Figure 17. Here, we are given thirty figures. I

---

[10] Olson, "A Proposal for a Symbolic Interpretation," 58.
[11] Ibid., 54.

know these numbers look random when you are skimming over them in your Bible, but observe them closer here. They are all divisible by 5 or end in a 2 or a 7 (with the single exception of Methuselah whose age can be derived by adding multiples of 5 and 7).

These sorts of statistics don't occur at random. That's not theological opinion; it's math. The probability that

	Age at fatherhood	Remaining years lived after son's birth	Total lifespan
Adam	130	800	930
Seth	105	807	912
Enosh	90	815	905
Kenan	70	840	910
Mahalalel	65	830	895
Jared	162	800	962
Enoch	65	300	365
Methuselah	187	782	**969**
Lamech	182	595	777
Noah	500	450	950

Figure 17. The genealogical figures from the Masoretic Texts of Genesis 5.

the distribution of numbers in Genesis 5 represents an arithmetically natural distribution has been calculated at .00000006%.[12]

Imagine you are one of the original patriarchs. One day you peruse your genealogy and notice that you can only die on a year divisible by 5 or on a year ending on a 7 or a 2. The grim reaper can't put his boney flippers on you until you hit one of those dates. You then realize that you and your ancestors unfailingly have supernatural birth control—again, until you hit a year divisible by 5 or ending on a 7 or a 2. A third time, you deduce from the pattern of your ancestors that the remaining years you will live in the space between the birth of your son and death must, again, be dictated by a year that is divisible by 5 or ends with a 7 or a 2! Outside of those numbers, you're effectively immortal! I have

---

[12] Sparks lays out this math in Kenton L. Sparks, "Genesis 1-11 as Ancient Historiography" in Charles Halton and Stanley N. Gundry (eds.), *Genesis: History, Fiction, or Neither? Three Views on the Bible's Earliest Chapters* (Grand Rapids: Zondervan, 2015), 120.

bolded Methuselah's total lifespan, the only outlier (undoubtedly, because he died in the year of the Flood).

Isn't it also a little odd that these men range from 65 to 500 with respect to the time that they had their firstborn? Did Noah use ancient birth control because he didn't want to have his three kids until his half-a-thousandth birthday? To treat these numbers as if they are a natural genealogy devoid of stylization seems to ignore what the Bible is openly trying to do. Are we going to cram this passage into *our* cultural mold of what *we think* a genealogy "should be," or do we care about figuring out what the biblical authors were up to?

The evidence indicates that the biblical authors, like their neighbors, loved playing with number symbolism. The fact that this math appears in the same book as the numerological cathedral of the first chapter of Genesis is probably significant. The fact that Enoch's lifespan is 365, the same number of days in a solar calendar, is probably significant. The fact that Lamech, the seventh born in Gen 4, would be avenged "seventy-seven times" (verse 24) and died at age 777 is probably significant.[13] The fact that there are a total of 10 names in this genealogy, corresponding with the overall numerological scheme (i.e. 10 is divisible by 5), is probably significant.

Additionally, Genesis 5 is not the only genealogy in the Bible that does all this. All the figures in the genealogy in Genesis 11, from Shem to Terah, also follow another noticeable, but somewhat different mathematical cipher. When we compile the rest of the genealogical stats given from Abraham to Joshua throughout Genesis and Deuteronomy, we also find that these figures are divisible by 5 or end in a 7.[14]

So what does it all mean? Scholars have ventured many theories. The task involves complex investigative work into the significantly different readings we find throughout the Old Testament's major manuscript families. However, for our more modest purposes, I will only draw

---

[13] Genesis 4 has Lamech as the seventh from Adam according to the following begetting sequence: Adam, Cain, Enoch, Irad, Mehujael, Methushael, Lamech.

[14] Noted in L. R. Bailey, "Biblical Math as *Heilsgeschichte?*" in R. D. Weis and D. M. Carr (eds.), *A Gift of God in Due Season: Essays on Scripture and Community in Honor of James A. Sanders.* JSOTSup 225 (Sheffield: JSOT Press, 1996), 85. Namely, Abraham had his son at 100 and lived to be 175, Sarah gave birth at 90 and died at 127. Isaac had his son at 60 and died at 180. Ismael died at 137 and Jacob died at 147. For Joseph, Moses and Joshua we have lifespans of 110, 120 and 110, respectively. Additionally, both Isaac and Esau married at 40.

attention to some of the particularly obvious patterns to which scholars have frequently pointed.

First, why do so many of these figures end in 2 and 7? The number 7 is a classic Hebrew symbol of completion, so there's no surprise there, but why 2? Observe the Genesis 5 table again. Excluding Methuselah's age of death, we are left with twenty-nine genealogical figures. Of these, twenty-one end in a number divisible by 5. All the rest end in a 2 or 7. It is interesting that by subtracting 7 from any of these numbers ending in a 2 or 7, *they all become divisible by 5*. For example, if you subtract 7 from Lamech's 777 it becomes 770. If you subtract 7 from Jared's 962, it becomes 955. This is strong evidence that *all* these figures were originally nice, round numbers divisible by 5, but that some came to be increased by an addition of the sacred number 7. In the single exception of Methuselah's death, it is plausible that his lifespan might have originally been 955 with 7 added twice to arrive at 969.

Another strange pattern: Scan down the column that provides the ages of the patriarchs during their year of fatherhood, and you will notice that it starts with Adam at 130. Gradually, the numbers decrease as you go down the list—105, 90, 70, and 65. This pattern of diminishing is then abruptly broken, leaping up even beyond the Adam figure to 162 with Jared, 187 with Methuselah, and 182 with Lamech. What gives? Is there a reason for this breach of pattern?

The explanation seems to be the following: According to Gen 7:11, the Great Flood occurred, "in the 600th year of Noah's life." In other words, the Bible doesn't tell us the date of the Flood but has it chronologically attached to Noah. As Etz has pointed out, if Jared, Methuselah, or Lamech had fathered their sons at age 65 in the above chart like Mahalalel and Enoch, then their sons would have been born sooner. This would have reduced the span of time between Adam and the Flood—mathematically leaving us with these three men outliving the date of the Flood.[15] Even if the genealogy had Jared, Methuselah, and Lamech fathering their sons at the higher age of 130, like Adam, it would still mathematically result in Methuselah and Lamech outliving the Flood. Consequently, it is likely that Jared, Methuselah, and Lamech had their years of fatherhood significantly increased by a scribe into the 160s and 180s to make the chronology fit with the Noah story.

---

[15] Donald V. Etz, "The Numbers of Genesis V 3-31: A Suggested Conversion and its Implications," *Vetus Testamentum* 43.2 (1993), 172.

Powerful support for this theory is found in the fact that other ancient biblical manuscript families, with independent transmission histories, solved this same Flood-overlap problem by intentionally modifying the numbers in different ways. An ancient transmission group of the Jewish Scriptures called the Samaritan Pentateuch doesn't contain the above highly augmented fatherhood ages. It records them as quite similar to Mahalalel and Enoch's 65—giving 62 for Jared, 67 for Methuselah, and 53 for Lamech. But how then does the Samaritan version solve the issue of people outliving the Flood that aren't supposed to? Its scribes did this by dramatically subtracting off these three men's *total lifespans*. Roughly, the Septuagint tackles this same problem by making the ages at fatherhood of nine different patriarchs 100 years higher than what appears in the Masoretic version. All of this is evidence that these numbers were transmitted with some fluidity, perhaps because they seek to adjust an initial, lost source that didn't mathematically cohere with the chronology of the Flood.[16]

Bailey points us to other fascinating observations about the lifespan totals. For example, Joseph and Joshua are associated with living in the land of Egypt. Particularly, Joseph's body was embalmed and placed in a sarcophagus (Gen. 20:26). Both of these men's lifespans happen to correspond with the ideal age of 110, which we find used in ancient Egyptian literature as a symbol for a full, blessed life.[17]

Moses lived 120 years (Deut 34:7), and Sarah lived 127 (Gen 23:1). It's probably not a coincidence that in ancient Semitic culture 120 was also considered the ideal lifespan.[18] Sarah is so honored in the text that

---

[16] Ibid., 172-176.

[17] Regarding the ideal Egyptian age of 110, Abrami points us to lines from the Precepts of Petah-Hotep and the Westcar Papyrus. Leo Michel Abrami, "The Ages of the Personalities in Genesis," *Jewish Bible Quarterly* 39.4 (2011), 261.

[18] There is a cuneiform tablet from Emar reading, "One hundred twenty years (are) the years of mankind—verily it is their bane." See, Jacob Klien, "The Bane of Humanity: A Lifespan of One Hundred Twenty Years," *Acta Sumerologica* 12 (1990), 59. This idea may also be found in Genesis 6:3, which says God's spirit will only abide in man for 120 years. The primary hurdle for this interpretation, however, is that so many people are given as having lived well over 120 years after the Flood—such as Arphaxad's 403 years (Gen 11:12), Eber's 430 (11:17), or Reu's 207 years (11:20). A second possibility is that the 120 years of Genesis 6:3 refers not to God shortening the lifespan of humanity, but to the length of time God had decreed before finally initiating the flood. The evidence for this comes from *Atrahasis* where periods of 1,200 years are allowed to transpire before Enlil

she not only attains 120, but 120 plus 7! When looking at these culturally symbolic numbers, it doesn't seem "arrogant" for us to ask, "Did it 'just happen that way,' or is the text saying that 'They lived life to the full' regardless of their actual ages?'"[19]

Many biblical scholars also believe that the genealogy in Genesis 5 shares certain mathematical affinities with an ancient Near Eastern text called the Sumerian King List.[20] Our versions of this ancient tradition list the names of kings that supposedly lived before the Flood. Where Genesis 5 gives stylistic lifespans in the hundreds of years, the Sumerian List claims that Sumer's kings before the Flood reigned for stylistic units of tens of thousands of years.

Some of these versions give a figure named Enmenduranna as the seventh king in the list. In Genesis 5, Enoch is the seventh. It's no surprise that his placement should correspond with that number of perfection considering he was so beloved by God that tradition based on Gen 5:24 maintained that he was snatched up into heaven. Later in Jewish belief, compiled in books like 1 Enoch, we read that this sage was given celestial knowledge on a tour of heaven. Enmenduranna was also brought to heaven before the assembly of the gods Adad and Shamash to be taught divination techniques, which he used to establish what the texts call his *baru*-priesthood.[21]

---

finally becomes annoyed enough with humanity to send the flood (as noted in Joshua John Van Ee, "Death and the Garden: An Examination of Original Immortality, Vegetarianism, and Animal Peace in the Hebrew Bible and Mesopotamia" [PhD diss., University of California, 2013], 190).

[19] Lloyd R. Bailey, *Genesis, Creation, and Creationism* (New York: Paulist Press, 1993), 63.

[20] In an article appearing on the Answers in Genesis website, López agrees with the conclusion that between the Sumerian King List and Genesis 5, "The probability that the resemblance is fortuitous is very small...." Raúl López, "The Antediluvian Patriarchs and the Sumerian King List," *Answers in Genesis*, Dec 1998. Accessed Jun 2017, www.answersingenesis.org/bible-history/the-antediluvian-patriarchs-and-the-sumerian-king-list/. Though he explains the data differently, Finkel also opines, "The attempt by some scholars to treat the Genesis Great Ages tradition as if it had nothing to do with the cuneiform world seems to me utterly absurd." Irving Finkel, *The Ark Before Noah: Decoding the Story of the Flood* (New York: Double Day, 2014), 251.

[21] See Bailey, *Genesis*, 59. For further parallels with Enoch and Adapa, who is also sometimes credited as the seventh king, see Amar Annus, "On the Origin of the Watchers: A Comparative Study of the Antediluvian Wisdom in Mesopotamian and Jewish Traditions," *Journal for the Study of the Pseudepigrapha* 19.4 (2010), 286.

As has frequently been noted by scholars, a connection may likewise be at play here in how Enoch lived 365 years—the number of days in a solar calendar. It happens that Enmenduranna had a close relationship with the sun god and ruled over the ancient city of Sippar, an important center of the solar cult and its temple.[22] Most scholars, therefore, believe that Enoch functioned, in the Bible and later literature, as the Hebrew answer to the seventh Mesopotamian king and that, "The people of the ancient Near East engaged in what might be called 'competitive historiography' to show how their national heroes outshone the heroes of other peoples or were the true and most ancient founders of culture."[23] Whether intentionally associated particularly with Enmenduranna's solar significance or not, Enoch's calendrical age should probably be understood in some way as a monotheistic symbol for the divine administration of the cosmos.

As a final example, I have also pointed to Lamech's seventh placement in Genesis 4 and death at 777 years. A third connection with him and this sacred number can be found in Genesis 4:24: "If Cain is avenged seven times, then Lamech seventy-seven!" If that isn't enough, Hess has even suggested a possible fourth connection between Lamech and the number seven: Lamech does not receive the seventh spot in the Genesis 5 genealogy, that honor falls to Enoch. However, Seth's son Enosh, whose name simply means *man*, is interpretively often considered a "new Adam" and Lamech's position in Genesis 5 *is seventh from Enosh*.[24] Considering that this number is repeatedly associated with

---

[22] This possibility is noted by James C. VanderKam, *Enoch: A Man for all Generations* (Columbia: University of South Carolina, 1995), 6. For the scholarly consensus on this interpretation see Amar Annus, "On the Origin of the Watchers," 278. In relation to a possible Enmenduranna connection, Day likewise adds, "Enoch's solar connection is further highlighted later in the so-called Astronomical Book of Enoch, *1 Enoch* 72-82, where he appears as an advocate of the solar calendar." John Day, "The Flood and the Ten Antediluvian Figures," James K. Aitken, Katharine J. Dell and Brian A. Mastin (eds.), *On Stone and Scroll: Essays in Honour of Graham Ivor Davies* (Berlin: Gruyter, 2011), 217. Scholars like Kugel have cast some healthy skepticism on the Enmenduranna connection, but he maintains the solar connection with his lifespan. James L. Kugel, *Traditions of the Bible: A Guide to the Bible as it was at the Start of the Common Era* (Cambridge: Harvard University Press, 1998), 191.

[23] John J. Collins, *The Apocalyptic Imagination: Introduction to Jewish Apocalyptic Literature*, 3 ed. (Grand Rapids: Eerdmans, 2016), 57.

[24] Richard S. Hess, "Lamech in the Genealogies of Genesis," *Bulletin for Biblical Research* 1 (1991), 22-3.

Lamech in four different ways, it would be absurd to deny that literary symbolism is involved.

Therefore, "It is plausible to suppose that others (if not all) of the ages in the Genesis list have non-literal, mystic, symbolic significance. Keen, playful, creative minds apparently have been at work in the fashioning of this system, but much of the key to the result remains opaque to interpreters in the present."[25]

If I understand him fairly, Ham has objected that viewing these genealogies in Genesis as a symbolic-numerological construct is an invitation for trouble. Just where do we draw the line between symbolism and history? He challenges, "When do the genealogies become trustworthy again?"[26] In response, I would suggest that the genealogies should be treated as "trustworthy"—that is, intended as literally accurate, when they start to at least look like they are trying to be *literally* accurate. For example, contrast with these highly stylized and symbol-laden numbers can be made with the *actual random* numbers given for the reigns of Israel and Judah's kings. Starting with Rehoboam in the books of Kings, we read of the following periods of reigns expressed in years: 17, 3, 41, 2, 24, 7 days, 12, 22, 25, 2, 8, 1, 28, 40, 17, 16, 29, 52, 41, 6 months, 1 month, 10, 2, 20, 16, 16, 9, 29, 55, 2, 21, 3 months, 11, 3 months, and 11.[27] Obviously, this set *is* concerned with literal accuracy. It doesn't conform to the blatant mathematical ciphers and symbolism explored above.

Starting from the assumption that these genealogies are literally historically accurate, an Answers in Genesis article concludes, "Using the Bible, well-documented historical events, and some math, we find that the Flood began approximately 4359 years ago in the year 1656 AM or 2348 BC."[28] Hodge agrees that "the Flood of Noah's day...occurred around 2350 BC."[29] Andrew Snelling, one of the leading young-earth

[25] Bailey, *Genesis*, 64.
[26] Ham, "Christian Academics," n.p.
[27] I have taken this argument and reproduced these figures according to the example in Bailey, "Biblical Math," 88.
[28] David Wright, "Timeline for the Flood," *Answers in Genesis*, Mar 9, 2012. Accessed Jun 28, 2017, www.answersingenesis.org/bible-timeline/timeline-for-the-flood/.
[29] Bodie Hodge, "Were the Pyramids Built Before the Flood?" *Answers Magazine*, Oct 1, 2012. Accessed Jun 28, 2017, www.answersingenesis.org/archaeology/ancient-egypt/were-the-pyramids-built-before-the-flood/.

geologists featured in the popular documentary *Is Genesis History?*, has also co-written an article headlining an issue of *Answers Magazine* in which he attempts to biblically date the Ice Age. The authors work from the assumption that "the Flood of Genesis 6…occurred roughly 4300 years ago…."[30] Again, that's 2300 BC—the Sixth Dynasty of the Egyptian Old Kingdom following the "golden age" of the pyramid builders in the Fourth Dynasty. It also happens to land smack in the middle of Sargon of Akkad's well-documented military conquests of Mesopotamia that impacted most of the Near East. The Egyptian Abydos and Turin king lists cover the rulers of this period and are oblivious about a world-destroying global flood.

It's historically outrageous to suppose a global flood in these centuries is supposed to have managed to blast out the Grand Canyon in North America and fossilize the dinosaurs in Uzbekistan but couldn't put a dent in the Sphinx at Giza or other hundreds of Egyptian sites and entire civilizations constructed far earlier and well documented as alive and well through this period. If you accept the calculation that a global flood occurred in 2300 BC, you absurdly end up having to compress or explain away nearly all of the world's chronological and archaeological evidence dating to before the middle of the Egyptian Old Kingdom period.[31] This is intolerably conspiratorial. Using these genealogies, which we understand very little, as literal chronologic markers is foolish, both literarily and historically.

CONCLUSION

This chapter opened with five cases where interpreting the long lifespans of the patriarchs in Genesis as literal numbers generate significant problems in the biblical text itself. Second, I have argued for

---

[30] Andrew A. Snelling and Mike Matthews, "When was the Ice Age in Biblical History," *Answers Magazine*, Apr. 1, 2013. Accessed Jun 28, 2017, www.answersingenesis.org/environmental-science/ice-age/when-was-the-ice-age-in-biblical-history/.

[31] Hodge's argument that essentially all Egyptian civilization and monuments must be dated after 2300 BC (on the basis that Noah's son Mizraim didn't occupy the Nile Delta until after Babel) is astonishing. The hieroglyphs on the Creation Museum's displayed Narmer Palette are nearly a millennium older than that date. Hodge, "Were the Pyramids Built Before the Flood?," n.p.

evidence of a high degree of mathematical contrivance and symbolism for at least some of these numbers.

In Bailey's assessment, "analysis and comparison [of the biblical genealogies] does not suggest that the biblical figures are not 'true.' Rather, it raises the possibility that they depict a mode of 'truth' that differs from modern concern with chronological accuracy."[32] These words strike me as excessively optimistic, and I have no theological interest in "explaining away" or rendering scientifically palatable the biblical authors' apparent belief in remarkably long lifespans possessed in former ages. Yet there is certainly some truth in Bailey's words. To even claim the numbers have been derived by rounding literal lifespans stretches credulity because you have features like Noah having his firstborn at the remarkably late age of 500 and the fact that some of these figures are obviously derived from literary motivations (like Enoch's 365 or Lamech's 777). When some creationists take these numbers as chronologically accurate, to the point of having "a precision of one year" (as one *Answers* article claims),[33] they overlook these red flags that the biblical authors themselves are openly waving at us.

What would the original readers of Genesis have taken away from its genealogies? Bailey suggests that these ages perhaps symbolize divine oversight. The stylized figures given for the lifespans of the patriarchs seem designed to symbolize that history is not random, but regulated by God. For the Jews sitting in exile, wondering if God's covenant promises were void, that concept would have been no trivial message.[34]

---

[32] Bailey, *Genesis*, 93.

[33] Raúl López, "The Antediluvian Patriarchs and the Sumerian King List," n.p.

[34] This is the thesis in Bailey, "Biblical Math," 101-2. Lambaard's conclusion is quite close as well: "The post 586 [BC] identity of Israel is fed, in this genealogy, by a text that uses the continuity of past generations to give security in the present." Christo Lombaard, "Genealogies and Spiritualties in Genesis 4:17-22, 4:25-26, 5:1-32," *Acta Theologica Supplementum* 8 (2006), 159.

CHAPTER 11

ANIMAL DEATH BEFORE THE FALL

WHEN you first enter the main hall of the Creation Museum, you see depictions of raptors playing next to a lifelike human child. Along the tour, you enter the Garden of Eden to see a wax figure of Adam hugging a lamb in one arm as he invitingly extends the other toward a predatory cat. A few feet away waddles a penguin. In the Garden path is a large, beaked dinosaur chowing on what appears to be some sort of prehistoric pineapple. A sign next to the creature poses the question: "What did Dinosaurs Eat?" It answers: "Before man's Fall, animals were vegetarians. In a 'very good' creation, no animal would die, so there were no carnivores. All the beasts of the earth, not just the 'beasts of the field' that God brought to Adam to name, ate only plants."

Continuing the tour, we see Adam and Eve sharing the forbidden fruit, and things immediately spiral into mayhem. Expelled from the Garden, we are promptly taken before an animatronic raptor hunched over a torn carcass. A sign explains again how nature "Red [in] Tooth and Claw" only came about as a consequence of humanity's original transgression. It claims, "Before Adam's sin" there was "no struggle for survival" among animals.

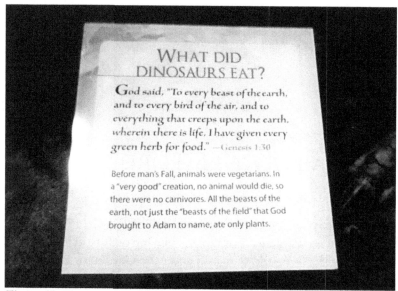

Figure 18. Museum sign claiming that animals only ate plants before the Fall. Photo by Joel Kramer, 2014.

Figure 19. A dinosaur eats a kill after the Fall. Photo by Joel Kramer, 2014.

These ideas have become canonical within young-earth literature. Tim Clarey, who has published a book intended as a Christian alternative to secular school science textbooks, writes, "In God's original creation, even the mighty *T. rex* was a vegetarian, as were all animals. It wasn't until after the sin of man and the resulting Curse that *T. rex* became a meat-eater."[1] *The New Answers Book* (Figure 20) contains a picture of a Tyrannosaurus holding a watermelon in its jaws and teaches the idea that cutting fruit rind may have been their pre-Fall function (Apparently, the involved museum staff ironically haven't reflected on the fact that modern watermelons are the invention of artificial selection and looked little like this in recent antiquity.)[2] Ham states: "When God completed His work of creation, …[p]eople and animals were all vegetarian."[3] Morris said the same.[4]

Many young-earth thinkers will admit that this idea is one of young-earth creationism's more difficult doctrines given the state of our present world.[5] Nearly everywhere in nature, we see creatures exquisitely equipped with all sorts of creative means to inflict death and suffering

---

[1] Tim Clarey, *Dinosaurs: Marvels of God's Design: The Science of the Biblical Account* (Green Forest, AR: Master books, 2015), 79.

[2] Image is found in Bodie Hodge, "How Did Attack/Defense Structures Come About?" in Ken Ham (ed.), *The New Answers Book: Over 25 Questions on Creation Evolution and the Bible* (Green Forrest, AR: Master Books, 2006), 266. Modern watermelons are estimated to have emerged in Mediterranean agriculture from an incredibly smaller and less fleshy form several thousand years ago. Even Giovanni Stanchi's painting of a watermelon in the seventeenth century illustrates how much the crop has changed only recently. See Harry S. Paris, "Origin and Emergence of the Sweet Dessert Watermelon, *Citrullus Lanatus*," *Annals of Botany* 116.2 (2015), 133-148.

[3] Ken Ham, *The Lie: Evolution/Millions of Years (25th Anniversary Edition)* (Green Forest, AR: Master Books, 2012), 54.

[4] Henry M. Morris, *The Biblical Basis for Modern Science: The Revised and Updated Classic!* (Green Forest, AR: Master Books, 2002), 103.

[5] As the young-earth ecologist Gordon Wilson admitted, "It may seem unthinkable that scorpions, divinely designed predators, could have once lived on vegetation, but in Genesis 1:30 God says, 'Everything that creeps on the earth, in which there is life, I have given every green thing for food.' A world where animals didn't eat other animals is almost impossible to imagine." Gordon Wilson, "Scorpions—Armed and Dangerous Created Creature," *Answers Magazine*, 1 Jan 2013. Accessed 29 Jul 2018, https://answersingenesis.org/creepy-crawlies/scorpions-armed-and - dangerous/.

upon one another. If animals never harmed or consumed each other before Adam's sin, what exactly did scorpions look like before the Fall? Why is their whole body decked out in plate armor like medieval knights? Why do they need those massive pincers? Why are their hind legs and mesosoma designed to coil forward, putting their hulkish claws within access of a segmented tail attached to a bulbous, hooked syringe capable of injecting complex neurotoxins and enzyme inhibitors? Did God create them like this, or were these structures post-Fall developments?

If these biological structures were all post-Fall developments, it is difficult to imagine the unspeakable changes these organisms had to undergo after the Fall. That sounds suspiciously like evolution.

If one chooses the first option instead, that God did create animals with all of these predatory biological structures, then we have to confront the massive issues associated with the fact that all sorts of creatures were frolicking around the Garden eating vegetation that they had little or no biological capacity even to digest properly.

It's also strange (and seems deceptive in scientific retrospect) to think that God might have created the natural world with all these deadly structures that had no purpose other than anticipation of Adam and Eve's rebellion.

One wonders what Adam would have thought of them as he was naming the animals. What exactly would vipers be using their chemical receptors, hollow fangs, and venom sacks for in Eden? To stalk and chew broccoli?

Figure 20. An image shown in *The New Answers Book* and in Creation Museum lectures shows a *T. Rex* eating a watermelon. Image used under fair use.

Another problem for the original vegetarian view: The whole narrative purpose of the Tree of Life in Genesis 3 assumes that without access to it humanity was mortal. That is why God's strategy for sentencing the man and woman to death was simply to kick them out of the Garden. The text directly explains that God did this so that man could not, "reach out his hand, and take from the Tree of Life and live forever" (Gen 3:22). So humanity, God's highest creation, was created inherently mortal (they needed access to the tree to prevent them from dying) but all the lower animals were made inherently immortal, like gods? This seems tremendously inconsistent.

Third, there are obvious issues with population control. On the view of young-earthers like Ken Ham, if Adam had never sinned, every species would presumably be reproducing unchecked by death. If things were permitted to continue in this state it would create a situation of literally exponential overpopulation—an ecological nightmare.

Of course, young-earthers have developed clever responses to these sorts of concerns: Maybe God placed the genes for lethal structures inside the animals at the time of creation but didn't allow them to be expressed physically until after the Fall.[6] (So God evolved them at warp speed—causing them to manifest countless major morphological changes and suppressing their old genes exclusive to vegetarian living?) Maybe God would have supernaturally seen to it for all eternity that no dinosaur would ever accidentally step on an ant or a lizard? (I'm not constructing a strawman. Answers in Genesis has an article entitled, "Did Adam Step on an Ant Before the Fall?" that proposes this answer.)[7] With respect to overpopulation, maybe God planned to effectively supernaturally sterilize all the animals after the earth was full

---

[6] As Wilson proposes for the stingers of scorpions. Wilson, "Scorpions—Armed and Dangerous," n.p.

[7] Foley states: "Surely the God who could uphold the shoes, clothes, and feet of every wandering Israelite and who protected His servants from the fire could sustain the perfect pre-Fall world in such a way that no ant accidentally got squished. This would not be hard for the all-powerful God.... [A]ccidents never happen in a perfect world." Avery Foley, "Did Adam Step on an Ant Before the Fall?," *Answers in Genesis*, 4 Dec 2015. Accessed 26 Jul 2018, https://answersingenesis.org/death-before-sin/did-adam-step-on-an-ant-before-fall/.

as an article by Bodie Hodge claims.[8] (Good luck finding the Bible verse for that one.)

We can sit around and dream up *deus ex machina* answers like these to explain away all of the problems in a theory. However, when I was a young-earth creationist, I found myself growing ever more uneasy as I read apologetics books that endlessly contrived more and more of these miraculous textually baseless solutions to resolve basic logistic issues with the young-earth view. In terms of the continual addition of *ad hoc* supernatural bailouts, the young-earth view of the origin of animal predation seemed to me as elegant as a shaved gorilla. This struck me as especially odd because none of these logical puzzles that kept me awake at night even seemed to have crossed the minds of the Old Testament authors. If the biblical authors shared the Creation Museum's view, why didn't they show evidence of even registering these things as a problem?

Something was missing.

The three major passages young-earthers cite in support of a universal state of original vegetarianism in the animal kingdom are given below:

Gen 1:29-30

And God said, "Behold! I give to you every seed-bearing plant that is upon the face of all the earth and every tree of which is in it the fruit of a tree bearing seed—to you it shall be for food. And to all the beasts of the earth, and to all the birds of the sky, and to all the creeping things upon the earth, of which is in them the breath of life, are all green plants for food." And it was so.

Gen 9:1-5

And God blessed Noah and his sons and said to them, "...[A]ll moving which lives will be to you for food. Like a green plant, I give to you everything. Only meat of which blood is in it you may not eat. And for your own lifeblood, I will require a reckoning: from the

---

[8] He states, "The command was to populate until the earth was full, and then reproduction would cease." Bodie Hodge, "Didn't the Curse Prevent Overpopulation?" *Answers in Genesis*, 11 May 2010. Accessed 26 Jul 2018, https://answersingenesis.org/bible-questions/didnt-the-curse-prevent-overpopulation/.

hand of every beast I will require it. I will require it from the hand of every beast and from the hand of a man...."

Isa 11:1-9

And a shoot will come from the stump of Jesse...and the wolf will sojourn with the lamb, and the leopard with the young goat will lie down, and the calf and young lion and the fatted calf will be together, and a little child shall drive them. And the cow and the bear will graze together, and their young ones will lie down. And the lion will eat straw like the ox. And the suckling child will play on the den of the asp and the infant will put his hand on the adder's den. None will hurt nor destroy in all my holy mountain....

Just browsing over these passages, readers should appreciate how tremendously compelling the young-earth interpretation of them appears.

In Gen 1:29-30, it is obvious that God is granting vegetation to all animals and humans for food. Put that next to Gen 9:1-5, a contrasting but parallel passage after the Flood, and it seems that only in this later passage does God first grant humans the right to eat meat. Its terminology appears to imply that Gen 1:28-30 was indeed pronouncing universal vegetarianism to be the original status of creation.

After these comes the knockout punch! Isaiah speaks of how the New Creation will feature lions eating straw like oxen and wolves befriending lambs. Surely, the prophet is drawing this imagery from his understanding that, before the Fall, the created order included no animal hostility and no death!

This is the traditional interpretation I was taught since childhood, however, my understanding of these passages radically changed when I discovered a doctoral thesis dedicated entirely to this subject by J. J. Van Ee. Van Ee's work is a model of quality scholarship—the most erudite and linguistically sophisticated interpretive study of this subject that currently exists. I believe his research blows the original vegetarianism view out of the water. His dissertation concludes: "An analysis of the relevant texts indicates that such a view of the original created state is not present in Mesopotamian literature or the Hebrew Bible.... Neither restrict original human or animal diets to vegetation. And neither portray a time of perfect peace between humans and animals or among animals themselves."[9]

In this chapter, I'm not attempting to argue that we can find evasive ways to weasel our way out of the obvious meaning of the above-mentioned Bible passages (a charge of which, I think most old-earth commentaries might legitimately be judged guilty), nor do I want to argue that the original vegetarianism view is simply one of several plausible options. Instead, I will argue that the Creation Museum's view of original vegetarianism is a demonstrably inferior interpretation of the Old Testament data. It isn't how the Bible's original northwest Semitic audience would have intended or understood the text at all. Likewise, the centuries of traditional theology based on the original vegetarianism view must be reassessed. We will examine the three aforementioned passages in turn.

GENESIS 1:28-30

The problem with the idea that Genesis 1:29-30 teaches the original creation was free of all animal death lies in the verse that immediately precedes it. In verse 28, God commands the man and woman to "subdue" the earth and to "rule" its animals.

You've probably heard many sermons teaching that these words *subdue* and *rule* exhort us to steward and care for the earth. This is a load of nonsense. While a message of ecological stewardship and compassion towards animals can be powerfully defended from other passages in the Bible, you're not going to come up with that specific message from a proper interpretation of the Hebrew words translated *subdue* and *rule* in Genesis 1:28.

The reality is, in Hebrew, these specific verbs are shockingly harsh, even militant with connotations of violent force. If that comes as news to you, welcome to the club. As Old Testament scholar Daniel Stulac comments, theologians are guilty of "persistent underreporting of the violence implied by the text's key terms.... It is clear from

---

[9] Joshua John Van Ee, "Death and the Garden: An Examination of Original Immortality, Vegetarianism, and Animal Peace in the Hebrew Bible and Mesopotamia" (PhD diss., University of California, 2013), xiii.

context…that these terms are not benign."[10] The biblical text in question reads:

> And God blessed them [the man and woman] and God said to them, "Be fruitful and multiply and fill the earth and subdue [כבש] it and rule [רדה] over the fish of the sea and the birds of the air and over all animals which move upon the earth." And God said, "Behold! I give to you every seed-bearing plant…."

The first verb translated "subdue" here, *kavash*, occurs thirteen other times in the Bible. Surveying its usage comprehensively, in six of these cases, it refers to military conquest of hostile lands.[11] Five other instances use it to speak of forcing people into slavery.[12] Among the remaining two, Mic 7:19 uses it of God aggressively trampling sin underfoot,[13] and Esther 7:8 uses it to speak of sexual assault. War, enslavement, trampling, and assault! It's no wonder Christians and Jews

---

[10] Daniel J. Stulac, "Hierarchy and Violence in Genesis 1:26-28: An Agrarian Solution," Submission for Ecological Hermeneutics Open Section at SBL Annual Meeting 2013, 4, 6, www.academia.edu/5186990/Hierarchy_and_Violence_in_Genesis_1_26-28_An_Agrarian_Solution.

[11] Num 32:22, 29; Josh 18:1; 2 Sam 8:11, 1 Chron 22:18, and Zech 9:15, which uses it in the context of Israel plowing down her national enemies as an expression of God's judgment.

[12] These are 2 Chron 28:10; twice in Neh 5:5; Jer 34:11, and 34:16.

[13] The NIV has, "tread our sins underfoot." The ESV has, "tread our iniquities underfoot," identical to the NASB and similar to the ERV. The HCSB reads, "He will vanquish our iniquities," and the NET Bible uses the conquest language of: "conquer our evil deeds." Claiming that *kavash* in Genesis 1 must be non-violent, Turpin argues that Micah 7:19 shows that *kavash* can have a non-violent meaning: "[I]n Micah 7:19 God subdues our sins which is a sign of God's compassion." Although God's trampling of Israel's sin is motivated by his compassion in the verse, Turpin is plainly wrong in implying that God's trampling of sin here is therefore non-violent. (How does one even trample non-violently?) God's aggressive subduing of sin is particularly emphasized by the second parallel poetic couplet of the verse: "You will tread our sins underfoot / and hurl all our iniquities into the depths of the sea." Simon Turpin, "Did Death of Any Kind Exist Before the Fall: What the Bible Says About the Origin of Death and Suffering," *Answers Research Journal* 6 (2013), 104. www.answersingenesis.org/arj/v6/death-before-fall.pdf.

concerned about ecological abuse have sought ways to mitigate the harshness of this term in the creation mandate.

In opposition to our prejudices, Karl Möller, retired professor of Old Testament at the University of Gloucestershire, rightly warns us: "We need to be careful not to sanitize the text to make it conform to our modern sensibilities regarding issues such as force and violence…. [T]he harshness implied in the terms כבש and רדה ב should not be explained away."[14]

Some have complained that these thirteen uses of this word for "subdue" in the Bible are not a large enough sample size for linguists to adequately extract the word's meaning. But the term also shows up in an Akkadian cognate that has proven equally harsh.[15]

The takeaway: Humanity was commanded to conquer and take rulership over the animals with language similar to Israel's mandate to conquer Canaan through military combat.[16] What about God's other command that humanity should "rule" the animals? The verb here, *radah*, is not the more docile sort of term Genesis 1 uses, for example, to speak of the sun's ruling over the day.[17] *Radah* occurs at least twenty-six

---

[14] Quoted in Van Ee, "Death and the Garden," 333. Originally, Karl Möller, "Images of God and Creation in Genesis 1-2," in Jamie A. Grant, Alison Lo, and Gordon J. Wenham (eds.), *A God of Faithfulness: Essays in Honour of J. Gordon McConville on His 60th Birthday* (New York: T & T Clark, 2011), 20-21.

[15] Van Ee quotes the *Chicago Assyrian Dictionary* entry on *kabāsu*: "to crush, defeat an enemy, to bother, to make people do work, to press people." ("Death and the Garden," 203.) In order to make the creation mandate comport with an idea of original vegetarianism, scholars like Lohfink have tried to argue that the Akkadian *kabāsu*, which refers to treading over, might be an idiom for taking symbolic possession of something. Van Ee (ibid, 202-204) rejects this analysis because: 1) It must be implied without any textual confirmations that such a meaning was implied by it (i.e., we have no texts confirming its discrete use as such an idiom). 2) It is strange to supply that meaning in the perfect *Niphal* stem in conjunction with the preposition לפני in a passage like Josh 18:1. If *kavash* in that passage is simply an idiom for taking possession and doesn't refer to conquest, then the passage would have to be translated something like, "The land *had been* stepped on (i.e. possessed) in front of them." What does it mean that the Israelites had already stepped on and come to possess what was in front of them? And, 3) Josh 18:1 and 3 seem to contrast the Hebrew word for "possess" with the term for "subdue."

[16] Ibid., 207.

[17] Environmentalist theologians sometimes cite Psa 8:6-8 where *mashal* is interchanged with *radah* in the divine mandate. This linguistic methodology should be rejected because the notion of governance is obviously circumscribed by

other times in the Bible and seems to derive from an etymology either of "descending upon" or of "treading" (as in a winepress).[18] It "is used to communicate a highly coercive form of control. The verb by itself can be used to communicate harshness or injustice.... The focus is on having power over someone and not on executing administrative or bureaucratic functions."[19]

My comprehensive survey of the term in the Old Testament confirms this conclusion.[20]

---

reading *radah* with a harsh connotation of rule. Equating *radah* with *mashal* contradicts the connotation of *radah* in our other texts and still has to deal with the harsh preceding terminology for "subdue" which makes the rulership possible. Finally, as Van Dyk points out, Psa 8 speaks of the animals being "put...under foot." *Radah*, he says, "has the meaning of 'vigorous conquest by a superior force'. The image of a conquering king striking down his enemies (e.g. Psa 18:38) is invoked here.... It can therefore not be denied that Psalm 8 strengthens the idea that humans have the power to act as repressive forces within nature...." Peet Van Dyk, "Challenges in the Search for an Ecotheology," *Old Testament Essays* 22.1 (2009) 191-2.

[18] Van Ee, "Death and the Garden," 208-9. Although he thought P believed in original vegetarianism, Westermann agreed with the "basic meaning is 'to tread down.'" Claus Westermann, *Genesis 1-11: A Commentary*, trans. John J. Scullion S.J. (Minneapolis: Augsburg Publishing, 1984), 158-9. Joel 4:13 uses the term of treading a winepress.

[19] Ibid., 207.

[20] These twenty-six occurrences follow (note, the term is used twice in both Judg 5:13 and 14:9): Outside of its two uses in Genesis, Lev 25:43, 46 and 53 all use it of "ruling with severity"; Lev 26:17 of being ruled by "those who hate you"; Num 24:19 of a ruler who would "destroy survivors," and Judg 5:13 of military retaliation against Canaan. 14:9 uses a form of the word for Samson coercing honey out of a lion carcass. The term is used in 1 Kgs 4:24 with reference to tribute paying vassals under Solomon designated in verses 21-23; 1 Kgs 5:16, 9:23 and 2 Chron 8:10 of foremen over what the texts specify were Solomon's forced laborers; Neh 9:28 of Israel being ruled by "enemies," from whom they cried out to be delivered; Psa 49:14 of the righteous treading over the wicked in Sheol. 68:27 praises the tribe of Benjamin in the context of the military conquest of verses 11-23. 72:8 uses the term of Israel's king ruling those who would "bow before him" and "lick the dust"; 110:2 of the king who would make his "enemies" a "footstool"; Isa 14:2 of Israel "possessing" and "enslaving" its enemies, verse 6 speaking of God judging those who were "ruling" the nations with "unceasing anger," and 41:2 of a "ruler" who will "subdue kings" and "turn nations to dust by the sword." Jer 5:31 is a castigation against the evil rulership of Israel's priests. Lam 1:13 uses the term of God "overpowering" the lamenter by casting down fire

Due to the negative connotations associated with it, the term "is not used for someone ruling over his own people unless that rule involves some sort of oppression or injustice."[21] Surely, the term's use in dyad with *kavash* reinforces an austere connotation.[22] Again, however uncomfortable the terminology may appear to us theologically from a modern environmentalist standpoint, the verbs Genesis uses in the creation mandate carry overtones of military conquest and dominating rulership.[23] In the extremely harsh, resource-scarce world of the Bible, humanity's struggle against the lethal forces of nature was far more immediate and pressing than it is for the majority of us in our modern

---

on him out of his "fierce anger." Ezek 29:15 is a judgment against Egypt—that she will never again rule other nations, and 34:4 speaks of ruling "with force and harshness."

[21] Ibid., 210. Alter likewise acknowledges in his notes that, "in most of the contexts in which [the verb *radah*] occurs it seems to suggest absolute or even fierce exercise of mastery." Robert Alter, *The Five Books of Moses: A Translation with Commentary* (New York: Norton, 2004), 19.

[22] Contrary to Stambaugh's argument that the term "subdue" syntactically refers to the earth and not the animals, just as being fruitful is a necessary condition (and is, therefore, conceptually linked) with filling the earth, subduing is the necessary precondition upon which man's rulership is logically based. (Van Ee, "Death in the Garden," 198). Therefore, man's subjugation of the earth should be understood as partial metonymy circumscribing the animals who are parts of "the earth" and cannot be ruled until the precondition of subjugation is brought about. We wouldn't, for example, say God's command for the Israelites to "subdue the land" of Canaan would exclude the Canaanites who are members of it. Jim Stambaugh, "Creation's Original Diet and the Changes at the Fall," *Journal of Creation* 5.2 (1991), 130-138. https://answersingenesis.org/animal-behavior/what-animals-eat/creations-original-diet-and-the-changes-at-the-fall/.

[23] Ibid., 217. Van Ee directs us to Postell's comment: "The militaristic overtones of the creation mandate, therefore, make sense only when understood as the prototypical mandate to conquer the Promised Land." Seth D. Postell, *Adam as Israel: Genesis 1-3 as the Introduction to the Torah and Tanakh* (Eugene: Pickwick Publications, 2011), 102. As an aside, Gen 2:18 says Eve was created as an *'ezer kenegdo*—what the King James translated as a "help-meet" for Adam. Robert Alter has pointed out that the translation "help," "is too weak because it suggests a merely auxiliary function, whereas 'ezer elsewhere connotes active intervention on behalf of someone, especially in military contexts, as often in the Psalms." Eve was created as Adam's "sustainer"—again, a term suggesting a military connotation with respect to humanity's function. See note on verse 18 in Alter, *The Five Books*, 22.

post-industrial environment where this struggle is already won and demands opposite balancing concerns.

Peet Van Dyk at the University of South Africa agrees:

> When reading the verse, the first inclination of the ecologically sensitive reader is to try and interpret the words 'subdue' and 'rule over' in a less damaging way.... However, within its immediate context the Hebrew words...cannot be softened in any way. Even Tucker['s study]...acknowledged that the term 'subdue' is a potentially violent verb, referring to 'trampling under one's feet' in absolute subjugation.[24]

Beyond the lexical analysis, there are also logistic reasons for inferring this use of violence from the text as well. Notice that God commands humanity to subdue and rule over three categories of creatures in Gen 1:28: "the fish of the sea," "the birds of the air," and "all animals which move upon the earth." It is easy to understand how and why a man might subdue and rule over a cow or sheep without harming it, but as the Talmud asks, how do ancient people subdue and rule over birds or fish? What does it look like to rule a fish? Is Adam going to hook it up to a yoke? Is he going to have a dolphin plow his field? One imagines subdued fish and birds were generally fairly useless to ancient man unless found in a net or lodged in some birdlime.

For this reason, those who claim that we should interpret the verbs subdue and rule in Genesis 1 differently than we would in *every other* passage in the Bible based on the pre-fallen world's unique *context* are wrong.[25] *Contextually*, it only makes sense for human beings to subdue and rule over two out of the three categories of referenced animals if they were to kill them for food or other purposes. Even for the third category of animals, livestock types represent an extreme minority of "all animals which move upon the earth." What does it mean to "subdue" vipers, lions, or leopards if they were originally as vegan as San Francisco yoga instructors and meek and harmless?

---

[24] Van Dyk, "Challenges in the Search for an Ecotheology," 190. Footnote citations removed from within quotation.

[25] This is in response to writers like Stambaugh, who claim, "Nowhere is a violent fulfillment of these imperatives ever implied within the text or context." Stambaugh, "Creation's Original Diet," 132.

The military terminology of the creation mandate permits use of human force and violence against the animal world. Consequently, *it seems most reasonable to also conclude violence existed between animals before the Fall*. Three justifications for this inference follow:

1) The military conquest terminology of "subduing" and establishing "rulership" strongly implies struggle against an opposing force. Arguably, in the thirteen instances of *kavash* we have surveyed in the Bible, that is always its connotation. (Particularly, the dual usage of this terminology harkens to Israel's mandate to subjugate Canaan.) If animals were considered armed enough to present a struggle with man, surely their hostility expressed itself against other animals in the natural world.

2) If human violence upon animals was a feature of God's original creation, consistency would lend to the probability that animal violence upon other animals was a feature of God's original creation.

3) The following point cannot be emphasized enough: Genesis 3 formally spells out the consequences of the Fall. The origin of animal death and predation is never even hinted at in the passage (despite plainly falsified attempts of some creationists to read it into the curse on the serpent).[26] Given the unimaginably

---

[26] Attending to the curse on the serpent in Gen 3:14, Foley's article (as well as an article by Hodge and McIntosh in the *New Answers Book*) claims that the phrase "you are cursed from among all [מִכָּל] cattle, and from among all beasts of the field" means that the curse on the serpent implies the cattle and beasts of the field were also cursed (with newly introduced death). This interpretation is soundly falsified by the immediately occurring explanatory parallel clauses that define the serpent's curse as being humbled to the ground below all beasts: "Upon your belly you shall go, and dust you will eat all the days of your life." The text specifies that the serpent was more cursed compared to all (Hebrew lit. "*from all*") the beasts of the field in the sense of relative ignobility—that he was brought lower than they are. There is, therefore, nothing in the text upon which to predicate an additional curse of death upon the animals. Avery Foley, "Did Adam Step on an Ant," n.p. ; Bodie Hodge and Prof. Andy McIntosh, "How Did Attack/Defense Structures Come About?" *The New Answers Book 1*, 27 Dec 2018. Accessed 27 Jul 2018, https://answersingenesis.org /evidence-for-creation/design-in-nature/how-did-

dramatic changes this would necessitate in the structure of the natural world, including for agricultural man (aren't predatory animals a curse on agricultural man?), it seems remarkable that the author should omit any reference to it, instead focusing on things like the scourge of thorns and weeds! The fact that the author of Genesis 3 doesn't connect the Fall with the origin of all animal death and predation (where one should greatly expect him to) lends considerable probability that he didn't maintain such a connection.

GENESIS 9:1-5

Many defenders of the original vegetarianism view believe their interpretation is bolstered by Genesis 9:1-5, [27] a passage where God speaks to Noah and his sons immediately after the waters of the Great Flood had receded:

> And God blessed Noah and his sons and said to them, "Be fruitful and multiply and fill the earth, and your fear and your dread will be upon all animals of the earth and on all birds of the sky, in all which creeps on the earth, and in all the fish of the sea. *In your hand they are given. All moving which lives will be to you for food. Like a green plant, I give to you all.* Only meat of which blood is in it you may not eat. And for your own lifeblood I will seek: from the hand of all life I will seek. I will seek it from the hand of every beast and from the hand of a man...."

---

defense-attak-structures-come-about/. Alternatively, Hodge and McIntosh's piece also claims that the statements, "dust you are, and to dust you will return" (Gen 3:19) implies that the curse introduced the change that "creatures would return to dust." This inference plainly exceeds the data of the text since Gen 3:19 is addressed particularly to humanity, not animals.

[27] For example, according to Mortenson, "...Genesis tells us that man was not given permission to eat meat until after the Flood (Genesis 9:3)." Terry Mortenson, "The Fall and the Problem of Millions of Years of Natural Evil," *Answers in Depth*, July 18, 2002. Accessed 8/20/17, www.answersingenesis.org/theory-of-evolution/millions-of-years/the-fall-and-the-problem-of-millions-of-years-of-natural-evil/; Hodge and McIntosh, "How Did Attack/Defense Structures Come About?," n.p. Also, Ham citation in following footnote.

The parallel language here to the previous passage we examined is undeniable, so it is sometimes argued that this passage marks the first time in history that God gave humanity permission to start eating animals.

Proponents of this interpretation understand God to be saying, "All moving which lives will be to you for food. Like [I previously granted you the right to eat] a green plant, I [*now*] give to you everything." As the CEO of the Creation Museum states, "After the event of Noah's flood, God told Noah that now humans could eat meat, could eat animal flesh. But before that time, they are instructed only to be vegetarian."[28]

However, a significant problem with this interpretation is that the gap of chapters between the opening creation account and this passage implies that man was already eating meat at God's pleasure. Three texts evidencing this follow:

1) Gen 3:21 has God himself making Adam and Eve leather clothes. Theologians like to imagine this leather was a by-product of God dramatically initiating the first animal sacrifice in history, but the text never actually mentions a sacrifice. The author is only interested in specifying the purpose of providing clothing.[29] The fact that God has no objection in this passage to using the flesh of a dead animal to supply for one of humanity's physical needs seems to lend evidence that this prerogative would have also extended to physical needs like consumption.

2) In Gen 4:2, we are told that Abel was a keeper of flocks, and *in 4:4 he is depicted bringing the fat of the firstborn of his livestock* to God as a pleasing offering to the Lord. What? Did Abel go to all that trouble of keeping flocks so he could butcher the animals, cut away the fat off the inner flesh, then throw the meat away to rot

---

[28] "What Really Happened to the Dinosaurs?" YouTube video, 4:13, interview with Ken Ham, posted by "Answers in Genesis," Jun 21, 2014, www.youtube.com/watch?v=7hzLvWlTzLs. Accessed Oct. 1, 2017 and stated at 1:30 mins into video.

[29] Citing parallel themes in three other ancient Near Eastern texts, Westermann states, "The connection of clothing made out of skins with the killing of animals and so with sacrifice can well operate in the ancient pattern which lies behind 3:21, but it plays no role in the present context." Claus Westermann, *Genesis 1-11: A Commentary*, trans. John J. Scullion, S.J. (Minneapolis: Augsburg Publishing, 1984), 270.

in a field? His paralleled brother Cain tilled the soil to produce crops (that the family could subsist on) but Abel spent an enormous amount of time and resources raising flocks that he couldn't eat? The fact that Abel went through the work of separating "fat portions" from the rest of his livestock kill (as opposed to simply sacrificing the entire animal) evinces that the rest of the kill was used for consumption, as was standard in sacrificial practice elsewhere.

3) In Genesis 7:2, God tells Noah to gather "seven pairs of all clean animals" and a single pair of "unclean animals" onto the ark. God's command for Noah to sort the animals according to what is usually dietary language would imply animals were eaten before the Flood.

Given this evidence that humanity was consuming meat after the Fall, why does Gen 9:1-5 seem to go out of the way to declare man's right to eat meat after the Flood? Isn't it strange for God to declare humanity's right to do what, it appears, people like Abel were already doing without any negative judgments from God?

In the past, many scholars have simply concluded that the biblical authors were contradicting each other. I believe Van Ee has found a far more coherent solution. Namely, Genesis 9 is written as it is because it's following a classic Hebraic formula for introducing *prohibitive legislation* in which, "an entire class of animals is designated as proper for food (or as improper) with the following restrictive clause providing the exceptions."[30]

Though it occurs in several contexts,[31] the most obvious uses of this Hebraic formula are Levitical. Leviticus 11 repeats it several times (for example, verses 3-4 and 9-10). It also occurs in parallel passages in Deut 14 in verses 6-7, 9-10, and 11-12. Like Genesis 9, these particular examples give a broad scope of categories of things *already permitted* for consumption, but then immediately follow with prohibited exceptions. Figure 21 illustrates these and other variations of the formula.

---

[30] Van Ee, "Death and the Garden," 245.

[31] Ibid. Van Ee cites the laws of redemption in Lev 27:26, 28 and Num 18:15.

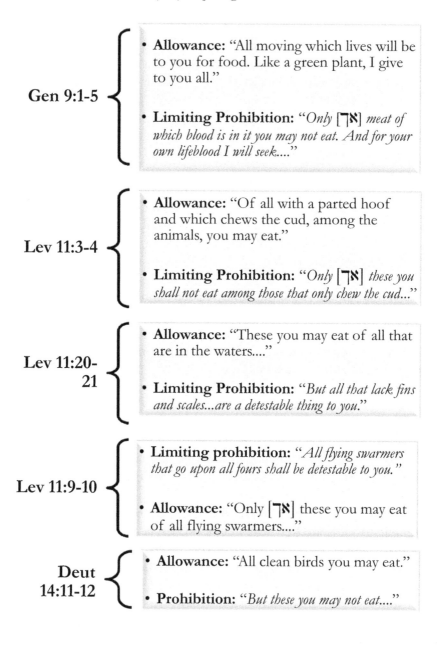

Gen 9:1-5

- **Allowance:** "All moving which lives will be to you for food. Like a green plant, I give to you all."

- **Limiting Prohibition:** *"Only [אך] meat of which blood is in it you may not eat. And for your own lifeblood I will seek...."*

Lev 11:3-4

- **Allowance:** "Of all with a parted hoof and which chews the cud, among the animals, you may eat."

- **Limiting Prohibition:** *"Only [אך] these you shall not eat among those that only chew the cud..."*

Lev 11:20-21

- **Allowance:** "These you may eat of all that are in the waters...."

- **Limiting Prohibition:** *"But all that lack fins and scales...are a detestable thing to you."*

Lev 11:9-10

- **Limiting prohibition:** *"All flying swarmers that go upon all fours shall be detestable to you."*

- **Allowance:** "Only [אך] these you may eat of all flying swarmers...."

Deut 14:11-12

- **Allowance:** "All clean birds you may eat."

- **Prohibition:** *"But these you may not eat...."*

Figure 21. Genesis 9:1-5 in parallel with other Hebrew Prohibitive legislation formulas. Typically, although not always, such formulas introduce a thing already well recognized as permitted for use or consumption before introducing a limiting prohibition with an אך.

Put simply, modern readers have long misread this passage because it follows a conceptual style of literary formulation we don't possess in Western languages. Gen 9:3's affirmation of man's right to eat meat is part of a formal Hebraic device setting up the *immediately following prohibitions* regarding consumption of blood (see Lev 17) and the violence described in the next verse, likely because this sort of disrespect for "lifeblood" (9:4) is what motivated God to flood the earth in the first place.[32]

There is, therefore, no implication that eating meat was previously prohibited. On the contrary, the particular prohibitive formula of this passage assumes that the creation mandate must have originally circumscribed the consumption of meat (in the same way that Israelites were already consuming cattle, birds, or fish before the introduction of the parallel Levitical restrictions). The author's purpose for reiterating this original prerogative is to emphasize the newly introduced exception of consuming blood.

ISAIAH 11:1-9

If, as Van Ee's study concludes, the notion of an original state of vegetarianism is absent in Mesopotamian literature in general[33] and contradicts the evidence in our two Genesis passages above, we have good reason to reconsider from where Isaiah might actually be taking his New Creation imagery about lions eating straw like oxen and wolves reposing with lambs. This part of Van Ee's thesis is the most fascinating because of the tremendous influence these Isaiah texts have historically exerted over our understanding of Genesis.

Going through Isa 11:1-9, note carefully what creatures will be freed from harm when the Messiah comes:

> And a shoot will come from the stump of Jesse...and the wolf will sojourn with the *lamb*, and the leopard with the *young goat* will lie down, and the *calf* and young lion and the *fatted calf* will be together, and a *little child* shall lead them. And the *cow* and the bear will graze

---

[32] This seems circumscribed by the term "violence" in Gen 6:11, given as one of the conditions motivating the flood judgment. Ibid., 246. Later, the Enoch corpus took up the same themes.

[33] This thesis comprises the first half of Van Ee's dissertation.

together, and their young ones will lie down. And the lion will eat straw like the *ox*. And *the suckling child* will play on the den of the asp and the *infant* will put his hand on the adder's den. None will hurt nor destroy in all my holy mountain....

We find here lambs, goats, variations of cattle, children, and infants. Notice all of these creatures in the passage are, "not taken from nature in general but from a specifically human context."[34]

Trinity College archaeologist John J. Bimson, who has specialized in the Bible's ecological theology, agrees:

> The prophet is not concerned with predation among animals as such, but with the danger certain animals pose to human welfare. This is clear from the fact that the animals that enjoy safety from former predators are the lamb, the goat, the calf and the cow—*domesticated* animals that were vital to the ancient Israelite economy.[35]

Isaiah is not saying that a day will come when there will be no hostility between any animals within the animal kingdom. Instead, he is saying there will come a day when predators will no longer plague humans *and their domestic property.*

Throughout the Bible, animal harm upon the human domain is frequently associated with divine cursing. When the children of Israel complained in the desert God cursed them with venomous serpents. Among the blessings and curses God sets before the Israelites in Lev 26, he tells them in verse 22 that if they don't obey him, he will, "send among you the beasts of the field and they will bereave you of your children and destroy your livestock and make you few and your roads will become desolate."

Van Ee also points to passages like Deut 32:24: "[T]he teeth of beasts I will send among them, along with venomous crawlers in the dust."[36] Tellingly, Jeremiah also lists the same animals described by Isaiah in the context of divine curses. In Jer 5:6 we read:

---

[34] Ibid., 300. Footnote citations omitted from quotation.
[35] John J. Bimson, "Reconsidering a 'Cosmic Fall,'" *Science and Christian Belief* 18.2 (2006), 70.
[36] Van Ee, "Death and the Garden," 308.

A lion of the forest shall slay them. A wolf of the desert plains will destroy them. A leopard lies watching upon their cities. All that go out from them will be torn to pieces because their transgressions are many....

After this, Jer 8:17 has God sending venomous snakes. Other examples of animals being used in curse contexts can be found in Job 20:16, 1 Kgs 13:26, Isa 15:9, or Hosea 2:14.

Of course, biblical divine curses usually came with their opposites attached in the form of blessings—provided Israel was obedient. If we go back to examine Leviticus 26 again we find in verse 6 that God says he will reward obedience to his laws by "ridding evil beasts from out of the land." In Psa 91:13, we read that the one who follows Yhwh's commands will "trample the lion and adder." In Job 5:23, Eliphaz speaks of how the righteous will be at "peace" with the "beasts of the field." In Hos 2:18 we read the prophecy: "I will cut a covenant for them on that day with the beasts of the field...."[37]

Considering there is no confirmed Old Testament tradition about original animal peace in Eden (and good biblical reasons to reject such a notion), it is more reasonable to conclude Isaiah is indulging in the same blessing-curse theme between dangerous animals and *the human domain* that we find presented throughout the prophets. All these blessings will be fulfilled when the Messiah comes, and God's people will be in a "covenant" with beasts of the earth.

A final question remains. How literal is Isaiah intending when he says lions will dine on straw like oxen? Does he really mean to say that people will one day lead out wolves, leopards, and bears to pasture with their goats and sheep?

I think the text itself provides evidence of intended hyperbole. These types of oracles of eschatological blessings characteristically employ the device. Amos 9:13 is one example pointed to us by Van Ee.[38] It says in the new creation, "the mountains will drip sweet wine and all the hills

---

[37] Ibid., 312. This passage is located alternately in verse 20 of the Masoretic texts. Andersen and Freedman state, "The beneficiaries are the children, and the pacification of the animals reverses the threat made in v 14, where the wild beasts were likely to eat them.... In Hos 2:20 it is people who are promised safety from the animals...." Francis I. Andersen, David Noel Freedman, *Hosea: A New Translation with Introduction and Commentary* (Doubleday: New York, 1980), 281.

[38] Van Ee, "Death and the Garden," 314.

will flow." Like Amos' stark visual image of wine flooding the hills, Isaiah may simply be taking known eschatological blessings from the Bible and exaggerating them beyond belief as a form of literary emphasis. It's not apparent that his point is literally that God's people will one day keep and farm bears and lions for agriculture.

Last of all, the fact that Isaiah probably isn't reflecting here on a state of original vegetarianism shouldn't be surprising because there are other texts in the Old Testament that praise certain aspects of the violence of the animal kingdom as beautiful. Psalm 104 is the classic example. That creation hymn opens with God stretching out the heavens, laying the foundations of the earth and raising it from the sea. Going through a tour of the created order, we read (v.19-21): "He set the moon for seasons. The sun knows when to go down. You make darkness and it is night, in which all the beasts of the forest creep. The young lions roar for their prey and seek their food from God."

The creation text in Job 38-39 likewise implies that God gives lions their prey and caps-off in 39:27-30 by praising the grandeur of the Middle Eastern griffon vulture: "By your mouth does the vulture mount up on high.... On the rock she dwells.... From there she spies food. From afar behold her eyes! His young ones gulp down blood, and where the fallen are, there he is."

In these passages, at least, the cycle of animal life being sustained by death is viewed as something peculiarly majestic.

ROMANS 8:19-22

Young-earth creationists additionally frequently cite a handful of New Testament verses for their interpretation of animal death as well. Frequently it is claimed that Rom 5:12 demonstrates that animal death would not be compatible with God's good creation ("sin entered the world through one man, and death through sin, and in this way death came to all men because all sinned"). Also, 1 Corinth 15:26 is cited for the same purpose ("The last enemy to be defeated is death"). This interpretation rather blatantly atomizes these two verses from their context and would likely not cross our minds as objections if we treated them properly like sentences pulled from a letter instead of the vague theological dictums we memorized in Sunday school. Both of these passages occur in the context of a long discourse on the introduction of human death brought about through Adam and how Christ's resurrection saves humanity and makes Jesus a second Adam. That is, the "death" they discuss is emphatically addressing humanity. To extend them to animals requires reading into the text what isn't there.

A more credible objection raised by young-earthers derives from Rom 8:19-22. Doesn't Paul here imply that animal death is the result of the Fall? The ESV reads:

> For the creation waits in eager expectation for the children of God to be revealed. For the creation was subjected to frustration, not by its own choice, but by the will of the one who subjected it, *in hope that the creation itself will be liberated from its bondage to decay* and brought into the freedom and glory of the children of God. We know that the whole creation has been groaning as in the pains of childbirth right up to the present time.

Hahne has written a book-length treatment on these few verses as they relate to extra-biblical Jewish literature written around the time of Paul. Sifting through the texts he surveys, I have failed to find any that explicitly links the origin of animal death to Adam's fall.[39] The closest seems to the Babylonian Talmud, Sanhedrin 59b, where several second and third century rabbis are quoted as teaching that Adam was not

---

[39] See Harry Alan Hahne, *The Corruption and Redemption of Creation: Nature in Romans 8.19-22 and Jewish Apocalyptic Literature*. Library of New Testament Studies 336 (New York: T&T Clark, 2006). Josephus' recounting of the Fall at the opening of *Antiquities* mentions nothing of animal death, though he does say that God deprived animals of speech. Jubilees (3:1-35) follows the same idea and focuses on human death. According to Hahne (p. 95), in 2 Enoch, "God did not curse the earth or animals after the fall."

Curiously, 2 Baruch 56:6 and 73:3 speak of Adam bringing "untimely death." The document speaks in broad terms of the corruptibility of creation with a bent towards discussing the human condition. Although it picks up on Isaiah's concept of animals becoming tame towards humans at the eschaton, there seems to be silence as to whether Adam's sin is responsible for the origin of death in the animal kingdom.

This likewise seems to be the case with 4 Ezra, although that text does have animal suffering as a consequence of the natural disasters God brings upon the earth in judgment (5:10-13; 14:17-18). The *Apocalypse of Moses* and *Life of Adam and Eve* do speak of animals changing after the Fall, but not in terms of death. Rather, they suggest that the animals became rebellious towards humanity's authority over them (148).

originally permitted to eat meat (though some of the arguments the Rabbis gave were astonishingly fanciful, perhaps intentionally humorous, beyond what any modern young-earth scholar would approve).[40]

Given that Jewish texts of the period generally omit reference to a state of original animal peace, even though they frequently speak of creation in parlance similar to Romans 8, we lack sufficient warrant for presuming that Romans 8 is making an off-hand allusion to a commonly assumed original state of animal peace.[41]

Contextually, in Romans 8:19-22, it seems Paul has Isaiah 24-27 running in the back of his mind. As Moo has demonstrated, the motifs Paul uses here are nowhere else, "brought together and linked in quite the same way as they are in Isaiah 24–27."[42] In Isaiah 24, we read the following (NASB):

> The earth mourns and withers, the world fades and withers…. The earth is also polluted by its inhabitants, for they transgressed laws, violated statutes, broke the everlasting covenant. Therefore, a curse devours the earth, and those who live in it are held guilty…. The new wine mourns. The vine decays. All the merry-hearted sigh. The windows above are opened, and the foundations of the earth shake.

---

[40] For example, in examining the creation mandate in Genesis 1, I posed the question, "What does it look like to rule over a fish? Is Adam going to have a dolphin plow his field?" The Talmud notices the same problem and takes that objection to the chin: *Yes*, one could pull a wagon by harnessing a fish and goat to it (59b). In the case of birds, the Talmud proposes that one could use them to help thresh grain. The section then immediately launches into a legend claiming before the Fall snakes had legs and could be used as beasts of burden like mules (their explanation of Adam's original command to rule the "animals which creep upon the earth").

[41] Here, the Pauline scholar George Carraway (Assistant Professor of Religion at Westminster, South Carolina) assures me (personal email correspondence, Jan 8, 2018):

> [I]n my estimation, there is nothing in Romans 8:18-22 to address your issue of animal peace, predation or vegetarianism. I don't believe a positive answer to the question…should be forthcoming from the passage. For Paul to make a point about animal peace at that point would be far removed from his point in Romans, and I see nothing in the passage to suggest he had anything like that in mind.

[42] Jonathan Moo, "Romans 8.19–22 and Isaiah's Cosmic Covenant," *New Testament Studies* 54.1 (2008), 84.

The earth is broken asunder. The earth is split through. The earth is shaken violently. The earth reels to and fro like a drunkard, and it totters like a shack. For its transgression is heavy upon it, and it will fall, never to rise again.[43]

We clearly see strong parallels here to Paul's language. Following this, in Isa 26:9, we read of how the righteous "yearn" for God and "eagerly seek" for God's judgment. Despite this, at present, the righteous suffer, "like a pregnant woman close to delivery cries out in her pangs" (v.17). This is strikingly parallel to Paul's language of anticipation and his birth pang analogy. Like Paul, Isaiah then immediately describes how God's people will rise from the dust, and "the earth will disclose the blood shed on it, and will no more cover its slain" (v. 21). This is the "swallowing up of death" mentioned in 25:8.

In addition to these conceptual parallels, Romans 8 also includes at least two verbal parallels that seem to put the association between these two passages beyond question:[44]

1) Paul says the creation is "in bondage to decay." The Greek translation of Isa 24:3 uses this same Greek word translated "decay" when it says that, "the earth mourns, and *withers*."

2) The Greek version of Isa 24:7 speaks of the vine mourning and follows that immediately with a rather striking statement about the merry-hearted sighing or groaning. This word, translated "sigh" or "groan," is the same uncommon term Paul uses for the "groaning" of creation.

Therefore, Paul's language of creation being in "bondage to decay" likely has its referent in Isaiah 24, and the content of the Isaiah passage doesn't circumscribe a state of original animal peace, but things like the ground, fruit vine, and God's bringing forth natural and other judgments—linking well with the curses enumerated in Genesis 3.

The distinguished historian of theology Gijsbert van den Brink at Leiden University agrees:

---

[43] I have made necessary grammatical emendations to the NASB here without bracketing them for the sake of reformatting the original poetry layout.

[44] I derive the following from Moo, "Romans 8.19-22," 85.

The reference in these texts is to the flora ("thorns and thistles," etc.) rather than to the animal world. Where the animal world is involved, such as in Gen 3:14 and in the eschatological passages like Isa 11:6-9 and 65:25, there is no indication that the suffering, death and extinction of animals in the present dispensation is seen as the result of human sin…. When we apply such texts to the animal world as well, it seems that we are extending their meaning beyond what they intend to say within their original context.[45]

To suppose Romans 8:19-22 circumscribes a presumed lost state of peace among animals seems to exceed the textual data of that passage and its most probable referent.

CONCLUSION

I understand how controversial these conclusions and their implications are because many in the church have been theologizing for centuries off the assumption that animal death is a perversion of the created order caused by Adam's sin. Modern readers come to Genesis thinking we know what Paradise should be, but we need to exercise great discipline in limiting our interpretation in accord with the Near Eastern data, especially to safeguard against imposing traditions onto the text.

When we examine Genesis 1 and 9, and Isaiah 11 with care, we find they do not suggest that creation was originally vegetarian and free of death. Considering the almost unavoidable conclusion that Paul is reflecting in Romans 8 on Isaiah 24-27, the idea that Romans 8 may be alluding to a state of original vegetarianism seems similarly doubtful. Besides this, even humanity was created mortal by default (in the sense that they required access to the Tree of Life to stave off death).

Regardless of how theologians choose to sort out the implications of the exegesis, I would suggest at least one religious benefit to the view I have presented. If Jews or Christians believe humans were designed by God to work in a blissful garden paradise devoid of any suffering, violence, or encounter with animal death, they will tend to view

---

[45] Gijsbert van den Brink, "God and the Suffering of Animals," in Koert van Bekkum, et al. (eds.) *Playing with Leviathan: Interpretation and Reception of Monsters from the Biblical World.* Themes in Biblical Narrative 21 (Netherlands: Brill, 2017), 189-190.

themselves as a creature designed for a soft, docile world. On the other hand, if one believes the biblical God designed human beings to serve as conquering warriors to face a world that included a degree of hostility and violence from the start, then the implication is that humanity possesses strength for handling the world's monsters, a strength not born from a place of sin or a perversion of human nature, but indigenous to it.[46]

As antagonistic as this chapter may seem towards some young-earthers, one need not necessarily abandon their young-earth views at all to agree with its argument. I suspect that many YECs secretly or openly find the original vegetarian doctrine to be a nuisance. If you are convinced that the earth is within 10,000 years old, and I'm unable to convince you otherwise, it is still worth knowing that you aren't biblically compelled also to believe that Tyrannosaurus originally used his nine-inch long, serrated teeth, set in a jaw capable of exerting some 8,000 of pounds of force,[47] to eat melons.

---

[46] The modern psychological data best seems to comport with this view of human nature. George A. Bonanno, "Loss, Trauma, and Human Resilience: Have We Underestimated the Human Capacity to Thrive After Extremely Aversive Events?" *American Psychologist* 59.1 (2004), 20-28.

[47] Nell Greenfieldboyce, "Tyrannosaurus Rex's Bite Force Measured 8,000 Pounds, Scientists Say," *NPR*, May 17, 2017. Accessed, Sept 18, 2017, www.npr.org/sections/thetwo-way/2017/05/17/528677883/tyrannosaurus-rexs-bite-force-measured-8-000-pounds-scientists-say.

SECTION III

A Path Forward

CHAPTER 12

WHY THE HOLY SPIRIT ISN'T YOUR BIBLE COMMENTARY

I THINK it is fair to say that many, if not most, young-earth creationists strongly oppose the way that I have been arguing from ancient Near Eastern contextual material at many points in this book.

In an *Answers* article, the popular young-earth scholar Dr. Terry Mortenson warns Christians against scholars who claim that specialized technical knowledge is necessary to understand major elements of biblical scripture. Mortenson particularly calls out John Walton, Professor of Old Testament at Wheaton College. Walton has conducted research comparing ancient Near Eastern creation myths to Genesis 1 and has concluded that there are some key ways in which our modern (and often Western) cultural assumptions have been disposing us to misread parts of the biblical creation story for centuries.

If I understand Mortenson fairly, he believes it is theologically unacceptable to claim that God would have inspired the human authors of scripture in such a way that modern archaeological or linguistic discoveries about the ancient world would be necessary to recognize major themes in the Bible's creation account. He says that scholars like Walton are becoming equivalent to evangelical "popes": "The implication is 'you can't understand the Bible on your own, so let the scholarly experts explain it to you.'"[1]

---

[1] Terry Mortenson, "Evangelical Popes," *Answers Magazine*, Apr 1, 2012. Accessed Jun 2017, www.answersingenesis.org/christianity/evangelical-popes/. For this reference, I am indebted to Susan L. Trollinger and William Vance Trollinger, Jr. *Righting America at the Creation Museum* (Baltimore: John Hopkins University Press, 2016), 133.

Ken Ham also fears that Walton has become one among many "Protestant popes" and quotes 1 Corinthians 8:1 with its caution against "knowledge [that] puffs up."[2] Suspecting that Walton is really motivated by a desire to make the Bible palatable to modern science, he writes:

> Walton believes that a person needs to understand ancient Near-Eastern thinking and culture in order to understand Scripture. He argues that such an understanding has been lost for ages, but that academics like himself have been able to regain an understanding of this ancient Near Eastern thinking so the rest of us in the church can finally (after thousands of years) understand what Genesis 1 means.[3]

Another Answers in Genesis article by Simon Turpin expresses similar disapproval: "These scholars come to the biblical account, read all the ostensible associated ANE creation parallels, and then interpret the passage in light of the parallels…thereby reading the parallels into the text. Evangelical scholars, such as Lamoureux and Longman, are guilty of reading Genesis in light of ANE texts."[4] As a final example, Steve Ham writes: "If our interpretation of the historical setting of the ancient Near East is required for determining biblical meaning, we are placing authoritative weight on an external source rather than in the very inspiration of Scripture."[5]

These writers believe their God wouldn't place information necessary to understand important themes of the Bible in some "external source" outside of it, especially when a majority of believing saints in the past had little or no access to that source. They ask, what would be the point of God inspiring things that only the original audience and Christians living after the archaeological discoveries of the twentieth century would be able to understand?

---

[2] Ken Ham, "*The Genesis Flood*—The Battle Still Rages!," n.p., *Ken Ham Blog*, Feb 20, 2011. Accessed Jun 2017, www.answersingenesis.org/blogs/ken-ham/2011/02/20/the-genesis-flood-the-battle-still-rages/.

[3] Ibid, n.p.

[4] Simon Turpin, "The Creation of Adam: Unique Revelation or Ancient Myth?" *Answers in Depth* vol 12 (2017). Accessed Jun 23, 2017, www.answersingenesis.org/genesis/creation-adam-unique-revelation-or-ancient-myth/.

[5] Steve Ham, "Is the Meaning of Genesis Lost in the Ancient Near East?" *Answers in Genesis*, Aug 2015. Accessed Jun 2017, www.answersingenesis.org/the-word-of-god/genesis-in-ancient-near-east/.

As attractive as these comments may sound to the democratic spirit of our age, I would advise treading with careful humility because the stakes are high. If these young-earth writers are wrong, then adopting their stance would result in the inclination to reject an emerging wealth of discoveries about the Bible's fuller meaning that has been privileged to modern readers. Consequently, failing to integrate these gifts of modern archaeology and linguistics would, and I believe has, stagnated the religious in many disproven interpretive traditions.

Second, the biggest problem I perceive with their argument is that it treats a monstrously complex issue as if it is simple and self-evident. I don't buy their presumed authority on the matter. How do Ham, Mortenson, and Turpin claim to know that the God of the universe wouldn't reserve the accurate interpretation of important parts of sacred texts to the work of trained scholars living after the discovery of some modern archaeological sources? Do they claim to understand the complexities of God's intentions in history in this specified regard?

Perhaps God enjoys the antique depths of his words unfolding in higher resolutions of clarity throughout history. Isn't this a major internal theme within the pages of the Bible itself and the substance of its epic beauty—the Israelite sacrificial system, prophecy, the centuries of unfolding typology of the Messiah, the whole book of Revelation? Doesn't the New Testament claim centuries of Jewish sages failed to grasp or only dimly comprehended important passages alluding to the incarnation until its occurrence in history? Perhaps God might have had good reasons for delaying the discovery of the Dead Sea Scrolls only until the twentieth century, or the translation of the Rosetta stone—the key which only unlocked Egyptian hieroglyphs in the nineteenth century.

And why should anyone expect God to make Bible interpretation fully or easily accessible to current, English lay readers when the New Testament was originally delivered to the overwhelmingly illiterate people of the Roman Empire—wasn't their interpretation of the Bible highly dependent on the few educated elites among them? Wasn't their scriptural access severely limited by the incomplete access their particular churches had to the forming New Testament canon for centuries?[6] And why should it matter that a majority of the devout until

---

[6] In addition to bringing up the point that, "all the NT cultures were by and large oral cultures, not cultures of texts," Ben Witherington has remarked, "One of the things I find most troubling as a historian about the usual debates about the

now have not had access to the modern archaeological discoveries that scholars like Walton use? The children of Israel didn't have access to the theology of the New Testament or the gospels *across the entire span of Old Testament history*. Would these young-earth authors fault God for this apparently unfair decision? Even then, for most centuries of Christian history, the average Christian didn't even have access to a personal Bible in their own language (books were not cheap before the emergence of printing). One might likewise suppose that God wouldn't see it as necessary to grant the ancients certain information available to modern readers because they faced different struggles or needs than we do at present.

The claim that the Bible is divinely revealed in such a way that all of its significant themes and passages have been accessible to all believers of all ages is logically absurd and historically easily falsified.

But let us consider Ham, Mortenson, and Turpin's claim in a more concrete fashion because it is not unique to them, but is a popular idea among Christians. Do we indeed sometimes require scholarly experts like Walton or Longman to set us straight? Is it sometimes necessary to have specified knowledge in the Bible's ancient Near Eastern context to understand its major themes?

THE HOLY SPIRIT AND INTERPRETATION

I have found that perhaps most Christians have been taught that the Holy Spirit's role is to function for them as their Bible commentary. Many therefore conclude that it is unnecessary to consult scholars—because the Holy Spirit is their interpreter. This is undoubtedly a core belief among most young-earth traditionalists that minimize the necessity of the Bible's Near Eastern context for understanding its meaning. But is it even justified by the texts of the Bible itself?

What follows is a discussion of what I believe Paul, in part, actually believed about the Holy Spirit's role in interpreting the Bible. However,

---

inerrancy of the Bible in evangelical circles is that it is an *ex post facto* debate. What I mean by this is that it is a debate about something that did not really exist as a collection before the fourth century AD— namely, the 27-book canon of the NT." Ben Witherington III, "The Truth Will Win Out: An Historian's Perspective on the Inerrancy Controversy," *Journal of the Evangelical Theological* Society 51.1 (2014), 22-3.

first I must clarify what I mean by "meaning." By the "meaning" of a text, I am referring to, "The paradigm or principle that the author consciously willed to convey by the sharable symbols he or she used."[7] In other words, we have interpreted a text accurately when we have understood what thoughts its author was *intending* to convey into the minds of his readers through the words ("shareable symbols") he wrote down. The paradigms and principles an author consciously intends to convey into the minds of others when he writes something can't be changed. The author's intended meaning is frozen in the amber of history. However, this is not to deny that the *implications* of the author's meaning cannot change.

For example, the command to "love my neighbor" is a concept with a fixed, particular *meaning*, but what it *implies* about how I should conduct myself in the fluctuating circumstances of my life can change. Or consider Paul's warnings against drunkenness. Although Paul never condemns the use of destructive drugs that were unknown to him like meth or cocaine, it would be absurd to claim that his teachings on the dangers of drunkenness have no implications that apply to the use of these other drugs. (This is why, by the way, those who claim ancient texts are ethically irrelevant in our modern age are wrong. The fact that the Bible doesn't discuss the ethics of internet usage, nuclear weapons, or genetic manipulation doesn't mean it cannot comment on the core moral implications of such topics.)

So the meaning of a text is to be defined as the thoughts an author *intended* to convey with their words into their reader's minds, and the implications of a text have to do with how one properly applies those communicated thoughts. With this in mind, we can return to our original question: what did Paul believe the Holy Spirit's role is in interpreting a biblical passage's meaning and therefore, of a correct understanding of its implications?

---

[7] Robert H. Stein, "The Benefits of an Author-Oriented Approach to Hermeneutics," *Journal of the Evangelical Theological Society* 44.3 (2001), 457. On the author as determiner of meaning see also, Eric J. Douglass, *Reading the Bible Ethically: Recovering the Voice in the Text*. Biblical Interpretation Series 133 (Leiden: Brill, 2014). Unlike some exegetes, I affirm that the New Testament authors do not always take a historical-grammatical hermeneutic of the Old Testament, but I have narrowed my focus here to that aspect of the text for the sake of simplicity.

1 CORINTHIANS 2:14

Historically, a critical place where this argument over the Holy Spirit's role in interpretation has taken place is 1 Cor 2:14:

> But the natural man does not accept the things of the Spirit of God; for they are foolishness to him, and he is not able to know them, because they are spiritually appraised.

I think it's clear and undisputed that Paul believed the Holy Spirit certainly helps Christians apply the *implications* of a scripture's meaning to their lives—that without him, a person could not even come to embrace the Christ. However, if you are like me, you grew up hearing this passage interpreted to mean that a person can't even intellectually comprehend the *meaning* of scripture without being indwelt by the Holy Spirit.

I believe conservative seminary textbook authors are correct in rejecting this view.

To begin with, there are several Greek words Paul could have used in 1 Cor 2:14 when he says the natural man doesn't "accept" the things of God. Instead of the common term *lambano*—which broadly and generically means "to take" in any number of senses, Paul used the word *dechomai*. As a leading Greek dictionary clarifies, *dechomai* is a precise term that implies the acceptance of a requested offering.[8] In other words, the natural man doesn't just fail to receive the things of the Spirit of God because he can't intellectually comprehend the offer of them. The connotation of the Greek term is that he intellectually *does* receive the offer, but chooses to reject it.

Second, as Robert Stein, Professor of New Testament Interpretation at Southern Seminary, points out, the term translated "foolishness" in the above verse is also used again by Paul in the very next chapter. Does this term refer to something being *incomprehensible* in that context? In 1 Cor 3:19 we read, "For the wisdom of this world is *foolishness* with God."

---

[8] Kittle notes this "distinction from the common → λαμβανειν" in that "the verb thus expresses the 'reaction to action on the other side.'" See "Δεχομαι" in Kittle and Bromiley, eds., *Theological Dictionary of the New Testament*, vol. II (Grand Rapids: Eerdmans, 1999), 50.

Obviously, God intellectually comprehends the presumed wisdom of the world, but the reason that God rejects it as foolishness is that he doesn't *accept* it as true.[9] For these reasons, 1 Cor 2:14 is implying that a non-believer *is* able intellectually to *comprehend* what the Bible is talking about, but that he is incapable of willingly *accepting* its teachings into his life without the Holy Spirit.

When Paul says the unbeliever "is not able to know" the "things of the Spirit of God," because "they are spiritually appraised," he is saying the unbeliever cannot *embrace* them and come to an *experiential knowledge* of such things. He needs the Holy Spirit to appreciate their value. Paul isn't saying that scripture is unintelligible babble to non-believers. Rather, as Larkin notes, non-believers in this passage *are* capable of mentally comprehending scripture, and it is this very capacity that causes them to *dislike* what it says, to consciously *reject* its message.[10] In order consciously to reject the content of a message, you must first be able to comprehend its content.

This interpretation of 1 Cor 2:14 accords with common sense. Most Christians know someone who could give an accurate intellectual explanation of major features of Christian doctrine or the gospel even though they reject them. If non-Christians can't *understand* the Bible, then it would be impossible for religious Jews or agnostic scholars to engage in Bible translation or to write technical commentaries. Yet, in reality, they sometimes produce some of the finest work in the field. For example, I have found that the Jewish scholar Robert Alter has produced what may be the best translation of the Book of Genesis in the English language. The evangelical scholar Grant Osborne concludes in his massive classic work, *The Hermeneutical Spiral*: "[T]he Bible does not state that the unbeliever cannot intellectually interpret it quite accurately."[11]

So, in 1 Cor 2:14, Paul is *not* claiming that it is the Holy Spirit's usual role to teach people the *meaning* of a given text. Rather, the claim is that the Holy Spirit helps believers to accept the text's meaning as true, and to apply its implications to their lives. A biblical scholar antagonistic to

---

[9] See discussion in Robert H. Stein, *A Basic Guide to Interpreting the Bible: Playing by the Rules*, 2 ed. (Baker Academic: Grand Rapids, 2011), 66.

[10] William J. Larkin Jr., *Culture and Biblical Hermeneutics: Interpreting and Applying the Authoritative Word in a Relativistic Age* (Grand Rapids: Baker, 1988), 289.

[11] Grant R. Osborne, *The Hermeneutical Spiral: A Comprehensive Introduction to Biblical Interpretation*, 2 ed. (Downers Grove: InterVarsity Press, 2006), 341.

Christianity like the best-selling skeptic Bart Ehrman can certainly interpret and articulate Paul's teachings about the gospel without the Holy Spirit's supernatural aid, but Paul would probably say someone like Ehrman is not capable of embracing this gospel and living it out without supernatural aid.

Consider this practically: How convincing would my interpretations be to you if I ditched Greek word study and simply asserted in an airy voice that I felt God told me 'in my heart' that my interpretations are correct? What if someone else claimed that they had a Holy Spirit-inspired feeling that I was wrong? If a Jehovah's Witness claims the Spirit impressed on his heart (whatever that means) that the grammar of John 1:1 doesn't say Jesus "was God" and someone else objects, on the same grounds, that it says the opposite: how can the stalemate be broken?

In order for the church to sort out interpretive disputes, it has to be able to appeal to objective things like Greek and Hebrew grammar, lexical study, historical analysis, and ancient manuscript analysis. The implication is clear. Creationists should come to recognize that their biblical scholars serve a unique role in the body of their church. Christians have a biblically internal moral obligation not to eclipse or disparage the unique role of their scholars (for example, by replacing them with material scientists, philosophers, or pastors), even as the church maintains a healthy skepticism of scholars and critiques their arguments.

Baptizing Laziness

Most of the Bible is certainly simple enough for even a casual reader to understand. Human nature is so uniform that, provided we have a decent translation, even the alien culture of the biblical authors shares enough with ours for us to understand most of what we read. But, to fully understand it, some portions of the Bible do require homework.

Using the Holy Spirit as an excuse for academic laziness in Bible study isn't going to help someone understand what the Hebrew words "subdue" and "rule" mean, why the wheels in Ezekiel's vision were covered in eyeballs, or what on earth Peter is getting at when he says in 1 Peter 3 that Jesus "preached to the spirits in prison" after his crucifixion. It won't help a person uncover why Paul says women should wear head coverings "because of the angels" in 1 Cor. 11:10, or what the "baptism of the dead" is in 1 Cor. 15:29. That method won't reveal to you why Moses' wife in Exodus 4 saved Moses' life from the wrath of God by touching Moses' feet with his son's freshly severed foreskin and pronouncing him a "bridegroom of blood." People can pray for God supernaturally to reveal to them the meaning of these passages all they want. However, biblically and practically speaking, the granting of this request would seem to constitute a miraculous exception in Paul's mind to the Holy Spirit's usual role, and it is, therefore, foolish to depend on it as one's standard operating interpretive method.

Unspiritual?

I claim the opposite. Expecting God supernaturally to drop the Greek clause structure of a passage into your lap without having to study some Greek is not far off from expecting God supernaturally to give you money, a healthy marriage, or a good school exam grade without having to do the work that corresponds with them. If someone told you they are too holy to study for their college linguistic, history, or anthropology exams and instead insisted that they are just going to pray for the Holy Spirit to show them the answers on the test, you wouldn't applaud them. Why do we praise people for treating Bible study this way?

The same goes for John 16:13, which 3:00 AM televangelists sometimes like to invoke when they are peddling slick theology. When John has Jesus telling the disciples in that verse, "The Holy Spirit will guide you in all the truth," the context refers to the disciples applying the memory of Christ's teachings for the establishment of the church. As the New Testament linguist Urban von Wahlde comments, when we look at the Greek grammar in that verse, the "reading favored by scholars would not assert that the Spirit will teach them all truth, but that his teaching will be 'in all the truth,' i.e. will stand completely in the truth."[12] It is not legitimate to deduce from passages like this that the

---

[12] Urban C. von Wahlde, *The Gospel and Letters of John*, vol 2 (Grand Rapids: Eerdmans, 2010), 608.
On a different level of analysis, O'Day's commentary adds that the "verb...points to the teaching role the Paraclete will have in the future life of the faith community. Its combination with 'truth' is a direct echo of 14:6, 'I am the way, and the truth, and the life,' and thus specifies the content of the Paraclete's

Holy Spirit gives you immediate supernatural access—without study of specialized resources—to all the technical information or theological knowledge you want concerning the Bible. Nor does it suggest that everything in the Bible can be understood given our present state of knowledge.

There is also a second observation that is relevant here: Christians often assume that pastors or theologians who are especially virtuous will, as a result of their godliness, be excellent sources for interpreting passages that are culturally or linguistically abstruse.

How should we understand Genesis 1:1? Let's consult Thomas Aquinas. What are the gods mentioned in Psalm 82? A man as intimate with the Holy Spirit as John Calvin must know. Why does God speak in the plural when he says, "Let us make man in our image?" If anyone has figured it out, surely a holy man like Luther would know!

Of course, I've chosen these examples because they are all cases where we can prove these men got these wrong, not through some moral fault or spiritual deficiency, but due to lack of grammatical and archaeological data only discovered after the twentieth century.

The golden age of biblical interpretation wasn't with the patristic fathers. It wasn't with Augustine. It wasn't with Calvin, Luther, the Puritans, or the founding of your denomination. At the opening of the nineteenth century, no one on earth could read Egyptian hieroglyphs. The great Mesopotamian libraries, like the vast majority of the over 130,000 cuneiform tablets currently sitting in the British Museum basement (of which only a fraction have even yet been translated) remained buried in the desert until the middle of that century.

Our iconographic data was next to nothing. George Smith had yet to translate and publish the Babylonian creation epic until 1876. It would be decades before the French began excavating the library at Ugarit or we gained our associated intimate knowledge of Baal-worship—the primary religion the Bible polemicizes against. The Dead Sea Scrolls wouldn't be discovered until the end of WWII, and, contrary to what your Sunday school teacher may have told you, the Dead Sea Scrolls

---

teaching. To say that the Paraclete will guide the disciples into all the truth is to say that in the future the Paraclete will lead the community into the life-giving revelation of God in Jesus." Gail R. O'Day, "The Gospel of John: Introduction, Commentary, and Reflections," in Leander E Keck (ed.), *The New Interpreter's Bible*, vol 9 (Nashville: Abingdon Press, 1995), 773.

didn't match perfectly with the 1,000 year later medieval manuscripts Old Testament translators had been using, particularly in books like Job and Jeremiah. They also granted us unprecedented access to some extra-canonical texts invaluable to the world of New Testament scholarship.

It was only recently that high resolution and infrared images of the Dead Sea Scrolls have been made available worldwide to anyone with an internet connection, or the same has been done with thousands of ancient New Testament texts by the Center for the Study of New Testament Manuscripts. Using computerized linguistic databases, modern biblical scholars can even run syntax searches across the entire body of biblical and other ancient texts that would take years for someone before the nineteenth century to conduct by hand with pen and paper.

The golden age of Biblical interpretation is now.

I am not saying that we shouldn't study church and rabbinic history and try to gain perspective in our interpretations from the 'democracy of the dead.' We have much to learn from ancient scholars. I am merely pointing out that they didn't have access to the *hundreds of thousands* of lines of contextual material for the Bible that have been discovered by modern archaeology, and Christians shouldn't assume God would have been obligated to supernaturally zap that information into their spiritual forebears' heads because Paul implies that's not his usual role. Moral virtue is not necessarily correlated with the ability to conduct a historical-linguistic analysis of Iron Age West Semitic religion and culture, and when it comes to Bible passages that are technically difficult, pastoral commentaries generally tend to be among the poorest resources.

CONCLUSION

Do you need ancient Near Eastern history, stout commentaries by linguists, lexicons, journal articles, and other contextual resources to understand Genesis? In many places, the answer is *yes*. Contrary to what is often claimed in the name of the doctrine of the "perspicuity of Scripture" (which chiefly pertains to issues concerning salvation), the belief that God inspired the Bible knowing people in the twenty-first century would use it does not logically imply that all its content should be expected to be non-obscure to people in the twenty-first century. It also doesn't mean that the interpretation that seems most obvious to twenty-first century Westerners on what they consider a "common sense" reading will therefore always be the correct one. We can prove with modern advancements in linguistics and archaeology that Jewish and Christian sages have sometimes misunderstood important parts of the Bible for centuries.

To be sure, most of the Bible is plain enough to understand, just as much as any other classic ancient text, but occasionally we need to have the humility to defer to scholars who have invested significant portions of their lives into understanding its context. We owe it to them to make use of their hard-earned contributions rather than citing the Holy Spirit as an excuse to sacralize our laziness and trivialize the significance of their role. If we want our theology to be accurately informed by the biblical world, then:

> Neither piety nor speculation—both of which are excellent in their own ways when properly controlled—can substitute for careful historical and exegetical investigation. Nor can traditional views of either the right or left be allowed to stand unscrutinized in the light of recent discoveries.[13]

---

[13] Richard Longenecker, *Biblical Exegesis in the Apostolic Period*, 2 ed. (Grand Rapids: Eerdmans, 1999), 185-86. I owe this citation to Peter Enns, "A Christotelic Approach to the New Testament Use of the Old in Its First-Century Interpretive Environment" in Stanley N. Gundry, Kenneth Berding, Jonathan Lunde (eds.), *Three Views on the New Testament Use of the Old Testament* (Grand Rapids: Zondervan, 2008), 172.

CHAPTER 13

HOW POPULAR VIEWS OF INSPIRATION PROTECT READERS FROM THEIR BIBLE

T HE relationship between the Bible and science has featured so prominently in this book that it is appropriate in this last chapter to draw together some concluding thoughts on the subject in the interest of my undoubted majority of Christian readers. I'm not a theologian, either formally or temperamentally. However, as a textual analyst, I offer a modest observation that I believe religious articulations of divine inspiration must account for if they are to match what we observe in the Bible itself. How theologians wish to integrate this fact is their task, and frankly, this is a circumstance where Christians could stand to learn from modern Judaism.

Namely, if the Bible is inspired, it is inescapable from studying it that any belief in its inspiration must account for God sometimes incorporating the false ancient cultural beliefs of its authors into the texts (a view historically termed "divine accommodationism" by theologians).[1]

THE APOSTLE PAUL'S AMBULATING BOULDER

Consider the following example: In his book, *The Bible Tells Me So*, the Old Testament scholar Peter Enns recounts a story from when he was conducting his doctoral studies at Harvard.[2]

---

[1] Wayne Grudem, *Systematic Theology: An Introduction to Biblical Doctrine* (Grand Rapids: Zondervan, 1994), 97.

[2] See following citations. Peter Enns' technical article exegeting the following is entitled: "The 'Movable Well' in 1 Cor 10:14: An Extrabiblical Tradition in an Apostolic Text," *Bulletin for Biblical Research* 6 (1996), 23-38.

To help pay the bills, Enns took a job as an assistant to a Jewish professor teaching an undergraduate course in how Jews interpreted the Bible in the centuries before Christ. One day in class, the professor came upon the familiar biblical story of how the Hebrews wandered forty years in the desert. If you remember, the homeless children of Israel were threatened by starvation and dying of thirst. To solve the starvation problem God sent them quail and manna. To solve their thirst problem, we read that Moses struck a rock with his staff and God miraculously sent water gushing out at a place called Rephidim. Later in the story, we read that Moses did this same thing again *forty years later* in a different location called Kadesh. So, the Hebrews acquired water from a rock at the start of their journey and again from a rock at the end of their forty years of wandering. But what did they drink in the decades between? The Bible doesn't answer that question. However, this didn't stop ancient Jews from reading in solutions between the lines.

Enns writes:

> And here is where things get bizarre.... Some creative, ancient Jewish interpreters came up with the perfectly insane idea that the rock at the beginning and the rock at the end were actually *one and the same rock*. "How can that be?" (asks any normal person). "Simple" (say these ancient Jewish interpreters of the Bible): that one rock had "obviously" been *following the Israelites around in the desert for forty years*, sort of like a movable drinking fountain.[3]

There's your answer: a supernaturally ambulating water fountain boulder tagging along with the Hebrews as they trekked around in the Sanai Peninsula for four decades![4] Enns recounts how ridiculous he found this early Rabbinic solution.

Then the unthinkable happened.

The professor with whom Enns was working had the class flip in their Bibles to 1 Corinthians 10 where Paul is recounting this same story of

---

[3] Peter Enns, *The Bible Tells Me So: Why Defending Scripture has Made Us Unable to Read It* (New York: HarperOne, 2014), 16-17.

[4] See Enns ("The 'Movable Well,'" 23-38) for the early texts maintaining this. Three he cites are *Pseudo-Philo's Book of Biblical Antiquities* 10:7; 11:15; 20:8, *Tosephta Sukka* 3.11, and *Targum Onqelos to Num* 21:16-20.

the wilderness wanderings. In this passage, Paul talks about how the children of Israel passed through the sea with Moses, how they followed God's cloud and were fed with manna. He recounts how God became angry and killed many of them in the wilderness—likening these things to the life of a Christian. Then, in the fourth verse, come these words: "For they drank from the spiritual *following rock*, and the rock was Christ."

The "*following rock*." These words left Enns in shock:

> Why was this moment so significant and unsettling for me? These early Jewish interpreters were interesting to read about, maybe even a little entertaining, like when they talked about a movable water-producing rock. But Paul?! No, not Paul!! He's a Christian. He's on *our side*. He is speaking for God and so he's not supposed to say stupid things like rocks follow people around in the desert to give them drink.
>
> I had met Paul for the first time, it seemed, and it struck me that this Paul probably wouldn't be allowed to teach biblical interpretation at the seminary that first introduced me to Paul.[5]

In the context of reflecting on all these other understood historical events, Paul just assumes and indirectly affirms on canonical record, some idea about the Israelite wanderings that probably did not happen. For good measure, it even turns out that he's tied this crazy reference to a direct analogy about his Lord and Savior Jesus.

Should churches start compelling their members to believe the rock story is literal history? Should people be accused of being snooty theological liberals for doubting it? Does doubting the literalness of the boulder story logically discredit Paul's associated point that Christ saves his people? If not, this passage suggests that any articulation of inspiration must be capable of accommodating false cultural ideas to express a greater main point (after all, it is written *to* that culture by those *within* that culture).

Are there other cases where we can observe Paul behaving in a similar manner—particularly in the scientific realm? I believe there is, and it's in one of the oddest passages in the entire New Testament—Paul's teachings on head coverings.

---

[5] Enns, *The Bible Tells Me So*, 17.

HEAD COVERINGS: A CASE STUDY IN THE STRANGE

I bring up head coverings in a book about creationism because it's an excellent case study demonstrating how articulations of the inspiration of the New Testament need to be held to account for how the Bible interfaces with its cultural context.

Thanks to three articles to which Michael Heiser points us in the *Journal of Biblical Literature*, I believe we now know why Paul expected women to cover their hair during worship in 1 Corinthians 11.[6]

Greek medical and biological texts like Hippocrates and Aristotle, Greek plays, and other ancient literary works imply female hair was considered a sexual organ.

Unfortunately, for me to explain why they thought this will require getting a bit PG-13 (in a book about the Bible where I've already pressed my luck with half a chapter dedicated to Behemoth's reproductive anatomy). So I will attempt to tackle the subject with the academic solemnity of a veteran gynecologist.

In short, as the Pauline scholar Christopher Mount says, "a woman's long hair, [was] conceived as part of the female genitalia in ancient biological theory."[7] More specifically, the ancient Greeks believed the tissues of women's internal bodies were especially "rarefied" [ἀραιόν] and "porous" [χαυνον]—absorbent to fluid (Hippocrates, *On Glands* 16). Head hair was thought hollow and enhanced the vacuum that tended to attract fluid upwards into the body.[8] For this reason, Greek medical experts maintained that a woman with long hair could better draw a

---

[6] See Michael S. Heiser, "Naked Bible 86: The Head Covering of 1 Corinthians 11:13-15," *The Naked Bible Podcast*, Feb 7, 2016. www.nakedbiblepodcast.com/naked-bible-86-the-head-covering-of-1-corinthians-1113-15/. These articles are: Troy W. Martin, "Paul's Argument from Nature for the Veil in 1 Corinthians 11:13—A Testicle Instead of a Head Covering," *Journal of Biblical Literature* 123.1 (2004), 75–84; Mark Goodacre, "Does περιβόλαιον Mean 'Testicle' in 1 Corinthians 11:15?" *JBL* 130 (2011), 391-96; and Troy Martin, "Περιβόλαιον as 'Testicle' in 1 Corinthians 11:15: A Response to Mark Goodacre," *JBL* 132.2 (2013), 453-465.
[7] Christopher Mount, "1 Corinthians 11:3-16: Spirit Possession and Authority in a Non-Pauline Interpolation," *Journal of Biblical Literature*, 124.2 (2005), 333.
[8] Martin, "Paul's Argument from Nature," 77 (citing Hippocrates, *On the Nature of Children* 20).

man's seed upwards into her womb where it might congeal and form a fetus.[9] The ancients believed long hair contributed to female fertility.

The main Hippocratic test for female sterility, which we also find mentioned by Aristotle (*Generation of Animals* 747a) and the first-century Greek physician Soranus (*Gynecology* 1.9), was to place a scented suppository in a woman's uterus and smell her breath the next day. If the doctor could detect the scent of the suppository on her mouth, this indicated she was still fertile. If the scent couldn't be detected, she was pronounced sterile, "because the channels connecting her uterus to her head are blocked. The suction power of her hair cannot draw up the semen through the appropriate channels in her body."[10] Aristophanes even references similar logic for detecting infidelity.[11]

Whereas long hair contributed to a woman's fertility, esteemed scholars like Aristotle, Plato, Diocles, and Hippocrates affirmed that male seminal fluid is stored in the brain.[12] It therefore followed that, if a man's hair was long, its upward suction power would tend toward making him impotent. In other words, it was in accordance with the nature of man as the emissive sex to have short hair, and it is the glory of a woman's nature to wear her hair long to embody the opposite, complementary function necessary for reproduction.[13] Put another way, standard Greco-Roman science maintained that a woman's hair is the female physiological counterpart to the testicles— acting as that member which draws reproductive fluid into the womb.

The Greeks also believed that hair growth occurred by the congealing of male or female sexual fluids, which are attracted to the tips of the follicles (since these fluids were conceived as stored in the

---

[9] Ibid., 81. See his footnote 23.

[10] Ibid., 80. Thus Aristotle (*Generation of Animals* 747a): "Women are tested (*a*) by means of pessaries: the test is whether the scent of the pessary penetrates upwards from below to the breath which is exhaled from the mouth.... If the required result is not forthcoming, it is proved that the passages of the body through which the residue is secreted have got obstructed and have closed up...." A. L. Peck (trans.), *Aristotle: Generation of Animals*. Loeb Classic Library (Cambridge: Harvard University Press, 1943), 247.

[11] See Martin's notes on the Greek of Aristophanes' *Ecclesiazusae* (523-24), wherein the character Praxagora challenges Blepyrus to test her fidelity by smelling her hair. Martin, "Paul's Argument from Nature," 80.

[12] Ibid., 78.

[13] Martin compares Paul here with a passage in Pseudo-Phocylides: "Long hair is not fit for males, but for voluptuous women." Ibid., 79.

channels of the head, hair thus grows there strongest). Hippocrates' *On the Nature of Children* (20:1-6) comes to this conclusion based on observations made of eunuchs and balding men. Recognizing that female hair should be categorized as a sexual organ, the important early church father Tertullian (writing around AD 208) therefore advised in accordance with the modesty customs of Greek culture, "Let her whose lower parts are not bare have her upper likewise covered" (*On the Veiling of Virgins*, 12).[14] Just as girls were expected to take up a head covering upon puberty, boys often had their hair cut as a pubescent rite of passage.[15]

Martin points out that Old Testament law explicitly required the covering of sexual organs during worship. Paul, therefore, seems to be extending this reasoning to female hair. In 1 Cor 11:13-15 Paul writes:

> Judge for yourselves: is it proper for a revealed woman to pray to God? Does not even nature itself teach you indeed that if a man has long hair it is a dishonor to him, but if a woman has long hair, it is glory to her? For that long hair is given to her in place of [or "for" ἀντὶ] a covering [περιβολαίου].

Why does Paul pronounce at the conclusion of his argument that hair is given to women, "in place of" a covering? Why do women need a covering like he has told us earlier if their hair *already* functions as one? The answer is that the term περιβόλαιον in verse 15 is used in Greek texts as a euphemism for male anatomy—the σαρκος περιβολαι "bags of flesh" which one Greek author calls the, "outward signs of puberty."[16] And so, nature teaches us that a woman's hair is given to her *in place of* the male testicles.

I appreciate how bizarre Martin's contextual argument may seem, but this is only the case because we moderns lack the ancient cultural mindset that allowed Paul to tactfully use this euphemism. Paul cleverly

---

[14] Translation from Alexander Roberts et al., *The Ante-Nicene Fathers Volume IV: Fathers of the Third* Century (New York: Cosmo Classics, 2007), 34.

[15] Martin, "Paul's Argument from Nature," 82.

[16] Ibid., 77. The term is used to describe Hercules' "bags of flesh" [σαρκος περιβολαι] which are the outward signs of puberty...." Achilles Tatius (*Clitiphon and Leucippe* 1.15.2) also uses the term in conjunction with female hair in an erotic description of two lovers.

words things in the most dignified manner possible without sacrificing the persuasiveness of his argument.

Martin's use of the ancient medical data and contextual linguistics to explain Paul's argument is so arresting because it tidily accounts for the complications in the passage that previous studies that have understood Paul's euphemism as literal have failed to explain for centuries.[17]

DEFINING "LYING" AND "ERROR"?

Many Christians are uncomfortable with the sort of interpretations I have presented in the two previous examples and earlier parts of this book. This is because they think that God would never allow Paul to include historically or scientifically "false" notions, either essential or non-essential, to a passage's primary message. They don't believe God would accommodate the Bible to the scientific place of its readers in this way. For example, Wayne Grudem, author of the most popular Systematic Theology textbook used by evangelical seminaries, raises the following objections:

[W]e must respond that such "accommodation" by God to our misunderstandings would imply that God had acted contrary to his character as an "unlying God" (Num. 23:19; Titus 1:2; Heb. 6:18)…. Furthermore,…if the accommodation theory is correct, then God *intentionally* made incidental affirmations of falsehood in order to enhance communication. Therefore, would it not also be right for us intentionally to make incidental affirmations of falsehood whenever

---

[17] Besides explaining the apparent contradiction in Paul's argument (i.e. he advises that women should wear a covering, then states that their hair has *already* been given to them to serve as one). This interpretation would also explain the strange line in verse 10 (ESV): "That is why a wife ought to have a symbol of authority on her head, because of the angels." As Tertullian maintained, Paul is probably alluding to a stream of legend reflected in Genesis 6 understood by ancient Jews to refer to divine beings who sought to fulfill their lustful desires for human women. In Paul's day, this tradition was a major theme in works like the Book of Enoch and was taken much more seriously than we moderns are inclined to recognize (e.g. Jude 6 and 2 Pet 2:4). Noted in D. F. Tolmie, "Angels as Arguments? The Rhetorical Function of References to Angels in the Main Letters of Paul" in *HTS Teologiese Studies/Theological Studies* 67.1, 825 (2011), 4-5. See also Michael S. Heiser, *Reversing Hermon: Enoch, the Watchers, and the Forgotten Mission of Jesus Christ* (Defender Publishing, 2017).

it would enhance communication? Yet this would be tantamount to saying that a minor falsehood for a good purpose (a "white lie") is not wrong. Such a position, contradicted by…Scripture…concerning God's total truthfulness in speech, cannot be held to be valid.[18]

Biblically and philosophically, I think this objection reflects an intolerably low-resolution understanding of what constitutes lying and truthful speech. In response to Grudem's rhetorical questions, *actually yes*, to be a virtuous person you *do* have to learn how to occasionally accommodate your speech to meet people where they are in their warped or simplistic perceptions. Sometimes you *should* permit people to remain in certain states of ignorance, and the Bible does imply on rare occasions that to speak and act virtuously and in accordance with truth, you must even be capable of engaging in strategic forms of deception.

Truth is hierarchical (meaning some truths are more important than others), and this fact means that speaking and acting truthfully often requires tact and sophistication as we weigh the relative value of different truths. For example, a person who enjoys going around telling people "true" things as a way of merely expressing cruel intentions and causing harm (that is, telling "black truths"—the opposite of "white lies") isn't living and speaking in truth. The individual statements they are uttering may be "true" in the proximal sense that they factually happen to correspond with reality, but they are lies insofar as they aren't being spoken in a manner accurately organized in proportion with other truths.

Conversely, there are plenty of circumstances where it is appropriate to utter "a minor falsehood for a good purpose," as Grudem disparagingly words it. If proverbial Nazis knock on your door and ask if you are hiding Jews, you *should* deceive them. By deceiving them you are using your speech in greatest alignment with truth in the sense that what you are saying *is accurately proportioned to reality in its full scope*. It also isn't wrong when Christians in dangerous war zones wear camouflage to protect themselves (camouflage is basically a way of lying about your location), or when Christian undercover cops lie to work their way into human trafficking rings so they can save lives.[19] You might be thinking,

---

[18] Wayne Grudem, *Systematic Theology*, 97.
[19] I owe these examples to Michael S. Heiser, "Lying and Deception," The Naked Bible blog (Mar 26, 2010). Accessed Sept 28, 2020. https://drmsh.com/lying-and-deception/.

"These examples may be an unfortunate necessity of living in a fallen world, but surely the biblical God himself is above such behavior."

You'd be wrong.

A fascinating paper by Yael Shemesh from Bar-Illan University provides no shortage of examples.[20] For example, in 1 Kgs 22:19-23 God is floating ways to kill king Ahab among his divine council members. At the recommendation of one of the spirits in his assembly, God commands "a lying spirit" to deceive Ahab's prophets to entice him to go into battle. A similar statement is made in Ezk 14:9: "If the prophet is deceived and speaks a word, I, the LORD, have deceived that prophet" (ESV). In 2 Thes 2:11 Paul says of certain recalcitrant non-believers—that "God sends them a strong delusion, so that they may believe what is false" (ESV). In 1 Sam 16:2, God commands Samuel to deceive Saul's men with the half-truth that he had come to Bethlehem to sacrifice a heifer. He did do this, but it was to disguise his greater intention of anointing one of Jesse's sons. Or consider Exod 1:15-21, where God blesses the Hebrew midwives for lying to the pharaoh after the Egyptian government commanded them to murder Hebrew newborns (that is, God approves of them lying to pharaoh for the sake of avoiding murder). For that matter, didn't God deceive Abraham when he told him he wanted him to slaughter Isaac as a sacrifice?

Were the New Testament authors aware of these Hebrew passages when they wrote things like, "It is impossible for God to lie?" (Heb 6:18). Did they skip the days these stories were covered in Synagogue? These examples illustrate that those who don't accommodate truth's hierarchical nature (and its associated necessity for tact and accommodation in communication) into their understanding of what qualifies as lying are proposing a view so sanctimoniously restrictive that it ironically renders the biblical God a liar.[21]

---

[20] Yael Shemesh, "Lies by Prophets and Other Lies in the Hebrew Bible," *Journal of the Ancient Near Eastern Society* 29 (2002), 81–95.

[21] Shemesh's nuanced conclusion is appropriate (Ibid., 95), "In contrast to those theologians and philosophers who reject any kind of lying, under any circumstances, the Bible recognizes that certain situations justify and even require deceptive measures. This is true even regarding God and God's prophets. Nevertheless, as we have seen, the Bible avoids ascribing outright, undisguised falsehood to the deity or to the prophets (and on occasion is equally reticent in regard to other positive figures)."

Consider the following analogy provided to us by Michael Heiser:[22] Imagine your five-year-old daughter asks where her newborn baby brother came from. If you have any sense, you will accommodate your answer to her context as a child. Perhaps you might simply respond that God fashioned her baby brother inside her mother. And so, you permit her to falsely infer that God literally, materially assembled her baby brother in the womb in your act of communicating to her your main point that human life ultimately comes from God. Are you a liar for accommodating your message to her in this way? Have you broken the ninth commandment? To claim that this answer is a lie or even an intended sub-truth seems absurd because we all recognize the necessity of accounting for intent, context, and tact in truthful speech.

Grudem's critique contains a last objection that will further permit us to diagnose this issue:

> God is the Lord of human language who can use human language to communicate perfectly without having to affirm any false ideas that may have been held by people during the time of the writing of Scripture. [Accommodationism] essentially denies God's effective lordship over human language.[23]

I don't deny that an omnipotent, all-knowing God should be capable of marshaling the control of language necessary to explain and correct all the false scientific assumptions of an author. In the same sense, I suppose that given enough time and effort one could even probably explain embryology to a five-year-old. Rather, the point is that it would often seem pointless, and often counterproductive or outright silly, to expect God or anyone else to have to behave in this manner.

But vague speculation is cheap. Look at the head covering episode as a concrete thought experiment. Given what we know about the motivations for head covering in relation to ancient Greek medical science, how do Christians think this situation should have played out? Was God supposed to have Paul just dodge the whole subject? This would certainly prevent him from repeating the scientifically false views

---

[22] Occurs 26 minutes into Michael S. Heiser, "Genesis and Creation: Old Testament Cosmology" YouTube video, 1:13:21, church lecture, posted by "HaibaneXIII," https://www.youtube.com/watch?v=bSG2s17VooQ&t=2435s.

[23] Wayne Grudem, *Systematic Theology*, 97.

of his culture, but this theologically imposed expectation seems unreasonable because head covering was clearly a controversy for which the church was seeking moral guidance.[24] What? Is God supposed to inspire Paul to ignore addressing a moral controversy the church was struggling with?

If we apply the same sort of expectations most Christians impose on the creation account in Genesis to this passage, one might suggest that God would have simply uploaded into Paul's head a supernatural crash course in human physiology so that he wouldn't repeat this false framework shared by his culture.

Let's play out how that would go down.

Imagine you are an ancient Corinthian. You and all your polytheistic neighbors in the Las Vegas of the ancient world think that female hair is an extension of reproductive anatomy (thanks Aristotle). Partially as an extension of this, your culture has instituted that women are to wear head coverings as the norm out in public as a symbol of modesty (and according to the ancient sources, *it was the norm*, contrary to what some modern pastors have sometimes claimed).[25] Imagine then, some guy named Paul comes to your city and claims a new God you've never heard of gave him a divine science lesson. Paul then goes around telling women not to care about covering their heads because it's bad science. Now you have a situation in which the church is exposing what their neighbors think are extensions of their sexual anatomy during worship in the name of the Holy Spirit!

Maybe some Christians might propose God should have revealed a divine anatomy lesson to Paul so Paul could have informed the church that the medical science of their day was wrong but that they should wear head coverings anyways for PR reasons.

This implies a situation in which the church has been catapulted centuries ahead of the ancient world in their comprehension of sexual anatomy, all for the sake of giving their God the license to tell them to carry on wearing head coverings *anyways*. This strategy would be like

---

[24] Finney emphasizes that Paul's style indicates that he is very likely addressing members who have not been keeping the practice as was ordered at a previous time. Mark Finney, "Honor, Head-coverings and Headship: 1 Corinthians 11.2-16 in its Social Context," *Journal for the Study of the New Testament* 33.1 (2010), 32-33.
[25] Ibid., 35-36.

using a sledgehammer to crack a peanut. Not only could the same result be achieved without the necessity of revealing advanced anatomy to the church (which they had no spiritual need for in the context of this letter, and so, would be *ad hoc*), but it seems unnecessarily restrictive to suppose that God should be morally compelled to correct all the false cultural assumptions involved in an instance of communication with people before being permitted to influence in them a message that isn't about those cultural assumptions (modesty, not science is the point of this passage).

If it's apparent David wasn't supernaturally cut off with a lesson in physiology when he wrote, "O Lord...test my kidneys..." (Ps 26:2), wouldn't expecting God to give Paul a divine lesson in advanced physiology be equally unnecessary here?

If you were transported back in time to be a leader in the Corinthian church with your modern knowledge of science, what would you advise the church to do? Would you have them engage in behavior that could signal sexual immodesty within that culture, or would you simply instruct them to continue using this accustomed dress for the sake of its moral implication in their culture?

I've written an edition of the Stoic philosopher Epictetus. Like Paul, Epictetus was a first century Roman who primarily discussed theology and ethical instruction, but on a few occasions, he happened, incidentally, to allude to ideas that we know today are scientifically false. For example, in his *Discourses* (III.23), he teaches his students that wise men shouldn't be concerned with trying to make people like them, because doing so gets in the way of the philosopher's obligation to show people what their moral faults are. He tells his students that if they only look to promote virtue in others, then good men will naturally be attracted to them, "like the sun which draws sustenance to itself."
What does Epictetus mean by this? Ancient Romans believed that the sun's rays were comprised of vapor that the sun attracted to itself as fuel for its fire.[26]

Knowing this, imagine I gave someone a copy of Epictetus and a day later, he returned it to me objecting: "This man believed the sun was fueled by the earth's vapor. He uses Aristotle's falsified theory of elements. He mistakes something about the flowering cycle of fig trees.

---

[26] Benjamin Stanhope, *The Golden Sayings of Epictetus: In Contemporary English with Explanatory Notes* (Charleston: Stanhope, 2016), 84.

Clearly, Stoicism and its writings are barbaric and outdated for our modern age."

My sense is that most modern antagonism people hold towards the Bible is similar to this. But why is this so? Ironically, I believe Christians bear most of the blame for endlessly training the public to think criticizing the Bible in this mode is legitimate.

When Epictetus says that a good man attracts virtuous men, "like the sun which draws sustenance to itself" is he even really wrong? Is David necessarily wrong when he says that God 'instructs [his] kidneys'? Is Job wrong when he says God "set the foundations" of the earth upon the slain dragon of chaos? Is it an error when the biblical authors speak of God's dwelling as if it is a geography located in the sky—above our mundane terrestrial world?

Consider a more contemporary example: Imagine I tell my landlord that the water spot on my ceiling has been growing, and he's blind as a bat if he can't see it himself. If he cuts me off with a "but actually" speech about bat ophthalmology and how bats actually have great vision, has he falsified the actual message I was attempting to communicate to him about the abhorrent state of the plumbing in my apartment? Has he shown my statement was actually in error?

It is important in all communication to distinguish the primary message of a given statement from the incidental elements that may be used to express it. When I say that certain elements in a biblical text are "incidental," I am referring to cultural assumptions in a passage that may be literally false yet don't invalidate the truth of the statement's primary intended message. Michael Heiser and the Semitist John Hobbins have sought to incorporate this sort of distinction in drafting what has been called, "The Bellingham Statement of Faith."[27] My personal religious views aside, the results, based on actual case studies in the text, seem much more respectable and interpretively useful than the vague sort of philosophical assumptions that currently dominate most pedestrian Christian theology.

---

[27] The Bellingham Statement and Heiser and Hobbin's interaction can be accessed through the original 24 posts generating their exchange: "Inspiration," *The Naked Bible blog* (2008-2009). Accessed May 1, 2017. http://drmsh.com/naked-bibles-inspiration-discussion/.

CONCLUSION

I argued in the first section of this book that creationists are wrong when they claim the Bible contains eyewitness accounts of prehistoric reptiles, a theme that I expand upon further in Appendix A.

In section two, I argued that the Bible can exegetically accommodate an ancient universe, and the following cosmological chapters of this book securely demonstrate that Genesis 1's material view of the heavens and earth was not scientifically advanced for its time. The seven days of creation in Genesis were intended to be understood literally, but most creationists have misunderstood the significance of the creation week in the sense that its primary function was to serve theological and literary purposes. Theological and literary purposes likewise underlie the genealogies of the patriarchs and have been largely misunderstood by concordists of all stripes. Finally, I have argued that the Creation Museum's view that there existed an original state of universal vegetarianism in the animal kingdom before the Fall is biblically unsupported.

In section three, I have argued that many (if not most) evangelical Christians are wrong about how they view the Bible's contextual relationship with the ancient world. Much of Genesis *is* cryptic, and some of it requires specialized knowledge to accurately understand, even in the case of some major themes like Genesis 1's presentation of creation as a Near Eastern temple or its assumptions on animal death.

Following this, I have examined a biblical caveat for articulating divine inspiration that I believe will help Christians avoid repeating many of the problems generated by the currently dominant view in evangelicalism and the Creation Museum.

FALSE ARTIFACTS, HOAXES, AND MISINTERPRETATIONS: YOUNG-EARTH CREATIONISM'S USE OF DRAGON LEGENDS

WHEN I first visited the Creation Museum, news media and attractive billboards announced that the state-of-the-art complex had constructed a new exhibit themed upon dragons. These visually stunning displays, brilliantly designed to engage children, are the first thing you see while in the admittance line. On visual layouts, in display cases, and on signs, visitors are shown numerous examples of dragon legends around the globe, from the Beowulf legends to Saint George the dragon slayer, to ancient Roman texts. This entire portion of the museum argues that ancient dragon lore is evidence that man and dinosaurs once coexisted. I will here demonstrate that many of these claims intended to bolster the young-earth position are wrong.

COWBOYS AND DRAGONS

As I made my way through the hall, one display, in particular, stood out. Inside a glass case sat a rifle, some spurs, and a cowboy hat. Big red letters grabbed my eye: "Cowboys and Dragons" (Figure 22). "On April 26, 1890," the placard said, "the *Tombstone Epitaph* newspaper [related an] incredible report." It then continued with a story of how several ranchers on horseback outside of Tombstone, Arizona, between the Whetstone and Huachuca mountains, shot and killed a giant flying reptile with membranous wings using Winchester rifles.

243

Figure 22. Display at the Creation Museum entitled, "Cowboys and Dragons."
Photo by author.

This same story often appears in popular young-earth creationist publications. In the *New Answers Book*, Hodge writes:

It was not until the 20th century that dragons were seen as myths. In 1890, a large flying dragon was killed in Arizona (in the United States), and samples were sent to universities back east. This was recorded in a newspaper under "A Strange Winged Monster Discovered and Killed on the Huachuca Desert," *The Tombstone Epitaph*, on April 26, 1890. No one seemed to entertain the idea they were myths then.[1]

Duane Gish said much the same:

> The description fits the Pteranodon family of flying reptiles rather closely. However, it especially fits the description of the *Quetzalcoatlus* fossil found in Texas in 1972. Those two cowboys may have shot the last living *Quetzalcoatlus* just a little over 100 years ago. It is an unlikely story, but who knows?[2]

The problem here is that the important details of this account are frequently omitted (laudably, the Creation Museum display does quote them).

Thanks to the internet, anyone with a laptop can go read a digital photograph of the archived paper in full.[3] We learn that two men (never named) were traveling home on horseback in the Huachuca desert when they saw a giant reptile in the sky that was apparently physically exhausted in its pattern of flight. They pursued, then, "after an exciting chase of several miles succeeded in getting near enough to open fire with their rifles and wounding it." The creature turned and went on the attack, but the two cowboys claimed they evaded and landed several critical shots. The beast rolled over and died. The newspaper then continues:

---

[1] Bodie Hodge, "Dragons…Were They Real?" in Ken Ham (ed.), *The New Answers Book Volume 4: Over 30 Questions on Creation/Evolution and the Bible* (Green Forest, AR: Master Books, 2013), 40.

[2] Duane T. Gish, *Dinosaurs by Design* (Green Forest: Master Books, 1992), 16.

[3] "Tombstone Epitaph (Tombstone, Ariz.), 26 April 1890," *Chronicling America: Historic American Newspapers. Library of Congress*, www.chroniclingamerica.loc.gov/lccn/sn95060905/1890-04-26/ed-1/seq-3/. See page three under, "A Strange Winged Monster Discovered and Killed on the Huachuca Desert."

They then proceeded to make an examination and found that it measured about ninety-two feet in length and the greatest diameter was about fifty inches.... The head, as near as they could judge, was about eight feet long. Its eyes were as large as a dinner plate and protruded about half way from the head.... They had some difficulty in measuring the wings as they were partly folded under the body, but finally got one straightened out sufficiently to get a measurement of seventy-eight feet, making the total length from tip to tip about 160 feet. The wings were composed of a thick and nearly transparent membrane and were devoid of feathers or hair, as was the entire body. The men cut off a small portion of the tip of one wing and took it home with them. Late last night one of them arrived in this city for supplies and to make the necessary preparations to skin the creature, when the hide will be sent east for examination by the eminent scientists of the day. The finder returned early this morning accompanied by several prominent men who will endeavor to bring the strange creature to this city before it is mutilated.[4]

These absurd measurements are what published young-earth retellings of this account often miss: 92 feet from head to tail, eyes as big as dinner plates, and the 160-foot wingspan. 160 feet (49 meters) is 80% of the size of the wingspan of a Boeing 747!

Duane Gish said this thing sounds like *Quetzalcoatlus*, the largest of the flying reptiles ever discovered. But *Quetzalcoatlus* had a wingspan roughly comparable to a fighter jet. The wingspan of the tombstone monster was claimed to be four times larger!

So what became of the remains of this creature? Were photographs ever taken? What about the "several prominent men" who went to go haul it back into Tombstone for display?

The facts are these: This story was tucked away on page three of a four-page newspaper. No photograph was printed of the creature and the reporter never actually said he saw it. Its remains were never brought to the town or any other. The competing Tombstone newspaper, *The Nugget*, never even mentioned the story, and, despite the *Answers Book*, samples of it were never sent to eastern universities. In fact, the *Epitaph* never said anything else again about this 92-foot flying Godzilla in the desert with wingspan specs comparable to an international cargo jet.

---

[4] Ibid.

Jana Bommersbach's excellent investigation into the Tombstone dragon concludes:

> So maybe there really was a giant bird in Arizona Territory at the end of the 19th century, and maybe two ranchers really did track it down and shoot it, and maybe they did come into town and get some "prominent" men to go with them to bring it back. But whatever happened next was so unspectacular, so uninteresting and so unremarkable that nobody ever spoke of it again, Would that have been the response if there really had been a dead dinosaur-like bird outside of town? Hardly.[5]

THE NARMER "DINOSAURS"

Another display case in the Creation Museum, labeled "Dragon Depictions around the World," contains a reproduction of an Egyptian artwork. This famous artifact known as the Narmer Palette, the original

of which is currently housed at the Cairo Museum, dates to 3,000 BC. One side is dominated by the image of two creatures on four legs with long intertwined necks (Figure 26). The use of this artifact in the museum's dragon exhibit implies that it may have ultimately been derived from human encounters with creatures like brachiosaurs.

Figure 23. Narmer Palette reproduction displayed in the Creation Museum. The museum's caption reads: "The Narmer Palette contains some of the earliest hieroglyphs ever found as well as two long-necked creatures that resemble sauropod dinosaurs." Photo by the author.

---

[5] Jana Bommersbach, "Tombstone's Flying Monster: The Old West Cold Case on the Thunderbird Photo is Solved in Our Eyes," *True West Magazine* (Jun 1, 2007), www.truewestmagazine.com/tombstones-flying-monster/.

Tim Clarey, a research associate at the Institute for Creation Research, also shows an image of the tablet in his book, agreeing that the artifact, "suggests that dinosaur-like animals coexisted with humans."[6] Although countless young-earth books and websites cite this stone, I have yet to see them specifically challenged on it. Sadly, their fantastic interpretation dissolves immediately if one only consults introductory literature on Egyptian art: The stone depicts serpent-necked *lions*, a motif common to Egypt and Mesopotamia.[7]

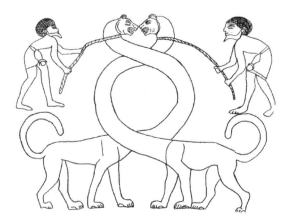

Figure 24. Detail from verso of Narmer Palette by author. Egyptian Museum, Cairo.

It's usual for Egyptian palettes like this to have a depressed circle in the center in which cosmetics were mixed. On the Narmer stone, this mixing cavity is cleverly made by the circle gap between the exaggerated intertwining necks (therefore serving as a partial functional explanation for their exceptional exaggeration on the pallet).[8] It turns out these mythical creatures are quite typical on other Egyptian palettes and apotropaic wands carved from hippopotamus ivory, especially during the Middle Kingdom. It doesn't make sense to interpret them as dinosaurs because they are always depicted with feline features.

The tails, feet, bodies, ears, faces, eyes, and noses in the Narmer Palette are themselves obviously leonine, but other Egyptian carvings are even more emphatic. Consulting museum archives, I've reproduced

---

[6] Tim Clarey, *Dinosaurs: Marvels of God's Design: The Science of the Biblical Account* (Green Forest, AR: Master books, 2015), 21.

[7] See Manfred Lurker, *The Gods and Symbols of Ancient Egypt* (Britain: Thames and Hudson, 1980), 17.

[8] Ibid.

several (primarily from Egyptian ivory wands) for contextual comparison in Figure 25.

Figure 25. Egyptian serpent-necked leopards. Top left: EA181755 British Museum, Late Middle Kingdom. Top right: UC16381 Petrie Museum, London. Bottom left: E. A. W. Budge, *The Gods of the Egyptians*, vol. 1 (London: Gilbert and Rivington, 1904), 59. Bottom right: 12.1519 Museum of Fine Arts, Boston, Middle Kingdom.

THE BLACK DRAGON CANYON PTEROSAUR

Does this Native American pictograph in Utah depict a pterosaur?

Figure 26. Display in the Creation Museum of the Black Dragon Canyon "pterosaur." Photo by author.

Another one of the first signs in the Museum (Figure 26) suggests a different claim. A corresponding article on the Answers in Genesis website claims:

> In Utah's San Raphael Swell there is other suggestive evidence for man's coexistence with pterosaurs. In the Black Dragon Canyon there is a beautiful pictograph of a pterosaur. The Indians of the Swell apparently saw a bird-like creature with enormous wings, a tail, a long neck and beak, and a vertical head crest, which some flying reptiles sported.[9]

---

[9] Bill Johnson, "Thunderbirds: Did American Indians See 'Winged Dinosaurs'?," *Answers in Genesis*, March 1, 2002. Accessed Feb 19, 2018, www.answersingenesis.org/dinosaurs/dragon-legends/thunderbirds/.

The Black Dragon Canyon pictograph is at least 1,000 years old. In the 1940s, a man named John Simonson used chalk to outline what he thought the edges of the painting were, seeing in it a winged monster. Though it was commonly practiced at the time, chalking the outline of pictographs is now illegal, and Simonson's abominable white border effacing the piece encouraged many visitors to the site to perpetuate his interpretation.

As I write, there is a photograph of the alleged pterosaur rock painting exhibited in the Creation Museum in the previously mentioned display case entitled, "Dragon Depictions around the World." The same photo also appears in the organization's *New Answers Book*.[10]

For years, experts have disagreed with this identification. It became such a subject of interest that in 2015 the rock art experts Jean-Loïc Le Quellec, Paul G. Bahn, and the archaeological chemist Marvin Rowe decided to use modern technology to put an end to the debate. The scientists used a pictographic digital enhancement program called DStretch to parse the original form of the image. The enhancement tool showed that the "pterosaur" was actually composed of five discrete figures (Figure 27). Rowe then corroborated the accuracy of the DStretch parsing by using an x-ray fluorescence gun to measure the iron concentration of the red ocher pigment at various points in the painting—establishing the original boundaries of its application.

The published study shows the pictograph isn't meant to depict a large flying reptile, but, rather, a group of classic subjects that centuries of decay have blurred to give the appearance of a single image.[11] The pterosaur's "head" is actually a figure with arms stretched forward, and its "wings" are composed of a bending anthropoid figure and a serpent. Part of the reason the left "wing" looks so deformed is that it was originally two quadrupeds.

---

[10] Hodge, "Dragons…were they real," 36.
[11] Jean-Loïc Le Quellec, Paul Bahn, and Marvin Rowe, "The Death of a Pterodactyl," *Antiquity*, 89.346 (2015), 872-884.

Figure 27. Recent computer enhancement demonstrates that the "pterodactyl" of Black Dragon Canyon is actually composed of several classic subjects depicted in the Barrier Canyon style. Image courtesy of Jean-Loïc Le Quellec of *Le Centre national de la recherche scientifique*. Used with permission and gratitude.

AN ABORIGINAL PLESIOSAUR

Figure 28. A purported painting of a plesiosaur by the Kuku Yalanji of Australia. (Image used under fair use.)

Figure 28 shows a painting presented in a Creation Museum Legacy Hall lecture by Answers in Genesis' "Curriculum Specialist" posted in 2018.[12] The painting is also endorsed in a 2011 article by Bodie Hodge last featured by Answers and Genesis in 2019.[13] The image is fairly popular in young-earth articles and presentations and seems to have first been published in the magazine *Creation*, in which the author, Rebecca Driver, cited it as evidence that Australian Aboriginals must have observed a living plesiosaur.[14] Driver's article reported that a missionary named Dennis Fields acquired this painting from a member of the Kuku Yalanji people of North Queensland and later donated it to Answers in Genesis.

There is little excuse for Creationists to still be citing this image because an excellent article published by Philip J. Senter in 2017 in the *Skeptical Inquirer* has conclusively revealed its source. Senter writes:[15]

How could a Kuku Yalanji artist depict a plesiosaur so well without his ancestors having coexisted with them? With a little help from a children's book. The Kuku Yalanji painting is a copy of Rudolph Zallinger's painting of the plesiosaur Elasmosaurus from page forty-seven of Jane Watson's *The Giant Golden Book of Dinosaurs* (Watson 1960). The Kuku Yalanji artist added the digestive tract and vertebral column, but the outline of the animal is a precise reproduction of Zallinger's painting, right down to the orientation of the neck, the bend in the middle of the left pectoral and pelvic fins, and the domed shape of the head. The fin in the painting that Goertzen (2001) mistook for a dorsal fin is actually the right pectoral fin,

---

[12] "Dinosaurs and the Bible with Bryan Osborn," YouTube video, 1:06:21, recorded presentation given by Bryan Osborn, posted Jul 11, 2018 by "Answers in Genesis," https://www.youtube.com/watch?v=Y80wHFoYrrQ. Image discussed at 48 mins.
[13] Bodie Hodge, "Dragon Legends—Truths Behind the Tales: Special Dinosaur Section," *Answers and Genesis*, 1 Oct 2011; last featured 24 Mar 2019. Accessed 4 Sept 2020, https://answersingenesis.org/dinosaurs/dragon-legends/dragon-legends-truths-behind-the-tales/.
[14] Rebecca Driver, "Australia's Aborigines...Did They See Dinosaurs?," *Creation* 21.1 (Dec 1998), 24-27.
[15] Philip J. Senter, "Did Australia's Aborigines See Plesiosaurs? Yes-In a Children's Book," *Skeptical Inquirer* 41.1 (2017), 34-6.

which the Kuku Yalanji artist depicted with the same shape and dimensions as in Zallinger's painting....[16]

Senter's article shows the outline overlay of the two images is virtually identical. Additionally, he points out that the Kuku Yalanji painting reproduces the domed shaped skull of Zallinger's old painting—a feature actual plesiosaurs lack.[17] The Kuku Yalanji painting inserts the elements of vertebrae and intestines. However, as Senter points out, "each of the vertebrae of the torso bears a prominent, downward-pointing spike, a feature absent in actual plesiosaur trunk vertebrae. Also, the intestine in the painting is short, broad, and straight, un-like the long, narrow, coiled intestines of reptiles."[18]

THE AGAWA ROCK MONSTER

Answers in Genesis' *New Answers Book* also shows us an old Native American painting from what is called the Agawa Rock site in Lake Superior Provincial Park.[19] This image is likewise promoted by Clarey as evidence that men lived with dinosaurs.[20]

On a flat stone surface off the bank of Lake Superior's Agawa Bay, one can find the well-preserved representation of a bull-horned quadruped with spikes along its back painted in red pigment. On the same surface, one can also see depicted five canoes, several snakes, and a man on horseback among other mundane animals.

The New Answers Book compares the bull-horned cryptid to *Kentrosaurus* or *Amargasaurus*. Besides the fact that this creature with a round head, ears, and buffalo horns looks almost nothing like *Kentrosaurus* or *Amargasaurus* (or any other known dinosaur), the problem with this identification is that every element of this rock art is already known.

In the early 1800s a local Indian explained to an American ethnographer that the panel commemorates the four-day crossing of the lake by a war party in five canoes. The man on horseback was the

---

[16] Ibid., 36.
[17] Ibid.
[18] Ibid.
[19] Hodge, "Dragons...were they real," 36.
[20] Clarey, *Dinosaurs*, 19.

leader, named Myeengun, and the creationists' bull-horned *Kentrosaurus* is the depiction of a spirit the natives call Underwater Panther or *Mishipizhiw*.[21]

This identification is even more certain considering the location of the image on the bank of a lake and the fact that Underwater Panther is one of the most attested images among the tribes of that region found on medicine bags, in petroglyphs, and on war clubs. Of these, I have reproduced several line details for contextual comparison (Figure 30).

Figure 29. Agawa rock paintings, Lake Superior Provincial Park. Photograph by D. Gordon E. Robertson.

---

[21] Phil Senter, "More 'dinosaur' and 'pterosaur' rock art that isn't," *Palaeontologia Electronica* 15(2.22A) (2012), 9-10. www.palaeo-electronica.org/content/2012-issue-2-articles/275-rock-art-dinosaurs.

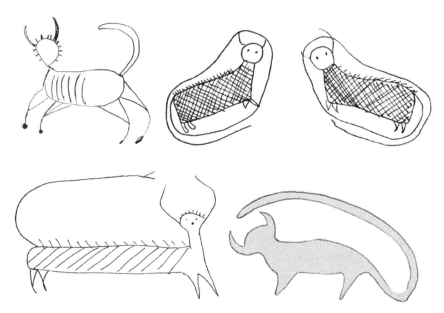

Figure 30. Top left: Anishinaabe club 3/4643, National Museum of the American Indian. Two figures top right: Winnebago war club 62-15-1, University of Pennsylvania Museum. Bottom left: Lake Winnebago rock carving. Bottom right: Rock painting, Basswood River Falls, Minnesota.

Senter tells us that the name "panther" is an archaism for the mountain lion and that this spirit was believed to dwell in the depths of capricious lakes. Because the Native Americans believed he controlled marine storms by the thrashing of his tail, they frequently petitioned the spirit, offering him sacrifices of dogs to ensure safety during their perilous voyages over large bodies of water like Superior.[22]

The paleontological folklorist Adrienne Mayor points out that early French explorers to the Great Lakes recount that when the natives encountered the remains of mastodons eroding out of marshes and riverbeds, they attributed them to horned marine monsters.[23] Perhaps the great buffalo horns of *Mishipizhiw* are an example of this.

Senter lists several reasons why it is foolish to mistake the feline spirit for a dinosaur. To start with, the spirit is universally depicted with

---

[22] Ibid.

[23] Adrienne Mayor, *Fossil Legends of the First Americans* (Princeton: Princeton University Press, 2005), 13. I owe this citation to Senter.

a round, catlike head and buffalo horns. In the Agawa painting, it clearly has ears.

Second, there is a horse and rider among the paintings. Therefore, the paintings must be dated to colonial times after horses were imported from the Old World. If the Indians were seeing quadruped dinosaurs loitering around Ontario at this time, it seems fair to have expected literate travelers to mention them as well. Finally, the creationist interpretation is strongly dependent on the spikes along the creature's spine. The problem here is that these lines were occasional symbolic adornments and are frequently excluded in other works of art of similar provenance.[24]

THE ILLINOIS PIASA

The same mentioned Answers in Genesis article tells us of yet another amazing eyewitness account of a living pterosaur:

In the Midwest, the Illini Indians of Illinois were once terrorized by a creature they called "Piasa", which means "bird that devours man". The Piasa was so large that it could allegedly carry off a full-grown deer. When it finally acquired a taste for human flesh, no Indian was safe. The Illini, as well as other Indian tribes in the area, greatly feared the Piasa and sought to destroy it.[25]

I'm not a Native American linguist, but I find it suspicious that a five-letter word can encode the phrase "bird that devours man." The author goes on to tell us a detailed account of how the Illini Indians hid 20 warriors at the opening of a cave and used their chief named Ouatoga as human bait in order to kabab the giant bird to death with arrows. Sound too good to be true? Well, the author assures us that a writer named John Russell in 1848 tracked down the cave where it was said the creature once lived. Upon exploring it, he reported that the 20-by-30 foot floor was entirely covered with human bones.

The origin of this urban legend seems to have come from an evangelical magazine in 1848. Kent Hovind, one young-earth advocate (not associated with Answers in Genesis), appears to have found the

---

[24] Senter, "More 'Dinosaur' and 'Pterosaur' Rock Art," 10.
[25] Johnson, "Thunderbirds."

story and believed it was an historical account. Other young-earth creationists took his word for it and have been mistakenly repeating his error ever since.

It is said Russell intimated its fanciful creation to the ethnographer W. McAdams.[26] According to Russell's son, the idea came to Russell after reading an old description of a painting of Underwater Panther recorded in a travel journal by the Jesuit missionary Jacques Marquette.[27] Marquette speaks of how, at the time he was living, in the late 1600s, there was a large Indian painting on a bluff on the Mississippi river of a terrifying quadruped creature with horns, a humanoid face, scales, and a tail that circled the entire image ending with fish fins. The addition of wings was supplied by Russell's imagination.[28]

The frequent YEC preoccupation with identifying pterosaurs with American Midwestern thunderbird mythology is also strange considering our myths and native drawings explicitly mention the fact that the creatures were feathered. If native oral legends about thunderbirds interface with the ancestral memory of any ancient living creature at all, they would far more plausibly correspond with *Teratornis merriami*, a condor-like North American species with a 12-foot (3.6 meter) wingspan that actually did once live alongside American Indians according to standard paleontology.[29]

HERODOTUS' FLYING SERPENTS

What other alleged eyewitness accounts of pterosaurs do some young-earth creationists cite? Ken Ham writes, "In the fifth century before Christ, Herodotus, the famous Greek historian, wrote about the 'winged serpents' of Arabia. Their descriptions fit what we know about pterodactyls."[30]

---

[26] See Frederick E. Voelker, "The Piasa," *Journal of the Illinois State Historical Society* 7.1 (1914), 89.

[27] Senter, "More 'Dinosaur' and 'Pterosaur' Rock Art," 11-12.

[28] Voelker, "The Piasa," 82-84.

[29] This has been proposed by Mayor, *Fossil Legends*, 103-105.

[30] Ken Ham, *Did Eve Really Have an Extra Rib? And Other Tough Questions About the Bible* (Green Forest, AR: Master Books, 2002). See the section question, "What about Flying Dragons? Aren't they Just Mythical?" Also stated by Ham in *The Great Dinosaur Mystery Solved: A Biblical View of these Amazing Creatures* (Green Forest, AR: Master Books, 1998), 51.

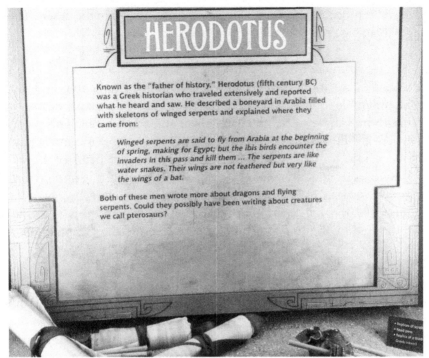

Figure 31. Display in the Creation Museum suggesting that Herodotus' winged serpents might be pterosaurs. Photo by author.

I can remember once at my own former church years ago, our youth were shown a popular young-earth documentary called *Dragons or Dinosaurs*. I found it no surprise that in his companion book the producer of the film also emphasizes this passage from the Greek historian. In discussing Herodotus' description of the serpents' wings, he shows us a picture of a pterodactyl that lurks like a gargoyle over the Creation Museum gift shop entrance, pronouncing the resemblance, "uncanny."[31]

These "winged serpents" are also emphasized and illustrated in Hodge's children's book,[32] as well as in a Creation Museum display case depicted in Figure 31.

---

[31] Darek Isaacs, *Dragons Or Dinosaurs? Creation Or Evolution?* (Alachua, FL: Bridge Logos, 2010), 33-34.

[32] Bodie Hodge and Laura Welch, *Dragons: Legends and Lore of Dinosaurs* (Green Forest, AR: Master Books), 21.

Indeed, Herodotus does tell us about winged serpents in the desert. The original passage reads as follows:

> Not far from the town of Buto, there is a place in Arabia to which I went to learn about the winged serpents. When I came thither, I saw innumerable bones and backbones of serpents; many heaps of backbones there were, great and small and smaller still. This place, where lay the backbones scattered, is where a narrow mountain pass opens into a great plain, which is joined to the plain of Egypt. Winged serpents are said to fly at the beginning of spring, from Arabia, making for Egypt; but the ibis birds encounter the invader in this pass and kill them. The Arabians say that the ibis is greatly honoured by the Egyptians for this service, and the Egyptians give the same reason for honouring these birds.[33]

After telling us a little about the ibis, Herodotus adds that "The serpents are like water-snakes. Their wings are not feathered but most like the wings of a bat."[34] At first, this passage may be very tantalizing to the cryptozoologist in all of us. Unfortunately, many young-earth creationists have rarely read another passage in Herodotus that elaborates further upon them. It is there where things unravel.

To begin with, in the passage above, Herodotus says the Arabians showed him "bones and backbones of serpents; many heaps of backbones...great and small and smaller still." He doesn't specify that he saw the bones of their wings (that feature which would be most worthy of remark) but emphasizes their spines.

Second, though he has never seen one alive, Herodotus says he was *told* they look like "water-snakes." If he were describing a species of pterosaur, with its elongated beak, feet, a torso ribcage structure, and usually a head crest, he picked a remarkably bad analog.

In the other passage, Herodotus' Arabian sources also informed him that the reason these creatures can only be found deep into the Arabian spice route is that they don't lay eggs like other vipers. During copulation, the female kills the male by biting through his neck. "But," Herodotus continues, "the female is punished for his death; the young

---

[33] *Histories* II.75. A.D. Godley (trans.), *Herodotus with an English translation by A.D. Godley.* Loeb Classical Library 117 (Cambridge: Harvard University Press, 1981), 361-363.

[34] *Histories* II.75-76. Ibid.

avenge their father, and gnaw at their mother while they are yet within her; nor are they dropped from her till they have eaten their way through her womb."[35]

He informs us that they don't proliferate in other lands like egg-laying serpents because their numbers are kept in check by the lethal process of reproduction. I should hardly need to point out that unlike these serpents, pterosaurs, of course, did lay eggs. We've discovered beautifully preserved pterosaur eggs, including one in China fossilized alongside its *Darwinpterus* mother.

Recall that Herodotus is getting all this from Arabian spice traders? They also told him that these snakes make it perilous to collect their frankincense:

> Arabia…is the only country which produces frankincense and myrrh and cassia and cinnamon and gum-mastich. All these except myrrh are difficult for the Arabians to get. They gather frankincense by burning that storax which Phoenicians carry to Hellas; they burn this and so get the frankincense; for the spice-bearing trees are guarded by small winged snakes of varied color, many around each tree; these are the snakes that attack Egypt. Nothing except the smoke of storax will drive them away from the trees.[36]

Herodotus immediately follows this with another unlikely tale about how the Arabians claim they acquire the spice cassia: They claim they wrap themselves from head to toe "in oxhides and other skins" as protection. This is because cassia "grows in a shallow lake," and as they wade out, there are clawed "winged creatures" of a different species living in and around the water, "very like bats, that squeak similarly [to bats]" and attack the intruder.

Ever wonder how cinnamon is harvested? Well, the spice traders won't say what land they acquire it from, but giant birds find the rare sticks and build them into their nests on inaccessible cliffs. So the spice traders have to cut large, dead animals (oxen and donkeys) into massive chunks and lay them out for the winged terrors. These titan birds fly off with the meat, which is so heavy that when they plop it into their nests, the nests break, causing the cinnamon sticks to drop to the ground.

---

[35] *Histories* III.109. Godley, *Herodotus*, 137.
[36] III.107. Ibid., 135.

"Thus is cinnamon said to be gathered, and so to come from Arabia to other lands."

The winged snake story occurs as a feature in the immediate midst of several fanciful tales about how to acquire certain spices.

It is telling that these stories given to Herodotus were spun by the spice traders to highlight how difficult or perilous it was to acquire the products they were selling and to presumably hide their actual source. The boring reality is that cinnamon and cassia were produced in South Asian plantations by peeling and drying the bark of a species of laurel. It was then imported and distributed by the Arabian monopoly.[37] Instead of this, we are sold a bill-of-goods about deadly winged snakes, ornery, bat-infested lakes, and big birds that hoard cinnamon sticks on cliffs in secret lands. The message is likely that one needs guts and technical skills to obtain these commodities. Outsiders ought to therefore keep their paws out of the spice harvesting business and appreciate the economic value of these things.

The first century Roman historian Pliny, who wanted to interrupt the spice monopoly, attempted to expose these tales, stating that the "winged serpents," "clawed bats," and "cinnamon birds" were clearly "invented by the natives to raise the price of their commodities."[38] The researcher Karen Radner goes so far as to compare the winged snake story to the old Scythian tale that griffins haunted the Gobi. The Scythians, who prospected the area for gold, had an economic incentive to use the gold-guarding griffon legend to discourage others from venturing into the area. As with our winged snakes, those traders could cite the frequent fossilized remains of *proceratops* in certain parts of the desert as proof of the dangers of the endeavor.[39]

Assuming Herodotus was indeed shown the myriad skeletal remains he mentions. The real mystery is trying to figure out what exactly he was shown. Adrienne Mayor points out that his account calls to mind several Egyptian sites archaeologists have uncovered along the Nile. The Egyptians there piled up thousands of pounds of fossilized bones at two

---

[37] See Ayelet Gilboa and Dvory Namdar, "On the Beginnings of South Asian Spice Trade with the Mediterranean Region: A Review," *Radiocarbon* 57.2 (2015), 265-83.

[38] Pliny the Elder, *Natural History*, Book XII:XLII. Trans. H. Rackham, Leob Classical Library 370 (Cambridge: Harvard University Press, 1945), 63.

[39] Karen Radner, "The Winged Snakes of Arabia and the Fossil Site of Makhtesh Ramon in the Negev," *Wiener Zeitschrift für die Kunde des Morgenlandes* 97 (2007), 361.

shrines.[40] Rader locates the region Herodotus describes within a fossiliferous site in the Negev called Makhtesh Ramon. She suspects that a few petrified species, easily distinguished among the rock, lend themselves to be interpreted as a flying snake, especially an ancient elongated salamander with bat-like front digits called *Ramonellus longispinus*.[41]

Herodotus emphasizes twice that he was shown many "backbones, great and small"—the only feature of their anatomy he describes as having seen. I believe it is therefore plausible he was shown the abundance of Middle Triassic ammonites common to areas like Makhtesh Ramon. "In antiquity ammonites were commonly related to enrolled snakes. They were used as amulets and protectors and as antidotes against snake bite."[42] Identifying the historian's serpent graveyard as a desert fossil valley is attractive since it would lend great enough permanence to the site for the legend to embed itself as well as it did, but given the brevity of Herodotus' description, it is difficult to be certain.

What we do know is that the historians' description of the creatures doesn't at all correspond with pterosaurs. Beyond that, their existence in Herodotus comes embedded within a fistful of other tall-tales received from the same source. These others are demonstrably false and would have served the economic interests of those spreading them. It is therefore unfortunate to see this story so frequently cited in YEC literature without acknowledgment of these contextualizing facts.

---

[40] Adrienne Mayor, *The First Fossil Hunters: Paleontology in Greek and Roman Times* (Princeton: Princeton University Press, 2000), 136.
[41] Radner, "The Winged Snakes," 361.
[42] M. S. Barroso, "Bezoar stones, magic, science and art," in Duffin, Moody, Gardner-Thorpe (eds.), *A History of Geology and Medicine*. Geological Society Special Publication 375 (London: Geological Society, 2013), 194.

WHY ARE THERE DRAGON LEGENDS ALL AROUND THE GLOBE?

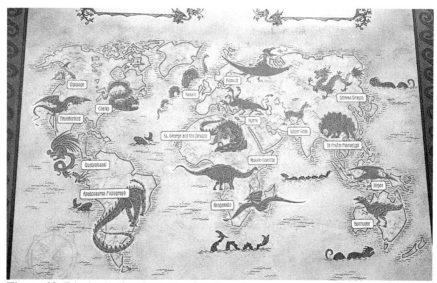

Figure 32. Display in the Kentucky Creation Museum mapping out dragon legends around the world. Photo by author.

One of the most engrossing biographies I've ever come across is that of the American Apache Geronimo. The US government pursued the warrior for many long years, but the Chiricahua successfully resisted the encroachment of their land despite the tremendous cost and failed military efforts made by the United States. As an old man, Geronimo came to be held at Fort Sill in Oklahoma. S.M. Barrett, a local superintendent of education, happened to befriend the Indian and found his stories so fascinating that he eventually entreated President Theodore Roosevelt for permission to take down his biography—a firsthand account of the warrior's life in the Native American West. Geronimo begins the story of his life by providing us the Apache origin myth.

The Apache say when the earth was young, it was filled with evil beasts, especially one tremendous and wise dragon that constantly devoured the early human population and prevented it from growing beyond a meager number. One woman, in particular, had many children, but each time she gave birth, the great dragon would sniff them out and gobble them up.

It came to pass that she managed to succeed in hiding one child in a cave who grew into an especially precocious young man. Disregarding his mother's will, one day the boy left the safety of the cavern with a little bow desiring to hunt his first buck. As he was exploring a nearby mountain, the ancient reptile quickly discovered him. The beast was amazed to find that the youth displayed no sign of fear. In fact, the boy with the tiny bow challenged the reptilian colossus to the terms of a dual. The agreement was that both parties would be permitted to take four shots at the other.

Geronimo continues:

> Then the dragon took his bow, which was made of a large pine tree. He took four arrows from his quiver; they were made of young pine tree saplings, and each arrow was twenty feet in length. He took deliberate aim, but, just as the arrow left the bow, the boy made a peculiar sound and leaped into the air. Immediately the arrow was shivered into a thousand splinters, and the boy was seen standing on the top of a bright rainbow over the spot where the dragon's aim had been directed. Soon the rainbow was gone and the boy was standing on the ground again. Four times this was repeated, then the boy said, "Dragon, stand here; it is my time to shoot." The dragon said, "All right; your little arrows cannot pierce my first coat of horn, and I have three other coats—shoot away." The boy shot an arrow, striking the dragon just over the heart, and one coat of the great horny scales fell to the ground. The next shot another coat, and then another, and the dragon's heart was exposed. Then the dragon trembled, but could not move…. [The boy] sped the fourth arrow with true aim, and it pierced the dragon's heart. With a tremendous roar the dragon rolled down the mountain side—down four precipices into a canyon below…. [F]ar down in the canyon below, they could see fragments of the huge body of the dragon lying among the rocks, *and the bones of this dragon may still be found there.* This boy's name was Apache.[43]

I don't think it is at all illegitimate for people who believe the earth is under 10,000 years old to point out that there are dragon legends in

---

[43] My emphasis. Geronimo, *Geronimo's Story of his Life*, S. M. Barrett (ed.) (New York: Duffield & Company, 1915), 9-10.

nearly every civilization across the globe. It's not at all obvious that different, disassociated cultures would make up legends about the same monster. At the same time, I'm tremendously skeptical of the common YEC claim that man's coexistence with dinosaurs is a satisfying explanation for the ubiquity of these ancient myths.

Although I will not dwell on the subject here, the current evolutionary timeline requires that serpent recognition must be deeply and significantly embedded in the most primitive architecture of the human brain. This is because it has snakes as one of our most ancient and longstanding enemies exerting high predatory selective force on our early mammalian ancestors. Nearly five decades of research has reinforced the biological evidence that "snakes remain special stimuli for humans." Humans "learn snake fear more easily than fear of most other stimuli through direct or vicarious conditioning."[44] Therefore, it has been argued by primatologists and neuroscientists that reptiles would be expected to manifest as the most prominent predatory archetype within the human imagination and unconscious.[45] That is, there are good evolutionary-biological reasons to expect that if human beings attempt to dream up a "super-predator," cross-culturally, the product will usually be a creature with serpentine aspects.

ANCIENT FOSSIL INTERPRETATION

Beyond this proposed explanation from evolutionary psychology, another more humble suggestion has often been overlooked. Namely, as in the case of the Apache myth, we can prove that many of these legends were ultimately the product of ancient people discovering and attempting to interpret fossils—that the discovery and interpretation of

---

[44] Arne Öhman and Susan Mineka, "The Malicious Serpent: Snakes as a Prototypical Stimulus for an Evolved Module of Fear," *Current Directions in Psychological Science* 12.1 (2003), 5.

[45] See the thesis of Lynne A. Isbell, *The Fruit, the Tree, and the Serpent: Why We See So Well* (Cambridge: Harvard University Press, 2011). Öhman and Mineka agree: "Because reptiles have been associated with danger throughout evolution, it is likely that snakes represent a prototypical stimulus for activating the fear module." "The Malicious Serpent," 7. The Psychologist Jordan B. Peterson at the University of Toronto has advocated a similar theory. "The Cat-Snake-Bird and Innate Fears | Jordan Peterson," YouTube Video, 05:30, interview, Dec 15, 2017. Posted by "Jordan B. Peterson Clips," Jan 9, 2018, https://m.youtube.com/watch?v=UxR2FkKEjys.

petrified dinosaur remains didn't start with eighteenth and nineteenth century Europeans.

The leading researcher on this subject is a folklorist at Stanford University named Adrienne Mayor. Mayor has published several fascinating books in which she pinpoints the geographic origins of dragon and other popular myths. She has found that these locations overlap heavily with known fossil beds.

Her pioneering research traces ancient fossil hunting history and mythology in regions like Native North America, Mongolia, Greece, and Rome. And the stories don't end with dragons. People in the ancient world are known to have given accounts of uncovering the skeletal remains of giant birds, griffins, the grotesque giants who waged war upon Olympus, and other fantastic beasts. Many examples of this phenomenon in the ancient world are undeniable, and it is worth reviewing a few here for sake of illustration.

CHINESE FOSSIL MEDICINE

According to mentions made in ancient texts like the *I Ching*, people in fossiliferous regions of China have been intentionally digging up and consuming "dragon bones" as medicine since possibly earlier than 1,000 BC.

Supplying apothecaries, ancient Chinese fossil mining was a lucrative and sophisticated business, and many important nineteenth century paleontological discoveries in China were made by Europeans, not in the field, but in the words of one paleontologist, "in the drugstores of large Chinese cities."[46]

China is so rich in fossils, and its use of them in traditional medicine is so prominent, that Mayor noticed imperial customs records of 1885 that reported *twenty tons* of these petrified "dragon bones" were *exported* that year alone.[47] In 2007, the National Geographic Society reported that this practice is still going in rural areas. A paleontologist named Dong Zhiming discovered that villagers in Henan were grinding up and drinking the massive fossilized remains of herbivorous dinosaurs:

---

[46] Quoted by Mayor, *The First Fossil Hunters*, 39.
[47] Ibid.

"When Dong arrived, the villagers told him they believed that the bones were from dragons flying in the sky...."[48]

GRIFFINS IN THE GOBI

Our ancient reports of griffons are usually strangely unembellished. The winged but flightless beaked creatures spoken of by Scythian nomads were said to reside in the deserts of the East, and it was rumored that they jealously guarded stashes of gold. Mayor traced the geographic origins of these myths to regions like the Red Desert in Uzbekistan and the Western Gobi where it turns out that beaked dinosaurs are the most abundant known. The fossils, exposed by desert winds, are so conspicuous and abundant against the red earth that one paleontologist described them as, "ridiculously easy to find," even to the point of being a "nuisance" for paleontologists.[49] A 1922 expedition to the Gobi followed ancient caravan trails in the Altai Mountains and discovered over one hundred *Protoceratops* and *Psittacosaurus* skeletons in two summers.[50]

Mayor explains that not only do the remains correspond with the geography and abundant ancient depictions we have of the griffin, but it is significant that regions like Altai are rich in gold sand that washes down from the mountains and becomes scattered by desert winds. Modern visitors report this phenomenon, and the ancient authors Theophrastus and Pliny also tell us that desert dwellers would rush to search the ground for glittering precious gems after shifting winds. It would be absurd to suspect that ancient desert traders wouldn't have noticed and attempted to interpret these abundant petrified skeletons, and, given our ancient data, the morphology of the griffon fits the profile of a *protoceratops* quite well.

INDIAN DRAGONS

Mayor also points us to the biography of the travels of Apollonius of Tyana.[51] The third century author Philostratus informs us that dragons in his day were common in India. It was even said that an array of their

---

[48] Kevin Holden Platt, "Dinosaur Fossils Part of Longtime Chinese Tonic," *National Geographic News*, July 2007. Accessed Jun 2017, www.news.nationalgeographic.com/news/2007/07/070713-china-dinos.html.
[49] Quoted by Mayor, *The First Fossil Hunters*, 43.
[50] Ibid., 40.
[51] Ibid., 130.

skulls were exhibited in a shrine in the center of a city called Paraka. He relates this in the course of recounting Apollonius' travels following through the Siwalik Hills paralleling the Himalayas.

Modern paleontologists have noted just how rich in late Tertiary fossils this region is: "On the slopes, in eroding cliffs, and along marshy streambeds, from Kashmir to the banks of the Ganges, the local people would have observed a host of strange skeletons...."[52]

The first significant European excavation of the region by Hugh Falconer, "collected more than 300 big bones in six hours." On a second expedition, Falconer amassed over 250 skulls from these exposures. Then, in 1848, "he shipped over five tons of fossils from this area to London museums."[53] Natives of the region were perfectly aware of these exposures, and Falconer reported some of the mythology surrounding them that he received from a local rajah.[54] Mayor informs

Figure 33. *Giraffokeryx punjabiensis* skull discovered in Siwalik Hills. Photo by Nikos Solounias. Used with permission and gratitude.

---

[52] Ibid.

[53] Ibid., 135.

[54] Ibid., 133. On the mythology of this region, see also, Alexandra Van Der Geer, Michael Dermitzakis, and John De Vos, "Fossil Folklore from India: The Siwalik Hills and the Mahâbhârata," *Folklore* 119.1 (2008), 71-92. www.jstor.org/stable/30035461.

us that in this region one finds the fossils of giant crocodiles, tortoises up to the size of small cars, all manner of prehistoric elephants, chalicotheres, and anthracotheres, and numerous species of giraffes. Several of the images Mayor provides of extinct giraffes from this region are stunningly dragon-like, such as the *Sivatherium* (named after the Hindu god Shiva) first discovered in this region, and especially the four-horned *Giraffokeryx* (Figure 33 and Figure 34).

It is particularly telling that Philostratus says that the Indians hunted dragons because their heads contained inside them flashing gems of iridescent hues.[55] As Mayor notes, Falconer and modern paleontologists have frequently been amazed at how fossils in the geology of this region frequently contain beautiful calcite and selenite crystals.[56]

Figure 34. Size of *Giraffokeryx* skull discovered in Siwalik Hills. Photo by Nikos Solounias. Used with permission.

---

[55] Philostatus, *Life of Apollonius*, III.6-10.
[56] Mayor, *The First Fossil Hunters*, 133.

A GREEK MONSTER

Fossil interpretation among the Greeks dominates the subject of Mayor's first book. A brief illustration of the phenomenon may be found in the following story.

Homer tells a legend of the king Laomedon of Troy. It is said that the god Poseidon, angry with the monarch for failing to square a debt, sent a great sea monster to destroy his city. Seeking to appease the creature, Laomedon chained his daughter to the rocks outcropping the sea. Hercules, just arriving from an expedition, saw the distressed princess and defeated the beast in combat.

What makes this case compelling is that this legend came to be depicted on a Corinthian vase dating to the 500's BC—an image of which can be seen on the cover of Mayor' book. The artist who created the vase depicts the Trojan monster as a large, toothy animal skull eroding out of a rocky outcrop. Certainly, the artist was aware that such a fossil in his day was being associated with the story.[57] Again, we see an example of how mythological stories were invoked to explain these petrified alien forms.

DRAGONS IN NORTH AMERICA

Finally, many curious examples of ancient fossil legends have been documented in North America.

Interestingly, the Pit River people, the Navajo, and the Zuni intuited that the world must be extremely old in their creation myths. Mayor relates to us a story from one Pit River Indian who recalls encountering young-earth creationist teachers as a young boy in school. The Indian children refused to accept the earth is young and sarcastically "clashed head-on" with their teachers because it contradicted their geological intuitions.[58] As one Lakota holy man wrote: "What you people call fossils, these too are used by us. Deep in the Badlands we find the bones of the water monster, which lived before human beings appeared."[59]

The Zuni explained the petrified skeletons on their lands as the work of two Hero Twins. As in the Apache story, in primordial times, the

---

[57] Mayor, *Fossil Legends of the First Americans*, 160-161.

[58] Ibid., 150.

[59] I am indebted to Mayor for this citation. John Fire Lame Deer and Richard Erdoes, *Lame Deer, Seeker of Visions: The Life of a Sioux Medicine Man* (London: Touchstone, 1972), 134.

earth was teeming with terrible predators. But the Sun gave special lightning to two twins with which to fight these beasts. They swept the land with their new power, blasting the bizarre foes wherever they found them, crying out: "We have changed you into rock everlasting!"[60]

One ethnologist, adopted into their tribe, stated that it is for this reason, "we find, here and there, throughout the world, their forms, sometimes large like the beings themselves, sometimes shriveled and distorted. And we often see among the rocks the forms of many beings that live no longer."[61]

The Hopi and Pueblo were much more religiously comfortable with approaching the remains of these ancient enemies than the Navajo. Their potters say that the most prized stones for polishing pottery come from dinosaur skeletons. "These 'dinosaur stones' were passed down over generations of craftspeople. Potters describe going out with elders to areas where dinosaur bones are found, to search for rounded, smooth pebbles inside rib cages."[62] This practice of collecting what paleontologists call gastroliths (stones swallowed by animals to aid in digestion) is quite ancient. In Wyoming and Montana, paleontologists have discovered several sites where Clovis people also intentionally sought out and fashioned tools from the gastroliths obtained from dinosaur exposures.[63]

In his biography, a Lakota medicine man named Lame Deer recounts how in the early 1900s, while crossing the Badlands of the Rosebud Reservation in the Dakotas, he was caught in a terrible hailstorm. The clouds blotted out the landscape in darkness and Lame Deer's hair stood on end from the electricity in the air—what he took as the great Thunder Birds overhead. Fearing flash flooding, he scuffled up a ridge and straddled it in the dark, clinging to it all night as he awaited the warming break of dawn. As his surroundings became visible, he made a frightening discovery: "I was straddling a long row of petrified bones, the biggest I had ever seen. I had been moving along the spine of the

---

[60] Mayor, *Fossil Legends of the First Americans*, 112.

[61] Ibid.

[62] Ibid., 157. Examples of this are frequent in archaeology. For example, Susan C. Ryan (ed.), *The Archaeology of Shields Pueblo (Site 5MT3807): Excavations at a Mesa-Top Community Center in Southwestern Colorado* [PDF Title], (Crow Canyon Archeological Center, 2015), 251. Accessed Jul 20, 2017. Available at www.crowcanyon.org.shieldspueblo.

[63] Mayor, *Fossil Legends of the First Americans*, 157-8.

Great Unktehi [water dragon].... [R]iding the ridge like a horse was spooky, like riding the monster."[64]

Later, Lame Deer reported finding other ridges where "you can see vertebrae sticking out in a great row of red and yellow rocks."[65] Indeed, mosasaurs are common in the terrain spanning from Kansas to the Dakotas.

In the 1800s, the paleontologist Othniel Marsh commented that once, while seated on his horse in the badlands, he could count, "the remains of five huge monsters spread upon the plain."[66] According to Mayor, "skeletons of marine creatures and flying reptiles in the Kansas-Nebraska chalk beds certainly contributed to Plains Indian myths about Thunder Birds and Water Monsters."[67]

A story similar to Lame Deer's comes in a final example worthy of recounting from the childhood memory of a Crow medicine woman named Pretty Shield in the 1800s.

Before horses, Indians frequently hunted buffalo by routing them off cliffs. In her old Montana village, Pretty Shield and some other children were playing at the base of one of these buffalo jumps, collecting the old bones and making little tipis with them. One of the children got the idea to dig into a peculiar, black streak she noticed in the soil at the base of the cliff. She quickly happened to unearth a massive skull, unlike anything the children had seen before. By her descriptions and the general geology of the area, it was likely reptilian.

The girls ran home greatly disturbed and told their father of the nightmarish relic before guiding him to its location. The medicine man had them stand some distance away. He approached the ancient one and lit up his tobacco pipe. Between puffs, the Indian offered the end of the pipe up to its mouth. He explained that the girls were only playing and had not intended to disturb his rest. He then reverently wrapped it in fine buffalo leather and reburied it.[68] Such is the attitude of many tribes concerning large fossils. As Mayor observes, some believe, "it would be a grave hazard to disturb these ancient enemies, for fear of breaking the spell of their entrapment."[69]

---

[64] Ibid., 223-4.
[65] Ibid., 224.
[66] Ibid., 191.
[67] Ibid., 178.
[68] Ibid., 282-3.
[69] Ibid., 131.

I have only produced a meager handful of examples here from the hundreds of fascinating stories detailed between Mayor's two books. Surely, an in-depth study of other indigenous people in other fossiliferous parts of the world like Africa would likewise turn up the same sort of proclivities for fossil interpretation.

The bottom line is that the mere cross-cultural, independent existence of dragon legends doesn't automatically demand a massive overhaul of modern paleontological chronology. Mainstream scientists and anthropologists aren't helplessly flummoxed by dragon legends like many young-earth publications so frequently claim.

CONCLUSION

I have bitten hard in this section because I wish to encourage more caution among those who make claims from artifacts purporting to overturn the paleontological timeline affirmed by the vast majority of relevant scientists.

To review what we have seen, the Creation Museum, the late chemist Duane Gish, and Answers in Genesis' *Answers Book* have passed around a dragon hoax from a nineteenth century coal town newspaper. The Museum and other popular publishing scientists present a false interpretation of the Egyptian Narmer tablet, and we have seen a rock art display in the Museum that has been proven for years to be a misinterpretation by a published scientific journal.

Answers in Genesis possesses a purported aboriginal painting often cited as evidence for man's coexistence with living plesiosaurs, including in a Creation Museum Legacy Hall lecture by their Curriculum Specialist. However, a year before this presentation, it was already demonstrated that this painting had been copied from a children's book by a major magazine in an easily accessible online article.

Answers in Genesis' *Answers Book* and a young-earth geologist misinterpreted a pictograph of a Native American mountain lion spirit as a spiny dinosaur, despite how widely known the history of the image is. The Answers in Genesis website article also mistook a nineteenth century fiction magazine story as a serious historical account of a pterodactyl gobbling up Indians. Ken Ham, the Museum, and a popular young-earth astrophysicist, Bodie Hodge, among plenty of others, have also misused an old tale Herodotus passed on from Arabian spice traders in order to back up their belief that pterosaurs and human beings must have coexisted.

It is also worth mentioning that several articles on the Answers in Genesis' website, originally published in the magazine *Creation* in 1997 and 2002, took an optimistic stance on what are known as the Ica Stones.[70] Even at the time these articles were published it had long been demonstrated that the stones were hoaxed.[71]

Similar grievances could be cited of uncritical assertions from indigenous folklore currently being upheld in Answers in Genesis' life-sized Ark Encounter.[72]

---

[70] Swift's article emphasized the weathering, patina and pictorial deformation on a stone shown to him by Cabrera as "evidence against a modern forgery." Dennis Swift, "Messages on Stone," *Answers in Genesis*, March 1997. Accessed June 2017, www.answersingenesis.org/extinct-animals/ice-age/messages-on-stone/. Johnson's previously cited "Thunderbird" article claims there is no proof of forgery and that, "The stones remain a mystery, and reinforce the intriguing possibility that the ancient Amerindians knew of such creatures."

[71] On the history and forgery of the stones see Karen O. Bruhns, Nancy L Kelker, *Faking the Ancient Andes* (New York: Routledge, 2010), 183ff. According to Feder, Professor of Anthropology at Central Connecticut State University, in the *Encyclopedia of Dubious Archeology*, the stones "represent one of the most transparent and absurd archaeological hoaxes ever perpetrated.... They're simply inane." Kenneth L. Feder, *Encyclopedia of Dubious Archaeology: From Atlantis to the Walam Olum* (Santa Barbara: Greenwood, 2010), 141.

[72] For example, a sign in the Ark Encounter Museum (entitled, "Legends Around the World") claims to report indigenous legends from various cultures about the Tower of Babel. These are reproduced nearly word-for-word from the book *Searching for Adam* produced by Answers in Genesis' publisher (Tim Chaffey, "Humanity's Shared History Reflecting the Truth of Genesis 1-11," *Searching for Adam: Genesis 1-11 the Truth About Man's Origin* [Green Forest, AR: Master Books, 2016], 451). The Museum claims that the Choctaw of the United States, the Mikir of Burma, and the Papago of Arizona all had a legend about a tower built to heaven and a subsequent confusion of languages. The sign then flatly asserts, "These legends do not seem to be the result of missionary influence, as skeptics often allege." But the author's paper contains no independent analysis of these specific myths to assess them for missionary influence. With regards to the Choctaw legend, the Native American ethnographer David I. Bushnell Jr. took it for granted that the "Choctaw undoubtedly heard the story from the early missionaries.... [C]onsequently it may be that we have here their own ancient myth combined with, or modified by, the story told them by the missionaries" ("Myths of the Louisiana Choctaw," *American Anthropologist*, 12.4 [1910], 531). The author gives Frazer as his source for the Mikir Myth, yet Frazer likewise maintained, "There can be little doubt that this story is merely an echo of

If leading young-earthers want their highly minority positions in the physical sciences to be taken seriously, it is in their interest to avoid being negligent with ancient texts, folklore, and artifacts. It is difficult to trust such organization's stances on complex scientific topics like evolutionary biology, paleontology, and geology when any layperson with an internet connection can quickly see they have been prone in the past towards indulging in outlandish claims in simpler domains.

---

missionary teaching" (Sir James George Frazer, *Folk-lore in the Old Testament: Studies in Comparative Religion, Legend and Law vol 1* [London: MacMillan, 1918], 384). As for the Papago myth, I've tracked down what may be the earliest recorded version related in a government report in 1865 (M. O. Davidson, "Arizona Superintendancy" in *Annual Report of the Commissioner of Indian Affairs, for the Year 1865* [Washington: Washington Government Printing Office, 1865], 128-140. www.digital.library.wisc.edu/1711.dl/History.AnnRep65a). Besides the fact that this tribe long had missionary contact by this time, every version of the story has the first man named Montezuma—a name brought to the Papago by the Catholic Spaniards, whom our earliest missionary informants say they retained memory of in very old traditions. In the absence of contrary demonstration, the indigenous provenance of the Museum's related versions of these myths is doubtful.

APPENDIX B

MISUSE OF FLOOD LEGENDS

YOUNG-EARTH creationists frequently cite the existence of flood legends around the globe as evidence that the Great Flood was historical and universal. I've combed through many of these sources and can say with certainty that they are indeed a frequent feature of many mythologies.[1] The question that folklorists have asked in the past is whether these particular stories are the product of cultural transmission, independent local floods, or one global cataclysm. Several realizations have emerged: First, it is undeniable that many of these legends were the product of local floodings. How could one infer such a thing? One reason for inferring this is that only a comparative few flood legends remember the event as having occurred in some distant land. In most indigenous cultures, the given flood is remembered from the standpoint of the people group's present geography. Second, folklorists who have plotted the distribution of these legends geographically have discovered that there is a tendency for them to coincide with major bodies of water. For example, in North America, a massive cluster of flood legends curiously hug the West Coast, and there is an abnormal distribution along the Mississippi River and Great Lakes.[2] I would suggest that the disproportionate concatenation stretching California might be correlated with the fact that it was submerged under the ocean for much of its geological history, and we know Native Americans reasonably associated out-of-place marine fossils on land with their ancient flood stories.

---

[1] See for example, Dang Nghiem Van, "The Flood Myth and the Origin of Ethnic Groups in Southeast Asia," *The Journal of American Folklore* 106.421 (1993), 304-37.
[2] Bernhard Lang reproduces a chart of this in "Non-Semitic Deluge Stories and the Book of Genesis: A Bibliographical and Critical Survey," *Anthropos* 80, 4.6 (1985), 610.

Another consideration that should temper our citation of these legends is that Christian missionaries historically tended to reach many uncontacted people groups before the ethnographers did. In probably most cases, cultures were already exposed to Bible stories before their indigenous oral mythology had the opportunity of being recorded.[3] (Most often, missionaries brought the means of recording.) One example of this merging of native and biblical material can be observed in Hawaii.

A HAWAIIAN NOAH?

At the time of writing, Answers in Genesis' Ark Encounter Museum website features a page with beautiful graphics entitled, "World Flood Myths." One of the headings speaks of a Hawaiian flood account.[4] An Answers in Genesis article likewise claims:

> Hawaiians have a flood story that the world became a wicked...place. Only one good man was left, and his name was Nu-u. He made a great canoe with a house on it and filled it with animals.... [O]nly Nu-u and his family were saved.[5]

It truly would be impressive if this myth were indigenous, but according to an old article in the *Journal of the Polynesian Society*, at the time this legend was recorded, "many Hawaiian had become Christianized and familiar with biblical history."[6] This particular legend is related to us in Fornander's collections published in the early 1900s. We even have a

---

[3] For example, in his survey of Mesoamerican flood traditions, Horcasitas concluded, "The biblical account has exerted an overwhelming influence on indigenous deluge stories, no matter how remote the native cultures have been from European groups." Fernando Horcasitas, "An analysis of the Deluge Myth in Mesoamerica," in Alan Dundes, *The Flood Myth* (Berkeley: University of California Press, 1988), 216.
[4] "World Flood Myths" under the heading, "Hawaii," *Ark Encounter*, 2017. Accessed Sept 2, 2017, www.arkencounter.com/flood/myths/.
[5] Monty White, "Flood Legends: The Significance of a World of Stories Based on Truth," *Answers Magazine*, 2007. Accessed Jun 2017, www.answersingenesis.org/the-flood/flood-legends/flood-legends/.
[6] Bruce Cartwright, "The Legend of Hawaii-Loa," *The Journal of the Polynesian Society* 38, 2.150 (1929), 105-121.

record of the older version of the legend before the biblical additions were inserted. I dug up the Hawaiian travel journal of the missionary William Ellis in 1823. Midway through, Ellis mentions he talked to some Hawaiians who told him "their fathers…had never before heard of a ship, or of Noah" like the later Christianized Fornander version of the myth.[7] The significant biblical parallels weren't indigenous. Unfortunately, you can find creationist books and websites everywhere repeating the later legend as if it's the original. Duane Gish had illustrations of it made for his children's book.[8] Kent Hovind repeated it in lecture slides. It is on a panel in the Creation Evidence Museum in Texas,[9] and it is presently featured on the website of the Kentucky 100 million dollar ark museum.

A HINDU NOAH?

Another Answers in Genesis article refers to a very ancient Indian flood legend recorded in the Satapatha Brahmana and Mahabharata.[10] This one predates the first century, so Christian missionaries couldn't have been the source of the parallels between it and the Bible. However, the problem with taking the Indian Manu fish story as evidence of a global flood is that it sides with Mesopotamian mythology *against* the biblical story on certain details. Most notably, in the Mesopotamian myth, there are seven gods called *apkallu* who deliver culture to humanity before the Flood.

---

[7] William Ellis, *A Narrative of a Tour through Hawaii, or Owhyhee: With Remarks on the History, Traditions, Manners, Customs and Language of the Inhabitants*, The Advertiser Historical Series No. 2 (Honolulu: Hawaiian Gazette Co., 1917), 333. See digital version at www.archive.org/details/journalofwilliam000434mbp.

[8] Duane T. Gish, *Dinosaurs by Design* (Green Forest: Master Books, 1992), 74.

[9] This is reported by Julie Anne Duncan, "Faith Displayed as Science: The Role of the 'Creation Museum' in the Modern American Creationist Movement" (Student Thesis Harvard University, 2009), 75.

[10] Troy Lacey and Lee Anderson, "The Genesis Flood—Not Just Another Legend," *Answers Magazine*, 2013. Accessed Jun 2017, www.answersingenesis.org/the-flood/flood-legends/the-genesis-flood-not-just-another-legend/.

Annus has catalogued Mesopotamian inscriptions demonstrating that Genesis 6 was intentionally polemicizing *against* the *apkallu* tradition,[11] but these figures are similar to the seven *rishis* in the Indian myth. In an article in the *Journal of Indian History*, Stavig affirms, "In both the Indian and Mesopotamian narrative the seven sages survived the flood since [the god] Marduk sent the seven sages to Apsu during the deluge."[12] He further cites heavy correspondences between the Indian and Babylonian creation myths.[13] Indeed, archaeology confirms contact between Southern India and Mesopotamia.[14] "Given the strength of these arguments, it can be assumed that the two versions of the flood story in the Satapatha Brahmana and the Mahabharata were likely influenced by Mesopotamian traditions."[15] A historical global flood doesn't seem necessary to explain the data here because the Indian legend has idiosyncratic details indicating a transmission from the particular Mesopotamian version.

A CHINESE NOAH?

The Answers in Genesis piece also claims: "Another flood story is from China. It records that Fuhi, his wife, three sons, and three daughters escaped a flood and were the only people alive on earth. After the Great Flood, they repopulated the world."[16] I spent several days trying to find a primary source for this online and in ethnographic journals. All I could find were references in creationist websites and books that

---

[11] Amar Annus, "On the Origin of the Watchers: A Comparative Study of the Antediluvian Wisdom in Mesopotamian and Jewish Traditions," *Journal for the Study of the Pseudepigrapha* 19.4 (2010), 277–320. I am indebted to Michael Heiser for making this study known to me.

[12] Gopal Stavig, "Historical Contacts Between Ancient India and Babylon," *Journal of Indian History*. Platinum Jubilee Volume (2001), 2.

[13] Ibid., 3-5

[14] Ed Noort, "The Stories of the Great Flood: Notes on Gen 6:5-9:17 in its Context of the Ancient Near East" in Martínez and Luttikhuizen, *Interpretations of the Flood*, Themes in Biblical Narrative (Leiden: Brill, 1998), 11-2. Stavig, "Historical Contact," 12. V. R. Ramachandra Dikshitar, *The Matsya Purana: A Study*. Bulletins of the Department of Indian History and Archaeology 5 (University of Madras, 1935), 14.

[15] Noort, "The Stories of the Great Flood," 12.

[16] White, "Flood Legends," n.p.

pointed back to a book entitled *Dinosaurs by Design* by the late Duane Gish. I promptly ordered this hoping that Gish might have provided the primary Chinese text. I didn't expect to receive an illustrated children's book in the mail. Flipping through the pages, towards the end, I came to an illustration of a Chinese man next to an oriental version of the ark, the same image I had seen on the Answers in Genesis website article.

The text reads:

> One ancient Chinese classic called the "Hihking" tells the story of Fuhi, whom the Chinese consider to be the father of their civilization. This history records that Fuhi, his wife, three sons, and three daughters escaped a great flood. He and his family were the only people left alive on earth. After the great flood they repopulated the world. An ancient temple in China has a wall painting that shows Fuhi's boat in the raging waters. Dolphins are swimming around the boat and a dove with an olive branch in its beak is flying toward it.[17]

The '*Hihking*,' certainly refers to the *I Ching*—the ancient Chinese *Book of Changes*. The *I Ching* isn't a collection of Chinese mythology but a 3,000-year-old technical divination manual. I tracked down a translation of the book and combed every page, both by hand and using digital searches. I found no flood account.

Frustrated, I finally contacted Mark Edward Lewis at Stanford University, a leading historian of ancient China and Professor of Chinese Culture. His 2006 book, *The Flood Myths of Early China*, is described in a review in the *Journal of Folklore Research* as the most comprehensive Western monograph on the subject.[18] When I shared with him the above quote circulated in creationist literature, he assured me, "No early text has any myth of this nature." He then pointed out that Gish's 'Fuhi' refers to Fu Xi—a serpent bodied deliverer of culture. He and his twin sister became associated with a flood myth in a third or fourth century AD text, though they were not generally associated with flood mythology before that time. In the story, the twins survive the deluge and repopulate the earth. I failed to locate any mention of "three

---

[17] Gish, *Dinosaurs by Design*, 74.
[18] Xiaohong Chen, "The Flood Myths of Early China (Review)," *Journal of Folklore Research Reviews* (2008), accessed Apr 2, 2018.
https://scholarworks.iu.edu/journals/index.php/jfrr/article/view/2543/2419.

sons and three daughters" who endured with them. In regards to the painting that Gish claimed exists in some unspecified "ancient temple in China," Lewis responded, "If the temple that you describe exists anywhere, and I have no knowledge of it, it is certainly not 'ancient.'"[19]

I hope that challenging unfounded claims such as these will additionally encourage creationists to exercise greater caution with how they use indigenous flood legends.

---

[19] Personal email correspondence on Feb 13, 2017.

APPENDIX C

COSMOLOGY AND TRADITIONAL
WORLD CULTURES

THE following survey closes this book and examines how traditional cultures around the globe have interpreted the physical cosmos. In contextualizing ancient Judah's cosmic geography, this book has prioritized the *Sitz im Leben* of the Near East. However, it can be independently demonstrated that the interpretations supplied from this specified context comport with cognitive dispositions that are found to be anthropologically universal. The ubiquity of belief in an essentially flat earth and solid sky vault in traditional cultures rebuts a poplar apologetic narrative that exaggerates the astronomical sophistication of ancient peoples and provides a secondary level of analysis in support of this book's interpretations.

THE QUR'AN

The Yale philologist Kevin van Bladel has published a fascinating paper on the historical context of the Qur'an's cosmology.[1] We know from Christian writings leading up to and during Muhammad's life that the spherical earth hypothesized by Ptolemaic cosmology was still controversial in some geographies despite being nearly universally embraced by the West. In the early 400s, Severian, the Bishop of Gabala in Syria published six sermons on creation where he vehemently

---

[1] The following examples are from Kevin Van Bladel, "Heavenly Cords and Prophetic Authority in the Quran and Its Late Antique Context," *Bulletin of the School of Oriental and African Studies, University of London* 70.2 (2007), 225-46. www.jstor.org/stable/40379198.

defended a flat earth interpretation of the Bible. From him we read statements like the following: "'[It] is He…that stretcheth out the heavens as a curtain and spreadeth them out as a tent to dwell in'; the Scripture says that it has a top, which a sphere has not." Severian believed, like many ancient Rabbis, that the earth was flat and the sun didn't submerge under it at night, but retrogressed back to its starting place behind the dome, "as if hidden by a wall."[2]

Later, Cosmas Indicopleustes, a Syrian trained churchman, wrote an impressively large collection entitled *Christian Topography* around 550. In it, he also attempted to prove that the earth is essentially flat with a solid sky—against the opinion of other Christians like John Philoponus who accepted the Ptolemaic model. Like Severian, Cosmas often cited the tent language in Isa 40:22 and Psa 104:2 to demonstrate this, and he constantly refers to the idea of a spherical earth with pejoratives like "pagan error."

Other sixth century Syrian Christians who defended the flat earth included a theologian named Narsai, the head of the school of Nisibis, and Jacob of Serugh.[3] We even have a Syriac hymn from the middle of the sixth century that implies the physical dome of a church is similar to the sky.[4]

All this is significant because the Christianity the Qur'an most interacts with was the Syriac church. Not only do early Islamic sources tell us this, but scholars recognize that there are a large number of Syriac words and phrases in the Qur'an which have been translated into Arabic.[5] The evidence indicates that Muhammad assumed some cosmological notions shared by the Syriac Christian writings we have. Probably the most explicit example of this is contained in a fascinating story the Qur'an relates about Alexander the Great (called here "The

[2] Quoted J. L. E. Dreyer, "Medieval Cosmology" in Milton K. Munitz (ed.), *Theories of the Universe: From Babylonian Myth to Modern Science* (New York: The Free Press, 1957), 119.
[3] Bladel, "Heavenly Cords," 226.
[4] Ibid.
[5] See comments on Muhammad's contact with the Syrian Church in Sidney Griffith, "Christian Lore and the Arabic Qur'ān: The 'Companions of the Cave' in *Sūrat al-Kahf* and in Syriac Christian Tradition" in Gabriel Said Reynolds (ed.), *The Qur'ān and Its Historical Context*. Routledge Studies in the Qur'ān (New York: Routledge, 2008), 110, 114-116.

Two-Horned One") in surah 18. I've lightly modified Bladel's exceptionally clear translation as follows:[6]

83. And they are asking you about the Two-Horned One.
Say: I will relate for you a glorious record about him.
84. We [Allah speaking] granted him power in the earth
and gave him a heavenly course (*sabab*) out of every thing.
85. So he followed a heavenly course
86. until, when he reached the place of the sun's setting,
he found it setting in a putrid spring
and he found by it a people.
We said, "O Two-Horned One, either you will punish (them) or do them a favor."
87. He said, "Whoever does wrong, we will punish him,
and then he will be sent back to his Lord
and He will punish them in an unknown way."

There are several reasons one can imply the Qur'an is being literal here:

1) A Hadith reports that one of Muhammad's close companions named Abu Dharr had a conversation with the prophet about the setting of the sun, and Muhammad purportedly told him that it sets in a spring of water.

2) We know what tradition stream the Qur'an is drawing this story from, and that source is emphatically describing the sun literally setting in water.

Concerning the first: *Sunan Abu Dawud* is the name of one of the more popular Hadith collections recorded a couple of centuries after Muhammad's death. In it, Abu Dawud recounts an early story about Muhammad attributed to one of Muhammad's closest companions named Abu Dharr:

---

[6] I have modified Bladel's translation here by excising a footnote, two Arabic transliterations and by exchanging his phrase "fetid spring" with "putrid spring." In Kevin Van Bladel, "The Alexander Legend in the Qur'ān 18:83-102," in Gabriel Said Reynolds (ed.), *The Qur'ān in Its Historical Context*. Routledge Studies in the Qur'an (New York: Routledge, 2008), 177.

Narrated Abu Dharr: I was sitting behind the Messenger of Allah [peace be upon him] who was riding a donkey while the sun was setting. He asked: Do you know where this sets? I replied: Allah and his Apostle know best. He said: It sets in a spring of warm water.[7]

Some avoid the implications of this Hadith by arguing that it's unhistorical, but for our purposes, the historicity of this account is irrelevant. Whatever the case may be, the literal cosmology appears to have been taken seriously enough for Abu Dawud to pass it on in Muhammad's name, evidence that in Muhammad's recent context it would have been a live option.

More importantly, as I mentioned, the tradition stream from which the Qur'an takes this story is known. It was recorded in a more detailed account composed sometime after AD 628 (Muhammad died in 632) in a Syriac text called the *Alexander Legend*. The *Alexander Legend* is important because it contextualizes the strange elements in the Qur'anic telling. For example, Alexander is called the "Two-Horned One" in the Qur'an because God puts iron horns on his head in the Syriac version. The Qur'an tells how Alexander discovered the putrid sea at the edge of the earth. The Syriac version uses a similar odd description. In the Qur'an, when Alexander reaches the putrid waters, Allah cryptically tells him he can either "punish the people or do them a favor." In the Syriac version, one finds this corresponds with Alexander testing the deadliness of the waters by casting in convicts.

The Qur'an also uses the term "heavenly course" (*sabab*) to describe the heavenly conduit that Alexander follows. This is paralleled with the Syriac "window of heaven" that Alexander takes to traverse the sky vault (much like the old Gilgamesh motif).[8] Later in the Qur'an, Alexander builds a barrier wall out of metal to protect an ambiguous people in a foreign land. We find in the Syriac narrative that this was accomplished by thousands of workers he borrowed from Egypt— created to protect the Persians from two Hun kings. Bladel summarizes:

---

[7] I have excised a transliteration at the end of this quotation. *Sunan Abu Dawud*, Book 31, Hadith 3991. "Dialects and Readings of the Qur'an (Kitab Al-Huruf Wa Al-Qira'at)" *Sunnah.com*, accessed Jan 2017. www.sunnah.com/abudawud/32/34.

[8] Bladel, "Heavenly Cords and Prophetic Authority," 227-9.

They relate the same story in precisely the same order of events using many of the same particular details. Every part of the Qur'anic passage has its counterpart in the Syriac, except that in the Qur'an the story is told through the first-person account of God.[9]

It is undeniable that the two traditions contextualize each other and they both adhere to some of the same cosmology in their interface. In short, even after the dissemination of the Ptolemaic model, seventh century Middle Christians and Muslims were still taking ideas about the literal "ends of the earth" seriously.

NATIVE AMERICAN LEGENDS

Levy-Bruhl writes, "In North America, in Indian belief, the earth is a circular disc usually surrounded on all sides by water and the sky is a solid concave hemisphere coming down at the horizon to the level of the earth."[10] Hartley's *Native American Mythology* agrees that indigenous North Americans believed the earth, "is flat and round below and surmounted above by a solid firmament in the shape of an inverted bowl."[11]

There are no shortages of wonderful North American stories that convey this cosmology. In 1908, an ethnographer named David I. Bushnell Jr. spent five months visiting some of the few Choctaw still living near Bayou Lacomb in Louisiana. The following is one of the legends he received firsthand:

Tashka and Walo were brothers who lived long ago. Every morning they saw the sun rise above the horizon, pass high overhead, and late in the day die in the West. When the boys were about four years old they conceived the idea of following the sun and seeing where he died. So the next day, when he was overhead, they started to follow him; but that night, when he died, they were still in their own

---

[9] Bladel, "The Alexander Legend in the Qur'ān," 182.

[10] I owe this citation to Paul Seely, "The Firmament and the Water Above: Part I: The Meaning of *raqia*ʿ in Gen 1:6-8," *Westminster Theological Journal* 53 (1991), 229. Originally in B. Sproul, *Primal Myths* (New York: Haper & Row, 1969), 61.

[11] Hartley Burr Alexander, *Native American Mythology* (New York: Dover Publications, 2005), 249.

country, where they knew the hills and the rivers. Then they slept, and in the morning when the sun was again overhead they once more set off to follow him. And thus they continued for many years to wend their way after the sun in his course through the heavens.

Long, long afterward, when the two boys had become men, they reached a great expanse of water, and the only land they could see was the shore on which they were standing. Late that day, when Sun died, they saw him sink into the water; then they also passed over the water and entered Sun's home with him.[12]

As the story progresses, we learn that the two young men make their way above the sky and they are aided by a massive buzzard to return to their home on earth.

The Navaho story of creation better describes the solid dome (apparently made of stone) and claims that a race of blue-headed people lives above it in a second blue world. It speaks of an earthly tribe who,

> ...went in circles upward till they reached the sky. It was smooth. They looked down.... [Some]one having a blue head thrust out his head from the sky and called to them, saying: "In here, to the eastward, there is a hole." They entered the hole and went through it up to the surface (of a second world). The blue one belonged to the...Swallow People.... A great many of their houses, rough and lumpy, lay scattered all around.[13]

The Shishoni relate a remarkably clever conception. They imagined the sky was made of a great dome of ice and that the spirit of a giant serpent (the rainbow) produced rain by rubbing its back against this surface, grating off ice that melted as it precipitated.[14] Discussing the clearly stated Cherokee belief that the sky was a "vault of solid rock," a nineteenth century Smithsonian ethnographer among the Cherokee tells us that this vault was believed to be in a state of "constantly rising and

---

[12] David I. Bushnell, Jr., *The Choctaw of Bayou Lacomb St. Tammany Parish Louisiana.* Smithsonian Institution Bureau of American Ethnology (BAE) Bulletin 48 (Washington: Government Printing Office, 1909), 35.
[13] Washington Matthews, *Navaho Legends.* Memoirs of the American Folk-lore Society Vol. V (New York: G. E. Stechert & Co, 1897), 64-5.
[14] Peter Metevelis, "The Lapidary Sky over Japan," *Asian Folklore Studies* 59.1 (2000), 83.

falling at the horizon and crushes those who try to go beyond." This concept was expressed, "in the mythologies of the Iroquois of New York, the Omaha, and the Sioux of the plains, the Tillamook of Oregon and other widely separated tribes."[15] An example of this theme is the Tillamook myth where six men travel to the other side of the sky but upon returning one gets cut in half by its slamming shut.[16]

There's also a common motif of myths surrounding the theme of people piercing the heavenly vault, especially among tribes of the Plateau and Northwest Coast. Like Australian Aboriginal myths involving a chain of spears, a Tlingit story has a boy creating a ladder of arrows by successively shooting them into the vault. He then climbs up these to reach the other side of heaven.[17]

AUSTRALIA

As unlikely as it may seem, Australian Aboriginal cosmology also shares some general commonalities with ideas found in the Bible, showing that these ideas arise naturally as ancient people attempt to interpret the world with the naked eye. Dianne Johnson, in her book *Night Skies of Aboriginal Australia,* writes:

> Despite my cautionary notes about different cosmologies, it is occasionally possible to identify universal themes. Most Australian Aboriginal people held a common view of the earth as a flat disc surrounded by the boundless water of an ocean. Above this earth-disc was a solid vault or canopy. Beyond this vault was the sky-world, a vast, plentiful and beautiful place.[18]

In the Australian Alps, the sky dome was conceived to be held up by trees. Among a people from the Great Australian Bight, it is reported that they said the dome was supported by "a great tree, known as

---

[15] James Mooney, *Myths of the Cherokee*. The Smithsonian Institution BAE Annual Report 19 (Washington: Government Printing Office, 1897-98), 440.

[16] Ibid.

[17] John Reed Swanton, *Tlingit Myths and Texts*. The Smithsonian Institution BAE Bulletin 39 (Washington: Government Printing Office, 1909), 439.

[18] Dianne Johnson, *Night Skies of Aboriginal Australia: A Noctuary* (Sydney: Sydney University Press, 2014), 23.

Warda," and on the New South Wales coast, the mythology speaks of supporting "solid wooden pillars watched over and guarded by an old man."[19] One anthropologist reports that the Karadjeri conceived of the sky dome as made of "rock or shell."[20] Johnson also mentions the many Aboriginal stories of people finding ways to climb up to and walk around upon the heavenly vault.[21] For example, she tells us, "Among some Victorian groups there was a view that people used to be able to climb up an immense pine tree...up through its branches to the topmost ones which reached the sky. They could walk about, indeed live on the starry vault."[22] In the Adelaide area, there is a myth about a man who threw a massive spear that stuck in the vault. He then threw another with such terrific aim that it stuck in the butt of the first spear, and so, throwing spear after spear, they eventually extended to the ground, and he was able to climb up them to the sky, on the other side of which, he decided to live.[23] The Mandalbingu people of Arnhem Land tell a story about how the sky was originally lifted and separated from the earth by magpie birds with the help of wooden props of graduating length.[24]

OCEANIC PEOPLE GROUPS

Seely points us to a naturalist who spent time living among the Dayak headhunters of Borneo in the early twentieth century. He reports that these people:

> ...consider the earth to be a flat surface, whilst the heavens are a dome, a kind of glass shade which covers the earth, and comes in contact with it at the horizon. They, therefore, believe that, traveling straight on, always in the same direction, one comes at last, without any metaphor, to touch the sky with one's fingers. Now as they know that Europeans come from far away over the sea, the

---

[19] Ibid., 23-4.
[20] Ibid., 24.
[21] Ibid, 24-7.
[22] Ibid., 24-5.
[23] Related in Philip A. Clarke, "The Aboriginal Cosmic Landscape of Southern South Australia," *Records of the South Australian Museum* 29.2, 128.
[24] Johnson, *Night Skies of Aboriginal Australia*, 26.

supposition that we are nearer heaven comes naturally to them…. It was with real sorrow that they heard me assert that in Europe the sky was quite as far from the earth as in Borneo.[25]

Seely draws our attention to another report from the Mortlock Islands:

[I]n reply to our question as to what land lay beyond these islands, the natives drew a line to the west of them and explained in a very clear and simple way that yonder, beyond the Paloas Islands, the dome of the sky was too close to the earth to permit navigation; the utmost that could be done was to crawl along the ground or swim in the sea.[26]

Among the Melanesians we are told, "Many of the natives thought that if they could only reach [the horizon] they would be able to climb up to the sky."[27] The Māori of New Zealand tell how the sky father *Rangi* and earth mother *Papa* once lovingly embraced, leaving little space and no light for their terrestrial children. In order to create more living space and let in light, one of their offspring called *Tāne-toko-rangi* ("Tāne who propped up the sky") dropped on his back and used his feet to push the sky father and earth mother asunder. In some versions, the two were then retained with props. It is said that rain drops are the tears of *Rangi*, who still longs to embrace his terrestrial bride.[28]

In Fiji, we find represented the motif of the warrior who climbs a tree to reach the vault in a previous age when it was much lower.[29] A Hawaiian legend compares the universe with a calabash gourd. "They speak of the earth—*paa ilalo*, the 'solid below'—and the heavens—*paa iluna*, the 'solid above.'"[30] Citing a wealth of anthropological studies

---

[25] Odoardo Beccari, *Wandering in the Great Forests of Borneo: Travels and Researches of a Naturalist in Sarawak*. Trans. Enrico H. Giglioli (London: Archibald Constable & Co, 1904), 337-8.

[26] L. Levy-Bruhl, *Primitive Mentality* (Boston: Beacon, 1966), 53-55.

[27] Ibid.

[28] Stephen Robert Chadwick and Martin Paviour-Smith, *The Great Canoes in the Sky: Starlore and Astronomy of the South Pacific* (Switzerland: Springer, 2006), 183.

[29] See Ev Cochrane "The Ladder-to-Heaven," 7. Available from Cochrane at www.maverickscience.com/myth-ladder.pdf. Originally in his *Martian Metamorphoses: The Planet Mars in Ancient Myth & Religion* (Aeon: 1997).

[30] Maud W. Makemson, "Hawaiian Astronomical Concepts," *American Anthropologist* 40.3 (1938), 370.

conducted in the early twentieth century, the great Italian religious historian Raffaele Pettazzoni wrote the following:

> The notion of the firmament as a solid vault made of a hard, blue, transparent substance is quite wide-spread in Polynesia, from the Tonga Islands to Mangaia, from Tahiti to the Marquesas. Such a notion is also to be found among the Andamanese, where the Supreme Being Puluga is believed to live in a large stone house in the sky. The same idea is found in Africa…and in Madagascar….[31]

The people of Busama in New Guinea believe the bowl of heaven "is as strong and solid as roof-thatch." Sometimes the Melanesians fear it will become old and one day break.[32] In Western New Guinea the Yali also say it is "solid and as hard as a rock."[33]

CHINA AND JAPAN

A Chinese text called *The Mathematical Classic Concerning the Dial and Gnomon* includes material that may date as early as 1,000 BC. It talks about the *gai tian* or Celestial Lid—a dome with attached celestial bodies. The ancient Chinese thought of the earth as surrounded by an ocean like the Hebrews, but unlike them believed the earth was square instead of a disk, a view partly motivated by Taoist geometrical harmony.[34] By around AD 200, there arose three Chinese astronomical schools: The *kai thien* school believed heaven to be a solid dome. The *hun thien* understood the heavens to be a solid but rotating sphere somewhat like the Western model, and the last school, the *hsüan yeh*, posited an atmospheric model of "infinite space." The appearance of this atmospheric model by this time evinces that the Chinese were

---

[31] Raffaele Pettazzoni, *Essays on the History of Religions*. Trans. H. J. Rose (Leiden: Brill, 1967), 40-41.
[32] Bo Flood, Beret E. Strong, William Flood, *Pacific Island Legends: Tales from Micronesia, Melanesia, Polynesia, and Australia* (Honolulu: Besspress, 1999), 90-91.
[33] Freerk C. Kamma, *Religious Texts of the Oral Tradition from Western New-Guinea*. Religious Texts Translation Series: Nisaba, vol. 8 (Leiden: Brill, 1978), 118.
[34] Joanne Conman, "It's about Time: Ancient Egyptian Cosmology," *Studien zur Altägyptischen Kultur* 31 (2003), 34-35.

remarkably advanced relative to the rest of the world.[35] Needham emphasizes, "It is obvious…that the *hsüan yeh* conception was a very enlightened one. It was really more enlightened than the Aristotelian-Ptolemaic conception of concentric crystalline spheres, which was dominant in European thought for a thousand years or more."[36] In fact, the Chinese were so ahead of their time that in 1595 a Jesuit missionary named Matteo Ricci wrote back home a letter enumerating a number of the "absurdities" of the Chinese. Among them, he listed their belief that the sky is empty (and not solid) and that the stars move in a void![37]

Despite all this, we should not minimize the tenacity of the solid dome idea in China. A chronicle as late as the Liang dynasty (AD 502-556) relates a creation myth in which a demiurge chisels the sky out the primordial rock, separating them with chisel and hammer.[38] In addition to the Chinese examples, Japan also had mythologies about the sun concealing itself in a rock-grotto in the sky, and we find that the stone firmament is represented in Shinto temples.[39]

INDIA

Unsurprisingly, Indian cosmology is complex, but the themes we have been tracing can be found here as well. The earliest source, the Rig Veda, dated roughly around 1,500 BC, clearly articulates a solid firmament. Seely cites examples that I here reproduce: One creation hymn speaks of the god "by whom the dome of the sky was propped up" (10.121.5). Another says, "Firm is the sky and firm is the earth" (10.173.4). There is also mention of people who "climb up to the sky" (8.14.14; 2.12.12; 1.85.7), language about the separation of the sky from

---

[35] Joseph Needham, "The Cosmology of Early China" in Carmen Blacker (ed.), *Ancient Cosmologies* (Great Britain: George Allen & Unwin, 1975), 87-9.

[36] Ibid., 91.

[37] Ibid., 92. Matteo Ricci was writing just as belief in the solid spheres of the Copernican model was dying out in the Western astronomical community. This shift is usually attributed to the work of the English astronomer Thomas Digges publishing in 1576.

[38] Metevelis, "The Lapidary Sky over Japan," 80. See also the myth of the sky created from the god Phan Ku's skull. David Adams Leeming and Margaret Adams Leeming, *A Dictionary of Creation Myths* (Oxford: Oxford University Press, 1994), 49.

[39] Ibid., 79-88.

earth (7.86.1), and the god Varona, who "pushed away the dome of the sky."[40]

Following these texts come the Sanskrit Brahmanas composed around 900-700 BC. In them, the world is compared to a tortoise shell. Its domed upper shell was compared to the heavenly vault and the flat underside held to be analogous to earth.[41] One also sees the sky compared to an eggshell accompanied by first attempts to estimate the height of the dome.[42] (The answer is a thousand cows stacked on one another, for those wondering.)[43]

AFRICA

One ethnographer writing an article on the cosmology of the Tswana of South Africa mentions the cosmology of the Babylonians, Egyptians, and Hebrews and tells us that the Tswana vision of the universe "departs little from this picture." He says, "It is interesting to observe that, regardless of where man has sought to reflect upon, and interpret the universe around him, he has come to roughly the same conclusions."[44] We find that "The Tswana universe is geocentric; the stars, sun and moon revolve round the earth which is flat. At the edge of the earth is water. The sky is made of stone, the stone of God, beyond which God lives. Water is beneath the earth and above the sky."[45]

---

[40] Seely draws our attention to this information ("The Firmament," 232), citing W. O'Flaherty (trans.), *The Rig Veda*, (New York: Penguin, 1981), 26, 28, 35, 36, 64, 160, 161, 165, 213.

[41] R. F. Gombrich, "Ancient Indian Cosmology" in Blacker, *Ancient Cosmologies*, 116.

[42] Ibid., 117. The reference is to *Pancavimsa Brahmana* XX. 1, 9.

[43] Ibid. Another example: The Minyong tribe in northeast India say that the earth is a woman and the sky a man. When the two married and desired to come together the lesser gods, man and animals held a council, "to consider how they could save themselves from being crushed between them." They say that one of the gods, Sedi-Diyor grabbed hold of the sky and gave him such a beating that he fled upwards and has stayed there ever since. Sproul, *Primal Myths*, 197.

[44] Andrew Clegg, "Some Aspects of Tswana Cosmology," *Botswana Notes and Records* 18 (1986), 33.

[45] Ibid., 33.

Pettazzoni observed that, "The same idea [of a solid vault] is found in Africa not only in Madagascar but also in southern Nigeria, and in the Cameroons, among the Pangwe, as likewise among the Djagga in the north-east of the African continent."[46] The Zulu people apparently believed the sky to be made of "a blue rock."[47] The Bantu believe it to be a "solid roof" and have numerous myths about people reaching the world above by climbing trees or ropes let down from the vault. Breutz notes that this form of legend is quite common. "The concept that the sky is solid and connected to the earth by a ladder, rope or chain" appears in the Niger bend, among the Yoruba in Nigeria, the Mamabolo, Lamba, Tsonga and Zulu.[48] A Yao story tells of how a poor woman, whose baby drowned, was able to climb a tree up to heaven and successfully appeal to the deity on behalf of her child.[49] The Bavenda and Bathonga also considered the earth a "large flat disk floating in water, roofed by the dome of the sky…which meets the circumference of the disk at the horizon."[50]

SCANDINAVIA AND RUSSIA

The grim personality of Norse mythology is built into its creation and corresponds with some Chinese mythology and a belief held by the ancient Celts. In verses 40-41 in *Grímnismál* of the Poetic Edda, we are told the giant Ymir was slain. His flesh became the earth, the ocean his blood, and the sky was created from his colossal skull.

The *Kalevala*, the national epic of Finland, speaks of the smith god Ilmarinen who, along with forging sun and moon from gold and steel,

---

[46] Pettazzoni, *Essays on the History of Religions*, 41.

[47] J. A. Farrer, *Zululand and the Zulus: Their History, Beliefs Customs, Military System, Home Life, Legends, Etc., Etc., and Missions to Them* (Kerby & Endean: Oxford, 1879), 144.

[48] P. Breutz, "Sotho-Tswana Celestial Concepts," in *Ethnological and Linguistic Studies in Honour of N.J. van Warmelo*. Department of Bantu Administration and Development Ethnological Publications 52 (Pretoria: South Africa Government Printer, 1969), 199-200.

[49] See the first chapter of Alex Werner, *Myths and Legends of the Bantu* (London: George G. Harrap, 1933).

[50] Hugh Arthur Stayt, *The Bavenda* (New York: Frank Cass & Co, 1968), 225.

"shaped the sky, hammered out the lid of heaven."[51] Fortson points out that the Proto-Indo-European "word for 'stone' secondarily refers to 'heaven' in Indo-Iranian and Germanic." He notes that this "may rest on a conception of the heaven as a stony vault, from which fragments might fall in the form of meteorites...."[52]

According to Couprie, the Lapland people thought that heaven was held fixed by a great north nail (*bohinavvle*), the polar star. On the Day of Judgment Arcturus will shoot it with his bow causing the heavenly vault to crash to earth.[53] The Siberian tribes speak of "sky-land" which Raven once took Man up to explore and first acquire fire from a star in its vault.[54] A Chuckchi legend tells of how the Creator made sunshine by creating a woodpecker that he commanded to bore a hole into the vault.[55]

CENTRAL AND SOUTH AMERICA

Like the majority of creation stories, the Mayan *Popol Vuh* and the Mixtec people describe how the earth was formed from the darkness of the primordial waters. In Central and Yucatec Maya thought, the earth was sometimes conceived as the back of a colossal caiman floating among these cosmic waters.[56] One also observes the Aztecs referring to it as a disk surrounded by a ring of water, as well as square with four cardinal posts upholding the sky like the construction of a house.[57]

From the early Olmec to the Late Classical Maya and the Spanish Conquest there are texts and explicit depictions of gods bearing up the sky. An early Olmec monument shows two stout deities supporting its

[51] Eino Friberg (trans.), *Kalevala: Epic of the Finnish People*, 4 ed. (Helsinki: Otava Publishing, 1988), 356.
[52] Benjamin W. Fortson IV, *Indo-European Language and Culture: An Introduction*, 2 ed. Blackwell Textbooks in Linguistics (Singapore: Wiley-Blackwell, 2010), 26.
[53] D.L. Couprie (trans.), *Heaven and Earth in Ancient Greek Cosmology: From Thales to Heraclides Ponticus*. Astrophysics and Space Science Library 374 (New York: Springer, 2011), 213-14.
[54] Sproul, *Primal Myths*, 225.
[55] Ibid., 230.
[56] Mary Miller and Karl Taube, *An Illustrated Dictionary of the Gods and Symbols of Ancient Mexico and the Maya* (London: Thames & Hudson, 1997), 69-70.
[57] Ibid., 83-84.

great weight with arms raised aloft.[58] The architecture of Mayan temples also depict gods supporting the roof of the physical building.[59] The *Historia de los mexicanos por sus pinturas* tells us the heavens were raised by the creator's four sons, and the four sky bearers can likewise be found in the Aztec Vaticanus B and the Borgia codices.[60] The *Chilam Balam* speaks of how in a previous age the four *Bacab* deities holding up the sky destroyed the earth by letting it fall.

Among the natives of South America, Cochrane cites legends about ascents to the sky using ladders or arrow chains in countries like Brazil, Bolivia, and Argentina among the Mataco, Chorote, Nivalke, Tupi, Shipaya, and Sikuani. Frequently these myths presume an ancient time when the vault was much closer to earth.[61] The Mataco even claim that in former times people would climb to heaven from a high tree. "The men of this earth climbed up it and went to hunt in the world above."[62]

The solid firmament is well attested in the Amazon. Modern anthropological work among the remote Yanomami has been fascinating. They consider it a primary job of their shamans to uphold the heavenly vault with rituals, envisioning that one day it will collapse and destroy the world. The Brazilian Yanomami Davi Kopenawa describes this first hand: "Sometimes, when the sky makes threatening noises, women and children whimper and cry in fear. These are not empty cries! We all fear being crushed by the falling sky...." Kopenawa proceeds to illustrate this with a story from his youth: On a seemingly clear night in the forest, his people were alarmed when they heard, "several loud cracks in the sky's chest. They came in rapid succession, each more violent than the last, and they seemed very close." Everyone in the camp was sent into a panic, yelling and weeping with fear: "'Aë! The sky is starting to collapse! We are all going to perish! Aë!' I was also scared! I had not become a shaman yet..., [but] there were still great shamans among us, for many of our elders were still alive." Immediately, these elders began working to uphold the vault. "Their

---

[58] See the photograph of Potrero Nuevo Monument 2 in Miller and Taube, *Gods and Symbols*, 154.

[59] Deena Ragavan (ed.), *Heaven on Earth: Temples, Ritual, and Cosmic Symbolism in the Ancient World*. Oriental Institute Seminars 9 (Oriental Institute: Illinois, 2013), 112.

[60] Miller and Taube, *Dictionary of Ancient Mexico*, 154.

[61] Cochrane, "The Ladder-to-Heaven," 4-5.

[62] Ibid., 7.

fathers and grandfathers had taught them this work long ago. This is how once again they were able to prevent its fall."[63]

GREECE

Finally, this book has already developed how, by the fourth century, figures like Plato, Eudoxus, and Aristotle influenced the shape of the classical model of the universe that would find enduring influence and expression in the writings of Ptolemy. This model envisioned the celestial bodies fixed to a series of rotating spheres that surround the earth—the stars embedded upon the outermost sphere. Before the Milesian philosophers began formulating various complex models beginning around the sixth century BC, we can see that the Greeks shared an understanding of the cosmos with parallels to the Near East. Our earliest descriptions can be found in the writings of Homer. Adams tells us that Homer pictured the earth, "as a circular, flat disc surrounded by the great river Ocean."[64]

The Illiad (XVII:425) and the Odyssey (XV:329) tell us the sky is made of iron, an idea which Pontani quotes throughout other Greek texts.[65] The Greeks conceived it, "as a bowl-like hemisphere…covering a flat earth."[66] Seely likewise cites five other Classical scholars who agree that among Homer and Hesiod, "The sky is a solid hemisphere like a bowl…cover[ing] the flat round earth."[67] This old conception is also found in figures like Thales, Anaximander, and Xenophanes of Colophon.[68] In his *Geographica* (7.3.8), Strabo relates an amusing account citing Alexander the Great's general Ptolemy. During one of Alexander's military campaigns, he received Celtic ambassadors

---

[63] Davi Kopenawa and Bruce Albert, *The Falling Sky: Words of a Yanomami Shaman.* Trans. Nicholas Elliott and Alison Dundy (Cambridge: Belknap Press of Harvard, 2013), 129-130.

[64] Quotation from Iliad XVIII:607 in Edward Adams, "Graeco-Roman and Ancient Jewish Cosmology" in Johnathan T. Pennington (ed.) *Cosmology and New Testament Theology* (New York: T&T Clark, 2008), 7.

[65] Filippomaria Pontani, "Bronze Heaven in Archaic Greek Poetry," *L'antiquité classique* 80 (2011), 157-162.

[66] Ibid.

[67] Paul Seely, "The Geographical Meaning of 'Earth' and 'seas' in Genesis 1:10," *Westminster Theological Journal* 59 (1997), 235.

[68] Ibid.

interested in striking a treaty. Inviting them to a round of drinking, Alexander asked them what was the greatest object of fear among their people, expecting himself to be the answer. Instead, the Celts insisted that it was not any man they feared, but that they were chiefly concerned that the sky would one day collapse and destroy the world.

CONCLUSION

This survey should be sufficient evidence that premodern cultures universally tend strongly towards belief in a solid sky, usually a dome vault. They also very frequently (with a few exceptions) propound an essentially flat earth model because it is so phenomenologically compelling to do so. Seely produces a considerable number of other sources unmentioned here which further instantiate this propensity.[69] The Hebrew Bible is no exception to this and certainly has heavenly waters suspended over the sky, as well as a disk of the earth surrounded by a ring of ocean. This book has developed how Israel's neighbors believed in similar notions, and it is significant that the Old Testament describes it in a way that reflects that Near Eastern context.

---

[69] Ibid., 240ff.

INDEX OF TERMS AND PHRASES

IMAGE ATTRIBUTIONS

BIBLIOGRAPHY

Abrami, Leo Michel. "The Ages of the Personalities in Genesis," *Jewish Bible Quarterly* 39.4 (2011), 258-262.

Adams, Edward. "Graeco-Roman and Ancient Jewish Cosmology" in Johnathan T. Pennington (ed.) *Cosmology and New Testament Theology* (New York: T&T Clark 2008), 5-27.

Alexander, Hartley Burr. *Native American Mythology* (New York: Dover Publications, 2005).

Allen, James P. "The Celestial Realm" in David P. Silverman (ed.), *Ancient Egypt* (Oxford: Oxford University Press, 1997), 114–31.

_____. *Genesis in Egypt: The Philosophy of Ancient Egyptian Creation Accounts.* Yale Egyptological Studies 2 (Yale University Press: New Haven, 1988).

Almansa-Villatoro, M. Victoria. "The Cultural Indexicality of the N41 Sign for *ḥjз*: The Metal of the Sky and the Sky of Metal," *The Journal of Egyptian Archaeology* 105.1 (2019), 73–81.

Alter, Robert. *The Book of Psalms: A Translation with Commentary* (New York: W.W. Norton & Company, 2007).

_____. *The Five Books of Moses: A Translation with Commentary* (New York: Norton, 2004).

_____. *The Wisdom Books: Job, Proverbs, Ecclesiastes; A Translation with Commentary* (New York: W. W. Norton & Co., 2010).

Amos, Clare. *The Book of Genesis.* Epworth Commentaries (Peterborough: Epworth Press, 2004).

Amzallag, Nissim. "Copper Metallurgy: A Hidden Fundament of the Theology of Ancient Israel?" *Scandinavian Journal of the Old Testament* 27.2 (2013), 151-169.

Andersen, Francis I. and David Noel Freedman. *Hosea: A New Translation with Introduction and Commentary* (Doubleday: New York, 1980).

Andersen, Francis I. "On Reading Genesis 1-3" in Michael Patrick O'Connor and David Noel Freedman (eds.), *Backgrounds for the Bible* (Winona Lake: Eisenbrauns, 1987), 137-150.

Anderson, Bernard W. "A Stylistic Study of the Priestly Creation Story" in George W.

Coats and Burke Long (eds), *Canon and Authority: Essays in Old Testament Religion and Theology* (Philadelphia: Fortress, 1977), 148-162.

Annus, Amar. "On the Origin of the Watchers: A Comparative Study of the Antediluvian Wisdom in Mesopotamian and Jewish Traditions" in *Journal for the Study of the Pseudepigrapha* 19.4 (2010), 277-320.

Arnold, Bill T. *Genesis*. New Cambridge Bible Commentary (Cambridge: Cambridge University Press, 2009).

Assmann, Jan. *Of Gods and Gods: Egypt, Israel, and the Rise of Monotheism* (Madison: University of Wisconsin Press, 2008).

Atwell, James. "An Egyptian Source for Genesis 1," *Journal of Theological Studies* 51 (2000), 441-477.

Averbeck, Richard E. "A Literary Day, Inter-Textual, and Contextual Reading of Genesis 1-2" in J. Daryl Charles (ed.), *Reading Genesis 1-2: An Evangelical Conversation* (Massachusetts: Hendrickson, 2013), 7-34.

____. "Ancient Near Eastern Mythography as it Relates to Historiography in the Hebrew Bible: Genesis 3 and the Cosmic Battle," *The Future of Biblical Archaeology* (2004), 328-356.

Baasten, Martin F. J. "First Things First: The Syntax of Gen 1:1-3 Revisited" in Martin F. J. Baasten, and Reinier Munk (eds.), *Studies in Hebrew Literature and Jewish Culture Presented to Albert Van Der Heide on the Occasion of His Sixty-Fifth Birthday* (Dordrecht: Springer, 2007), 169-88.

Bailey, L. R. "Biblical Math as *Heilsgeschichte?*" in R. D. Weis and D. M. Carr (eds.), *A Gift of God in Due Season: Essays on Scripture and Community in Honor of James A. Sanders*. JSOTSup 225 (Sheffield: JSOT Press, 1996), 84-102.

____. *Genesis, Creation, and Creationism* (New York: Paulist Press, 1993).

Barroso, M. S. "Bezoar stones, magic, science and art" in Duffin, Moody, Gardner-Thorpe (eds.), *A History of Geology and Medicine*. Geological Society Special Publication 375 (London: Geological Society, 2013), 193-207.

Barry, John D., Mangum, Brown and Heiser (eds.), *NIV Faithlife Study Bible: Intriguing Insights to Inform Your Faith* (Grand Rapids: Zondervan, 2017).

Batto, B. F. "Behemoth" in K. van der Toorn, Bob Becking, and Pieter Willem van der Horst (eds.) *Dictionary of Deities and Demons in the Bible* (Leiden: Brill, 1999), 165-169.

____. "The Sleeping God: An Ancient Near Eastern Motif of

Divine Sovereignty," *Biblica* 68.2 (1987), 157-177.

_____. *In the Beginning: Essays on Creation Motifs in the Ancient Near East and the Bible.* Siphrut 9 (Winona Lake: Eisenbrauns, 2013).

Beale, Gregory K. "Eden, the Temple, and the Church's Mission in the New Creation," *Journal of the Evangelical Theological Society* 48.1 (2005), 5-31.

Beccari, Odoardo. *Wandering in the Great Forests of Borneo: Travels and Researches of a Naturalist in Sarawak.* Trans. Enrico H. Giglioli (London: Archibald Constable & Co, 1904).

Ben-Dov, Jonathan. "The Resurrection of the Divine Assembly and the Title El in the Dead Sea Scrolls" in Andrea Ercolani and Manuela Giordano (eds.), *Submerged Literature in Ancient Greek Culture* (Berlin: De Gruyter, 2016), 9-32.

Bernat, David. "Biblical *Wasfs* Beyond Song of Songs," *Journal for the Study of the Old Testament* 28.3 (2008), 327-349.

Bimson, John J. "Reconsidering a 'Cosmic Fall,'" *Science and Christian Belief* 18.2 (2006), 63-81.

Bittel, K., R. Naumann, and H. Otto, *Yazilikaya: Architektur, Felsbilder, Inschriften und Kleinfunde, I* (Leipzig, 1941).

Black, Matthew and James C. VanderKam, *The Book of Enoch or I*

Enoch: A New English Edition with Commentary and Textual Notes (Leiden: Brill, 1985).

Bladel, Kevin Van. "Heavenly Cords and Prophetic Authority in the Quran and Its Late Antique Context," *Bulletin of the School of Oriental and African Studies, University of London* 70.2 (2007), 223-246.

_____. "The Alexander Legend in the Qur'ān 18:83-102," in Gabriel Said Reynolds (ed.), *The Qur'ān in Its Historical Context.* Routledge Studies in the Qur'an (New York: Routledge, 2008), 175-203.

Blidstein, Gerald J. "Rabbinic Judaism and General Culture: Normative Discussion and Attitudes" in Jacob J. Schacter (ed.) *Judaism's Encounter with Other Cultures: Rejection or Integration?* (Lanham, MD: Rowman & Littlefield, 1997), 1-53.

Block, Daniel I. *The Book of Ezekiel: Chapters 25-48.* The New International Commentary on the Old Testament (Grand Rapids: Eerdmans, 1998).

Bonanno, George A. "Loss, Trauma, and Human Resilience: Have We Underestimated the Human Capacity to Thrive After Extremely Aversive Events?" *American Psychologist* 59.1 (2004), 20-28.

Botterweck, Johannes, Helmer Ringgren, Heinz-Josef Fabry (eds.), *Theological Dictionary of the Old*

Testament Vol VII (Grand Rapids: Eerdmans, 1995).

Breutz, P. "Sotho-Tswana Celestial Concepts," *Ethnological and Linguistic Studies in Honour of N.J. van Warmelo*. Department of Bantu Administration and Development Ethnological Publications 52 (Pretoria: South Africa Government Printer, 1969), 199-210.

Brown, Francis S. R. Driver, and Charles A. Briggs (eds.), *A Hebrew and English Lexicon of the Old Testament* (Oxford: Clarendon Press, 1906).

Brown, William P. "'Let There Be Light!' The Genesis of Biblical Cosmology," *Journal of Cosmology* 9 (2010), 2187-2193.

_____. *Structure, Role, and Ideology in the Hebrew and Greek Texts of Genesis 1:1-2:3*. SBL Dissertation Series 132 (Atlanta: Scholars Press, 1993).

_____. *The Seven Pillars of Creation: The Bible, Science, and the Ecology of Wonder* (New York: Oxford University Press, 2010).

Brueggemann, Walter. *Genesis: Interpretation A Bible Commentary for Teaching and Preaching* (Louisville: Westminster John Knox Press, 1982).

Bruhns, Karen O., Nancy L Kelker, *Faking the Ancient Andes* (New York: Routledge, 2010).

Budge, E. A. Wallis. *The Gods of the Egyptians*. Vol. 1 (London: Methuen, 1904).

Bunta, Silviu. "The MESU-tree and the animal Inside: Theomorphism and Theriomorphism in Daniel 4," *Scrinium* 3.1 (2007), 364-384.

Bushnell Jr., David I. "Myths of the Louisiana Choctaw," *American Anthropologist*, 12.4 (1910), 526-535.

_____. *The Choctaw of Bayou Lacomb St. Tammany Parish Louisiana*. Smithsonian Institution Bureau of American Ethnology (BAE) Bulletin 48 (Washington: Government Printing Office, 1909).

Cartwright, Bruce. "The Legend of Hawaii-Loa," *The Journal of the Polynesian Society* 38.2(150) (1929), 105-121.

Chadwick, Stephen Robert and Martin Paviour-Smith, *The Great Canoes in the Sky: Starlore and Astronomy of the South Pacific* (Switzerland: Springer, 2006).

Chaffey, Tim and Jason Lisle, *Old Earth Creationism on Trial: the Verdict is in* (Green Forest: Master Books, 2008).

Chaffey, Tim. "Humanity's Shared History Reflecting the Truth of Genesis 1-11," *Searching for Adam: Genesis 1-11 the Truth About Man's Origin* (Green Forest, AR: Master Books, 2016), 145-158.

_____. "A Critical Evaluation of the Framework Hypothesis," Liberty University student paper (2007), 62-7.

Charles, R. H. (ed.), *The Apocrypha and Pseudepigrapha of the Old Testament, Volume Two.* Biblical Apocrypha Series (Berkeley: Apocryphile Press, 2004).

Charlesworth, James H. (ed.), *The Old Testament Pseudepigrapha: Volume One Apocalyptic Literature and Testaments* (Massachusetts: Hendrickson, 1983).

Chen, Xiaohong. "The Flood Myths of Early China (Review)," *Journal of Folklore Research Reviews* (2008), n.p. https://jfr.sitehost.iu.edu/review.php?id=350.

Clarey, Tim. *Dinosaurs: Marvels of God's Design: The Science of the Biblical Account* (Green Forest, AR: Master books, 2015).

Clarke, Philip A. "The Aboriginal Cosmic Landscape of Southern South Australia," *Records of the South Australian Museum* 29.2, 125-145.

Clegg, Andrew. "Some Aspects of Tswana Cosmology," *Botswana Notes and Records* 18 (1986), 33-7.

Clifford, Richard J. "The Tent of El and the Israelite Tent of Meeting," *The Catholic Biblical Quarterly* 33.2 (1971), 221-227.

_____. *Creation Accounts in the Ancient Near East and in the Bible.* The Catholic Bible Quarterly Monograph Series 26 (Washington: Catholic Bible Association, 1994).

Clines, David J. A. *Job 21-37.* Word Bible Commentary 18A (Nashville, TN: Thomas Nelson, 2006).

Cochrane, Ev. "The Ladder-to-Heaven," 1-47. Available from Cochrane at https://www.maverickscience.com/wp-content/uploads/ladder-to-heaven.pdf. Originally in his *Martian Metamorphoses: The Planet Mars in Ancient Myth & Religion* (Aeon: 1997).

Collins, John J. *The Apocalyptic Imagination: Introduction to Jewish Apocalyptic Literature*, 3 ed. (Grand Rapids: Eerdmans, 2016).

Comfort, Ray. *Nothing Created Everything: The Scientific Impossibility of Atheistic Evolution* (Los Angeles: WND Books, 2009).

Conman, Joanne. "It's About Time: Ancient Egyptian Cosmology," *Studien zur Altägyptischen Kultur* 31 (2003), 33-71.

Couprie, D.L. *Heaven and Earth in Ancient Greek Cosmology: From Thales to Heraclides Ponticus.* Astrophysics and Space Science Library 374 (New York: Springer, 2011).

Currid, J. D. "An Examination of the Egyptian Background of the Genesis Cosmology," *Biblische Zeitschrift* 35 (1991), 18-40.

_____. *Ancient Egypt and the Old Testament* (Grand Rapids: Baker Books, 1997).

Davidson, M. O. "Arizona Superintendency" in *Annual Report of the Commissioner of Indian Affairs, for the Year 1865* (Washington: Washington Government Printing Office, 1865), 128-140.

Davies, J.A. *A Royal Priesthood: Literary and Intertextual Perspectives on an Image of Israel in Exodus 19:6*, JSOTSup 395 (London: T&T Clark, 2004).

Day, John N. "God and Leviathan in Isaiah 27:1," *Bibliotheca Sacra* 115 (1998), 423-36.

Day, John. "The Flood and the Ten Antediluvian Figures," James K. Aitken, Katharine J. Dell and Brian A. Mastin (eds.), *On Stone and Scroll: Essays in Honour of Graham Ivor Davies* (Berlin: Gruyter, 2011), 211-224.

_____. *God's Conflict with the Dragon and the Sea: Echoes of a Canaanite Myth in the Old Testament* (Cambridge: Cambridge University Press, 1985).

_____. *Yahweh and the Gods and Goddesses of Canaan*. Journal for the SOTSup 265 (New York: Sheffield Academic Press, 2000).

del Olmo Lete, G. and Joaquín Sanmartín. *A Dictionary of the Ugaritic Language in the Alphabetic Tradition (DULAT)*. Trans. Wilfred

G. E. Watson. Handbuch der Orientalistik 67 (Leiden: Brill, 2003).

Dietrich, M. O. Loretz, and J. Sanmartín (eds.), *The Cuneiform Alphabetic Texts from Ugarit, Ras Ibn Hani and Other Places* (Münster: Ugarit-Verlag, 1995).

Dijk, H. J. van. *Ezekiel's Prophecy on Tyre (Ez. 26,1-28,19) A New Approach*. Biblica et orientalia 20 (Rome: Pontifical Biblical Institute, 1968).

Dijk, Renate Marian Van. "The Motif of the Bull in the Ancient Near East: An Iconographic Study" (M.A. thesis, University of South Africa, 2011).

Dikshitar, V. R. Ramachandra. *The Matsya Purana: A Study*. Bulletins of the Department of Indian History and Archaeology 5 (University of Madras, 1935).

Dillow, Joseph C. *The Waters Above: Earth's Pre-Flood Vapor Canopy* (Moody Press: Chicago, 1982).

Douglass, Eric J. *Reading the Bible Ethically: Recovering the Voice in the Text*. Biblical Interpretation Series 133 (Leiden: Brill, 2014).

Dreyer, J. L. E. "Medieval Cosmology" in Milton K. Munitz (ed.), *Theories of the Universe: From Babylonian Myth to Modern Science* (New York: The Free Press, 1957), 115-140.

____. *History of the Planetary Systems from Thales to Kepler* (New York: Cosimo Classics, 2007).

Driver, Rebecca. "Australia's Aborigines…Did They See Dinosaurs?," *Creation* 21.1 (Dec. 1998), 24-27.

Duncan, Julie Anne. "Faith Displayed as Science: The Role of the 'Creation Museum' in the Modern American Creationist Movement" (Student Thesis Harvard University, 2009): www.papers.ssrn.com/sol3/papers.cfm?abstract_id=2007942.

Dyssel, Allan. "Sea Monsters and Other Mythical Creatures Associated with the Primeval Flood in the Old Testament: A History of Denial," (D.Th., University of South Africa, 2017).

Eknoyan, G. "The Kidneys in the Bible: What Happened," *Journal of the American Society of Nephrology*, 16.12 (Dec 2005), 3464-3471.

Ellis, William. *A Narrative of a Tour through Hawaii, or Owhyhee: With Remarks on the History, Traditions, Manners, Customs and Language of the Inhabitants*, The Advertiser Historical Series No. 2 (Honolulu: Hawaiian Gazette Co., 1917).

Engle, Richard W. "Psalm 74: Studies in Content, Structure, Context and Meaning" (D. Th. thesis, Grace Theological Seminary, 1987).

Enns, Peter. "A Christotelic Approach to the New Testament Use of the Old in Its First-Century Interpretive Environment" in Stanley N. Gundry, Kenneth Berding, Jonathan Lunde (eds.), *Three Views on the New Testament Use of the Old Testament* (Grand Rapids: Zondervan, 2008), 167-217.

____. "The 'Movable Well' in 1 Cor 10:14: An Extrabiblical Tradition in an Apostolic Text," *Bulletin for Biblical Research* 6 (1996), 23-38.

____. *The Bible Tells Me So: Why Defending Scripture has Made Us Unable to Read it* (New York: HarperOne, 2014).

Epstein, I. (ed.), *The Babylonian Talmud: Seder Nezikin. Sanhedrin II*. H. Freedman (trans.) (London: Soncino, 1935).

Etz, Donald V. "The Numbers of Genesis V 3-31: A Suggested Conversion and its Implications," *Vetus Testamentum* 43.2 (1993), 171-189.

Farrer, J. A. *Zululand and the Zulus: Their History, Beliefs Customs, Military System, Home Life, Legends, Etc., Etc., and Missions to Them* (Kerby & Endean: Oxford, 1879).

Fathers of the English Dominican Province, The *"Summa Theologica" of St. Thomas Aquinas Part 1*, vol. 2. (London: R. & T. Washbourne, 1912).

Faulkner, Danny R. "Thoughts on the *rāqîa'* and a Possible Explanation for the Cosmic Microwave Background," *Answers Research Journal* 9 (2016), 57-65.

Feder, Kenneth L. *Encyclopedia of Dubious Archaeology: From Atlantis to the Walam Olum* (Santa Barbara: Greenwood, 2010).

Finger, Stanley. *Origins of Neuroscience: A History of Explorations into Brain Function* (Oxford: Oxford University Press, 1994).

Finkel, Irving. *The Ark Before Noah: Decoding the Story of the Flood* (New York: Double Day, 2014).

Finney, Mark. "Honor, Head-coverings and Headship: 1 Corinthians 11.2-16 in its Social Context," *Journal for the Study of the New Testament* 33.1 (2010), 31-58.

Fisher, L. R. "The Temple Quarter," *Journal of Semitic Studies* 8.1 (1963), 34-41.

Flood, Bo, Beret E. Strong, William Flood, *Pacific Island Legends: Tales from Micronesia, Melanesia, Polynesia, and Australia* (Honolulu: Besspress, 1999).

Foley, Avery. "Did Adam Step on an Ant Before the Fall?," *Answers in Genesis*, 4 Dec 2015. n.p. https://answersingenesis.org/deat h-before-sin/did-adam-step-on-an-ant-before-fall/.

Forton IV, Benjamin W. *Indo-European Language and Culture: An Introduction*, 2 ed. Blackwell Textbooks in Linguistics (Singapore: Wiley-Blackwell, 2010).

Frazer, Sir James George. *Folk-lore in the Old Testament: Studies in Comparative Religion, Legend and Law vol 1* (London: MacMillan, 1918).

Freedman, H. and Maurice Simon (eds.), *Midrash Rabbah: Complete in Ten Volumes. Translated into English with Notes* (New York: Soncino Press, 1983).

Frey, Mathilde. "The Sabbath in the Pentateuch: An Exegetical and Theological Study" (PhD diss. Andrews University, 2011).

Friberg, Eino (trans.). *Kalevala: Epic of the Finnish People*, 4 ed. (Helsinki: Otava Publishing, 1988).

Friedländer M. (trans.). Moses Maimonides, *The Guide for the Perplexed* (New York: Dover, 1904).

Fuller, Russell T., *Invitation to Biblical Hebrew: A Beginning Grammar* (Grand Rapids: Kregel, 2006)

Futato, Mark and George M Schwab, *Cornerstone Biblical Commentary: Psalms, Proverbs*, ed. Philip W. Comfort (Carol Stream: Tyndale, 2009).

Futato, Mark David, *Interpreting the Psalms: An Exegetical Handbook*. Handbooks for Old Testament

Exegesis (Grand Rapids: Krugel, 2007).

García, A. César González and Juan Antonio Belmonte (eds). "Thinking Hattusha: Astronomy and Landscape in the Hittite Lands," *Journal for the History of Astronomy* 42.4 (2011), 461-494.

Geronimo, *Geronimo's Story of his Life*, S. M. Barrett (ed.) (New York: Duffield & Company, 1915).

Gibson. John C. L. *Canaanite Myths and Legends*, 2 ed. (London: T & T Clark, 1956).

Gilad, Elon. "Why Hebrew has so Many Words for 'Penis,'" *Haaretz*. Jul 22, 2015. www.haaretz.com/jewish/features /.premium-1.667193.

Gilboa, Ayelet and Dvory Namdar, "On the Beginnings of South Asian Spice Trade with the Mediterranean Region: A Review," *Radiocarbon* 57.2 (2015), 265-83.

Gilmer, James Edward. *100 Year Coverup Revealed: We Lived with Dinosaurs* (Bloomington: AuthorHouse, 2011).

Gish, Duane T. *Dinosaurs by Design* (Green Forest: Master Books, 1992).

Godley, A.D. (trans.), *Herodotus with an English translation by A.D. Godley*. Loeb Classical Library 117 (Cambridge: Harvard University Press, 1981).

Goebs, Katja. "Crown (Egypt)" in van der Toorn et al. (eds), *Iconography of Deities and Demons in the Ancient Near East*. Electronic Pre-Publication 14 April 2015 (Zürich: University of Zürich, 2015), 10-1. http://www.religionswissenschaft. unizh.ch/idd.

Goodacre, Mark. "Does περιβόλαιον Mean 'Testicle' in 1 Corinthians 11:15?" *Journal of Biblical Literature* 130 (2011), 391-96.

Greenfieldboyce, Nell. "Tyrannosaurus Rex's Bite Force Measured 8,000 Pounds, Scientists Say," *NPR*, May 17, 2017. www.npr.org/sections/thetwo-way/2017/05/17/528677883/tyra nnosaurus-rexs-bite-force-measured-8-000-pounds-scientists-say.

Greenstein, Edward L. "God's Golem: The Creation of the Human in Genesis 2" in Henning Graf Reventlow and Yair Hoffman (eds.), *Creation in Jewish and Christian Tradition*. JSOTSup 319 (Sheffield: Sheffield Academic Press, 2002), 119-239.

Greenwood, Kyle. *Scripture and Cosmology: Reading the Bible Between the Ancient World and Modern Science* (Downer's Grove: InterVarsity Press).

Griffith, Sidney. "Christian Lore and the Arabic Qur'ān: The 'Companions of the Cave' in *Sūrat al-Kahf* and in Syriac Christian

Tradition" in Gabriel Said Reynolds (ed.), *The Qur'ān and Its Historical Context.* Routledge Studies in the Qur'ān (New York: Routledge, 2008), 109-138.

Grudem, Wayne. *Systematic Theology: An Introduction to Biblical Doctrine* (Grand Rapids: Zondervan, 1994).

Gunkel, Hermann. *Genesis.* Trans. Mark E. Biddle, Mercer Library of Biblical Studies (Macon: Mercer University Press, 1997).

Guthrie, W.K.C., *A History of Greek Philosophy: Volume 1, The Earlier Presocratics and the Pythagoreans* (Cambridge: Cambridge University Press, 1962).

Hahne, Harry Alan. *The Corruption and Redemption of Creation: Nature in Romans 8.19-22 and Jewish Apocalyptic Literature.* Library of New Testament Studies 336 (New York: T&T Clark, 2006).

Ham, Ken. "Christian Academics Telling God What He Got Wrong," *Answers in Genesis, Ken Ham Blog,* Jan 2014. n.p. www.answersingenesis.org/blogs/ken-ham/2014/01/25/christian-academics-telling-god-what-he-got-wrong/.

____. "Dinosaurs and the Bible," *Answers in Genesis,* Nov. 5, 1999. n.p. Last featured Jan. 5, 2015. www.answersingenesis.org/dinosaurs/dinosaurs-and-the-Bible/.

____. "Dinosaurs for Kids," YouTube video, 1:26:23, recorded presentation given by Ham, posted by "Answers in Genesis," Dec 18, 2014, www.youtube.com/watch?v=B-g_hk_KKro.

____. "Giant Siberian 'Unicorn' Discovered," *Ken Ham Blog,* Apr. 5, 2016. n.p. www.answersingenesis.org/blogs/ken-ham/2016/04/05/giant-siberian-unicorn-discovered/.

____. *"The Genesis Flood*—The Battle Still Rages!," *Ken Ham Blog,* Feb 20, 2011. n.p. www.answersingenesis.org/blogs/ken-ham/2011/02/20/the-genesis-flood-the-battle-still-rages/.

____. "What Really Happened to the Dinosaurs" in Ken Ham (ed.), *The New Answers Book 1: Over 25 Questions on Creation/Evolution and the Bible* (Green Forest, AR: Master Books, 2006), 149-177.

____. *Did Eve Really Have an Extra Rib? And Other Tough Questions About the Bible* (Green Forest, AR: Master Books, 2002).

____. *Dinosaurs for Kids* (Green Forrest: Master Books, 2009).

____. *The Great Dinosaur Mystery Solved: A Biblical View of these Amazing Creatures* (Green Forest, AR: Master Books, 1998).

____. *The Lie: Evolution/Millions of Years (25th Anniversary Edition)*

(Green Forest, AR: Master Books, 2012).

_____. *The New Answers Book 1: Over 25 Questions on Creation Evolution and the Bible,* Ken Ham (ed.) (Green Forest, AR: Master Books)

Ham, Steve. "Is the Meaning of Genesis Lost in the Ancient Near East?" *Answers in Genesis,* Aug 2015. n.p. www.answersingenesis.org/the-word-of-god/genesis-in-ancient-near-east/.

Hamilton, Victor P. *The Book of Genesis: Chapters 1-17,* The New International Commentary on the Old Testament (Grand Rapids: Eerdmans, 1990).

Handy, Lowell. *Among the Host of Heaven: The Syro-Palestinian Pantheon as Bureaucracy* (Winona Lake: Eisenbrauns, 1994).

Hartnett, J. *Starlight Time and the New Physics* (Powder Springs: Creation Book Publishers, 2007).

Hasel, Gerhard F. "The Polemic Nature of the Genesis Cosmology," *Evangelical Quarterly* 46 (1974), 81-102.

_____. "The Significance of the Cosmology of Genesis 1 in Relation to Ancient Near Eastern Parallels," *Andrews University Seminary Studies* 10 (Andrews University Press, 1972), 1-20.

Hatch, Durwood B., *God Did It: Not the Big Bang and Evolution*

(Oklahoma: Tate Publishing, 2010).

Hayes, Christine. "Lecture 3. The Hebrew Bible in its Ancient Near Eastern Setting: Genesis 1-4 in Context," YouTube Video, 47:42, university lecture, Dec 2012. Posted by "Yale Courses," May 8, 2017, www.m.youtube.com/watch?v=A NUD8IK12ms.

Heidel, Alexander. *The Babylonian Genesis: The Story of Creation.* 2 ed. (Chicago: University of Chicago Press, 1951).

Heine, Ronald E. (ed.) *Homilies on Genesis and Exodus.* Fathers of the Church 71 (Washington: Catholic University of America Press, 1982).

Heiser, Michael S. "Deuteronomy 32:8 and the Sons of God," *Bibliotheca Sacra* 158 (2001), 52-74.

_____. "Divine Council" in John D. Barry and Lazarus Wentz (ed.), *The Lexham Bible Dictionary* (Bellingham, WA: Lexham Press, 2012), 112-6.

_____. "Ezekiel's Vision, Part 2," *PaleoBabble,* 2008, n.p. www.michaelsheiser.com/PaleoBa bble/2008/08/ezekiels-vision-part-2/.

_____. "Inspiration," *The Naked Bible blog,* 2008-2009, n.p. http://drmsh.com/naked-bibles-inspiration-discussion/.

_____. "Jesus' Quotation of Psalm 82:6 in John 10:34: A Different View of John's Theological Strategy," Paper presented to the Society of Biblical Literature (2012).

_____. "Lying and Deception," The Naked Bible blog. Mar 26, 2010, n.p. https://drmsh.com/lying-and-deception/.

_____. "Naked Bible 86: The Head covering of 1 Corinthians 11:13-15," *The Naked Bible Podcast*, Feb 7, 2016, n.p. www.nakedbiblepodcast.com/naked-bible-86-the-head-covering-of-1-corinthians-1113-15/.

_____. "Should the Plural אלהים of Psalm 82 Be Understood as Men or Divine Beings?" Presented to the Annual Meeting of the Evangelical Theological Society (2010), 1-14, www.thedivinecouncil.com/ETS2010Psalm82.pdf.

_____. "The Divine Council in Late Canonical and Non-Canonical Second Temple Jewish Literature" (PhD diss. University of Wisconsin-Madison, 2004).

_____. "There's a Lot to Think About When Translating Genesis 1:1-3," *The Naked Bible Blog*, 2011, n.p. www.drmsh.com/theres-a-lot-to-think-about-when-translating-genesis-11-3/.

_____. "What is / are (an) Elohim?" Presented at the Evangelical Theological Society (2010), 1-12. www.thedivinecouncil.com/WhatisareanelohimETS2010.pdf.

_____. *Reversing Hermon: Enoch, the Watchers, and the Forgotten Mission of Jesus Christ* (Defender Publishing, 2017).

_____. *The Unseen Realm: Recovering the Supernatural Worldview of the Bible* (Bellingham: Lexham Press, 2015).

Hess, Richard S. "Lamech in the Genealogies of Genesis," *Bulletin for Biblical Research* 1 (1991), 21-25.

Hobbins, John. "A Response to Ellen van Wolde on Genesis 1," *Ancient Hebrew Poetry*, 2009, n.p. www.ancienthebrewpoetry.typepad.com/ancient_hebrew_poetry/2009/10/a-response-to-ellen-van-wolde-on-genesis-1.html.

_____. "Genesis 1:1-3: How it all Began," *Ancient Hebrew Poetry*, Apr 2008, n.p. www.ancienthebrewpoetry.typepad.com/ancient_hebrew_poetry/2008/04/genesis-11-3-ho.html.

Hodge, Bodie and Laura Welch, *Dragons: Legends and Lore of Dinosaurs* (Green Forest, AR: Master Books).

Hodge, Bodie and Prof. Andy McIntosh, "How Did Attack/Defense Structures Come About?" *The New Answers Book 1*, 27 Dec 2018, n.p. https://answersingenesis.org/evidence-for-creation/design-in-nature/how-did-defense-attak-structures-come-about/.

Hodge, Bodie. "Didn't the Curse Prevent Overpopulation?" *Answers in Genesis*, 11 May 2010, n.p. https://answersingenesis.org/bible -questions/didnt-the-curse-prevent-overpopulation/.

_____. "Dragon Legends—Truths Behind the Tales: Special Dinosaur Section," *Answers and Genesis*, Oct. 1 2011; last featured Mar. 24 2019, n.p. https://answersingenesis.org/dino saurs/dragon-legends/dragon-legends-truths-behind-the-tales/.

_____. "Dragons…Were They Real?" in Ken Ham (ed.) *The New Answers Book Volume 4: Over 30 Questions on Creation/Evolution and the Bible* (Green Forest, AR: Master Books, 2013).

_____. "How Did Attack/Defense Structures Come About?" in Ken Ham (ed.), *The New Answers Book: Over 25 Questions on Creation Evolution and the Bible* (Green Forrest, AR: Master Books, 2006).

_____. "The Collapse of the Canopy Model," *Answers in Genesis*, Sept 2009, n.p. www.answersingenesis.org/enviro nmental-science/the-collapse-of-the-canopy-model/.

_____. "Were the Pyramids Built Before the Flood?" *Answers Magazine*, Oct 1, 2012. n.p. www.answersingenesis.org/archae

ology/ancient-egypt/were-the-pyramids-built-before-the-flood/.

Hoffmeier, James K. "Some Thoughts on Genesis 1 & 2 and Egyptian Cosmology," *Journal of the Ancient Near Eastern Society* 15 (1983), 39-49.

Hoffner Jr., Harry A. "Song of Ullikummi," in *Hittite Myths*. Society of Biblical Literature Writings from the Ancient World 2 (Atlanta: Scholars Press, 1990), 55-64.

Holding, James Patrick. "Is the *Raqiya'* ('Firmament') a Solid Dome? Equivocal Language in the Cosmology of Genesis 1 and the Old Testament: A Response to Paul H. Seely," *Journal of Creation* 13.2 (Nov 1999), 44-51.

Holmstedt, Robert D. "Genesis 1.1-3, Hebrew Grammar and Translation," *Ancient Hebrew Grammar*, Nov 11, 2011, n.p. www.ancienthebrewgrammar.word press.com/2011/11/11/genesis-1-hebrew-grammar-translation/.

_____. "The Relative Clause in Biblical Hebrew: A Linguistic Analysis" (PhD diss, University of Wisconsin-Madison, 2002).

_____. "The Restrictive Syntax of Genesis i 1," *Vetus Testamentum* 58 (2008), 56-67.

Horcasitas, Fernando. "An Analysis of the Deluge Myth in Mesoamerica," in Alan Dundes (ed.), *The Flood Myth* (Berkeley:

University of California Press, 1988), 283-220.

Horowitz, Wayne. *Mesopotamian Cosmic Geography*, Mesopotamian Civilizations 8 (Winona Lake: Eisenbrauns, 1998).

Hugh, Ross. *The Genesis Question: Scientific Advances and The Accuracy of Genesis*, 2 ed. (Colorado Springs: NavPress, 2001).

Humphreys, D. Russell, *Starlight and Time: Solving the Puzzle of Distant Starlight in a Young Universe* (Green Forrest: Master Books, 1994).

Hurowitz, Victor. "The Genesis of Genesis: Is the Creation Story Babylonian?" in Sarah Yeomans (ed), *From Babylon to Baghdad: Ancient Iraq and the Modern West* (Washington DC: Biblical Archaeology Society, 2009), 2-10.

_____. *I have Built You an Exalted House: Temple Building in the Bible in Light of Mesopotamian and North-West Semitic Writings*. JSOT Series 115 (Sheffield: A&C Black, 1992).

Huse, Scott M. *The Collapse of Evolution*, 3rd ed. (Grand Rapids, Baker Books, 1997).

Isaacs, Darek. *Dragons or Dinosaurs? Creation or Evolution?* (Alachua, FL: Bridge Logos, 2010).

Isbell, Lynne A. *The Fruit, the Tree, and the Serpent: Why We See So Well* (Cambridge: Harvard University Press, 2011).

J. Larkin Jr., William. *Culture and Biblical Hermeneutics: Interpreting and Applying the Authoritative Word in a Relativistic Age* (Grand Rapids: Baker, 1988).

Johnson, Bill. "Thunderbirds: Did American Indians See 'Winged Dinosaurs'?," *Answers in Genesis*, March 1, 2002, n.p. www.answersingenesis.org/dinosaurs/dragon-legends/thunderbirds/.

Johnson, Diana et al. "Analysis of a Prehistoric Egyptian Iron Bead with Implications for the Use and Perception of Meteorite Iron in Ancient Egypt," *Meteoritics & Planetary Science* 48.6 (2013), 997-1006.

Johnson, Dianne. *Night Skies of Aboriginal Australia: A Noctuary* (Sydney: Sydney University Press, 2014).

Johnston, Gordon H. "Genesis 1 and Ancient Egyptian Creation Myths," *Bibliotheca Sacra* 165 (2008), 178-94.

Joines, K. R. "The Serpent in Gen 3," *Zeitschrift für die Alttestamentliche Wissenschaft* 87 (1975), 1-11.

Jones, Scott C. "Corporeal Discourse in the Book of Job," *Journal of the Society of Biblical Literature* 132.4 (2013), 845-863.

Kaiser, Walter C. Peter H. Davids, F. F. Bruce, Manfred Brauch, *Hard Sayings of the Bible*

(Downers Grove: InterVarsity, 1996).

Kamma, Freerk C. *Religious Texts of the Oral Tradition from Western New-Guinea.* Religious Texts Translation Series: Nisaba, vol. 8 (Leiden: Brill, 1978).

Keel, Othmar and Silvia Schroer. *Creation: Biblical Theologies in the Context of the Ancient Near East*, trans. Peter T. Daniels (Winona Lake: Eisenbrauns, 2015).

Keel, Othmar. *Altorientalische Miniaturkunst: Die ältesten visuellen Massenkommunikationsmittel. Ein Blick in die Sammlungen des Biblischen Instituts der Universität Freiburg Schweiz* (Universitätverlag Freiburg Schweiz: Vandenhoeck & Ruprecht Göttingen, 1996).

_____. *Jahwe-Visionen und Siegelkunst: Eine neue Deutung der Majestätsschilderungen in Jes, Ez 1 und 10 und Sach 4*, Stuttgarter Bibel-Studien 84/85 (Stuttgart: Verlag Katholisches Bibelwerk, 1984).

_____. *The Symbolism of the Biblical World: Ancient Near Eastern Iconography and the Book of Psalms.* Trans. Timothy J. Hallett (Winona Lake: Eisenbrauns, 1997).

King, L. W. *Enuma Elish: The Seven Tablets of Creation*, vol. 1 (London: Luzac and Co., 1902).

Kingsley, Peter. "Ezekiel by the Grand Canal: Between Jewish and Babylonian Tradition," *Journal of the Royal Asiatic Society* 2.3 (1992), 339-346.

Kittle, Gerhard and Geoffrey W. Bromiley (eds.). *Theological Dictionary of the New Testament*, vol. II (Grand Rapids: Eerdmans, 1999).

Klien, Jacob. "The Bane of Humanity: A Lifespan of One Hundred Twenty Years," *Acta Sumerologica* 12 (1990), 57-70.

Koch-Westenholz, Ulla. *Mesopotamian Astrology: An Introduction to Babylonian and Assyrian Celestial Divination.* The Carsten Niebuhr Institute of Near Eastern Studies 19 (Denmark: Museum Tusculanum Press).

Kopenawa, Davi and Bruce Albert. *The Falling Sky: Words of a Yanomami Shaman.* Trans. Nicholas Elliott and Alison Dundy (Cambridge: Belknap Press of Harvard, 2013).

Kopple, J. D. "The Biblical View of the Kidney," *American Journal of Nephrology*, 14 (1994), 279-81.

Korpel, Marjo and Johannes de Moor. "The Leviathan in the Ancient Near East," in Koert van Bekkum, et al. (eds.), *Playing with Leviathan: Interpretation and Reception of Monsters from the Biblical World.* Themes in Biblical Narrative 21 (Netherlands: Brill, 2017), 3-20.

Kovacs, Maureen Gallery. *The Epic of Gilgamesh* (Stanford, CA: Stanford University Press, 1989).

Kramer, Samuel Noah. *History Begins at Sumer* (New York: Anchor, 1959).

_____. *The Sumerians: Their History, Culture and Character* (Chicago: University of Chicago Press, 1963).

Kugel, James L. *Traditions of the Bible: A Guide to the Bible as it was at the Start of the Common Era* (Cambridge: Harvard University Press, 1998).

Kwakkel, Gert. "The Monster as a Toy: Leviathan in Psalm 104:26" in Koert van Bekkum, et al. (eds.), *Playing with Leviathan: Interpretation and Reception of Monsters from the Biblical World*. Themes in Biblical Narrative 21 (Netherlands: Brill, 2017), 77-89.

Lacey, Troy and Lee Anderson. "The Genesis Flood—Not Just Another Legend," *Answers Magazine*, 2013, n.p. www.answersingenesis.org/the-flood/flood-legends/the-genesis-flood-not-just-another-legend/.

Lambert, W. G., A. R. Millard, and Miguel Civil (eds.). *Atra-Hasis: The Babylonian Story of the Flood* (Winona Lake: Eisenbrauns, 1999).

Lame Deer, John Fire and Richard Erdoes. *Lame Deer, Seeker of Visions: The Life of a Sioux Medicine Man* (London: Touchstone, 1972).

Lang, Bernhard. "Non-Semitic Deluge Stories and the Book of Genesis: A Bibliographical and Critical Survey," *Anthropos* 80, 4.6 (1985), 605-616.

Leeming, David Adams and Margaret Adams Leeming. *A Dictionary of Creation Myths* (Oxford: Oxford University Press, 1994).

Levenson, Jon D. *Creation and the Persistence of Evil: The Jewish Drama of Divine Omnipotence* (Princeton: Princeton University Press, 1988).

Levy-Bruhl, L. *Primitive Mentality* (Boston: Beacon, 1966).

Lisle, Jason. "Dinosaurs and the Bible, Part 1," *Answers in Genesis*, 00:18:00. Video Lecture uploaded March 2009, www.answersingenesis.org/media/video/animals/dinosaurs-and-Bible/.

_____. *Taking Back Astronomy: The Heavens Declare Creation and Science Confirms It* (Green Forest, AR: Master Books, 2006).

Lombaard, Christo. "Genealogies and Spiritualties in Genesis 4:17-22, 4:25-26, 5:1-32," *Acta Theologica Supplementum* 8 (2006), 145-164.

Longenecker, Richard. *Biblical Exegesis in the Apostolic Period*, 2 ed. (Grand Rapids: Eerdmans, 1999).

López, Raúl. "The Antediluvian Patriarchs and the Sumerian King List," *Answers in Genesis*, Dec, 1998, n.p.

www.answersingenesis.org/bible-history/the-antediluvian-patriarchs-and-the-sumerian-king-list/.

Lurker, Manfred. *The Gods and Symbols of Ancient Egypt* (Britain: Thames and Hudson, 1980).

Lutz, Erik. "Contradictions: Hanging on Pillars of Nothing?," *Answers in Genesis*, Aug 9, 2011, n.p. www.answersingenesis.org/astronomy/earth/contradictions-hanging-on-pillars-of-nothing/?sitehist=1501457736342.

Makemson, Maud W. "Hawaiian Astronomical Concepts," *American Anthropologist* 40.3 (1938), 370-383.

Martin, Gary. "*Raqi'a*: Form and Function of the 'Firmament' as a Celestial līmes/līmen in Israelite Cosmology," graduate seminar paper, Washington University (2013), 1-30. www.faculty.washington.edu/garmar/Raqia.pdf.

Martin, Troy W. "Paul's Argument from Nature for the Veil in 1 Corinthians 11:13—A Testicle Instead of a Head Covering," *Journal of Biblical Literature* 123.1 (2004), 75–84.

_____. "Περιβόλαιον as 'Testicle' in 1 Corinthians 11:15: A Response to Mark Goodacre," *JBL* 132.2 (2013), 453-465.

Mathews, Kenneth A. *The New American Commentary*, vol 1A (Nashville: Broadman & Holman Publishers, 1996).

Matthews, Washington. *Navaho Legends*. Memoirs of the American Folk-lore Society Vol. V (New York: G. E. Stechert & Co, 1897).

Maul, Stefan M. "Der Sieg über die Mächte des Bösen: Götterkampf, Triumphrituale und Torarchitektur in Assyrien" in Erich Zenger (ed.), *Ritual und Poesie: Formen und Orte religiöser Dichtung im Alten Orient, im Judentum und im Christentum*. Herder's Biblical Studies 36 (Freiburg: Freiburg, 2003), 47-71.

May, Gerhard. *Creatio Ex Nihilo: The Doctrine of 'Creation out of Nothing' in Early Christian Thought*. Trans. A. S. Worrall (New York: T&T Clark, 2004).

Mayor, Adrienne. *Fossil Legends of the First Americans* (Princeton: Princeton University Press, 2005).

_____. *The First Fossil Hunters: Paleontology in Greek and Roman Times* (Princeton: Princeton University Press, 2000).

McCabe, Robert V. "A Critique of the Framework Interpretation of the Creation Account (Part 1 of 2)," *Detroit Baptist Theological Seminary Journal* 10 (2005), 49-51.

McDonald, Nathan. *Deuteronomy and the Meaning of 'Monotheism'* (Tübingen: Mohr Siebeck, 2003), 1-21.

Meier, S. A. "Angel I" in *Dictionary of Deities and Demons in the* Bible, K. van der Toorn, Bob Becking, and Pieter Willem van der Horst (eds.) (Leiden: Brill, 1999), 45-50.

Metevelis, Peter. "The Lapidary Sky over Japan," *Asian Folklore Studies* 59.1 (2000), 79-88.

Mettinger, T. N. D. "Seraph" in K. van der Toorn, Bob Becking, and Pieter Willem van der Horst (eds.) *Dictionary of Deities and Demons in the Bible* (*DDD*) (Leiden: Brill, 1999), 742- 744.

_____. "The Elusive Essence: YHWH, El and Baal and the Distinctiveness of Israelite Faith" in E. Blum, C. Macholz and E.W. Stegemann (eds.), *Die Hebräische Bibel und ihre zweifache Nachgeschichte: Festschrift für Rolf Rendtorff zum 65* (Neukirchen-Vluyn: Neukirchener Verlag, 1990), 393-417.

Middleton, J. Richard. "Created in the Image of a Violent God? The Ethical Problem of the Conquest of Chaos in Biblical Creation Texts," *Interpretation* 58.4 (2004), 341-355.

Miller, Mary and Karl Taube. *An Illustrated Dictionary of the Gods and Symbols of Ancient Mexico and the Maya* (London: Thames & Hudson, 1997).

Mitchell, Elizabeth. "Unicorns in the Bible?," *Answers in* Genesis, Feb 3, 2015, n.p. www.answersingenesis.org/kids/vi deos/unicorns-Bible/.

_____. "Unicorns in the Bible" in *The New Answers Book 3: Over 35 Questions on Creation/Evolution and the Bible*, ed. Ken Ham (Green Forest, AR: Master Books, 2009), 319-322.

_____. "Will the Real Unicorn Please Stand Up?," *Answers in* Genesis, Jun 15, 2011, n.p. www.answersingenesis.org/extinct-animals/will-the-real-unicorn-please-stand-up/.

Mitchell, Stephen. *The Book of Job* (New York: Harper Perennial, 1992).

Möller, Karl. "Images of God and Creation in Genesis 1-2," in Jamie A. Grant, Alison Lo, and Gordon J. Wenham (eds.), *A God of Faithfulness: Essays in Honour of J. Gordon McConville on His 60th Birthday* (New York: T & T Clark, 2011), 3-29.

Moo, Jonathan. "Romans 8.19–22 and Isaiah's Cosmic Covenant," *New Testament Studies* 54.1 (2008), 74-89.

Mooney, James. *Myths of the Cherokee.* The Smithsonian Institution BAE Annual Report 19 (Washington: Government Printing Office, 1897-98).

Morales, L. Michael. *The Tabernacle Pre-Figured: Cosmic Mountain Ideology in Genesis and Exodus* (Leuven: Peeters, 2012).

Morris, Henry M. *The Biblical Basis for Modern Science: The Revised and Updated Classic!* (Green Forest, AR: Master Books, 2002).

____. "The Young Earth Creationist Bibliography," *ICR.org*, www.icr.org/article/YoungEarth-creationist-bibliography/. Originally published in *Acts & Facts* 24.11 (1995).

____. *The Remarkable Record of Job* (Green Forest: Master Books, 2000).

Morrow, Jeff. "Creation as Temple-Building and Work as Liturgy in Genesis 1-3," *Journal of the Orthodox Center for the Advancement of Biblical Studies* 2.1 (2009), 1-13.

Mortenson, Terry. "Evangelical Popes," *Answers Magazine*, Apr 1, 2012, n.p. www.answersingenesis.org/christianity/evangelical-popes/.

____. "The Fall and the Problem of Millions of Years of Natural Evil," *Answers in Depth*, July 18, 2002, n.p. www.answersingenesis.org/theory-of-evolution/millions-of-years/the-fall-and-the-problem-of-millions-of-years-of-natural-evil/.

Mount, Christopher. "1 Corinthians 11:3-16: Spirit Possession and Authority in a Non-Pauline Interpolation," *Journal of Biblical Literature*, 124.2 (2005), 313-340.

Mulder, Michael. "Leviathan on the Menu of the Messianic Meal: The Use of Various Images of Leviathan in Early Jewish Tradition" in Koert van Bekkum, et al. (eds.) *Playing with Leviathan: Interpretation and Reception of Monsters from the Biblical World*. Themes in Biblical Narrative 21 (Netherlands: Brill, 2017), 118-130.

Mullen Jr., E. Theodore. *The Divine Council in Canaanite and Early Hebrew Literature*. Harvard Semitic Monographs 24 (Chico, CA: Scholars Press, 1980).

Müller, W. M. *The Mythology of All Races. Vol. 12: Egyptian* (New York: Cooper Square, 1964).

Needham, Joseph. "The Cosmology of Early China" in Carmen Blacker (ed.), *Ancient Cosmologies* (Great Britain: George Allen & Unwin, 1975), 87-109.

Nicolaidis, Efthymios. *Science and Eastern Orthodoxy: From the Greek Fathers to the Age of Globalization*, trans. Susan Emanuel (John Hopkins University Press: Baltimore, 2011).

Niehaus, Jeffrey Jay. *God at Sinai: Covenant and Theophany in the Bible and Ancient Near East* (Grand Rapids: Zondervan, 1995).

Niehr, H. "Zaphon," in K. van der Toorn, Bob Becking, and Pieter Willem van der Horst (eds.) *Dictionary of Deities and Demons in the Bible* (Leiden: Brill, 1999), 925-929.

Noegel, Scott B. "God of Heaven and Sheol," *Hebrew Studies* 58 (2017), 119-144.

Noort, Ed. "The Stories of the Great Flood: Notes on Gen 6:5-9:17 in its Context of the Ancient Near East" in Florentino Garcia Martínez and Gerard P. Luttikhuizen, *Interpretations of the Flood*. Themes in Biblical Narrative (Leiden: Brill, 1998), 1-38.

O'Day, Gail R. "The Gospel of John: Introduction, Commentary, and Reflections," in Leander E Keck (ed.), *The New Interpreter's Bible*, vol 9 (Nashville: Abingdon Press, 1995).

O'Flaherty, W. (trans.), *The Rig Veda*, (New York: Penguin, 1981).

Ogunlana, Babatunde. "Inspiration and the Relationship Between Genesis 1:1-2:4A and *Enuma Elish*," Paper presented to Jos-Bukuru Theological Society, Jos, Nigeria (July 11, 2013), 87-105.

Öhman, Arne and Susan Mineka. "The Malicious Serpent: Snakes as a Prototypical Stimulus for an Evolved Module of Fear," *Current Directions in Psychological Science* 12.1 (2003), 5-9.

Olson, Craig. "A Proposal for a Symbolic Interpretation of Patriarchal Lifespans" (PhD diss. Dallas Theological Seminary, 2017).

Osborn, Bryan. "Dinosaurs and the Bible with Bryan Osborn," YouTube video, 1:06:21, recorded presentation, posted Jul 11, 2018 by "Answers in Genesis," https://www.youtube.com/watch?v=Y80wHFoYrrQ.

Osborne, Grant R. *The Hermeneutical Spiral: A Comprehensive Introduction to Biblical Interpretation*, 2 ed. (Downers Grove: InterVarsity Press, 2006).

Paris, Harry S. "Origin and Emergence of the Sweet Dessert Watermelon, *Citrullus Lanatus*," *Annals of Botany* 116.2 (2015), 133-148.

Parker, Gary. *Building Blocks in Science: Laying a Creation Foundation* (Green Forrest: Master Books, 2007).

Parker, S. B. "Sons of (the) God(s)" in K. van der Toorn, Bob Becking, and Pieter Willem van der Horst (eds.) *Dictionary of Deities and Demons in the Bible* (Leiden: Brill, 1999), 794-800.

Pelikan, Jaroslav (ed.). *Luther's Works, Volume 1: Lectures on Genesis, Chapters 1-5*, trans. George V. Schick (St. Louis: Concordia, 1958).

Pelosi, Alexandra. *Friends of God: A Road Trip With Alexandra Pelosi*, HBO, Jan 25, 2007.

Pelt, Miles Van. "Exegetical Evidence for Non-Solar and Non-Sequential Interpretations of

Genesis 1 and 2 Creation Days" in Timothy D. Finlay and William Yarchin (eds.), *The Genre of Biblical Commentary: Essays in Honor of John E. Hartley on the Occasion of His 75th Birthday* (Oregon: Wipf and Stock, 2015), 199-216.

Pennington, Jonathan T. *Cosmology and New Testament Theology* (New York: T&T Clark, 2008).

Peterson, Jordan B. *Maps of Meaning: The Architecture of Belief* (New York: Routledge, 1999).

Pettazzoni, Raffaele. *Essays on the History of Religions.* Trans. H. J. Rose (Leiden: Brill, 1967).

Piankoff, Alexandre and Natacha Rambova. *Mythological Papyri,* Bollingen Series XI.3 (New York: Pantheon, 1957).

Platt, Kevin Holden. "Dinosaur Fossils Part of Longtime Chinese Tonic," *National Geographic News,* Jul 2007, n.p. www.news.nationalgeographic.com /news/2007/07/070713-china-dinos.html.

Pontani, Filippomaria. "Bronze Heaven in Archaic Greek Poetry," *L'antiquité classique* 80 (2011), 157-162.

Pope, Marvin. *Job: A New Translation with Introduction and Commentary by Marvin Pope,* The Anchor Bible vol. 15 (New York: Doubleday, 1965).

Postell, Seth D. *Adam as Israel: Genesis 1-3 as the Introduction to the Torah and Tanakh* (Eugene: Pickwick Publications, 2011).

Poythress, Vern S. "Rain Water Versus a Heavenly Sea in Genesis 1:6-8," *Westminster Theological Journal* 77 (2015), 181-91.

____. "Biblical Studies: Three Modern Myths in Interpreting Genesis 1," *Westminster Theological Journal* 76 (2014), 321-350.

Prichard, James. *Ancient Near Eastern Texts Relation to the Old Testament, (ANET)* 2 ed. (Princeton: Princeton University Press, 1969).

Provençal, Philippe. "Regarding the Noun שרף in the Hebrew Bible," *Journal for the Study of the Old Testament* 29.3 (2005).

Quasten, Johannes et al. (eds.). *The Literal Meaning of Genesis Volume 1.* Ancient Christian Writers (Mahwah: Paulist Press, 1982).

Quellec, Jean-Loïc Le, Paul Bahn, and Marvin Rowe. "The Death of a Pterodactyl," *Antiquity,* 89.346 (2015), 872-884.

Rackham, H. (trans.) Pliny the Elder, *Natural History,* Book XII:XLII. Leob Classical Library 370 (Cambridge: Harvard University Press, 1945).

Rad, Gerhard von. *Genesis: A Commentary (Revised Edition).* The Old Testament Library

(Philadelphia: Westminster Press, 1972).

Radner, Karen. "The Winged Snakes of Arabia and the Fossil Site of Makhtesh Ramon in the Negev," *Wiener Zeitschrift für die Kunde des Morgenlandes* 97 (2007), 353-365.

Ragavan, Deena (ed.). *Heaven on Earth: Temples, Ritual, and Cosmic Symbolism in the Ancient World.* Oriental Institute Seminars 9 (Illinois: Oriental Institute, 2013).

Rahmouni, Aïcha. *Divine Epithets in the Ugaritic Alphabetic Texts.* Trans., J.N. Ford, Handbook of Oriental Studies. Section I, The Near and Middle East (Leiden: Brill, 2008).

Rasmussen, Adam David. "How St. Basil and Origen Interpret Genesis 1 in the Light of Philosophical Cosmology" (PhD diss., The Catholic University of America 2013).

Reynolds, Edward H. and James V. Kinnier Wilson. "Neurology and Psychiatry in Babylon," *Brain* 137.9 (2014), 2611-9.

Roberts, Alexander and James Donaldson (eds.). *Ante-Nicene Christian Library: Vol. III. Tatian, Theophilus, and the Clementine Recognitions* (Edinburgh: T&T Clark, 1867).

Roberts, Alexander, et al. *The Ante-Nicene Fathers Volume IV:*

Fathers of the Third Century (New York: Cosmo Classics, 2007).

Roberts, John R. "Biblical Cosmology: The Implications for Bible Translation," *Journal of Translation* 9.2 (2013), 1-53.

Ronning, John L. "The Curse of the Serpent (Genesis 3:15) in Biblical theology and Hermeneutics," (PhD diss. Westminster Seminary, 1997).

Ross, Allen P. "Studies in the Life of Jacob Part 1: Jacob's Vision: The Founding of Bethel," *Bibliotheca Sacra* 142 (1985), 224-37.

Roth, Martha T. "Age at Marriage and the Household: A Study of Neo-Babylonian and Neo-Assyrian Forms," *Comparative Studies in Society and History* 29.4 (1987), 715-747.

___, **et al.** (eds.), *Chicago Assyrian Dictionary* 17.1 (Illinois: Oriental Institute, 1989).

Rouillard, H. "Rephaim" in K. van der Toorn, Bob Becking, and Pieter Willem van der Horst (eds.) *Dictionary of Deities and Demons in the Bible* (Leiden: Brill, 1999), 692-700.

Rowold, Henry. "מִי הוּא? לִי הוּא!" Leviathan and Job in Job 41:2-3," *Journal of Biblical Literature* 105.1 (1986), 102-9.

Rush, David E. and Larry Vardiman, "Pre-Flood Vapor Canopy Radiative Temperature Profiles" R.E. Walsh and C. L.

Brooks (eds.), *Proceedings of the Second International Conference on Creationism* (Pittsburgh: Creation Science Fellowship, 1990), 231–240.

Ryan, Susan C. (ed.), *The Archaeology of Shields Pueblo (Site 5MT3807): Excavations at a Mesa-Top Community Center in Southwestern Colorado* [PDF Title], (Crow Canyon Archeological Center, 2015). www.crowcanyon.org.shieldspueblo.

Saggs, H. W. F. *Civilization Before Greece and Rome* (New Haven: Yale University Press, 1989).

Sarna, Nahum. *Understanding Genesis: The Heritage of Biblical Israel* (New York: Schocken Books, 1966).

Sasson, Jack M. "Time…to Begin," in Michael Fishbane, Emanuel Tov and Weston W. Fields (eds.), *"Shaʿarei Talmon": Studies in the Bible, Qumran, and the Ancient Near East Presented to Shermaryahu Talmon* (Winona Lake: Eisenbrauns, 1992), 183-194

Savage, J. J. (trans.) Ambrose, *Hexaemeron*, IV.15 in, *Hexameron, Paradise, and Cain and Abel.* The Fathers of the Church, vol. 42 (Washington: Catholic University of America, 2003).

Schaff, Philip and Henry Wallace (eds.). *Nicene and Post-Nicene Fathers: Second Series, Volume VII Cyril of Jerusalem, Gregory Nazianzen.* Trans. Edward Hamilton Gifford (New York: Cosimo Classics, 2007).

Seely, Paul. "The Firmament and the Water Above: Part I: The Meaning of *raqiaʿ* in Gen 1:6-8," *Westminster Theological Journal* 53 (1991), 227-240.

_____. "The Geographical Meaning of 'Earth' and 'seas' in Genesis 1:10," *Westminster Theological Journal* 59 (1997), 231-55.

Senter, Philip J. "More 'dinosaur' and 'pterosaur' rock art that isn't," *Palaeontologia Electronica* 15(2.22A) (2012), 1-14. www.palaeo-electronica.org/content/2012-issue-2-articles/275-rock-art-dinosaurs.

_____. "Did Australia's Aborigines See Plesiosaurs? Yes-In a Children's Book," *Skeptical Inquirer* 41.1 (2017), 34-6.

Shemesh, Yael. "Lies by Prophets and Other Lies in the Hebrew Bible," *Journal of the Ancient Near Eastern Society* 29 (2002), 81–95.

Shuchat, Wilfred. *The Creation According to the Midrash Rabbah* (Jerusalem: Devora, 2002).

Simon-Shoshan, Moshe. "'The Heavens Proclaim the Glory of God…': A Study in Rabbinic Cosmology," *Bekhol DeraKhekha Daehu* 20 (2008), 67-96.

Smick, Elmer B. "Mythology and the Book of Job," *Journal of the*

Evangelical Theological Society 13.2 (1970), 101-106.

Smith, Mark S. "Mark S. Smith – The Birth of Monotheism," YouTube video, 1:59:52, lecture presented to the Tangier Global Forum, Feb 20, 2018. Posted by "Tangier Global Forum," Jan 27, 2017.
https://www.youtube.com/watch?v=PvOT6Kj8Yxk.

_____. "The Structure of Divinity at Ugarit and Israel: The Case of Anthropomorphic Deities versus Monstrous Divinities" in Gary Beckham and Theodore J. Lewis (eds.) *Text, Artifact, and Image: Revealing Ancient Israelite Religion* (Providence: Scholars Press, 2006), 38-63.

_____. *The Origins of Biblical Monotheism: Israel's Polytheistic Background and the Ugaritic Texts* (Oxford: Oxford University Press, 2001).

_____. *The Priestly Vision of Genesis 1* (Minneapolis: Fortress Press, 2010).

Snelling, Andrew A. and Mike Matthews, "When was the Ice Age in Biblical History," *Answers Magazine*, Apr. 1, 2013, n.p. www.answersingenesis.org/environmental-science/ice-age/when-was-the-ice-age-in-biblical-history/.

Sommer, Benjamin D. "An Anthology of Beginnings," *Parashat Bereishit 5776*. Produced by Jewish Theological Seminary (2015), www.jtsa.edu/an-anthology-of-beginnings.

_____. *The Bodies of God and the World of Ancient Israel* (Cambridge: Cambridge University Press, 2009).

_____. "Seraphs," *Bible Odyssey* presented by *The Society of Biblical Literature*, n.p. www.Bibleodyssey.org/en/tools/ask-a-scholar/seraphs.

Sparks, Kenton L. "Genesis 1-11 as Ancient Historiography" in Charles Halton and Stanley N. Gundry (eds.), *Genesis: History, Fiction, or Neither? Three Views on the Bible's Earliest Chapters* (Grand Rapids: Zondervan, 2015), 110-139.

Speiser, E. A. *Genesis: Introduction, Translation and Notes* (New York: Doubleday, 1964).

Sproul, B. *Primal Myths* (New York: Haper & Row, 1969).

Stambaugh, Jim. "Creation's Original Diet and the Changes at the Fall," *Journal of Creation* 5.2 (1991), 130-138.

Stanhope, Ben. "The Biblical Flat Earth: Responding to Objections," video presentation, Jun 19, 2018, Posted by "Ben S." http://m.youtube.com/watch?v=c8Jz4tvlhZM.

_____. "First Temple Hebrew Seals and Bullae Identifying Biblical Persons: A Study of their

Iconographic and Historical Significance" (M. A. Thesis, Hamburg University, Dec 2019). https://independent.academia.edu /BenStanhope.

_____. *The Golden Sayings of Epictetus: In Contemporary English with Explanatory Notes* (Charleston: Stanhope, 2016).

Stavig, Gopal. "Historical Contacts Between Ancient India and Babylon," *Journal of Indian History*. Platinum Jubilee Volume (2001), 1-16.

Stayt, Hugh Arthur. *The Bavenda* (New York: Frank Cass & Co, 1968).

Steel, Allan K. "Could Behemoth have been a Dinosaur?," *Journal of Creation* 15.2 (2001), 42–45.

Stein, Robert H. "The Benefits of an Author-Oriented Approach to Hermeneutics," *Journal of the Evangelical Theological Society* 44.3 (2001), 451-66.

_____. *A Basic Guide to Interpreting the Bible: Playing by the Rules*, 2 ed. (Baker Academic: Grand Rapids, 2011).

Strange, John. "Some Notes on Biblical and Egyptian Theology," in *Egypt, Israel, and the Ancient Mediterranean World* (Leiden: Brill, 2004), 345-358.

Stulac, Daniel J. "Hierarchy and Violence in Genesis 1:26-28: An Agrarian Solution," Submission for Ecological Hermeneutics Open Section at SBL Annual Meeting (2013), 1-14. www.academia.edu/5186990/Hier archy_and_Violence_in_Genesis_1 _26-28_An_Agrarian_Solution.

Swanton, John Reed. *Tlingit Myths and Texts*. The Smithsonian Institution BAE Bulletin 39 (Washington: Government Printing Office, 1909).

Swift, Dennis. "Messages on Stone," *Answers in Genesis*, March 1997, n.p. www.answersingenesis.org/extinct-animals/ice-age/messages-on-stone/.

Thomas, Brian. "What Were the 'Waters Above the Firmament'?" *Acts & Facts* 45.5 (2016), 20.

_____. *Dinosaurs and the Bible* (Oregon: Harvest House, 2015).

Tolmie, D. F. "Angels as Arguments? The Rhetorical Function of References to Angels in the Main Letters of Paul" in *HTS Teologiese Studies/Theological Studies* 67.1, 825 (2011), 1-8.

Trimble, M. and E. H. Reynolds. "A Brief History of Hysteria: From the Ancient to the Modern," in Michael J. Aminoff, François Boller, Dick F. Swaab (eds.), *Handbook of Clinical Neurology vol. 139* (Amsterdam: Elsevier, 2016), 3-10.

Trollinger, Susan L. and William Vance Trollinger, Jr.

Righting America at the Creation Museum (Baltimore: John Hopkins University Press, 2016).

Tsumura, David T. *Creation and Destruction: A Reappraisal of the Chaoskampf Theory in the Old Testament* (Winona Lake: Eisenbrauns, 2005).

Tsumura, David Toshio. *The Earth and the Waters in Genesis 1 and 2: A Linguistic Investigation.* JSOTSup 83 (Sheffield: Sheffield Academic Press, 1989).

Turpin, Simon. "Did Death of Any Kind Exist Before the Fall: What the Bible Says About the Origin of Death and Suffering," *Answers Research Journal* 6 (2013), 99-116.

_____. "The Creation of Adam: Unique Revelation or Ancient Myth?" *Answers in Depth* vol 12 (2017). www.answersingenesis.org/genesis /creation-adam-unique-revelation-or-ancient-myth/.

Uehlinger, Christoph. "Leviathan" in K. van der Toorn, Bob Becking, and Pieter Willem van der Horst (eds.), *Dictionary of Deities and Demons in the Bible (DDD)* (Leiden: Brill, 1999), 511-515.

Vail, Eric M. "Using 'Chaos' in Articulating the Relationship of God and Creation in God's Creative Activity" (PhD diss., Marquette University, 2009).

Van Der Geer, Alexandra. Michael Dermitzakis, and John De Vos. "Fossil Folklore from India: The Siwalik Hills and the Mahâbhârata," *Folklore* 119.1 (2008), 71-92. www.jstor.org/stable/30035461.

Van Dyk, Peet. "Challenges in the Search for an Ecotheology," *Old Testament Essays* 22.1 (2009) 186-204.

Van Ee, Joshua John. "Death and the Garden: An Examination of Original Immortality, Vegetarianism, and Animal Peace in the Hebrew Bible and Mesopotamia" (PhD diss., University of California, 2013).

Van, Dang Nghiem. "The Flood Myth and the Origin of Ethnic Groups in Southeast Asia," *The Journal of American Folklore* 106.421 (1993), 304-37.

VanderKam, James C. *Enoch: A Man for all Generations* (Columbia: University of South Carolina, 1995).

Vardiman, Larry and D. Russell Humphreys. "A New Creationist Cosmology: In No Time at All Part 1," *Acts & Facts* 39.11 (2010), 12-15.

Voelker, Frederick E. "The Piasa," *Journal of the Illinois State Historical Society* 7.1 (1914), 82-91.

Wahlde, Urban C. von. *The Gospel and Letters of John*, vol 2 (Grand Rapids: Eerdmans, 2010).

Waltke, Bruce K. and M. O'Connor. *An Introduction to Biblical Hebrew Syntax* (Winona Lake: Eisenbrauns, 1990).

Waltke, Bruce K. *Genesis: A Commentary* (Grand Rapids: Zondervan, 2001).

Walton, John and Tremper Longman III. *How to Read Job* (Downers Grove: Intervarsity, 2015).

Walton, John H. *The Lost World of Genesis One: Ancient Cosmology and the Origins Debate* (Downers Grove: InterVarsity Press, 2009).

_____. *The Lost World of Adam and Eve: Genesis 2-3 and the Human Origins Debate* (Downers Grove: IVP Academic, 2015).

Walton, Joshua Theodore. "The Regional Economy of the Southern Levant in the 8th-7th Centuries BCE" (PhD diss., Harvard University, 2015).

Ward, William A. "The Four-Winged Serpent on Hebrew Seals," *Rivista Degli Studi Orientali* 43.2 (1968), 135-43.

Watkins, Calvert. "The Golden Bowl: Thoughts on the New Sappho and its Asianic Background," *Classical Antiquity* 26.2 (2007), 305-324.

Waytt, N. "The Seventy Sons of Athirat, the Nations of the World, Deuteronomy 32.6b, 8–9, and the myth of divine election" in N. Waytt (ed.), *The Archaeology of Myth: Papers on Old Testament Tradition* (New York: Routledge, 2010) 69-77.

Wazana, Nili. "Anzu and Ziz: Great Mythical Birds in the Ancient Near Eastern, Biblical, and Rabbinic Traditions," *Journal of the Ancient Near Eastern Society* 31.1 (2009), 111-135.

Weeks, Noel K. "Cosmology in Historical Context," *Westminster Theological Journal* 68 (2006), 283-293.

_____. "The Bible and the 'Universal' Ancient World: A Critique of John Walton," *Westminster Theological Journal* 78 (2016), 1-28

Weinfeld, Moshe. "Sabbath, Temple and the Enthronement of the Lord - The Problem of the *Sitz im Leben* of Genesis 1:1-2:3," in André Caquot and Mathias Declor (eds.), *Mélanges bibliques et orientaux en l'honneur de M. Henri Cazelles* (Kevelaer: Butzon & Bercker, 1981), 501-511.

Werner, Alex. *Myths and Legends of the Bantu* (London: George G. Harrap, 1933).

Westermann, Claus. *Genesis 1-11: A Commentary*, trans. John J. Scullion, S.J. (Minneapolis: Augsburg Publishing, 1984).

_____. *Genesis: A Practical Commentary*. Text and

Interpretation, trans. David E. Green (Grand Rapids: Eerdmans, 1987).

Whitcomb, John C. and Henry M. Morris. *The Genesis Flood: The Biblical Record and its Scientific Implications* (New Jersey: Presbyterian and Reformed Publishing, 1961).

White, Ellen. *Yahweh's Council: Its Structure and Membership*. Forschungen sum Alten Testament 2 (Tübingen: Mohr Siebeck, 2014).

White, Joe and Nicholas Comninellis. *Darwin's Demise: Why Evolution Can't Take the Heat* (Green Forrest: Master Books, 2001).

White, Monty. "Flood Legends: The Significance of a World of Stories Based on Truth," *Answers Magazine*, 2007. www.answersingenesis.org/the-flood/flood-legends/flood-legends/.

Whitley, John B. "עיפה in Amos 4:13: New Evidence for the Yahwistic Incorporation of Ancient Near Eastern Solar Imagery," *Journal of Biblical Literature* 134.1 (2015), 127-138.

Wikander, Ola. "From Indo-European Dragon-Slaying to Isaiah 27.1: A Study in the *Longue Durée*" in Tommy Wasserman, Greger Andersson and David Willgren (eds.), *Studies in Isaiah: History, Theology, and Reception*. Library of Hebrew Bible/Old Testament

Studies 654 (Oxford: Bloomsbury T&T Clark, 2017), 116-135.

Williams, Michael. *Basics of Ancient Ugaritic: A Concise Grammar, Workbook, and Lexicon* (Grand Rapids: Zondervan, 2012).

Wilson, Gordon. "Scorpions— Armed and Dangerous Created Creature," *Answers Magazine*, 1 Jan 2013. https://answersingenesis.org/creepy-crawlies/scorpions-armed-and-dangerous/.

Wilson, Joshua D. "A Case for the Traditional Translation and Interpretation of Genesis 1:1 Based Upon a Multi-Leveled Linguistic Analysis" (PhD diss., The Southern Baptist Theological Seminary, 2010).

_____. "Have we Misunderstood Genesis 1:1?" *Answers in Depth*, Sept 11, 2013, n.p. www.answersingenesis.org/hermeneutics/have-we-misunderstood-genesis-11/.

Wilson, Leslie S. *The Serpent Symbol in the Ancient Near East: Nahash and Asherah: Death Life and Healing* (Lanham: University Press of America, 2001).

Witherington III, Ben. "The Truth Will Win Out: An Historian's Perspective on the Inerrancy Controversy," *Journal of the Evangelical Theological* Society 51.1 (2014), 19-27.

Wolde, Ellen van. "Why the Verb ברא Does Not Mean 'to Create' in Genesis 1.1-2.4a," *The Journal for the Study of the Old Testament* 34.1 (2009), 3-23.

Wood, Alice. *Of Wings and Wheels: A Synthetic Study of the Biblical Cherubim*. Beihefte zur Zeitschrift für die alttestamentliche Wissenschaft (New York: Walter de Gruyter, 2008).

Wright, David. "Timeline for the Flood," *Answers in Genesis*, Mar 9, 2012, n.p. www.answersingenesis.org/bible-timeline/timeline-for-the-flood/.

Wright, J. Edward. *The Early History of Heaven* (Oxford: Oxford University Press, 2000).

Younker, Randall W. and Richard M. Davidson. "The Myth of the Solid Heavenly Dome: Another Look at the Hebrew רָקִיעַ RĀQIAʿ," *Andrews University Seminary Studies* 1 (2011), 125-147.

Made in the USA
Monee, IL
12 October 2021

79857836R00187